CHRISTIAN THEOLOGY IN CONTEXT

SERIES EDITORS

Timothy Gorringe   Graham Ward

CHRISTIAN THEOLOGY IN CONTEXT

Any inspection of recent theological monographs makes plain that it is still thought possible to understand a text independently of its context. Work in the sociology of knowledge and in cultural studies has, however, increasingly made obvious that such a divorce is impossible. On the one hand, as Marx put it, 'life determines consciousness'. All texts have to be understood in their life situation, related to questions of power, class, and modes of production. No texts exist in intellectual innocence. On the other hand texts are also forms of cultural power, expressing and modifying the dominant ideologies through which we understand the world. This dialectical understanding of text demands an interdisciplinary approach if they are to be properly understood: theology needs to be read alongside economics, politics, and social studies, as well as philosophy, with which it has traditionally been linked. The cultural situatedness of any text demands, both in its own time and in the time of its rereading, a radically interdisciplinary analysis.

The aim of this series is to provide such an analysis, culturally situating texts by Christian theologians and theological movements. Only by doing this, we believe, will people of the fourth, sixteenth or nineteenth centuries be able to speak to those of the twenty-first. Only by doing this will we be able to understand how theologies are themselves cultural products—projects deeply resonant with their particular cultural contexts and yet nevertheless exceeding those contexts by being received into our own today. In doing this, the series should advance both our understanding of those theologies and our understanding of theology as a discipline. We also hope that it will contribute to the fast developing interdisciplinary debates of the present.

Ernst Troeltsch and Liberal Theology

RELIGION AND CULTURAL SYNTHESIS IN WILHELMINE GERMANY

Mark D. Chapman

OXFORD
UNIVERSITY PRESS

*This book has been printed digitally and produced in a standard specification
in order to ensure its continuing availability*

OXFORD
UNIVERSITY PRESS

Great Clarendon Street, Oxford OX2 6DP

Oxford University Press is a department of the University of Oxford.
It furthers the University's objective of excellence in research, scholarship,
and education by publishing worldwide in

Oxford New York

Auckland Bangkok Buenos Aires Cape Town Chennai
Dar es Salaam Delhi Hong Kong Istanbul Karachi Kolkata
Kuala Lumpur Madrid Melbourne Mexico City Mumbai Nairobi
São Paulo Shanghai Taipei Tokyo Toronto

Oxford is a registered trade mark of Oxford University Press
in the UK and in certain other countries

Published in the United States
by Oxford University Press Inc., New York

© Mark D. Chapman 2001

ISBN 0-19-924682-3

For

Jacob and Edmund

Preface

This book assesses the German liberal theological tradition in the early years
of the twentieth century, concentrating in particular on the work of Ernst
Troeltsch. It tries as far as possible to discuss theology in the context of the
broader history of ideas, and to situate it within broader social and political
movements. It also tries to avoid some of the pejorative interpretative categories (such as 'Culture Protestantism') and instead seeks to understand
the period on its own terms. Great theologians do not always deserve to be
read through the distorting lens of the First World War.

Some parts of this book have been published in an earlier form elsewhere:
Chapter 1 as 'Troeltsch, Kant and the Quest for a Critical Public Theology'
(*Zeitschrift für neuere Theologiegeschichte*, 5 (1998), 29–59); Chapter 2 as 'Reli-
gion, Ethics and the History of Religion School' (*SJT*, 46 (1993), 43–78);
Chapters 4 and 5 as 'Apologetics and the Religious *A Priori*: the Use and
Abuse of Kantianism in German Theology, 1900–1920' (*Journal of Theologic-
al Studies*, 43 (1992), 470–510); Chapter 5 as 'Theology within the Walls:
Wilhelm Herrmann's Religious Reality' (*NZSThRph*, 34 (1992), 69–84);
Chapter 8 as 'Polytheism and Personality—Aspects of the Intellectual Relationship between Weber and Troeltsch' (*History of the Human Sciences*, 6
(1993), 1–33).

Very many people have helped me in writing this book. My interest in
Troeltsch and liberal theology began when I was an undergraduate reading
philosophy and politics. Without the intelligent and critical preaching of
my college chaplain, Trevor Williams, I would never have become a theologian. I went on to write an Oxford doctorate on Troeltsch's philosophy of
religion, which bears a family resemblance to some of the material in
the present book. I benefited from a year as a German Academic Exchange
Service (DAAD) scholar in Munich from 1986–7 with Trutz Rendtorff
and Friedrich Wilhelm Graf. Graf, who succeeded to Rendtorff's chair, has
continued to help me in innumerable ways and I am much indebted to his
friendship. As Sir Henry Stephenson Fellow in Sheffield I was able to test
out various chapters on unsuspecting biblical scholars, who at least
appeared to be enthusiastic. Robert Morgan, my erstwhile doctoral super-
visor, has continued to read my work with a critical eye and an active pencil
and I owe him a special debt. My students at Cuddesdon have indulged my
taste for historical theology and have been a marvellous stimulation for my
own research.

I would like to thank my wife Linda for her support and love. Finally, I would like to thank my boys, Jacob and Edmund, for teaching me something about the modern world and the future hope. It is to them that this book is affectionately dedicated.

Mark D. Chapman

Ripon College, Cuddesdon
September 2000

Contents

Abbreviations

MdETG	*Mitteilungen der Ernst-Troeltsch-Gesellschaft*
MP	Robert Morgan and Michael Pye (eds.), *Ernst Troeltsch: Writings on Theology and Religion*
MWG xv. 1	*Max Weber Gesamtausgabe*, xv. 1
NDB	*Neue Deutsche Biographie* (Berlin: Duncker and Humblot, 1977–)
NF	*Neue Folge*
NZSThRph	*Neue Zeitschrift für Systematische Theologie und Religionsphilosophie*
PCE	Ernst Troeltsch, *Praktische christliche Ethik*. See under Primary Works (unpublished)
RGG[1]	*Die Religion in Geschichte und Gegenwart*, first edn. (Tübingen: J. C. B. Mohr (Paul Siebeck), 1907–).
RH	Ernst Troeltsch, *Religion in History: Essays Translated by James Luther Adams and Walter F. Bense* (Edinburgh: T. and T. Clark, 1991)
RPH	Ernst Troeltsch, *Religionsphilosophie*. See under Primary Works (unpublished)
SGT i	Wilhelm Herrmann, *Schriften zur Grundlegung der Theologie*, ed. Peter Fischer-Appelt, i (Munich: Kaiser, 1966)
SGT ii	Wilhelm Herrmann, *Schriften zur Grundlegung der Theologie*, ed. Peter Fischer-Appelt, ii (Munich: Kaiser, 1967)
SJT	*Scottish Journal of Theology*
TLZ	*Theologische Literaturzeitung*
ThR	*Theologischer Rundschau*
TS i	Horst Renz and F. W. Graf (eds.), *Troeltsch-Studien, i: Untersuchungen zur Biographie und Werkgeschichte* (Gütersloh: Gerd Mohn, 1985)
TS iii	Horst Renz and F. W. Graf (eds.), *Troeltsch-Studien, iii: Protestantismus und Neuzeit* (Gütersloh: Gerd Mohn, 1984)
TS iv	Horst Renz and F. W. Graf (eds.), *Troeltsch-Studien, iv: Umstrittene Moderne. Die Zukunft der Neuzeit im Urteil der Epoche Ernst Troeltschs* (Gütersloh: Gerd Mohn, 1987)
TS vi	F. W. Graf and Trutz Rendtorff (eds.), *Troeltsch-Studien, vi: Ernst Troeltschs Soziallehren. Studien zu ihrer Interpretation* (Gütersloh: Gerd Mohn, 1993)
ZThK	*Zeitschrift für Theologie und Kirche*

1

Theology in 1914

INTRODUCTION

In this book I offer an interpretation of the liberal theology of Wilhelmine Germany, concentrating in particular on its public profile and engagement with the broader social, philosophical, and political culture. In doing so, I resist the temptation to use anachronistic interpretative categories, especially the misleading notion of 'Culture Protestantism'.[1] It does not seem reasonable to dismiss a style of theology primarily on the basis of guilt by association with support for a war which nobody—including the military strategists—could possibly have predicted. Besides, the public activity of a large number of theologians, many of whom possessed a remarkably cosmopolitan outlook and worked towards greater understanding between the nations, was hardly warmongering. By looking at the work of some theologians and biblical scholars, who represent what can be loosely termed liberal theology,[2] and by focusing more closely on the leading theologian of the period, Ernst Troeltsch, this book outlines some underlying themes which indicate a shared desire to bring theology into a critical dialogue with contemporary culture. It should become clear that the stance of many pre-First

---

[1] On the concept of 'Kulturprotestantismus' see esp. Friedrich Wilhelm Graf, 'Kulturprotestantismus. Zur Begriffsgeschichte einer theologischen Chiffre'. The most important recent work on the subject is Gangolf Hübinger, *Kulturprotestantismus und Politik*. For a brief account in English see Rupp, *Culture Protestantism*. The term was used originally as a synonym for 'liberal theology' (itself a vague term) and for modern or 'new' Protestantism. However, it acquired a negative connotation in dialectical theology, even if, as Hartmut Ruddies (in 'Karl Barth im Kulturprotestantismus. Eine theologische Problemanzeige') has argued, Barth himself retained a similar critical stance towards 'culture' until 1926. No ecclesiastical or theological activity could fail to be at the same time a cultural activity (esp. 230). On this see also Bruce L. McCormack, *Karl Barth's Critical Realistic Dialectical Theology*.

[2] I have interpreted 'liberal' to embrace that group of theologians who were concerned to bring the Christian faith into some degree of reconciliation with modern thought. It stands in opposition to the other leading school of 'positivism' and also to confessionalism. There are, however, no hard and fast boundaries to the term, and it will become clear that there were many different shades of opinions among liberal theologians. In the second half of the nineteenth century, as Weinhardt shows (in *Wilhelm Herrmanns Stellung in der Ritschlschen Schule*, 7–15), the term was applied mainly, though not exclusively, to the successors of Hegel like Otto Pfleiderer. By the turn of the twentieth century, however, it was a much broader concept and

World War German liberal theologians towards their culture, as well as their many constructive efforts to reform and reshape that culture, have been seriously undervalued. Far from being concerned with the legitimation of Wilhelmine society, there was frequently an overriding interest in the future possibilities for Christianity under the changed conditions of the modern world. Indeed these conditions provided the given with which the theologian, politician, or sociologist had to work: they were the facts which shaped the contemporary possibilities for humankind. This book is intended to show that the practical and realistic theology which developed in Germany before the First World War, particularly that of Ernst Troeltsch, was rather more ambitious, and certainly more subtle, than may at first sight be apparent to those who have gazed at the past through Barthian spectacles (a subject which is discussed in more detail at the end of this chapter).

Although the spectre of the subsequent course of German history, with its virtually complete sacrificing of individuality in the national community during the Nazi period, cannot wholly be ignored, particularly given Barth's accusation that the Wilhelmine liberal theologians were frequently engaged in little more than cultural apologetics, it nevertheless becomes clear that many if not most liberal theologians took as a given the inalienable rights of the autonomous individual. Thus, instead of moving from the 'social whole' downwards, whether this was identified with Church or State, there was a tendency among those theologians active in the critical public sphere to start from below, from the position of the autonomous individual: integration became the chief task, but not at the expense of loss of autonomy. In the jargon of the time, this involved the formation of 'ethical personality' (*Persönlichkeit*) out of the fragmented individual by grounding it in an ethical whole which did not deny its difference.[3] Indeed liberal theology, unlike some other theological movements both before and after the First World War, bears little similarity to totalitarianism.

This emphasis on autonomy and integration in the concept of 'personality' meant that there could be no return to alternative integrative models which denied individuality. Thus, even though individuals were growing ever more isolated and society was becoming increasingly fragmented, there could be no simple repristination of some hallowed past, since the pre-Enlightenment structure of authority had thwarted autonomy, the very basis of human ethical activity. Troeltsch thus claimed that to see the individualism of the modern world as such a 'deadly poison that kills culture'

---

was associated with certain journals and particular theologians. Moreover, theological liberalism was closely connected to liberalism in all aspects of culture.

  [3] Thus Wilhelm Herrmann could write: 'The task, which will solve the riddle of the human world, can be nothing other than this: personality' (*Die Religion im Verhältnis zum Welterkennen und zur Sittlichkeit*, cited in Graf, 'Rettung der Persönlichkeit', 120).

would be to 'despair of the fundamental demands of morality'. The duty was rather to find a specifically modern solution to the problem of fragmentation. The task was therefore 'to discipline the individual ethically and thus to transfigure the natural powers of individualism' without thereby annihilating individuality itself.[4] Indeed the frequent forays by theologians into the public and political realm in pursuit of social transformation amply demonstrate the practical and critical character of much liberal Protestantism.[5] Such a critical stance throws into doubt the assumption that Culture Protestantism was merely another ideology of legitimation. Since this may be a contentious statement, the remainder of this chapter justifies this claim, and also outlines the complexity of the period by presenting a brief overview of the situation of liberal theology at the beginning of the twentieth century.

GERMAN PROTESTANT THEOLOGY IN 1914

In the years leading up to 1914 Protestant theology in Germany had achieved, at least on the surface, an unprecedented academic reputation both at home and abroad. Despite the growth in numbers of students and academic staff in the other faculties, over one-tenth of all the professorial chairs were occupied by Protestant theologians,[6] and about 8 per cent of all the students matriculated in the seventeen German universities with Protestant faculties were studying theology.[7] At the same time theology had moved far beyond the confines of the university and the Church. Indeed in the early years of the present century many theologians had attained a public profile which few other academics could match. Adolf Harnack (from

[4] Troeltsch, 'Das Wesen des modernen Geistes' (A1907/8b), 335; ET, 271. All references to Troeltsch follow the numbering system used by Graf and Ruddies in *Ernst Troeltsch Bibliographie*. Although most translations are my own, I have also usually given references to published English translations.

[5] See, for example, Troeltsch's essay, *Politische Ethik und Christentum* (A1904/6). The political activity of Culture Protestantism is discussed at length by Hübinger in *Kulturprotestantismus*, esp. chap. 4.

[6] In the summer semester of 1903 there were 112 ordinary Professors in Protestant Theology, together with a further 38 extraordinary Professors, and 30 University Lecturers (*Privatdozenten*). This amounts to 12.05 per cent of all professors in German universities at the time.

[7] The numbers of students studying in the seventeen Protestant Theology faculties in the German Empire remained relatively static from 1896 to 1910 at just over 2,000. Between 1910 and 1914, however, the number almost doubled, from 2,422 to 4,621. Overall the number of students in German universities increased from 29,467 to 53,143 in 1910 and 59,143 in 1914. In addition there were about 1,700 catholic students studying theology (approximately 4 per cent). As a comparison, in the winter semester 1830–1, Protestant Theology students constituted 27.04 per cent of all students, with a further 11.46 per cent matriculated in the Catholic faculties. For statistics on German universities see W. Lexis, *Das Unterrichtswesen im Deutschen Reich*; and Konrad H. Jarausch, *Students, Society and Politics in Imperial Germany*, 137.

1914 von Harnack), for instance, as well as being a professor at Berlin from
1888, was also Director both of the Prussian State Library from 1905 and of
the Kaiser-Wilhelm-Gesellschaft (the forerunner of the Max Planck Society
for the Advancement of Science) from 1911, positions which helped him
achieve unparalleled influence at court. With such a high public profile, theology was able to exert widespread influence on the broader culture through
what Gangolf Hübinger has called 'networks of cultural community'.[8]

Similarly many theologians, including Harnack and lesser-known figures
like Ernst von Dobschütz (1870–1934), had been able to build up a reputation beyond the boundaries of the German-speaking world:[9] before the First
World War German theologians were frequent contributors to British and
American theological journals, and there were also several successful col-
laborations in the production of international journals, most importantly
the *Constructive Quarterly*. There seems to have been little perception by foreign theologians before the war that (at least the more liberal) German theologians were in any sense apologists for the Wagnerian excesses of German
culture or for Prussian militarism. Indeed they were often seen as in some
degree hostile to German foreign policy. Thus Harnack (who admittedly
later made a significant contribution, to or possibly even wrote, the manifesto in support of Germany's war aims in 1914) was actively engaged in pre-
war international reconciliation, giving the keynote address to the first
meeting of the Associated Councils of the Churches of the British and
German Empires for the Fostering of Friendly Relations between the Two
Peoples, in 1911.[10]

Public Theology

Many leading liberal theologians, as well as some from other camps, sought
to influence the re-emergent 'public realm' (*Öffentlichkeit*),[11] one of the few
spheres of society which stood apart from the direct control of the State.
Thus, although the constitutional arrangements of the empire were only
semi-democratic (and have been variously characterized by historians as a
virtual military dictatorship[12] or as a 'semi-absolutist pseudo-constitutional

[8] Hübinger, *Kulturprotestantismus*, 16.

[9] As an example, at the 1904 Congress of Arts and Sciences which accompanied the Louisiana
Purchase Exposition in St. Louis the German contribution was unmatched by any other nation,
theology playing a significant role: Ernst Troeltsch, Harnack, and Otto Pfleiderer all took part.
See the report on German scholarship prepared for this congress by W. Lexis, *Das Unterrichtswesen im Deutschen Reich*, vol. i, p. iii.

[10] Cf. John A. Moses, 'The British and German Churches and the Perception of War', 32f. See
also Julian Jenkins, 'War Theology, 1914 and Germany's *Sonderweg*'.

[11] On the concept of the 'public domain' see Habermas, *Strukturwandel der Öffentlichkeit*.

[12] Cf. Thomas Nipperdey, *Deutsche Geschichte 1866–1918*.

monarchy'),[13] there was nevertheless a relatively pluralist public realm which allowed for constructive political and social debate. Although for the most part this existed alongside the official political culture, it nevertheless proved to be the case that at different times various causes were taken up into the political sphere. This public arena made possible a limited degree of criticism of the State, and also made an important contribution to the process of the adaptation of the political institutions to the massive social changes experienced during what was a period of extraordinary economic growth: some influential groups, including many theologians, were thus able to 'gain a purchase on the wall of authoritarianism (*Obrigkeit*)'.[14]

Thus, although it is important not to overemphasize the pluralist sphere in German culture before the First World War, there is nevertheless an inherent implausibility in H.-U. Wehler's thesis that cultural codes (including religion) were primarily concerned with regulating conflict and offered little more than an 'ideology of legitimation'.[15] Indeed the public activity of many liberal theologians provides an important counter-example to this view since, even though many were as equally concerned as the officers of the State with efforts at social integration, there was a tendency to rethink the nature of that integration *apart from* the State, while at the same time taking account of the constraining conditions of modernity. The public theology of Ernst Troeltsch, whose work will be discussed in detail in the course of this book, provides the most important example.

While it is important not to overestimate the influence of theologians in the critical public sphere,[16] many were concerned to reshape culture through engagement in public debate. A useful example of this is provided by the proliferation of new non-specialist religious journals from the beginning of the Wilhelmine period, which were dominated by a select band of more or less 'anti-authoritarian' liberal scholars. Perhaps most important is Martin Rade's *Die Christliche Welt*, which came to bear the subtitle, 'Protestant Journal for Cultured People of All Classes', and in which political, theological, and social debates carried equal prominence.[17] Theology, at least as

---

[13] H.-U. Wehler, *The German Empire 1871–1918*, 64–5.
[14] M. L. Anderson, 'Voter, Junker, *Landrat*, Priest', 1460.
[15] Wehler, *The German Empire*, 118.
[16] It is important to bear in mind that some 60 to 70 per cent of pastors saw themselves as 'positive' and consequently identified themselves with the inherited authoritarian and confessional political system.
[17] On the history and theological position of *Die Christliche Welt* see Hübinger, *Kulturprotestantismus*, esp. 132–42; and Rathje, *Die Welt des freien Protestantismus*. Supporters of the newspaper organized conferences and activities as well as contributing to a private news-sheet edited by Martin Rade which has recently been published in facsimile: Christoph Schwöbel (ed.), *An die Freunde*. This provides 'one of the best sources of the theological and political debates of

carried on in such journals, had distanced itself from a fixation on confessionalism and more generally on ecclesiasticism, exerting a direct influence
in the public domain. Thus Rade claimed to 'hate' church politics[18] and
resisted any attempt to establish a Church party, even refusing the term
'liberal' itself. Indeed the public profile of *Die Christliche Welt* makes any
appraisal in purely theological categories at best misleading.[19] Although in
comparison with the confessional press its circulation was small (about
5,400 in 1908), *Die Christliche Welt*, together with other new journals, excited
a politically aware and activist pastorate and a broader intellectual élite,
thereby exerting much greater influence on the public debate than might
have been expected.[20] On the fortieth anniversary of its foundation Harnack
described *Die Christliche Welt* as the 'only cosmopolitan church paper that
we Germans possess',[21] and it came to occupy a key position in raising the
awareness of the problem of social integration in a Christian readership in
pre-war Germany.

At a somewhat different level, university theologians were keenly aware
of the need to publicize their scientific scholarship, and a range of books was
produced which moved outside the traditional arena of university theology
to offer popular presentations of theological research. Thus, according to
the biblical scholar Hermann Gunkel (1862–1932), there was a widespread
feeling that scholars had a duty to discuss popular religion, rather than to
indulge simply in the esoteric study of literary and textual criticism. He
reminded his fellow-theologians: 'our people are thirsty for your words
about religion and its history'.[22] This tendency to spread the appeal of
theology to a broader educated audience is exemplified by the publishing

the Wilhelmine period' (Hübinger, *Kulturprotestantismus*, 52). *An die Freunde* circulated among
the *Freunde der Christlichen Welt* (who numbered up to 1,450), among whom were virtually
all the liberal theologians, pastors, and intellectuals of the Wilhelmine period, including
Troeltsch and Harnack, and, later, the dialectical theologians of the Weimar era including Bultmann and Barth. It provides an invaluable commentary on the various causes fought by liberal
theologians (like the Jatho and Traub cases), discussions of political and social problems, and
large numbers of programmatic essays. While avoiding blind affirmation of culture, the *Freunde*
and their private journal nevertheless typify a renewed attempt to find cultural unity under the
conditions of modernity against the various conservative and fanatical alternatives (Hübinger,
Kulturprotestantismus, 142).

[18] *An die Freunde*, 130.
[19] Hübinger, *Kulturprotestantismus*, 142. Cf. Rathje, *Die Welt des freien Protestantismus*. In
his introduction to the reprinted edition of *An die Freunde*, Christoph Schwöbel fails to locate
the theological context of *Die christliche Welt* in the wider setting of German culture, thereby
underestimating the political implications of what was ostensibly a theological discussion
journal.
[20] Hübinger, *Kulturprotestantismus*, 133. See also F. W. Graf, 'Rettung der Persönlichkeit',
108.
[21] [Martin Rade], *Vierzig Jahre 'Christliche Welt': Festgabe für Martin Rade*, 3.
[22] Gunkel in *CW* 14 (1900), 60, cited by Graf, 'Rettung der Persönlichkeit', 108.

policy of Paul and Oskar Siebeck at J. C. B. Mohr, who produced the 'spiritual emblem' of the era,[23] the first edition of *Die Religion in Geschichte und Gegenwart*, as well as the long run of popular works like the *Religionsgeschichtliche Volksbücher*, which were produced in their thousands.[24] The publisher's advertising material for this series (to which virtually all the leading liberal theologians contributed) claimed:

Through systematic studies the *religionsgeschichtliche Volksbücher* intend to satisfy the inquiry through a study that is radical in the sense of being thoroughgoing, popular in the sense of its unembellished clarity, comprehensive in the sense that nothing necessary is left out of consideration, and scientific in the sense that all the best-educated specialists (who are free from apologetic but also free from every other tendency) present it in such a way as the experts set it forth.[25]

The style of Protestantism characterized by the Mohr press clearly exemplifies the stress on the practical application of Christianity within the constraints of modernity.

The historical reasons for this theological engagement in the public sphere, which will be alluded to in the course of this book, are complex. Perhaps most crucial was the need to compete with the Social Democratic Party, which increased massively in support in the years before the First World War, becoming the largest party in the Reichstag by 1912. As a response to this perceived threat there was a growth in the number of Protestant organizations concerned with social policy, which sought to provide alternative models for social integration in industrial society. Indeed some theologians, including Ernst Troeltsch, Wilhelm Herrmann (1846–1922), and Martin Rade (1857–1940), viewed the growth of Social Democracy as a genuine reaction to the inability of the inherited political and social structures to provide social integration in an increasingly mobile and dislocated industrial society.[26] Similarly the rise of Social Democracy provoked something of a crisis in theological and political liberalism as it became increasingly clear that the liberal ideal of the autonomous individual seemed to lead to social fragmentation and bureaucratization.[27] This crisis awakened in many theologians a greater willingness to engage in social and political analysis and to enter into dialogue with social thinkers through such

---

[23] Hübinger, *Kulturprotestantismus*, 303. See also 190–218.

[24] The importance of Paul and Oskar Siebeck in the spread of the historical method has recently been reassessed in Hübinger, *Kulturprotestantismus*, 190–219. For circulation figures, see 208–19.

[25] Cited in Rühle, *Der theologische Verlag J. C. B. Mohr*, 119 n.39.

[26] Cf. Wilhelm Herrmann, 'Religion und Sozialdemokratie', 260; *Ethik*, 205–21. See also Troeltsch, *Die Soziallehren* (A1912/2), 473 n.215, ET, 835 n.215.

[27] See, for instance, Troeltsch's depressing account of modernity in 'Das Wesen des modernen Geistes' (A1907/8b).

organizations as the *Evangelischer Sozial Kongreß*[28] in the effort to find new principles for social integration.

Perhaps more importantly, the integrating social whole for many theologians was not to be conceived as a contemporary equivalent of the confessional *Obrigkeitsstaat* of the seventeenth-century religious settlement, but was instead understood as something dynamic, and constituted through the process of critical engagement and restructuring. Thus, far from being primarily concerned with the religious legitimation of the predecessor or prevailing culture, many theologians, of whom Troeltsch was again the leading representative, were engaged in its critical reconstruction: indeed, for Troeltsch, the 'greatness of religion lay in its opposition to culture [and] in its difference from science and from utilitarian ethics'.[29] In contrast to the often simplistic Utopianism of much earlier liberal theology (of, for example, Richard Rothe (1799–1867)), as well as the thought of most of the conservative theologians of previous generations, the 'social question', accompanied by a relatively sophisticated sociological and statistical analysis, began to dominate the public theological debate. Perceptive analysts like the sociologist Max Weber (1864–1920) and the politician and theologian Friedrich Naumann (1860–1919), as well as Troeltsch, were clear that Protestantism, if it was to retain any potency in contemporary debate, would have to reformulate its thinking under the new conditions of highly industrialized society with its class conflicts and unprecedented social problems. In turn, neither Church nor State could be understood simply as givens, but had themselves to be reshaped under modern conditions, a process which would continue into the future.[30] The double imperative for the modern theologian was thus to understand the distinctive strands of modernity as well as to engage in public debate, since it was only through intervention in the public sphere that there could be any hope of social integration on the basis of Christian ethics. The dominant questions for the liberal theologian, which were posed by Troeltsch (and by many other theologians in varying form), were thus: 'what are the characteristic fundamental currents of the modern world?'[31] and what constraints and opportunities do they offer for Christian social ethics?

---

[28] The *Evangelischer Sozial Kongreß* commissioned many important statistical surveys, which contributed to the development of sociology as a discipline in Germany.

[29] 'Die Kirche im Leben der Gegenwart' (A1911/8a), 100.

[30] On Troeltsch's understanding of the Church see Mark D. Chapman, 'Concepts of the Voluntary Church in England and Germany, 1890–1920'; and Bradley E. Starr, 'Individualism and Reform'.

[31] 'Autonomie und Rationalismus' (A1907/11), col. 199.

THEOLOGICAL HISTORY IN THE LIGHT OF 1914

The task of writing theological history is, however, far from straightforward. Many, if not most, historians of theology have adopted what might be described as a dispensationalist approach to history, whereby the old covenant with the heirs of Schleiermacher and Ritschl (like Harnack and Troeltsch) has been superseded by the new covenant with Barth and the dialectical theologians of the 1920s. In this version of the story, the redundancy of the old dispensation is marked by the siding of some of the leading liberal theologians with Germany's war aims in 1914.

In his influential account of German Protestant theology in the twentieth century, for instance, Heinz Zahrnt proclaimed that 'historically, the Twentieth Century began in August 1914 with the outbreak of the First World War'.[32] Zahrnt here is agreeing with Karl Barth, who saw as decisive the support of many of his intellectual mentors, including Herrmann and Harnack, for the manifesto of the intellectuals in favour of Germany's war aims. Although Barth had wrongly identified the 4 October 1914 petition of the intellectuals, 'Appeal to the Civilized World',[33] with the theologians' 'Appeal to Protestant Christians Abroad' which was issued at the end of August,[34] he regarded its publication as a 'black day' for theology, and responded by claiming that he could no 'longer follow either their ethics and dogmatics or their understanding of the Bible and of history. For me,' he went on, 'nineteenth-century theology no longer held any future'.[35] The theological tasks of the past, and indeed the pre-war activities of theologians which might have offered any contrary evidence of critical engagement with culture, had thus been rendered null and void by their behaviour during the war.

[32] Heinz Zahrnt, *The Question of God*, 15.

[33] 'An die Kulturwelt', *Berliner Tageblatt*, 4 October 1914. Among the ninety-three intellectuals who signed this appeal, several were leading theologians, including Adolf von Harnack, Wilhelm Herrmann, Adolf Deissmann, Reinhold Seeberg, and Adolf von Schlatter.

[34] 'An die evangelischen Christen im Auslande' (August, 1914); it was published in English in an appendix to a reply produced in Oxford: *To the Christian Scholars of Europe and America*, 19–23. This was a relatively moderate appeal endorsed by twenty-nine theologians, who pleaded that war should be confined to Europe so that the significant gains in the mission field should not be put at risk because of a dispute between the great missionary powers. It was dismissed in Britain as a cynical or a naïve attempt to safeguard the German colonies against invasion. For details of the various manifestos and counter-manifestos, see Charles E. Bailey, 'Gott mit uns', esp. 479–87, and 'The British Protestant Theologians'.

[35] 'Evangelical Theology in the Nineteenth Century', 14. For Barth's attitude to the First World War see McCormack, *Karl Barth's Critical Realistic Dialecticl Theology*, ch. 2, esp. 78–9, 112. The reaction of Germany's theologians to Germany's war aims was ambivalent, and often critical. Harnack and Troeltsch were among those who objected to Seeberg's 'Petition of the Intellectuals' of July 1915, and who signed a counter-declaration. On Troeltsch's involvement in politics in the First World War see Bernd Sösemann, 'Das "erneute Deutschland"'. For an interpretation of Germany's wartime theology see Mark D. Chapman, 'Theology, Nationalism and the First World War'.

Such a reading of theological history, with its emphasis on the abrupt caesura of 1914, means that the so-called 'Culture Protestants' of late nineteenth- and early twentieth-century Germany have usually been included amongst that group of theologians who made the interesting yet ultimately futile attempt to accommodate Christianity to the prevailing culture, in this case the militaristic and illiberal culture of Wilhelmine Germany. This becomes even more telling in Barth's account, where he points to another significant event which finally shook his faith in 'the good old days' of the nineteenth century: 'Accidentally or not,' he wrote, 'Ernst Troeltsch, the well-known professor of systematic theology and the leader of the then most modern school, gave up his chair in theology for one in philosophy'.[36] Although perhaps not an event of such world-historical proportions as the war, Troeltsch's defection from theology was considered by Barth to be as vital—at least symbolically—in sounding the death-knell for nineteenth-century theology.[37] Even if Barth had misunderstood Troeltsch's motives for changing faculty,[38] his move to Berlin (the capital city of the empire) and to the Faculty of Philosophy (the science of human reason) characterizes the logical culmination of any theology which starts from the human perspective.[39]

---

[36] Barth, 'Evangelical Theology', 14.

[37] Many of Troeltsch's critics, following Karl Barth, have seen him as a Culture Protestant (e.g. Reist, *Towards a Theology of Involvement*; and Bodenstein, *Neige des Historismus*). From a completely different perspective, Hans Bosse (*Marx–Weber–Troeltsch*, esp. 140ff.) compares Troeltsch and Marx, suggesting that for Troeltsch the conditions shaping human action were forever immutable. Troeltsch thus becomes guilty of Culture Protestantism, since any cultural synthesis would have to incorporate the status quo. Marx similarly recognized that certain economic conditions shape human action yet such conditions could be changed in revolutionary praxis. More recently McCormack (*Karl Barth's Critical Realistic Dialectical Theology*, 215) has depicted Troeltsch as the archetypal 'theologian of mediation' and Constance L. Benson (in *God and Caesar*) has painted an original if completely implausible picture of Troeltsch as a proto-Nazi and anti-Semite (e.g. 93, 215). However, such views, especially Benson's, entirely underestimate Troeltsch's critical distance from his own culture. As will become clear, Troeltsch's real position is rather more complex and is not so inherently conservative, since it allows for a reshaping of the forces that constrain human action in a synthesis *for the future*: compromise and assimilation are two very different principles. See also Rupp, *Culture Protestantism*.

[38] From 1910 Troeltsch had also taught in the Faculty of Philosophy at Heidelberg, and by 1915, on his transfer to Berlin, he claimed that he had 'outgrown' the confines of the theological faculty which he had earlier experienced as having 'a natural inclination towards fanaticism' (review of Jastrow (A1905/1), col. 14). There is little discontinuity in Troeltsch's concerns: even Amanda Seeberg could remark that Berlin got 'a believing philosopher rather than an unbelieving theologian' (*Lebensbild von Reinhold Seeberg*, cited in Bailey, 'Gott mit uns', 22). A move out of the ecclesiastically dominated theological faculty came as a great 'liberation and stimulus' (letter from Troeltsch to Herrmann, 10 March 1918) and gave space for an ever 'more exacting study of real life *Kultur* in general' (Troeltsch to Natorp, 4 July 1918). On Troeltsch's move to Berlin, see U. Pretzel, 'Ernst Troeltschs Berufung an die Berliner Universität'; and Gertrud von le Fort, *Hälfte des Lebens*, 122–3.

[39] In an autobiographical statement of 1927 (included in *Karl Barth–Rudolf Bultmann Letters*,

Barth's influential writing of theological history undoubtedly possesses the virtue of simplicity and may well point to certain dangers in a theology which fails to engage sufficiently critically with the culture in which it emerges. Nevertheless his rhetorical dismissiveness of his theological teachers as guilty by association, as well as the starkness of his dialectical terms, have served to isolate much earlier nineteenth-century German theology, and especially the theology of the early years of the twentieth century, from serious historical investigation. Indeed after Barth the the-ology of the 'long nineteenth century' may be seen as something of an aberration, all attempts to accommodate theology to post-Enlightenment patterns of thought being regarded as an intellectual cul-de-sac.[40] For Barth, and for many since, nineteenth-century theology has been seen as guilty not merely of idolizing a degenerate German culture, but also as equally in bondage to its eighteenth-century heritage, and thus to the Enlightenment's elevation of human reason as the measure of all things. This meant that theology had unwittingly become the servant of an anti-religious secularism, which, as Barth put it, was 'probably more pointed than the much praised or deplored secularism of today'.[41]

As a piece of powerful rhetoric Barth's (admittedly often surprisingly sympathetic)[42] dismissal of nineteenth-century theology has undoubtedly exerted a great deal of influence. And it is an interpretation that has a certain plausibility: the style of theology which will be discussed in this book may well lead to a dead end. However, before there can be any chance of deciding, it is important to return to the authors themselves. Over-bold interpretations have made it all too easy to overlook the subtleties of the period and the different strands of the many theologies that developed at least in part as responses to unprecedented social, political, and economic change. Furthermore, the Barthian approach also underplays the complex public profile and political activity of theologians themselves in the cultural and political debates in the years before 1914. This book is written in the

153) Barth claims that even while he was a student he had recognized Troeltsch as representing 'the limit beyond which I thought I must refuse to follow the dominant theology of the age'.

[40] For a recent popular account see A. E. McGrath, *The Genesis of Doctrine*, 199.

[41] See esp. Barth, 'Evangelical Theology', 15, 21. On this see K. G. Steck, 'Karl Barths Absage an die Neuzeit'.

[42] Barth at times stressed the importance of trying to understand the nineteenth century on its own terms. His history of *Protestant Theology in the Nineteenth Century*, while certainly not devoid of polemics, is rather less damning: 'To hear someone else always means to suspend one's own concerns ... If we are dealing with history—and before we pursue our own concerns and while we do so as theologians, we must also be occupied with history—this controversy originating in our own time must not be allowed to dominate the proceedings. We must always—under the presupposition of the unity of the Church—investigate the particular context and concern of the past and understand this from its own relative centre and not from ours' (24, 27).

2

The History of Religion School

The problems of history in relation to religion, which had been sensed so profoundly during the Enlightenment and throughout the nineteenth century, were taken up with great vigour by a group of biblical scholars in a thoroughgoing and rigorous way towards the end of the 1880s. This chapter and the next analyse the origins and teaching of the so-called 'History of Religion School',[1] which was of such vital importance in the development of liberal theology before the First World War. As this chapter shows, the reorientation of the dominant Ritschlian strand of liberal theology and its later dismemberment into a number of competing theological strands was achieved primarily through critical engagement with the Bible and with biblical religion.

There were, of course, huge problems associated with a thoroughgoing adoption of a historical method in theology. One of the leading members of the School, the New Testament scholar Wilhelm Bousset,[2] recognized this, observing that historical research was in 'danger of placing Christianity in the flux of development', of 'failing to give due worth to its special character and unique meaning, and thereby neutralizing and relativizing everything'.[3] 'The halo of the supernatural which had clung around "sacred history"', he

---

[1] I have translated *religionsgeschichtliche Schule* accurately as 'History of Religion School' for reasons that will become clear in the course of this chapter. For discussions of the History of Religion School see esp. Gerd Lüdemann, *Die religionsgeschichtliche Schule in Göttingen* and 'Die Religionsgeschichtliche Schule'; F. W. Graf, 'Der "Systematiker" der "kleinen Göttinger Fakultät"'; W. G. Kümmel, *The New Testament*, 245–324; G. W. Ittel, 'Die Hauptgedanken'; Anthonie Verheule, *Wilhelm Bousset*; W. Klatt, *Hermann Gunkel*; Martin Rade, 'Religionsgeschichte'; Dieter Sänger, 'Phänomenologie oder Geschichte'. Stephen Neill gives an inaccurate but influential treatment in *The Interpretation of the New Testament*, 157–67. The best recent discussion in English is by John K. Riches, *A Century of New Testament Study*, 42 ff. For an account of the development of New Testament theology following the School see David Way, *The Lordship of Christ*.

[2] Wilhelm Bousset (1865–1920), *Privatdozent* (PD) in New Testament (NT) in Göttingen (1889); *extraordinarius* (1896); *ordinarius* in Gießen (1916). For bibliography and comprehensive account of his life and work see esp. Verheule, *Wilhelm Bousset*; and Berger, 'Nationalsoziale Religionsgeschichte'.

[3] Wilhelm Bousset, 'Die Religionsgeschichte und das neue Testament', 364 f.

claimed, 'was destroyed',[4] which meant that history had become a 'labyrinth
for modern religious liberalism', where it threatened 'to betray itself'.[5]

All too often, however, the price paid for the escape from historical relativism was too high: a religion founded on personal spiritual experience, which
became the hallmark of the theory of religion adopted by most of the members
of the School, lost the power to change history. The very notion of a public
theology was thereby called into question. As a reaction to the dehumanizing
effects of Wilhelmine capitalism,[6] the escape into the individual was unsur-
prising, yet, as both Bousset and Troeltsch came to recognize, such 'mystical'
religion was ethically impotent. The second half of this chapter discusses the
ethical implications of the history of religion method in some detail: however
threatening history and the modern world might have become for Christian
faith, 'the most important question of life' was still, according to Troeltsch, the
'justification of the religious attitude to life against the all-devouring dominion
of modern naturalism'.[7] Ethics was thus central to the task of theology.

ALBRECHT RITSCHL AND THE FORMATION OF THE
HISTORY OF RELIGION SCHOOL

The Legacy of Ritschl

The most formative influence on the whole generation of German liberal
theologians working in the years before 1914 was Albrecht Ritschl,[8] whose
magnum opus, Justification and Reconciliation, presents a magisterial combination of religion, history, and ethics.[9] For Ritschl, God and the world had to be
united in an all-embracing system.[10] Thus, with his conviction that 'the pre-
eminent excellence of Christianity' was 'its view of the world as a *well-
rounded whole*',[11] Ritschl saw theology as centred on the combination of
'spiritual freedom and dominion over the world *and* labour for the Kingdom

---

[4] Bousset, *What is Religion?*, 288.   [5] Bousset, 'Der religiöse Liberalismus', 22.

[6] Cf. Troeltsch, 'Das Wesen des modernen Geistes' (A1907/8b), esp. 310 f.; ET, 249.

[7] Troeltsch, 'Meine Bücher' (A1921/29b), 5; ET, 367. These problems are explored briefly by
F. W. Graf in 'Religion und Individualität'.

[8] Albrecht Ritschl (1822–89), studied at Bonn, Halle, Heidelberg, and Tübingen; became *PD*
in NT in Bonn in 1846, and also in Church History and History of Dogma from 1848; *extraordinarius* from 1852 and *ordinarius* from 1859. From 1864 he was *ordinarius* in Göttingen, until his
death. For a bibliography of primary and secondary work see Zelger, 'Modernisierte Gemeindetheologie'. For biographical details see Otto Ritschl, *Albrecht Ritschls Leben*.

[9] On Ritschl's ethics see Helga Kuhlmann, *Die Theologische Ethik Albrecht Ritschls*.

[10] Cf. Hermann Timm, *Theorie und Praxis*, 24, 58, which maintains that Ritschl, although
critical of Hegel, nevertheless retained a quasi-Hegelian universal, inherited from his earlier
period when he had been under the influence of F. C. Baur, where both spiritual and natural
phenomena were part of the same reality.

[11] *JR* i. 188 f.

of God'.[12] Barth's insistence that Ritschl had completely ethicized the Gospel[13] along Kantian lines is therefore a misrepresentation since, according to Ritschl, 'if justification by faith is the basal conception of Christianity, it is impossible that it can express the relation of human beings to God and Christ without at the same time including a distinctive attitude of the believer to the world founded on that revelation'.[14] Ritschl thus held that faith and ethical activity were inextricably intertwined.

For Ritschl, the biblical and Reformation doctrine of the forgiveness of sins through the justification wrought by Christ meant that the Christian lived in a state of having been redeemed, which implied that the world did not constitute a lower reality from which the human was called upon to escape into a higher reality of faith, but it had instead to be incorporated into an all-embracing system. Thus Ritschl asked:

How can man, recognising himself as a part of the world and at the same time capable of a spiritual personality, attain to that dominion over the world, as opposed to limitation by it, which this capability gives him the right to claim?[15]

He answered by pointing to the centrality of the work of Christ for purposeful behaviour in the world, which alone would overcome the competing world-views of materialism and monism: 'In this *coherence* of the spiritual life the individual person possesses the significance of a *whole* which exceeds the significance of the entire world which is viewed as the ordering of a divided and naturally conditioned universe.[16] Ritschl summarized his theology most clearly in the first volume of *Justification and Reconciliation*:

Lordship over the world through trust in God, especially over the evils arising out of it, is the practical and purposeful correlate of justification, which Luther discovered in the footsteps of Paul and which Melanchthon was able to formulate in the classic documents of the Reformation. For whoever is reconciled with God is also reconciled with the course of the world which is conducted by God in one's best interest.[17]

However, all too often, according to Ritschl, the practical worldly aspects of the Reformation had been 'concealed', not least by the Reformers themselves.[18] As he maintained in his massive history of pietism:

Frankly it is shocking that there is no mention of the practical aims of justification by faith in the Fourth Article of the Augsburg Confession [i.e. that on 'justification by faith']. And if we explicate this aim in any other terms than blessedness, within present experience, and if we do not take the believer's attitude towards the world into consideration, how is it to be understood as distinctively Protestant?[19]

---

[12] *Instruction*, §47.
[13] Barth, *Protestant Theology in the Nineteenth Century*, 655. Cf. Christian Walther, *Typen des Reich-Gottes-Verständnis*, 163.
[14] *JR* iii. 168.   [15] *Instruction*, §8.   [16] *Instruction*, §50.   [17] *JR* i. 184 f.
[18] 'Festrede', 195.   [19] *GP*, 86; ET, 128.

In contrast to this position, Ritschl held that Protestantism had to centre on both religion and ethics without conflating the one with the other: a distinctive set of ideals (*Lebensideal*) had to lead to distinctive ways of behaviour (*Lebensführung*) if it was genuinely to be called Protestant.

The religious and the ethical, which Ritschl likened to two foci of an ellipse,[20] were thus united in the whole which formed the Protestant religion: Christian perfection was not achieved in some otherworldly sphere or through 'mystical escape', but in obedience to a 'worldly vocation [*Beruf*]' as the 'place for the practice of love'.[21] Indeed, according to Ritschl, this was the 'fundamental principle of Protestantism'.[22] The true meaning of the Lutheran doctrine of vocation was thus 'the practical expression for the fact that Christianity is not world-denying but world-fulfilling and world-pervading'.[23] Perfection was not to be found by Christians in some higher realm but precisely 'through continual intercourse with the world and within their distinctive vocations in worldly society'.[24] Nevertheless the highest end was still to order all ethical activity.[25]

The objective redemption effected by Christ had the practical result of inspiring activity motivated by love which led to a new organization of humanity, the kingdom of God,[26] as the earthly correlate of the love of God revealed for humankind in the reconciliation of Jesus Christ. Once again, Ritschl's theology is focused on the centrality of the community. He claimed: 'The community's faith . . . is the immediate object of theological cognition'.[27] Christianity was thus, according to Ritschl:

the perfected spiritual and ethical monotheistic religion, which, on the basis of the redeemed life and the kingdom of God established by its founder, consists in the freedom of divine adoption, and which includes the stimulus for activity from the motive of love which is directed to the ethical organization of humanity and which establishes blessedness both in divine adoption and in the kingdom of God.[28]

Divine purposes, however, could never be fully equated with worldly purposes; the motive of love would always 'point' beyond the world. 'It is an essential characteristic of the Kingdom of God,' Ritschl wrote, 'that the ultimate purpose in the world for created spirits reaches out beyond the world'.[29] All human activity pointed forwards to a future where reconciliation would be complete 'since the fullness of divine reward always reaches out beyond the measure of the presumed human achievement'.[30] In turn, Ritschl claimed, the Church could never be wholly identified with the kingdom of God but was rather a means to an end, representing the idea of the

---

[20] *JR* iii. 11.   [21] *GP*, 41; ET, 86.   [22] *GP*, 41; ET, 87.   [23] *GP*, 41; ET, 87.
[24] *GP*, 41; ET, 86.   [25] *Instruction*, §28.   [26] *JR* iii. 12 f.
[27] *JR* iii. 3. On this see also Zelger, 'Modernisierte Gemeindetheologie', 185–9.
[28] *JR* iii. 13 f.   [29] *JR* iii. 267.   [30] *JR* ii. 37.

'ethical unification of the human race through activity inspired by the motive of love'.[31] It thus fulfilled a function and was not merely an institution:

> Those who believe in Christ are a church in so far as they acknowledge in prayer their faith in God the Father and present themselves as human beings well pleasing to him through Christ. Those who believe in Christ are a kingdom of God in so far as, without observing the differences of sex, class or nation, they act reciprocally towards one another out of love.[32]

Ritschl's idea of the Christian community, as epitomized by the kingdom of God, thus rests on a vocational ethic; that is, on the need to live *within* a world which can be changed by the activity of love. Christian living does not leave the world untouched, but is capable of profound world-transforming possibilities. Thus, however much Ritschl might have seen God as the Prussian paterfamilias, and however much he might have equated worldly vocation with the maintenance of the status quo, he nevertheless provided the basis for subsequent attempts to reform the present for the sake of the future, to bring love as the highest motivation for action to its concrete realization. Against the other-worldly 'ascetic ethic' of the pietists who cut themselves off from the world, Ritschl's theology was based on a shaping of the world around higher ends.

Ritschl sought to ground his vision of a vocational theology in the historical figure of Christ, claiming that the 'idea of an ethical vocation . . . serves as a criterion for the public life of Christ as a visibly connected whole . . . His conduct . . . is as certainly in harmony with the universal moral law, as the end of the Kingdom of God, which he pursues in his special vocation as the founder, is the supreme end out of which the moral law arises'.[33] Thus the criterion for assessing history was drawn from the personality of Christ, who obediently fulfilled his vocation.[34] The kingdom of God, Ritschl contended, had been initiated by Jesus, who conceived of himself as Messiah,[35] and in his person revealed the highest human capacity for obedience to a divine vocation. It was thus Jesus himself who had founded a community on earth directed to the realization of the highest ethical good.[36] In short: 'The realization of the ultimate divine purpose in the world implies the messianic consciousness, and the success of education for the Kingdom of God is therefore dependent on the fact that the dominion of God which was to be realized ethically gained its archetype in [Christ's] person.'[37] It was the general thrust of Ritschl's vision, if not all its details, that served to attract many students to hear him in Göttingen.

---

[31] *JR* iii. 267.   [32] *JR* iii. 271.   [33] *JR* iii. 446.
[34] *JR* iii. 386 f., 476 f.; cf. *Unterricht*, §44.   [35] *JR* ii. 37.   [36] *JR* ii. 40.
[37] *JR* iii. 267.

The Attraction of Ritschl

Ritschl's son and biographer observed that it was Ritschl's efforts in systematic theology, rather than his labours in biblical theology,[38] that 'won over
his pupils to his view of Christianity'.[39] Ernst Troeltsch, for instance,
described his attraction towards Ritschl's theological concerns in his tribute
to his close friend Wilhelm Bousset,[40] published in 1920: while they were
both studying at Erlangen in the winter semester of 1884,[41] they had experienced a 'profound change' which led them to see the theological debate of
the time, particularly the conservative Lutheranism exemplified there,[42] as
failing to address what the two young colleagues saw as the real 'social and
political problems of the time' as well as the 'current natural-scientific
world-view'.[43] The problem with such theology, Troeltsch held, was its utter
failure to address the conditions of modernity. Its leading representatives,
including Ritschl's opponent F. H. R. Frank,[44] seemed to Troeltsch to be little more than 'relics of the fight between neo-pietism and the Enlightenment',[45] who sought refuge in what has been called the 'sectarian
mentality'[46] of the certainty of faith.[47] In such a theology there seemed to be
a huge gulf separating the intellect from the feelings. This dissatisfaction
with the Erlangen theology meant that Troeltsch was engaged in dispute
with his teachers ('nine tenths of whom were boring')[48] almost from the

[38] For a contemporary assessment of the weaknesses of Ritschl's biblical theology see Marsh,
Albrecht Ritschl.

[39] Otto Ritschl, *Albrecht Ritschls Leben*, ii. 260. What ought to be added, however, is that it was
precisely his failures as a biblical scholar that led many of his pupils into biblical studies.

[40] Troeltsch's friendship with Bousset has been well documented by Drescher (in *Ernst
Troeltsch*), who also makes many unpublished letters available for the first time (esp. 28–95).
Other letters were published in 'Briefe aus der Heidelberger Zeit an Wilhelm Bousset'
(G1976/2). On the student life of Troeltsch and Bousset see also Horst Renz, 'Troeltschs Theologiestudium'; and Graf, 'Der "Systematiker"'. To some extent at least, much of Troeltsch's
theology has to be understood in relation to Ritschl and even as a continuation of his basic system. Cf. W. Bodenstein, *Neige des Historismus*, 13; Yasukata, *Systematic Theologian*, 2.

[41] On Troeltsch's period in Erlangen see Drescher, *Ernst Troeltsch*, ET, 8–15.

[42] On the Erlangen theological tradition see F. W. Kantzenbach, *Die Erlanger Theologie*.

[43] Troeltsch, 'Die "kleine Göttinger Fakultät" von 1890' (A1920/8), col. 281. At Erlangen
Troeltsch was also influenced by the philosopher Gustav Claß (1836–1908), who probably
helped him move towards his own theological and philosophical position, particularly by point-
ing him in the direction of Kant, Lotze, and Schleiermacher. On Troeltsch and Claß see
Drescher, *Ernst Troeltsch*, ET, 30 f.; and H. Will, 'Ethik als allgemeine Theorie des geistigen
Lebens. Troeltsch' Erlanger Lehrer Gustav Claß'.

[44] Franz Hermann Reinhold Frank (1827–94). From 1857 Prof. in Erlangen. On Frank see
Falk Wagner, 'Lutherische Erfahrungstheologie'.

[45] 'Die "kleine Göttinger Fakultät" von 1890' (A1920/8), col. 281.

[46] Wagner, 'Lutherische Erfahrungstheologie', 228.

[47] Cf. Frank, *System der christlichen Gewißheit*.

[48] A remark given by Troeltsch in his qualifying examination for the ministry (14 June 1891),
cited in Drescher, *Ernst Troeltsch*, ET, 348.

outset of his theological education.[49] He experienced this deeply, as he wrote in a letter to Bousset in 1885:

There is no such thing as a consistent conception of the world. The combination of the two elements of the mechanical and the mental into an all-embracing construction will never be achieved: there will always be a massive unfathomable gulf between the two components. Research will always end with this statement: 'My understanding tells me this; my feelings tell me that' . . . The only systems which are consistent are those which deny one or other of these components.[50]

It was perhaps the pressing desire to find a solution to this split between feeling and intellect, and thus to bring Christianity into some kind of union with modern thought, that led Troeltsch, after a brief period in Berlin,[51] to study from 1886 to 1888 under Albrecht Ritschl in Göttingen. Ritschl, whose name was 'in the air everywhere',[52] had attempted (albeit in a quite different way from many of his students) to bring Christianity into a relationship with modernity. As Troeltsch later remarked: 'it was Ritschl who won us for theology; his powerful personality attracted us to Göttingen; we formed his last school'.[53] Similarly, in an autobiographical work, he could call Ritschl his 'teacher',[54] and in several of his letters to Bousset he reveals his sense of affection for Ritschl; indeed he was deeply shaken by Ritschl's death.[55]

Ritschl's influence on the group of young theologians who came together at Göttingen in the late 1880s was profound. However, many of his leading tenets were soon rejected,[56] which meant that the History of Religion School quickly became, in Hermann Gunkel's[57] words, a 'school without a teacher'.[58] This point is brought out by Hugo Greßmann, one of the School's early historians, who maintained that the word 'School' had to be 'understood in a general way' in order to have 'any meaning at all'.[59] Indeed, in the

[49] Drescher, *Ernst Troeltsch*. This biography is in many places deeply flawed. The best sections, however, concern Troeltsch's early intellectual development. See my review in *JTS* (1993), 437–40.
[50] Letter to Bousset (12 August 1885) (G1976/2), 22. The duality in Troeltsch's early thought between the intellect and the feelings is also brought out clearly in a letter of 30 July 1885 cited in Drescher, *Ernst Troeltsch*, ET, 34.
[51] On this see Drescher, *Ernst Troeltsch*, ET, 15–19.
[52] Letter to Bousset of 23 December 1885, cited in Drescher, *Ernst Troeltsch*, ET, 19.
[53] 'Die "kleine Göttinger Fakultät" von 1890' (A1920/8), col. 282. On Ritschl's influence in Göttingen see Jörg Baur, 'Albrecht Ritschl: Herrschaft und Versöhnung'.
[54] 'Meine Bücher' (A1921/29b), 5.
[55] Letter to Bousset of 23 March 1889, cited in Drescher, *Ernst Troeltsch*, ET, 20f.
[56] Cf. Gerd Lüdemann, 'Die Religionsgeschichtliche Schule', 325, 332.
[57] Hermann Gunkel (1862–1932), *PD* in NT in Göttingen (1888); *PD* in Halle (1889); Prof. in Berlin (1895); Prof. of Old Testament (OT) in Gießen (1907); Prof. in Halle (1920). See esp. Klatt, *Hermannn Gunkel* and J. C. O'Neill, *The Bible's Authority*, 231–47. For a fairly complete bibliography see Hans Schmidt (ed.), *ΕΥΧΑΡΙΣΤΗΡΙΟΝ*, 214–25.
[58] Gunkel, 'Gedächtnisrede an Wilhelm Bousset', 158.   [59] Greßmann, *Eichhorn*, 25.

opinion of Gunkel, one of the most important and original scholars associated with the School, it was little more than 'a many-sided friendship of a closely connected circle' of primarily New Testament scholars 'who found themselves in Göttingen at the professorial chair of Ritschl'.[60] Also among this circle of young academics were Ritschl's son-in-law Johannes Weiss,[61] Alfred Rahlfs,[62] Heinrich Hackmann,[63] later William Wrede[64] and, more distantly, Albert Eichhorn (who was nevertheless a key figure),[65] Wilhelm Heitmüller,[66] Hugo Greßmann,[67] Paul Wernle,[68] Heinrich Weinel,[69] and Richard Reitzenstein.[70] At a general level, it would be wrong to see the School as a homogeneous group, all of whom shared the same method: there were differences between and distinctive emphases in each of the scholars associated with the School and it cannot therefore be regarded as a monolithic academy of like-minded scholars.[71] They were united not so much by a common programme (although many of them were later to collaborate on the influential series of *religionsgeschichtliche Volksbücher*), but were rather, as Greßmann

[60] Gunkel, 'Gedächtnisrede an Wilhelm Bousset', 146.

[61] Johannes Weiss (1863–1914), son of Bernhard Weiss; PD in NT Göttingen (1888); Prof. (1890); Prof. in Marburg (1895); Prof. in Heidelberg (1908). On Weiss see Berthold Lannert, *Die Wiederentdeckung der neutestamentlichen Eschatologie*. Troeltsch was very pleased with Weiss's appointment at Heidelberg (see letter to Bousset of 1 March 1908 (G1976/2), 45).

[62] Alfred Rahlfs (1865–1935), PD in Göttingen (1891); Prof. (1901); OT textual critic. Alfred Rahlfs drew the attention of the young Göttinger to Lagarde. Troeltsch called him a 'friend' (letter to Bousset (G1976/2), 27) and remarked in another letter to Bousset: 'I shall never forget how much I owe to him and to Lagarde in terms of strictness and neatness, method and disposition which came to me through him' (27 May 1896, cited in Drescher, *Ernst Troeltsch*, ET, 349).

[63] Heinrich Hackmann (1864–1935), PD in Göttingen (1893–4); pastor in Shanghai; Prof. of History of Religion in Amsterdam (1913–33).

[64] William Wrede (1859–1906), PD in NT in Göttingen (1891); Prof. in Breslau (1893). See esp. introd. by A. Wrede in W. Wrede, *Vorträge und Studien*, pp. iii–xiv. For bibliography see G. Strecker, 'William Wrede'. Cf. W. Wiefel, 'Zur Würdigung William Wredes'; and Hans Rollmann, 'From Baur to Wrede'.

[65] Albert Eichhorn (1856–1926), PD in Halle (1886); Prof. in Halle (1888); Prof. in Kiel (1901–13). Suffered from severe illness. On Eichhorn see esp. Horst Renz, 'Albert Eichhorn'; and Greßmann, *Eichhorn*.

[66] Wilhelm Heitmüller (1869–1926), PD in Göttingen (1902); Prof. in Marburg (1902); Prof. in Bonn (1920); Prof. in Tübingen (1924); co-edited ThR with Bousset.

[67] Hugo Greßmann (1877–1927), Prof. of OT in Kiel (1902–6); Prof. in Berlin (1907–27).

[68] Paul Wernle (1872–1939), pupil of Bousset at Göttingen; PD of NT in Basel (1897); Prof. of Church History and Dogma at Basel (1900). He denied that he belonged to the school (cf. *Die Religionswissenschaft der Gegenwart in Selbstdarstellungen*, 228). The extensive correspondence from Troeltsch to Wernle has been edited by F. W. Graf, 'Ernst Troeltschs Briefe und Karten an Paul Wernle'.

[69] Heinrich Weinel (1874–1936), PD in NT in Berlin (1899); PD in Bonn (1900); Prof. of NT in Jena (1904); Prof. of Systematic Theology in Jena (1925). Particularly concerned with contemporary questions.

[70] Richard Reitzenstein (1861–1931), philologist; Prof. in Strassburg (1893); Freiburg (1911); Göttingen (1914–28). Published many works on Hellenistic religions.

[71] Cf. Lüdemann, 'Die Religionsgeschichtliche Schule', 325 ff.

suggested, a 'circle of researchers essentially of one mind, who worked under the guidance of the same spirit, shared a related problematic, and on the whole represented the same fundamental viewpoint'.[72]

In a letter of 1895 to Bousset congratulating him on the publication of his *Antichrist*, Troeltsch discussed this shared viewpoint, detecting a

> common current in the work of the young Göttingen school. This rests, if I might be permitted to say, on the unrestrained method of the history of religion which investigates the multifaceted religious movements which bear and surround Christianity in a purely historical manner. I have already noticed this in the book by Gunkel [i.e. *Schöpfung und Chaos*][73] and also in your work. Wrede also works in a similar way.[74]

A few years later Troeltsch spoke of this group as 'sharing' a method.[75] In an important article[76] F. W. Graf emphasizes the self-identification of the members of the School with a particular set of ideas, the 'conviction that theology must radically build on the basis of the historical consciousness',[77] thereby rejecting any artificial isolation of Christianity from its historical context. Although Graf maintains that the precise origins and the exact membership of the School give rise to more questions than answers,[78] he nevertheless asserts that 'what can be ascertained is that the group had a specific understanding of itself . . . and a sense of theological belonging which nevertheless did not deny the individuality of each of the young *Göttinger*'.[79]

By 1913, however, Troeltsch recognized that theology had changed: some form of historical method was far more widely accepted than had been the case at the outset of the History of Religion School in the late 1880s. Indeed, in his essay on the dogmatics of the History of Religion School, he claimed that the influence of the historical method had become so all-pervasive that 'these methods are used in scientific theology of every sort'.[80] Similarly, the Scottish theologian H. R. Mackintosh, who was very well versed in German theology, observed in 1909 that 'the new method of study, familiar to the Germans as the *religionsgeschichtliche Methode* is, in theology, the question of the hour'.[81] Troeltsch even doubted the possibility of speaking of a '*religionsgeschichtliche* School' at all.[82] He went on to say that:

[72] Greßmann, *Eichhorn*, 25.
[73] Troeltsch regarded Bousset's book as confirming Gunkel's conclusions.
[74] Letter to Bousset (G1976/2), 27.
[75] 'Geschichte und Metaphysik' (A1898/2), 5. On the development of the School see esp. F. W. Graf, 'Der "Systematiker"'; Gerd Lüdemann, *Die religionsgeschichtliche Schule in Göttingen*; and Horst Renz, 'Albert Eichhorn'.
[76] Graf, 'Der "Systematiker"'.   [77] Ibid., 289.
[78] Cf. Lüdemann, 'Die Religionsgeschichtliche Schule', 360.
[79] Graf, 'Der "Systematiker"', 289.
[80] Troeltsch, 'The Dogmatics' (A1913/2), 4; 'Die Dogmatik' (A1913/2a), 502 f.
[81] 'Does the Historical Study of Religion Yield a Dogmatic Theology?', 565.
[82] Troeltsch, 'The Dogmatics' (A1913/2), 4; 'Die Dogmatik' (A1913/2a), 502 f.

The only proper application of the term 'Religionsgeschichte' [was to] . . . designate those scholars who have given up the last remnants of a truth supernaturally revealed in the Bible and who work with the universally valid instruments of psychology and history. But even these form no school and have no common dogmatics. We may simply mention here such diverse spirits as Robertson Smith, Wellhausen, Lagarde, Gunkel, Weizsäcker, Wrede, Usener, Harnack, Holtzmann and Bousset.[83]

However, as the next section makes clear, even though the history of religion method was later to become so all-pervasive, there were nevertheless some distinguishing features and shared characteristics among the group of young theologians who gathered in Göttingen under the influence of Albrecht Ritschl and which shaped their overall theological vision.

DISTINGUISHING FEATURES OF THE HISTORY OF RELIGION SCHOOL

The Rejection of Ritschl

There was, first, a general dissatisfaction with Ritschl's theology. Indeed, in his assessment of the theses presented as part of the doctoral examination at Göttingen by the members of the History of Religion School, F. W. Graf has shown that there was a rapid rejection of Ritschl at the very outset of their careers.[84] In particular, Troeltsch's theses present clear criticisms of Ritschl, containing *in nuce* some of the most important charges he was later to level against Ritschl's successors. Thesis 15, for instance, asserts the need for metaphysics in theology, which amounts to a direct attack on Ritschl's vehement exclusion of metaphysics in his *Theologie und Metaphysik*. Thus Troeltsch claimed: 'Every positive *Glaubenslehre* includes a metaphysical philosophy of religion, even where the differences between religion and metaphysics are very clearly distinguished.'[85]

Troeltsch's fundamental breach with the most important tenets of Ritschl's theology can be dated from at least as early as 1891, with the publication of his dissertation.[86] The need for metaphysics is again brought out in Troeltsch's dissertation itself, where he points to the true task of dogmatics

---

[83] Troeltsch, 'The Dogmatics' (A1913/2), 4; 'Die Dogmatik' (A1913/2a), 503 f.

[84] 'Der "Systematiker"'. Cf. Drescher, *Ernst Troeltsch*, ET, 74–7.

[85] 'Thesen' (A1891/1a), 300.

[86] *Vernunft und Offenbarung* (A1891/3). Cf. H. R. Niebuhr, 'Ernst Troeltsch's Philosophy of Religion', 24. Becker also dates the break at the 'very beginning' (*Neuzeitliche Subjektivität*, 101). Drescher (in *Ernst Troeltsch*, ET, 19) detects a distancing of Troeltsch from Ritschl as early as 1888. However, in 'Ernst Troeltsch's Intellectual Development' he considers Troeltsch still 'to be operating on the basis of a Ritschlian theology' in 'Die christliche Weltanschauung' (A1894/1), 6,7, and sees the years 1895–6 as decisive for the rejection of Ritschl (cf. Drescher,

as the attempt to unify philosophy (or the prevailing scientific view of the world) with theology (as the religious interpretation of the world). Understanding the two together was the 'true meaning of dogmatics, which is of extraordinary importance for the life of religion'.[87] According to Troeltsch, a rejection of philosophy and thereby of metaphysics was nothing short of a rejection of the modern world, and thus the very possibility of synthesis. Perhaps more subtle is Troeltsch's Thesis 17,[88] where he called for the introduction of a new textbook for use in secondary schools. Since Ritschl had provided one of those currently in use (although it had proved rather too sophisticated for the average *Gymnasiast*), this was again a thinly veiled attack on the Göttingen professor.[89]

It soon became clear to the other members of the History of Religion School that Ritschl had stretched the New Testament material to breaking-point: a strictly historical method would reveal a completely different account of Jesus.[90] Indeed historical analysis would never yield what Ritschl demanded of it. Similarly there was a general perception by the members of the School that, in his isolation of Christianity from other religions as that religion where nature and spirit were most perfectly united, a fact he claimed to be able to prove on the basis of history, Ritschl had done little more than assert the uniqueness of Christianity dogmatically. Troeltsch asserted in distinction, however, that such a union could not be held to be qualitatively different in Christianity on the basis of a dogmatic judgement at the outset of research: the isolation of the Bible from the 'fabulously rich and interesting world of history'[91] was nothing more than unjustifiable 'assertion'.[92] He made a similar point as early as 1891 in the first of his doctoral theses:

Theology is a discipline of the history of religion, not as an ingredient in the construction of a universal history of religion, but as the determination of the content of

'Glaube und Vernunft', 47). Other commentators have set an equally arbitrary date for Troeltsch's 'rejection' of Ritschl. H. R. Mackintosh, for instance, suggests the break occurred some time around 1900 (*Types of Modern Theology*, 181). Sarah Coakley has plausibly shown, in a painstaking analysis of the different editions of *Die Absolutheit* (A1901/23), that Troeltsch rejected the different elements of Ritschl's theology at different times. Thus Troeltsch's work on historical periodization and his classification of Luther as medieval, his denial of supernaturalism, each meant a rejection of a different aspect of Ritschl's system (*Christ Without Absolutes*, ch. 2). Attempts to construct historical 'periodizations' of Troeltsch's thought thus suggest 'more conscious and consistent changes of direction than in fact occurred' (78).

[87] *Vernunft und Offenbarung* (A1891/3), 2f.; cf. 13.

[88] 'Thesen' (A1891/1a), 300; cf. *Vernunft und Offenbarung* (A1891/3), 7.

[89] Ritschl's rather grandiose intentions for his little book are indicated by the title, which is the same as that of the German edition of Calvin's *Institutes*. Swing's title, '*Instruction* in the Christian Religion', fails to capture this. Troeltsch was involved as a young lecturer in giving a class on this book at Göttingen (Drescher, *Ernst Troeltsch*, ET, 44).

[90] On this see Marsh, *Albrecht Ritschl*, 150–4.   [91] 'Meine Bücher' (A1921/29b), 5; ET, 367.

[92] 'Rückblick' (A1909/18a), 219 f.; ET, 74; cf. 'Die Selbständigkeit' (A1895/2), 373.

the Christian religion through comparison with the few great religions of which we have exact knowledge.[93]

Where Ritschl saw history as functioning merely to confirm the dogmatically fixed conception of Christianity, Troeltsch and his fellow members of the History of Religion School held that the very concept of Christianity itself had to be established on the basis of historical research and could not be dogmatically asserted beforehand. As Troeltsch maintained later, in an essay on the 'essence' of Christianity: 'a firmly delineated normative truth, presented as available in the Bible or in the Church and both accredited and recognisable on the basis of divine authority is dispensed with'.[94]

As will be shown in detail below, many of Troeltsch's early essays set about the task of justifying this claim for a historical comparative study of the history of religion within theology against the artificial isolation of Christianity from non-Christian religions. Thus he maintained: 'We have long given up the idea of tying Christianity exclusively to the Old Testament'.[95] Instead, he remarked, 'I want to place it in connection and comparison with all aspects of reality and with other religions'.[96] In short, as he maintained later in a lecture, 'the desire to see every form of non-Christian piety as an illusion is an impossibility'.[97] Wilhelm Bousset similarly rejected Ritschl's dogmatic isolation of Christianity. Looking back in 1919 he charted the changes since Ritschl's time. 'Only forty years ago we heard Ritschl say that everything was dependent upon the Old Testament'.[98] In distinction, Bousset held that it was only by placing Christianity and its biblical revelation fully in their historical context that there could be any chance of religion and theology coming to terms with the modern world.

Consequently religion, as the expression of the deepest feelings and longings of the human being, which was under threat from materialism and capitalism, would prove far more difficult to reconcile with the broader spectrum of culture than Ritschl, with his comfortable 'bourgeois'[99]

---

[93] 'Thesen' (A1891/1a), 299.   [94] 'Was heißt' (A1903/18a), 394; ET, 131.
[95] 'Geschichte und Metaphysik' (A1898/2), 5.   [96] Ibid., 53 f.
[97] *Glaubenslehre* (F1925/2), 11; ET, 17.
[98] 'Religion und Theologie', 41. Cf. Carsten Colpe, *Die Religionsgeschichtliche Schule*, 9: 'The History of Religion School's claim to theological legitimacy in the research of Israel and of Christianity is explicable in terms of a reaction to the scientific methods of the 'eighties'.
[99] Seeing Ritschl as the 'bourgeois' theologian *par excellence* is a typical criticism offered by many commentators. Karl Barth, for instance, sees Ritschl as standing 'with incredible clearness and firmness on the ground of his "ideal of life", the very epitome of the national-liberal German bourgeois synthesis of the age of Bismarck' (*Protestant Theology in the Nineteenth Century*, 656). Cf. Wolfgang Trillhaas, 'Albrecht Ritschl', 113: 'Ritschl embodied to the last threads of his existence the late bourgeois culture of the nineteenth century'. Such a view has been questioned by Weinhardt in *Wilhelm Herrmanns Stellung in der Ritschlschen Schule*.

synthesis, could ever have realized. Troeltsch makes his differences from Ritschl clear in the foreword to *Die Soziallehren*:

Trained in the school of Ritschl, I learned very early that two elements were united in the impressive teaching of this great and energetic scholar: a distinct conception of the dogmatic tradition by means of which modern needs and problems were met, and just as decided a conception of the modern intellectual and religious situation, by means of which it seemed possible to accept and continue the teaching of tradition, understood in the Ritschlian sense. The question arose, therefore, quite naturally, first whether this conception was true to the actual historical meaning of the dog-matic tradition and second, whether the present situation was being interpreted as it actually is. Then it became clear that from both sides a certain process of assimilation had been completed which did not correspond with actual facts and which did not permit the real contrast to appear in its full actuality. This naturally presented me with a double task: to make clear to myself both the ecclesiastical dogmatic tradition of Protestantism in its own historical sense, and the intellectual and practical situ-ation of the present day in its true fundamental tendencies.[100]

Ritschl's prime failure, therefore, according to Troeltsch, was that 'the burn-ing questions of the modern life or death struggle of religion received no answers or merely pretend answers'.[101] Instead, for Troeltsch, there had to be an ever greater degree of sensitivity towards these questions:

While the dogmatician [Ritschl] made clear the incomprehensibility of European intellectual history without knowledge of the long period of the all-pervasive domin-ion of theology, I have always maintained that the most important question of my life was the justification of the religious attitude to life against the all-devouring influ-ence of modern naturalism.[102]

Consequently if the theologian was called upon to help create a unified view of culture which rooted ethical action in a higher authority, a new method would have to be found which could embrace all the distinctive characteris-tics of the modern world.

Intellectual Influences

Perhaps the most important figure in the formation of a group identity between the members of the School was their *primus inter pares*, the enigmatic 'genius' Albert Eichhorn, a man whose spirit, according to Troeltsch, touched 'all the Göttingen *Privatdozenten* of these years'.[103] From beyond the theological faculty the young friends at Göttingen also found

---

[100]   *Die Soziallehren* (A1912/2), p. vii; ET, 19.   [101]   'Rückblick' (A1909/18a), 219; ET, 74.
[102]   'Meine Bücher' (A1921/29b), 5; ET, 367; cf. 'Theologie und Religionswissenschaft' (A1902/13), 116 ff.
[103]   Letter from Troeltsch to Greßmann cited in Klatt, *Hermann Gunkel*, 22.

great stimulation in Ritschl's opponent, the 'multifaceted and enigmatic'[104] Paul de Lagarde, Professor of Oriental Languages, whom Troeltsch described as 'one of the most stimulating and important of theologians, if at the same time one of the strangest',[105] and to whom he dedicated the second volume of his collected works.[106] After Lagarde, according to Troeltsch, 'science would not yield a philosophically exhausted religion devoid of all hope and power for prayer'.[107]

Lagarde's presence at Göttingen as Professor of Oriental Languages at the same time as Ritschl aroused a great deal of friction and heated debate. With his pleas for a historical science of religion, Lagarde was diametrically opposed to his Göttingen colleague, who had a very different understanding of the relationship of science and religion. The study of religion, Lagarde claimed, 'was simply an historical study, since Jesus, or if you prefer, the Gospel, appeared at a certain moment in history. Therefore our knowledge of Jesus and the Gospel can be obtained in no other way than that by which historical knowledge in general is acquired'.[108] Like Troeltsch, Gunkel regarded himself as Lagarde's pupil,[109] since he saw him as helping to free the study of history from the worst excesses of Hegelianism. Lagarde can thus justifiably be said to be the 'father'[110] or the 'true founder'[111] of the History of Religion School, since he 'divorced the evolutionary development of religion from all dogmatic and metaphysical application and called for the impartial dedicated study of the history of religion that would make use of every available means of conscientious research'.[112]

---

[104] Gunkel, 'Gedächtnisrede auf Wilhelm Bousset', 145 f.

[105] 'Die theologische und religiöse Lage' (A1903/16a), 19. Paul de Lagarde (real name, Paul Bötticher) (1827–91), *PD* in Oriental Studies in Halle (1851); *Gymnasium* teacher (1854); Prof. of Oriental Languages in Göttingen (1869). Especially remembered for his work on the Septuagint. Cf. Robert Hanhart, 'Paul Anton de Lagarde'; Fritz Stern, *The Politics of Cultural Despair*.

[106] *Zur religiösen Lage* (A1913/13). There has been little work on the direct influence of Lagarde on the History of Religion School (cf. Graf, 'Der "Systematiker"', 284 n.156). Troeltsch did not actually hear Lagarde (cf. Drescher, 'Ernst Troeltsch und Paul de Lagarde'). Constance Benson (in *God and Caesar*) sees this dedication as evidence of Troeltsch's excessive German nationalism and even anti-Semitism. There is, however, little (if any) other evidence in Troeltsch's published writings and unpublished papers to substantiate this claim.

[107] 'Theologie und Religionswissenschaft' (A1902/13), 20.

[108] Paul de Lagarde, 'Über das Verhältnis des deutschen Staates zu Theologie, Kirche und Religion', 47. The influence of the idea of a science of religion spread very rapidly, faculties of *Religionswissenschaft* being founded in Holland (1876) and Switzerland (1873). Chiefly because of Harnack's opposition, however, it was not until 1910 that a chair was established in Berlin. On this see Hans Rollmann, 'Theologie und Religionsgeschichte'. On the development of the science of religion see esp. Joseph M. Kitigawa and John S. Strong, 'Friedrich Max Müller and the Comparative Study of Religion', esp. 204 f.

[109] H. Gunkel, review of Reischle, col. 1103.   [110] Rade, 'Religionsgeschichte', col. 2189.

[111] Troeltsch, *The Absoluteness* (A1901/23d), ET, 78.

[112] Ibid.

There is, however, possibly a rather more subtle reason for the veneration of Lagarde by members of the History of Religion School, which again
reflects their distancing from Ritschl. As is emphasized by the eulogizing
Festrede which he gave to the University of Göttingen to celebrate the four-
hundredth anniversary of Luther's birth, Ritschl regarded the Reformer as
of supreme relevance for the contemporary balance between faith, history,
and ethics.[113] Lagarde, on the other hand, regarded Luther as a sectarian, and
objected to the celebration of his birthday altogether. Ritschl's speech was in
fact a step-by-step repudiation of Lagarde's views.[114] Thus, in honouring
Lagarde, Troeltsch and Gunkel were perhaps emphasizing the impotence of
a modern-day Protestantism which attempted simply to renew the tradition
of Luther. A return to the Middle Ages, as characterized by Ritschl's call for
a revitalization of Luther, was no longer possible. Where Ritschl considered
the reconciliation between religion and ethics in true community to be quite
straightforward even in the competitive situation of advanced capitalism,[115]
Troeltsch came to realize that capitalism threatened to rob the individual of
the capacity for fulfilment in community.[116] Thus he wrote that although
Ritschl had admittedly:

allowed attention to the modern picture of the world—i.e. its causal nexus of events
and the immeasurability of the world, which made anthropomorphism impossible
. . . it had become ever more obvious that forced and unhistorical interpretations
were being offered here and that in fact his procedure was silently to conform
traditional Christian ideas with those of modern science or ethics[117]

Troeltsch thus regarded Ritschl's understanding of the modern world as
highly defective. This is clear in *Die Soziallehren*, where again he argues
against Ritschl's attempt to apply Luther directly to the modern world.[118]

---

[113] Published in English in David Lotz, *Ritschl and Luther*, 187–202.

[114] Cf. Lotz, *Ritschl and Luther*, 166.

[115] On this see Zelger, 'Modernisierte Gemeindetheologie', 195.

[116] Ritschl did not regard Luther as founding the modern conception of autonomy,
but instead saw his idea of liberty as expressed in the notion of community: 'The freedom
which Luther has caused to shine forth brightly, namely Christian freedom, does not at all
involve a religious independence from communal norms and considerations' ('Festrede', 190).
Thus, far from seeing Luther as asserting a liberal conception of freedom (which stemmed
much more from Kant's emphasis on the autonomy of the person), Ritschl's ethic implied a
reconciliation between the world and God in obedience to a divinely appointed vocation within
the community.

[117] 'Rückblick' (A1909/18a), 217 f., ET, 73; cf. 'Die "kleine Göttinger Fakultät" von 1890'
(A1920/8), col. 282. However, it is also clear that Ritschl's attempt to provide a coherent syn-
thesis between religion and ethics displays a degree of continuity at least in purpose between
Ritschl and Troeltsch.

[118] Cf. *Die Soziallehren* (A1912/2), 440; ET, 470. Troeltsch had maintained this position from
the outset of his career (*Vernunft und Offenbarung* (A1891/3), 212).

For Troeltsch, Luther was very clearly part of the Middle Ages[119] and any coherent synthesis between the modern world and Christianity would have to rest upon another basis. Ritschl's error lay not so much in identifying Luther as the herald of the modern era, or even in artificially modernizing Luther, which Troeltsch felt he shared with many of his contemporaries,[120] as in his suggestion that the Reformation synthesis between Church and society, with its clearly delineated vocational ethic, could be reintroduced directly into or repristinated within the conditions of the modern world. For Troeltsch, however, even in its most modern form, the medieval synthesis could not adequately accommodate the modern conception of autonomy.

As well as Lagarde, Troeltsch and Gunkel also recognized the profound influence of another Göttingen figure, the Professor of Old Testament Bernhard Duhm.[121] As Troeltsch wrote in his brief account of his Göttingen years: 'In the background, Paul de Lagarde and Bernhard Duhm worked in quite a different direction from Ritschl, and drove us to the history of religion, bringing us to our fundamental break with Ritschl's conception of theology.'[122] Gunkel made a similar claim in his funeral oration for Wilhelm Bousset:

In the background of the new movement, but without any awareness of the new movement, there stood the multifaceted and enigmatic Lagarde and the profound Duhm, both of whom were without influence on the mass of their students in their own time, but nevertheless have exercized a quiet and enduring effect on individuals.[123]

The most important parallels between Duhm and the History of Religion School can be seen in his inaugural lecture given on his transfer to Basel in 1889, where he was deeply critical of the 'confusion of religion with theology, and the constriction of the former by the latter'.[124] Instead he saw 'the most important question of the present to be the definition of the independent essence of religion, its stages and, if possible, its laws of

---

[119] Luther was 'still a monk' (*Die Soziallehren* (A1912/2), 433 n.198; ET, 822 n.198). Cf. Dilthey, 'The Interpretation and Analysis of Man in the Fifteenth and Sixteenth Centuries', in L. W. Spitz (ed.), *The Reformation: Material or Spiritual*, 12.

[120] In *Die Soziallehren* (A1912/2), 441 n.202; ET, 471 n.202, Troeltsch remarks of both Herrmann's and Hermelink's Luther interpretation: 'Things could not have been contorted in a more mad (*toller*) and twisted fashion'. (My translation.)

[121] Bernhard Duhm (1847–1928), Prof. of OT in Göttingen (1877); Prof. in Basel (1888). On Duhm and the History of Religion School see esp. Graf, 'Der "Systematiker"', 25; Klatt, *Hermann Gunkel*, 34, 203. Cf. Bousset, *Die Lehre des Apostels Paulus vom Gesetz*, 90; H. J. Kraus, *Geschichte der historisch-kritischen Erforschung*, 275–83; and John Rogerson, *Old Testament Criticism in the Nineteenth Century*, 260.

[122] 'Die "kleine Göttinger Fakultät" von 1890' (A1920/8), col. 282.

[123] Gunkel, 'Gedächtnisrede auf Wilhelm Bousset', 145 f.

[124] Duhm, *Über Ziel und Methode der theologischen Wissenschaft*, 7.

development'.[125] For Duhm, religion was something distinct from dogmatic formulations and was marked by enthusiasm and inspiration, as he made clear in his influential book on the prophets, of 1875.[126] Indeed this book can justifiably be said to mark the rediscovery of the importance of the spirit which came to have a profound influence on the History of Religion School.

The Religion of the Spirit

This emphasis on the role of the spirit again marks a decisive reaction to Ritschl, who had downplayed the role of religious experience in favour of an ecclesiastical synthesis. This is perhaps clearest in his history of pietism,[127] which was written chiefly in response to the ecclesiastical circumstances of his own day, where an alliance between confessionalist Lutherans and pietists appeared to be threatening the balance between faith and ethics which formed the heart of his theology. For Ritschl, the pietist groups had severed links with culture in favour of individual experience, something which appeared to reject ethical vocation in the world in favour of world denial and asceticism. According to Ritschl, this contradicted the Reformation principle itself: the transfer of 'ascetic life over the walls of the monasteries into the society of lay people' was 'quite different from the intention of the Reformers of the sixteenth century'.[128] Consequently Ritschl refused to see religious 'ecstasy and inspiration' as anything more than a Catholic hangover from the Middle Ages: 'If mystical theology was at home in Anabaptist circles, this only goes to show that the Anabaptist Reformation obtained its leading motives from the Catholic-ascetic Christianity of the Middle Ages.'[129] In turn, Ritschl's Luther was very much the Luther of ethical calling as 'portrayed in his work *de libertate Christiana*', which was 'quite opposed to mysticism':

[Luther] confers the same value on the service of ethical activity towards other human beings as on those functions in which the character gains reconciliation with God. [Mysticism] teaches escape from the world and renunciation of the world and it places the value of the ethically good activity of human beings and of the formation of virtue, far beneath the ecstatic union with God. Luther taught that the Christian religion leads to spiritual dominion over the world.[130]

In contrast to Ritschl, the members of the History of Religion School emphasized the primacy of the spirit. Bousset, for instance, regarded Luther as essentially a mystical Reformer who had been 'held back by the theologian of Wittenberg',[131] and Rudolf Otto, who stood in close contact with the

---

[125] Ibid., 26.   [126] Duhm, *Die Theologie der Propheten*.   [127] Ritschl, *GP*.
[128] *GP* i. 7. My translation.   [129] *GP* i. 27 f.   [130] *GP* i. 28.
[131] Bousset, *What is Religion?*, 30.

History of Religion School from the outset, emphasized the priority of spirit over word in Luther in his *Promotionsschrift* of 1898. For Otto, the importance of the Word of God was that it should move the hearts of human beings.[132] In the same vein, both Gunkel and Bousset stressed the importance of the 'spirit-filled human being', rather than the scholastic theologian, in the development of religion. Thus, according to Gunkel: 'We recognize God's revelation in the great persons of religion who experience the holy mystery in their depths and speak in tongues of fire.'[133]

This emphasis on spirit, particularly the effects of the spirit on the individual and in the cultic community, forms one of the leading themes of the School. Gunkel, for instance, remarked in his dissertation of 1888 on the effects of the Holy Spirit that it was 'almost always in a spiritual form that epoch-making religious experiences come about; the most decisive religious persons' were 'those filled with the spirit (*Pneumatiker*) and the great epochs of religion' were 'filled with the spirit in many ways'.[134] So important was this emphasis on the spirit that Bousset traces the origin of the School to the publication of this dissertation.[135] Other works emphasizing the primacy of the spirit quickly followed.[136] Indeed only by seeing certain events as effects of the spirit could religion be truly explained since, according to Gunkel, 'one does not believe in the spirit in order to understand God's plan for the world but in order to be able to explain the presence of certain events which at first sight cannot be explained, in terms of a spiritual factor'.[137]

Unlike Ritschl, the History of Religion School was thus not primarily concerned with the analysis of theological and dogmatic statements, but with the explanation of what Wrede called 'appearances and moods'.[138] History of religion was thus not the 'history of dogma, but the history of piety . . . the enormous variety and the fulness of religious ideas and appearances which dominate human thought and the human heart and have determined human wills'.[139] Similarly, according to Gunkel, in the history of religion, 'the soul of man, the mysterious inner life which reveals itself to the external world when it expresses itself, is what is truly of value'.[140] For Bousset too,

---

[132]   Rudolf Otto, *Geist und Wort nach Luther*, esp. 36. According to H.-W. Schütte (in *Religion und Christentum in der Theologie Rudolf Ottos*), this book was at the basis of all Otto's subsequent theology and philosophy of religion. For Otto's relationship to the History of Religion School see esp. Graf, 'Der "Systematiker" ', 268.

[133]   Gunkel, *Israel und Babylonien*, 36.

[134]   Gunkel, *Die Wirkungen des heiligen Geistes*, p. xi (refs. are to the second edn. of 1899).

[135]   Bousset, 'Die Religionsgeschichte und das neue Testament', 272. Cf. H. R. Mackintosh, *Types of Modern Theology*, 183: 'The movement may be said to have opened with the publication of Gunkel's book on the operations of the Holy Spirit published in 1888.'

[136]   See, for instance, Weinel, *Die Wirkungen des Geistes*; Eichhorn, *Das Abendmahl im neuen Testament*; Heitmüller, *Taufe und Abendmahl bei Paulus*, 52.

[137]   Gunkel, *Die Wirkungen*, 20.   [138]   Wrede, *Vorträge und Studien*, 66.

[139]   Ibid., 65, 77.   [140]   Gunkel, *Reden und Aufsätze*, 12.

history of religion was concerned first and foremost not with the intellectual classes but with the 'piety of the broad masses'.[141]

Thus, against Ritschl's ecclesiasticism, the members of the History of Religion School showed the need to investigate the experience both of the masses and of the religious enthusiasts. Bousset, for instance, claimed:

One grows to realize that to attain a living conception of religion one does not only, and perhaps not even primarily, look at the clear world of ideas and concepts, at biblical injunctions, dogmas, and doctrines, but, rather, one looks at the broad stream of the religious life which flows along a different bed from that which we had previously imagined; it flows along the bed of moods and fantasies, of experiences and events of the most primitive kind which are often difficult to control: in ethics, custom, and cultus.[142]

In short, as Bousset remarked, 'research into piety is of the utmost importance for the understanding of Christianity'.[143] He reaffirmed this position in the introduction to his greatest work, *Kyrios Christos*, which sought 'to take as its starting-point the activity of the cultus and the community's worship of God, and the development of these things'.[144] In a bold statement he could thus claim that 'the beginnings of Christianity in which we might include Paul, John, and Gnosticism have nothing, I repeat absolutely nothing, to do with the distinctive philosophical literature of the educated classes'.[145] In a similar vein Gunkel asserted that '[this] dissolution of the letter allows the life-giving spirit to take hold'.[146] Paul Wernle, much influenced by the History of Religion School, went even further, seeing (with a certain anti-Jewishness quite distinct from Ritschl) all dogmatic theology as little more than a petrification of religious experience itself:

No one will blame the early Christians because of their transference of Jewish ideas to Jesus. The same hero-worship, the same faith which moved them to speak with tongues and enabled them to face the martyr's death, likewise impelled them to formulate their creed. The great picture presented in the first Jewish Christology, quaint and extravagant as it was, was inspired by pure love and enthusiasm. But in it lies the danger of all dogmatic thinking, viz., that dogma takes the place of the realities and represses them. What is new and emancipating in Jesus is embalmed in these Jewish ideas.[147]

---

[141] Bousset, 'Das Religionsgeschichte und das neue Testament', 360. Troeltsch too shared this concern with *Volksreligion* and with empirical psychology and sees one of his tasks as the reconciliation of *Volksreligion* with *Bildungsreligion*. Cf. esp. 'Die Selbständigkeit' (A1896/1), esp. 108; 'Religionsphilosophie' (A1904/7), esp. 132; 'Psychologie und Erkenntnistheorie' (A1905/7); 'Logos und Mythos' (A1913/8a).

[142] Bousset, 'Die Religionsgeschichte und das neue Testament', 271.

[143] Ibid., 355.

[144] Bousset, *Kyrios Christos*, 271.   [145] Ibid., pp. x–xi.

[146] Gunkel, *Zum religionsgeschichtlichen Verständnis*, p. vi.

[147] Paul Wernle, *Die Anfänge unserer Religion*, 27.

The History of Religion School was thus concerned first and foremost with research into the primordial experiences of religion, rather than with subsequent dogmatic formulations. It thereby returned to the Pauline (and Reformation) controversies of letter and spirit. Consequently, rather than concentrating on literary studies of the various books of the Bible, the primary object of investigation was the *religion* expressed by these books. Thus, for instance, Heitmüller emphasized the 'enthusiastic-mystic side' rather than the 'ethical-personal side' of the sacraments in Paul. The sacraments related 'to the possession of the spirit and to Christ mysticism. At the basis of the value of both acts lies a mystical natural conception of the religious relationship, which from the psychological point of view is a primitive, animistic, and simplistic way of thinking.'[148] The Ritschlian concept of theology, based on the religio-ethical idea of love as 'the practical expression that Christianity is not world-denying but world-pervading',[149] had thus been destroyed in the very study of religion itself. This history of religion method (distinct from history of *religions* method) is perhaps best expressed by Gunkel in the foreword to his collected addresses and essays:

From the outset we did not understand history of religion as the history of *religions* but as the history of *religion* . . . We were convinced that the ultimate purpose of our work on the Bible was to look in the hearts of the people of religion, to experience their thoughts inwardly and adequately to describe them. We did not chiefly want to occupy ourselves with the books of the Bible and their criticism, but rather we sought to read the living religion from these books. We are convinced that one grasps living religion not when one systematically orders the doctrines of the biblical authors together, but rather when one represents religion in its movement as it rises up out of the great people who are moved by the spirit of God. Thus no 'biblical theology' of the old kind, but 'history of religion'. This is a history of religion without breaches or window-dressing, carried out according to the strict rules of the rest of the discipline of history; it is a history of religion which shows the intricate picture of a religion as it stands in inmost connection to the political, cultural, and social milieux; it shows how religious ideas originate, how they grapple and unite among themselves, how the stuff of religion is transferred from one generation to the next, continually altered and bearing new ideas.[150]

Consequently, it can be claimed, it was not so much the pursuit of a thoroughgoing historical method as the shared understanding of the nature of religion that provided the leading common conviction of the members of the History of Religion School.

---

[148] W. Heitmüller, *'Im Namen Jesu'*, 253.   [149] Ritschl, *GP* i. 44.

[150] Gunkel, *Reden und Aufsätze*, pp. v f.

Religion and History

In opposition to Ritschl, then, the members of the History of Religion School viewed religion as something primarily of the spirit, and the history of religion was consequently the history of the spirit as it manifested itself in the great 'web of history',[151] in the religious experiences and personalities of the past.[152] As well as a concern for spiritual religion, there was thus naturally a focus on such religion as a phenomenon of human history. According to Gunkel, 'with the word "history" [Geschichte] we pronounce a whole world-view',[153] since 'whoever wants to see the revelation of God in history has quite decisively to place himself within the sphere of an idealist world-view'.[154] Revelation was not 'against history or outside history' but completed itself 'within the history of the spirit'.[155] Similarly, for William Wrede 'the movement of the revelation of God' could be seen in the 'whole of history'.[156] The spirit of God made contact with human beings in the human and historical phenomenon of religion, which meant, according to Gunkel, that history of religion was 'nothing other than a fresh wave in the powerful historical stream which has flowed from our great idealist thinkers and poets, throughout the whole life of the spirit, and indeed in theology for a long time'.[157]

The extent to which the picture of history in the History of Religion School was still coloured by the post-Hegelian view of necessary progress, however, varied between the members of the School. In dismissing Hegelianism, few went as far as Troeltsch, who came to consider it impossible 'to construct a theory of Christianity as the absolute religion on the basis of a historical way of thinking or by the use of historical means'.[158] In distinction Gunkel, for instance, considered that 'in Christianity there was a higher historical necessity'.[159] Similarly, he claimed, it was the convergence point of all that was best in historical religion:

---

[151] Bousset, 'Die Religionsgeschichte und das neue Testament', 364.

[152] It is this aspect which has been overlooked in most of the discussions of the School, which have tended to see the common conviction merely in the shared historical method. Ittel, for instance (in 'Die Hauptgedanken', 62), instead of seeing anything distinctive in the concept of religion itself, locates the common conviction of the School (somewhat anachronistically) in their shared appropriation of Troeltsch's method of probability, analogy, and reciprocity outlined in his response to Friedrich Niebergall ('Über historische und dogmatische Methode' (A1900/9a), esp. 731–5).

[153] Gunkel, 'Das alte Testament im Lichte der modernen Forschung', 55.

[154] Gunkel, Reden und Aufsätze, 15.

[155] Gunkel, review of Sellin, Die biblische Urgeschichte, in CW (1906), col. 176.

[156] Wrede, 'Das theologische Studium und Religionsgeschichte', in Vorträge und Studien, 66.

[157] Gunkel, 'Was will die "religionsgeschichtliche" Bewegung?', 356.

[158] Troeltsch, 'The Dogmatics' (A1913/2), 1 f.; 'Die Dogmatik' (A1913/2a), 500.

[159] Gunkel, Zum religionsgeschichtlichen Verständnis, 96.

Research into the history of religion—we might hope in confidence—must finally serve the end of allowing us to perceive the essence of Christianity more and more clearly, and to show in its full historical stature this incomparable and unique spiritual movement which is the best that mankind has been given.[160]

History, he went on, revealed a necessary progression towards an absolute revelation, since 'an eternal spirit moves in everything'. Thus he could confidently affirm:

With joyful certainty faith gives the answer: 'it is not chance that brings all this about'. Rather . . . it is the unity of the diverse; the union of all that is contradictory—it leads from a lower to a higher being. It draws those who follow it up to itself . . . So the concept of historical development leads to the idea of revelation. And, on the other hand, a revelation for those who think historically without history is not conceivable . . . It is in the nature of revelation that it develops in history.[161]

Similarly Bousset considered that the 'course of our wanderings through the history of religion' had revealed 'that the Christian religion is absolutely superior to all other religions, and that Christianity represents the highest point which religious development has reached'.[162] History of religion was thus 'a great work of God, a ceaseless upwards attraction, a continual discourse of God with humans and of humans with God'.[163] Indeed, in affirming the 'particular interpenetration of the abstract and the personal', the 'union of the religious principle with a person, who indeed walked here on earth and suffered death',[164] Bousset could at times sound almost Hegelian.

Most of the members of the School thus retained a strong idealist view of history and were frequently occupied with a hidden agenda which aimed to

---

[160] Gunkel, *Zum religionsgeschichtlichen Verständnis*, 4.

[161] Gunkel, 'Das alte Testament im Lichte des modernen Forschung', 64.

[162] Bousset, *What is Religion?*, 263. Cf. 289: 'History shows us that in many departments the heights already reached cannot be overstepped'. Cf. Weiss, *Die Predigt Jesu*, 7: 'Historical research can never prove the judgement of faith that in Jesus full revelation is given . . . But historical research can give this the necessary foundation'. Bousset sees religion as progressing through five stages: (1) the religion of the savages; (2) natural religions; (3) prophet reformers; (4) religions of the law; and (5) redemption religions. On their own, redemption religions paint too sharp a contrast to everyday life, and thus require an input from religions of the law: 'Wherever these two lines meet, where a religion can avoid the narrowness which characterizes both types of religion, and combines their good points, where redemption is united with the moral element—there we shall have the perfect form of religion. We shall now see whether the Christian religion satisfies these postulates!' (*What is Religion?*, 212). According to Bousset, Jesus freed religion from nationalism (218), and in the Gospel of redemption the individual finds salvation, yet it is only with the Reformation that Christianity 'accepts, in principle, human life and all the work appertaining to it because it accepts the morality revealed by it' (232). It thus turns out that the highest religion was revealed by the Reformers (just as for Hegel the goal of history was the Prussian State): 'The Reformation was a mighty act of freedom for Christianity accomplished by the German Spirit, a return to simplicity and truth'.

[163] Bousset, *Das Wesen der Religion*³, 17.   [164] Bousset, *Kyrios Christos*, 113.

show the absoluteness and the unsurpassability of the Christian religion. It was Troeltsch alone who drew the history of religion method to its logical conclusion by pointing out that the

modern understanding of history knows no evolutionary development in which an actual law-regulated universal principle produces laws that are universally authentic. It knows finally no absolute realization of such a universal principle within the context of history where as a matter of fact, only phenomena that are uniquely defined and thus possess individual character are brought forth at a given point.[165]

Although the idealist drive towards a synthesis of spirit and nature still dominated Troeltsch's thought, it was no longer to be settled in the artificial identification of the religious principle with the person, which was, he claimed, 'simply an abomination of historical realism'.[166] This understanding of history will be discussed at length in the next chapter.

The Interpretation of Paul, 'the Second Founder of Christianity'[167]

Both Gunkel and Bousset applied their understandings of the nature of religion, and of the historical method, to the study of the Bible. Like many other members of the School, they were particularly interested in St. Paul, a figure about whom they both wrote dissertations, in which the emphasis on the spiritual was already dominant. According to Gunkel, Paul was a 'man of the spirit of a particularly high grade',[168] for whom 'the whole life of the Christian' was 'a work of the spirit . . . revealing an overwhelming, supernatural divine power'.[169] 'The theology of the great apostle', he continued, was 'an expression of his experience, not his reading . . . Paul believes in the divine spirit because he has experienced it'.[170] In short, Gunkel concluded, 'the spirit is more powerful than anything else'.[171]

Similarly Bousset, in his dissertation of 1890 on Paul's doctrine of the law, emphasizes the vital impact of the saint's experience and personality on his writings. Indeed Bousset regarded it as his duty 'to show how it is psychologically comprehensible that the same man could write both Romans 1

---

[165] Troeltsch, *The Absoluteness* (A1901/23d), ET, 67.
[166] Troeltsch, review of Dorner (A1917/4), col. 87.
[167] Wrede, *Paulus*, 103 f; ET, 179 f.: 'As a rule even liberal theology has shied away from the conclusion that he refounded Christianity. But it is not to be evaded . . . True, he has not dominated everywhere, especially not in the life of simple, practical piety, but throughout long stretches of Church History—one need only think of the councils and the dogmatic controversies—he has utterly thrust into the background that greater person whom he meant to serve'.
[168] Gunkel, *Die Wirkungen*, 58.
[169] *Die Wirkungen*, 96. Cf. 96 f.: 'The spirit was the only power which could work definite miracles and was guarantor of certain miracles; with Paul the present possession of the spirit is all that the Christian possesses in time and eternity'.
[170] *Die Wirkungen*, 86. [171] Ibid., 96.

and 2 and Galatians 3 and 4'.[172] Such questions moved him far beyond
Ritschl's interpretations of the Pauline corpus, which suffered, he claimed,
'from the fact that the theological aspects of the apostle are seen as decisive'.[173] In his own studies of Paul, Bousset 'pointed to the fault of almost all
Pauline exegetes', who had 'far too rarely posed the question as to how Paul
came to this or that train of thought' and who thus neglected his syncretism,
enthusiasm, and his mysticism, and their connection to the broader history
of religion. 'Indeed, to some, the very question "how did Paul come to the
opposition between *erga* and *pistis?*"' was simply beyond comprehension.[174]

The essence of Pauline religion was thus not to be found in hard and fast
doctrines, but rather in the primordial religious experience of the individual.
The study of the historical origins of Christianity served to reveal a spiritual
essence which would endure despite all historical criticism. Thus, according
to Gunkel, 'just because the belief in resurrection and the conception of the
Messiah as "essential elements of the Christian religion" can be traced to
external influences, this is no reason to doubt the absoluteness of Christianity'.[175] Indeed, religion itself was beyond the scope of historical criticism.
Thus Gunkel claimed that although history could give a knowledge of the
origin and the development of religion, it could never yield any knowledge
of the 'mysterious and powerful in human life', which was to be found solely
in an immediate contact with the 'Spirit of God'.[176] Although admittedly
'[a]ppearances of the spirit' may have become less frequent since Paul's day,
Gunkel went on, 'they had never died out'.[177] In short, he concluded, religion was nothing other than 'the supernatural power which is sent from
God through Christ and works a miracle on those who believe'.[178]

The Mystical Solution

For most of the members of the History of Religion School, then, there was
an emphasis on the immediate grasp of the truth of religion which was not
dependent on the vagaries of history: the essence of religion was thus primarily to be found, according to Bousset, in 'the life-impulse . . . which in
actual fact emanated from the person of Jesus and touches and embraces us
in his community'. This alone allowed us to gain 'a firm and lasting hold on
the whole of the Gospel'.[179] Indeed the Christian Gospel 'proclaims a God
who in the first instance searches out and desires the individual human
soul'.[180] Similarly, according to Johannes Weiss, religious experience, as the

[172] Bousset, *Die Lehre des Apostels Paulus*, 93.   [173] Ibid., 91.
[174] Ibid., 119.   [175] Gunkel, *Zum religionsgeschichtlichen Verständnis*, 95.
[176] Gunkel, *Die Wirkungen*, 14.   [177] Ibid., p. viii.   [178] Gunkel, *Die Wirkungen*, 43.
[179] Bousset, *Die Mission und die sogenannte religionsgeschichtliche Schule*, 19.
[180] Bousset, *Unser Gottesglaube*, 20.

expression of the soul in union with the Spirit of God, 'is something which in the end resists analysis and rational explanation', a fact obvious to anyone 'who is accustomed to find fresh strength and uplift in prayer', and which 'no amount of scholarship is adequate to explain away'.[181]

Consequently, Bousset held, whatever the historical study of religion might reveal, the spiritual essence of religion was left intact, since 'faith teaches us that we are related to this essence of reality in the depths of our being, that we grasp it in our hearts, and our nature finds repose in it'.[182] 'This capacity to be grasped by the Spirit in our innermost being despite the vagaries of history was, according to Bousset, 'miraculous in the deeper sense of the word, the miracle of the individual spiritual life . . . What disappears is only the belief in miracles which affect the order of nature'.[183] Gunkel similarly recognized the miracle of the resurrection of Christ as that which 'illuminates life', and which 'we experience with him when we are mystically united with him'.[184] In this experience of redemption, the individual was thus 'liberated' from history 'and released from the natural, sensually determined self, which draws to itself the goal of its life and its strivings. Redeemed means being grasped by God'.[185]

In this teaching of the History of Religion School, it would seem that the old orthodox Lutheran doctrine of the *unio mystica* received new life in the idea of religion as a 'personal communion with the Godhead . . . a simple feeling of being drawn into the Godhead'.[186] Indeed this emphasis on the immediacy of feeling highlighted 'a kind of true knowledge free from all [historical] schematism',[187] which had a natural affinity with the epistemology stemming from J. F. Fries' Kantianism which was mediated to the later generation by Rudolf Otto. As will be shown in detail in Chapter 4, amongst the members of the History of Religion School it was Bousset who explored the philosophical presuppositions of spiritual religion in some depth.

In removing religion from history to its own unique sphere, however, there was a sense in which the History of Religion School had reduced the ethical importance of religion. Since it was no longer dependent on history, but was located instead in a deeper mode of perception, its effects in history, and consequently on ethics, were seriously questioned. Indeed, as Bousset remarked, 'in the last resort these researches lead man into the depths of his own being and demand this of him: affirm this depth of your own life'.[188]

---

[181] Johannes Weiss, *Earliest Christianity*, 42 f.
[182] Bousset, *Unser Gottesglaube*, 12.   [183] Bousset, *What is Religion?*, 287.
[184] Gunkel, *Zum religionsgeschichtlichen Verständnis*, 93. Cf. Klatt, *Gunkel*, 99: 'Gunkel wanted to elevate history to a new stringency; in the last resort he could not carry this through and fled into mysticism'.
[185] Bousset, *Unser Gottesglaube*, 48.   [186] Bousset, *Das Wesen der Religion*³, 17.
[187] Wrede, *Vorträge und Studien*, 37 f.   [188] Bousset, 'Anwendung', 479.

Religion, when conceived as its own independent sphere with little connection to the rest of reality, could no longer have much impact on the world of history, ethics, and science. Indeed, to some theologians, most importantly Ernst Troeltsch, such an emasculated religion deprived of its ethical power could never satisfy the demands of the modern world (an inadequacy which Bousset himself was later only too ready to recognize). As the next section will make clear, however, this tension between ethics and religion was, at least according to Bousset, to be traced back to Paul himself.

BOUSSET, RELIGION, AND ETHICS

In his *Kyrios Christos* of 1913, Bousset traces the development of the Church from its beginnings in St. Paul until Irenaeus' first great ecclesiastical synthesis. Whereas in Paul, Bousset claims, 'the effects of the spirit essentially come to life and experience in the community assembled for worship',[189] what begins as a product of devotion soon becomes an object of faith. Consequently, as the Church grows, so

the dogma of the divinity of Christ is on the march. We must never forget that behind the personal piety and the theology of Paul there is a living power and the reality of the cultic devotion of the Lord *Kyrios* in the community. What is worshipped must stand unconditionally on the side of God. Although Paul, following his Old Testament instincts, avoids the predicate of the divinity of Christ and looks to hold on to the distinction between *Theos* and *Kyrios*, the massive communal faith will quickly push the dogmatic distinction aside. It speaks consciously of the great mystery of the divinity of Christ and is placed in the centre of the Christian religion. For it is already there in cult and practice.[190]

Doctrine, thus, according to Bousset, did not develop in the conscious thought processes of the theologian, but acquired its own momentum in the worship of Christ in the cult: doctrine was thus an expression of practice. In the worship of the cultic Lord, however, the Jesus of history appeared constantly under threat as Christ-mysticism was soon translated into God-mysticism.[191]

Consequently by tearing Christianity from its historical and natural base, Paul, according to Bousset, threatened to remove the possibility of ethics from his system altogether:

On the one hand, the opposition between the world of spirit [*pneuma*] and that of *sarx* [flesh] is drawn to its logical conclusion, thereby pushing the Jesus of the Gospel to one side and transforming him into myth, tearing apart the worlds of creation and redemption. On the other hand, this opposition is so reduced that Christ no longer appears as

---

[189] Bousset, *Kyrios Christos*, 93.   [190] Ibid., 154.   [191] Ibid., 93.

the death and the annihilation of the natural man, the first Adam, but as his recreation, crowning, and completion, and thus a harmony is prepared between the world of creation and the world of redemption (Irenaeus and the ecclesiastical theology) . . . Yet Paul did not attempt to overcome the stream of the spiritual superman, and thus the dangers continually threatened. And thus Paulinism in its magnificence, with its body of inward mysticism, but also with the dangers which belong to this, became a one-sided redemption religion alongside the Gospel of Jesus with the forgiveness of sins.[192]

However, according to Bousset, the Christian experience of being in Christ, which was vital for Pauline religion, needed to be grounded in history, since, he claimed, 'present experience is as nothing if it cannot be tested alongside the historical appearance of Jesus of Nazareth'.[193]

Bousset had much earlier recognized the ethical implications of Pauline religion in his dissertation:

The breach with the old, with the past, is radical here; we can scarcely see how Paul could stand firm on the soil of the Old Testament revealed religion. The strength, indeed, if I might be permitted to say, the hatred of the law by the man of the spirit could have dubious ethical consequences. We have before us a one-sided religious viewpoint, which, despite all its splendour, its fervour, and its intensity, could also be destructive and could consume. We do not want to conceal from ourselves, and indeed Paul has not closed his eyes to, the dubious consequences of his thoughts.[194]

Thus, according to Bousset, in Paul himself there appeared to be no coherent attempt at a harmonization between faith and ethics. Indeed in the one-sidedness of his religion of the spirit, Paul had destroyed the possibility for a reconciliation between spirit and nature: whatever the glories of his writings, they were ethically ineffective.

The Pauline emphasis on experience of rebirth thus had to be brought into contact with the wider natural world, and it was this synthesis, on Bousset's account, that was first attempted by Irenaeus. For Paul, the dead and resurrected Christ was the decisive symbol for the elevation out of this world of the flesh, whereas for Irenaeus Christ became the effective symbol for the faithful—body and soul included.[195] Thus, in what Bousset called Irenaeus' 'clerically usable Paulinism',[196] there was a change of emphasis from the religious world of spirit cut off from that of nature towards an all-embracing synthesis. Irenaeus had thus succeeded, Bousset contended, in controlling 'that spiritual enthusiasm which was in the position of scattering and destroying an old world, but on which no new world could be built.'[197] Consequently, in his 'ecclesiastical review' of Paul, he paved the way for the future tasks of theology, which belonged in 'the simple and closed

---

[192] Ibid., 144 f.   [193] Bousset, 'Religion und Theologie', 43.
[194] Bousset, *Die Lehre des Apostels Paulus*, 122.   [195] Bousset, *Kyrios Christos*, 122.
[196] Ibid., 360.   [197] Ibid.

redemptive supernaturalism of Irenaeus in which *gratia* and *natura* are unified in a particular harmony and are determined by one another'.[198] Indeed, Bousset wrote elsewhere, without control, Paul's spiritual religion was in danger of developing into a Gnosticism which showed 'us what was possible in the development of the Christian religion before its consolidation in clerical dogmas'.[199] To avoid the excesses of a Marcion, Bousset concludes in *Kyrios Christos*, the initial enthusiasm and profound religious experience of the Christian movement required formulating into dogma. As he put it somewhat graphically: 'the volcano has cooled and the iodine lava masses have become the nourishing soils of the new world'.[200]

In forging his solution to the problems of religion and history, and of the rational regulation of religion through dogma, Bousset draws from the Pauline tradition of the cultic Christ, but points to the need to connect this with the historical Jesus. It was Paul who had ensured the 'guarantee of the unity and sociological exclusiveness of believers in Christ'.[201] Thus, as Bousset had written in *Kyrios Christos*, for Paul, to be *en kyrioi* was to stand in relationship with a communal expression of the exalted Christ, since the correlate of *kyrios* was always *ekklesia*.[202] Yet only if this cultic Christ could be connected with the *historical* Jesus of Nazareth, Bousset contended, could he function as the head of a community capable of world transformation. And only then could the community retain its links with wider culture and so prevent its degeneration into a sect.

In this way, Bousset maintained, the ethics of the Gospel could be united with the religious powers emanating from the figure of Christ. Bousset thus aimed to 'correct' Paul, who 'no longer had any place in his proclamation of the Gospel for the distinctive mark of the personal picture of Jesus, indeed for its very essence: Jesus' piety and his faith in God'.[203] It was 'not the historical Jesus, and also not primarily the Christ, who appeared on the road to Damascus, but rather it was the powerful reality of the Lord *Kyrios* as Paul had experienced him in the first Hellenistic communities and which ignited the fire of his Christ-piety'.[204] Bousset's purpose here was to retain this religious capacity to 'ignite' the soul of the believer, but without separating this power from its historical basis. The powers of the cultic Christ were thus seen as emanating from the very real figure of Jesus of Nazareth and in this way 'we may honour Jesus of Nazareth as the creative genius who fashioned the fundamental symbol for our faith, and in his person he has remained the powerful symbol for our faith'.[205]

[198]   Bousset, *Kyrios Christos*, 361.
[199]   Bousset, 'Die Religionsgeschichte und das neue Testament', 353 f.
[200]   Bousset, *Kyrios Christos*, 360.   [201] Bousset, 'Religion und Theologie', 32.
[202]   Bousset, *Kyrios Christos*, 87.   [203] Ibid., 90.   [204] Ibid., 106.
[205]   Bousset, *Die Bedeutung der Person Jesu*, 17.

According to Bousset, acceptance of Jesus meant entry into that historical community which was founded and nurtured by him. Indeed the Church had to become the proof of the power of the historical Jesus of Nazareth:

We modern people, with our leanings towards individuality and our great independence of mind, need to take to heart a warning against standing alone. We must place our feet firmly in the community which owes its origins to Jesus! It is only in the community—and history speaks clearly on this point—that man develops the wings and the capacity to soar into an invisible world . . . But we only find this community by joining an ecclesiastical organization based on an historical foundation.[206]

Most often, however, Bousset sought to unite the cultic and the historical in the elevation of Jesus as 'leader' or 'hero'. Thus, for instance, he wrote in *Kyrios Christos*: 'the religious superman (*Übermensch*), the *Theios Anthropos* in all his splendour which stirs Paul'[207] has to be connected with the historical Jesus in an effort to incorporate history and ethics into an all-embracing ecclesiastical system.[208]

In his faith that 'personalities make history',[209] Bousset thus accepts the leadership of Jesus as the universal figure capable of overcoming the anarchy and the anomie of contemporary life. It was as a charismatic leader, as one who incorporated universal ethical values and religious power, that the figure of Jesus was transferred into the present. As Bousset wrote in his book on the essence of religion:

God the Father, life in accordance with his will spent in joyful work for the service of the world, forgiveness of sins and eternal hope—all this hangs together and is crystallized in perfect clarity in the person of our Lord Jesus. And we speak this to him: 'Thou art our leader! There have been many leaders of men in different departments of life. Be thou our leader with whom no other is comparable, the leader of the highest, the guide of our souls to God, the way, the truth and the life.'[210]

In this leadership role, Jesus is compared with Bismarck, 'the one possessed of a magic word', and Goethe, in whom 'we have the picture of a life in accordance with universal laws—the picture of heroic, energetic, infinitely capable manhood'.[211]

---

[206] Bousset, *What is Religion?*, 299. Cf. Gunkel, *Schöpfung und Chaos*, 391: 'The Christian interpretation of eschatology is just as eclectic and inorganic as the Jewish. From the Christian standpoint also, the fact that the tradition, though so little understood, was nevertheless handed on is to be understood as a result of holy awe before the deep mystery of the revelation.'

[207] Bousset, *Kyrios Christos*, 119.

[208] In retaining this faith in the ethical message of the historical Jesus, Bousset steers clear of the eschatological message of Weiss and Schweitzer.

[209] Bousset, *What is Religion?*, 288.　　[210] Ibid., 298.

[211] Ibid., 274. Verheule (in *Wilhelm Bousset*, 369) suggests that Bousset saw Friedrich Naumann as the figure who was most fit to take on the mantle of Goethe and Bismarck. The importance of Carlyle's 'hero' should not be underestimated. For Bousset's eulogizing of heroes see

BOUSSET'S RETURN TO ETHICS

Over the years, however, Bousset grew increasingly dissatisfied with this solution. Models of charismatic leadership, however appealing, seemed to lack rational control and could easily degenerate into sectarianism. Thus, in a passionate lecture given immediately after the First World War to a group of intending theological students, Bousset returned to this problem of the relationship between religion and dogma, which he saw as a problem that had been 'made especially vital' in time of war.[212] Things had changed: the greatest danger for religion seemed to him to come no longer from history, but from the 'sectarianization' of religion; that is, from the removal of history and reason from faith altogether. Bousset thus made a plea for the rational regulation of religion against the prevailing mood of the time which glorified the irrational and stressed the immediacy of feeling.[213] Consequently he asked whether Jesus was not 'greater than the greatest of the prophets because in him the quiet rational element was stronger than in them'.[214] To rid religion of all connection with history and reason, however, was to run the risk of a degeneration into a self-indulgent mysticism where 'one begins to play about with erotic mysteries and brings these into the religious life; one speaks of androgynous humans—just as once was the case in Gnosticism'.[215]

Without a location in a historical tradition and without rational regulation, religion became, according to Bousset, nothing more than a 'rudderless ship'.[216] He contended, however, that theology was to serve as 'a gardener who tends the bush of religion', regulating (in another metaphor) 'the flow of the current to prevent it from becoming a raging torrent' and 'giving direction to the stream'.[217] In short, theology places religion in connection with the remainder of reality:

Theology has the task of placing piety in connection with the rest of human life. It has the task of unifying religion in every place with the popular life of a particular generation. Where it is ignored then there is necessarily the formation of the sect. And this is the definition of the sect: that in it the connection with human communal life is lost.[218]

---

esp. *What is Religion?*, 299, and *Die Bedeutung der Person Jesu*, 17. Cf. Heinrich Kahlert, *Der Held und seine Gemeinde*; and John K. Riches, *A Century of New Testament Study*, 42 ff.

[212] Bousset, 'Religion und Theologie', 29. On theology and the First World War see esp. W. Pressel, *Die Kriegspredigt*; G. Brakelmann, *Protestantische Kriegstheologie*.

[213] It was this message that was loudest in the Munich revolution, with its cry of 'Away with all historical ballast!' (Bousset, 'Religion und Theologie', 35).

[214] Bousset, 'Religion und Theologie', 37; cf. 33: 'As soon as mankind has reached the highest stage of prophetic religion, which strives after universalism, reason (*Ratio*) makes its presence felt'.

[215] Ibid., 36.   [216] Ibid.   [217] Ibid., 38.   [218] Ibid.

To prevent its collapse into sectarianism and to allow its survival as a potent force, Bousset contended, religion had to be incorporated into universal human reason. While recognizing that religious feeling or 'red-hot piety' would often be in conflict with theology,[219] and that theology was 'just as difficult for religion to bear as to dispose of',[220] he nevertheless gave theology a vital role. Similarly, while it was admittedly often important for religion to maintain its identity over and against the rest of culture, to sever all connection would lead to the end of religion altogether. Thus he wrote:

Religion has very often expressed a revolutionary 'No' to all human nature and culture. God be praised that it has done this! But, on the other hand, it becomes a weak power which merely sanctions what goes on. And we can look at the great events in the history of religion which first of all begin with something quite irrational but which develop the rational element ever more triumphantly.[221]

Bousset's earlier studies of Gnosticism, in *Kyrios Christos*, had revealed the severe problems of an unregulated religion. And they appeared to him to have parallels in the postwar situation. Thus he warned his students:

Beware when the pressure towards the formation of the sect is allowed in religion. This means nothing but chaos, dissolution, and barbarism. Have pity on the poor and afflicted German nation, if now the strongest religious powers are moving in the path of the sect, that is towards isolation and to an existence apart from the life of the nation. The greatest task of theology is the reconciliation of religion and the communal life of the nation.[222]

Such a task would not prove easy or indeed popular, Bousset maintained, yet it was of vital importance if Germany was to remain anchored in religion. The special task of theology was thus 'to find the language to proclaim the religion of the Gospel to the German nation so that it might be understood'.[223] The theologians would thereby become subject to '*noblesse oblige*'[224] as they helped prevent the nation from sliding into the anarchy of immediate feeling. Bousset concluded his lecture with a passionate plea:

Do not go the way of the sects ... It would now be a sacrilege to the soul of the German nation if the best religious powers of the present turned to the hidden mysteries and the arbitrariness of the sects. If you want to be leaders of the German nation with a universal mission, you will have to bear the pains and the tensions which theology demands. Yet if you attempt it they will be blessed pains and holy tensions. Those who sow with tears will reap with joy.[225]

After the First World War therefore Bousset came to regard his earlier solutions to the problems of faith and history, of religion and theology, as altogether unsatisfactory, not least because they seemed to make history

---

[219] Ibid., 31.   [220] Ibid., 29.   [221] Ibid., 36 f.   [222] Ibid., 39.
[223] Ibid., 43.   [224] Ibid.   [225] Ibid.

irrational. Before the war Bousset had not perceived history as the sphere in which reason might work itself out dialectically, but instead it had become the arena of great men, of irrational powers working on gifted individuals and great nations. In drawing on Carlyle and in sharing the idea of a charismatic leader which was prevalent in the Germany of his time,[226] Bousset presented a solution to the problem of faith and history which required the emergence of a new leader who alone could give meaning to the meaninglessness of history. In his earlier work Bousset thus sought the irrational acceptance of the power of the divine personality as the guarantee against anarchy, sectarianism, and individualism.

In his postwar lecture, however, he seems to be moving in a quite different direction, recognizing the need to regulate religion rationally if sectarianism in its modern guises of neo-mysticism and esotericism is to be avoided. In his final ethical solution, as will be shown in the closing chapter, Bousset shared much with Ernst Troeltsch. It did not take the war, however, to bring Troeltsch to the recognition of the need to connect religion, reason, and history: such an approach characterized his theology from the very beginnings of his career, and it is the reason why his relationship to the History of Religion School was always ambivalent. The next chapter analyses Troeltsch's early studies of the connections between history and religion, and his role in formulating a 'systematic theology' of the History of Religion School.

---

[226] Cf. Heinrich Kahlert, *Der Held und seine Gemeinde*. Bousset's ideas show a resemblance to those of Max Weber.

3

The Historical Method in Debate

THE SYSTEMATIC THEOLOGY OF THE HISTORY
OF RELIGION SCHOOL

Partly because of the large number of articles on doctrinal themes which he contributed to the first edition of the massive encyclopaedia *Die Religion in Geschichte und Gegenwart*, Troeltsch came to be considered the 'systematic theologian' of the History of Religion School. In the words of William Wrede, he was, in 'virtue of his all-embracing and thorough investigations, his great gifts, and the novelty of the way he puts the problems, the most important of the systematic theologians'.[1] It was this systematic interest which distinguished Troeltsch from most of the other members of the school: his major concern was to link the distinct form of life of religion with the rest of reality in an overarching unified vision.

Troeltsch outlined this particular systematic task most clearly in a programmatic article first published in the *American Journal of Theology*.[2] Echoing his work on the absoluteness of Christianity, where he remarked that 'theology is not concerned with the history of religion in general but normative knowledge acquired through study of religion',[3] he claimed that 'we are thrust back to history itself and the necessity of constructing from this history a religious world of ideas that shall be normative for us'.[4] He was thus concerned with the history of religion 'only in so far as it has been appropriated, or can be appropriated by theology'.[5] While Troeltsch's theology admittedly often emphasizes the almost mystical indwelling of the Christian in the Godhead, and thus reveals similarities with the major emphases of the History of Religion School discussed in Chapter 2, he nevertheless recognizes at the same time that such religious experience remains purely abstract unless there is a connection with history and ethics.

---

[1] Wrede, *Vorträge und Studien*, 66. Cf. Walter Bodenstein, *Neige des Historismus*, 37: '[Troeltsch] drew the consequences in a clear and sober fashion and thus became the systematic theologian of the History of Religion School'. Cf. also Reischle, *Theologie und Religionsgeschichte*, 11.

[2] 'The Dogmatics' (A1913/2).   [3] *The Absoluteness* (A1901/23d), ET, 25.

[4] 'The Dogmatics' (A1913/2), 1; 'Die Dogmatik' (A1913/2a), 500.

[5] 'The Dogmatics' (A1913/2), 3; 'Die Dogmatik' (A1913/2a), 502.

Indeed he remarks in *Die Soziallehren*: 'The doctrine of the mystical union or the indwelling of Christ is the kernel and the basis of all practical religious achievement, and the radiating centre of religious ethics.'[6]

In his essay on the dogmatics of the History of Religion School and in his lectures on *Glaubenslehre* ('doctrine of faith'), Troeltsch thus claimed that the first strand of any systematic theology after Schleiermacher[7] had to be a thoroughgoing 'historical investigation of the development of Christianity itself'.[8] Only after such an investigation could the theologian set about reaching criteria whereby Christianity could be shown to be 'universally supreme' in its own culture.[9] This moved on towards what Troeltsch regarded as the second strand of the systematic task of the History of Religion School: the attempt to discern the 'power which lies deeper than any historical formulation which it may have produced'.[10] This underlying power that emerged through historical investigation, and that functioned as a criterion to assess the truth of Christianity, was not, according to Troeltsch, strictly 'objective', but rather was related to Christianity's capacity to retain a genuine religious potency in the contemporary situation through subjective appropriation. Thus he came to the question: If the truth of Christianity could not be established either on the basis of a value judgement of faith or by an arbitrary isolation of a particular moment in history, then how could it be established? Troeltsch's early attempts to answer this question form the subject of this chapter.

The Difficulty of the Task

The task of theological appropriation was far from easy: the basic method of the History of Religion School (and later Troeltsch's work on the religious a priori) emphasized the independence and irreducibility of religion and consequently it was not easy to integrate religion into an all-embracing system or world-view. Nevertheless, Troeltsch argued, for Christianity to maintain its ethical potency it had to search for a unified vision, and thus had to be incorporated within the wider perspective. Indeed without a systematic theology the study of the history of religion could only ever 'contribute to an increase in the anarchy of historicism'.[11]

Thus, while sharing a similar understanding of religion to that of his colleagues, and while adopting a thoroughgoing historical method in its study, Troeltsch nevertheless sought to overcome what he considered their

---

[6] Troeltsch, *Die Soziallehren* (A1912/2), 857; ET, 737.   [7] *Glaubenslehre* (F1925/2), §1.
[8] 'The Dogmatics' (A1913/2), 3; 'Die Dogmatik' (A1913/2a), 502.
[9] *Glaubenslehre* (F1925/2), §1. 1.
[10] 'The Dogmatics' (A1913/2), 12 f.; 'Die Dogmatik' (A1913/2a), 511.
[11] 'Autonomie und Rationalismus' (A1907/11), col. 2760.

lack of a unified vision. An understanding of religion which apparently relegated it to the mystical sphere, and which interpreted religion solely in terms of an individual appropriation of the Godhead, appeared to Troeltsch to lack the possibility of an integrated social ethic: experience of union with the Godhead could not take place apart from a social, ecclesial, and historical context. He thus remarked in *Die Soziallehren*:

The distinctive nature of Christianity itself was never merely individualized mysticism, but also, at the same time, ethical driving power; a recognition of the divine will requires fellowship and a religion which can only be nourished by a living cultus. The cultus cannot be anything other than in some sense the worship of Jesus as the revelation of God. Thus even Schleiermacher moved back to the Church after the spiritualist-individualist ideas of his youth.[12]

Under such a conception, what was important for theology was not so much its defence of the independent sphere of religion, as its ability to find a connection with the rest of reality: '[The religious conviction] must always stand in connection with the great historical powers of religious history and community and, through this connection, attain the necessary depths and strengths and necessary organizational social effects.'[13]

Troeltsch had recognized the importance of this need for a historical expression of any spiritual religion in his earliest writings:

[r]eligion is not merely a kind of mystical suggestion of the divine life . . . 'Living religion' [is] never without *fides quae creditur* and such faith leads inexorably to a dialogue with the rest of the conceptual world, that is, to a dogmatics.[14]

Thus, from the beginnings of his career, Troeltsch distanced himself from the other members of the History of Religion School, who, he claimed, had failed to take adequate account of the social organization and ethical teaching of religion. As he wrote in *Die Soziallehren*:

The so-called 'History of Religion School' goes back entirely to spiritual religion (*Spiritualismus*), and is therefore ecclesiastically 'impotent'. My own theology is certainly spiritual but for that very reason it seeks to make room for the historical element, and for the cultic and sociological factor which is bound up with it. Naturally I am aware of the difficulties of such an undertaking.[15]

This chapter discusses Troeltsch's constructive efforts to unite the spiritual and the historical, which he developed in dialogue and dispute with Ritschlian theologians.

---

[12] *Die Soziallehren* (A1912/2), 939; ET, 979f.; cf. 'Schleiermacher und die Kirche' (A1910/16).
[13] 'Religionsphilosophie' (A1904/7), 131.
[14] *Vernunft und Offenbarung* (A1891/3), 3 n.1.
[15] *Die Soziallehren* (A1912/2), 936 n.504a; ET, 985 n.504a.

THE RITSCHLIAN SCHOOL AND
THE HISTORY OF RELIGION

Both the emphasis on spiritual religion and the recommendation of an unfettered historical method provoked often bitter hostility from other theologians, many of whom continued to identify to a greater or lesser extent with Ritschl. Ritschl's method had, however, undergone a significant transformation at the hands of many of his students. Indeed by the turn of the century there was agreement between the second generation of Ritschlians, led by Julius Kaftan and Wilhelm Herrmann, and Ritschl himself only in the 'shared pursuit of certain methodological axioms'[16] and certain 'fundamental aims and tendencies'.[17] Most importantly, it was only after Ritschl's death that the concept of the 'value judgement' of faith received its proper systematic treatment, which proved 'infinitely richer' as a 'theological principle' than anything else in his theological system itself. It was thus far more Ritschl's 'large and impressive personality'[18] than the 'agreement of the members over the content of the convictions of faith'[19] that provided a focal point of unity for this group of Ritschlian theologians. Indeed by 1891, when the History of Religion School was consciously distancing itself from Ritschl, his personal influence had, according to Kattenbusch, also begun to wane amongst his more self-conscious followers.[20]

In particular, it was under Herrmann, according to Johannes Wendland,[21] that Ritschl's unified system had broken down into 'divergent individual strands'.[22] Where Ritschl had maintained a unified vision with its concomitant vocational ethic (albeit with distinct tendencies towards dualism), there was instead almost complete agreement amongst the later generation of Ritschlians that religion and science[23] could no longer be united in an overall world-view. Instead each was to be restricted to its own separate sphere. It

[16] Gustav Ecke, *Die theologische Schule Albrecht Ritschls*, i. 76. See also Harnack's review of Ecke, 'Ritschl und seine Schule'; Arthur Titius, 'Albrecht Ritschl und die Gegenwart'; Robert Mackintosh, *Albrecht Ritschl and his School*, ch. 9.

[17] James Orr, *Ritschlianism*, 4; cf. Orr, *The Ritschlian Theology and the Evangelical Faith*, 11–28.

[18] Orr, *Ritschlianism*, 4.

[19] Gustav Ecke, *Die theologische Schule Albrecht Ritschls*, i. 76.

[20] F. Kattenbusch, *Die deutsche evangelische Theologie seit Schleiermacher*, 63.

[21] Johannes Wendland (1871–1947), assistant preacher at the Predigerseminar at Wittenberg (1898); Pastor in Görlitz (1901); *ordinarius* in Basel in Systematic Theology (1905–37).

[22] J. Wendland, *Albrecht Ritschl und seine Schüler*, 29. According to Horst Stephan, to accuse somebody of being a Ritschlian had virtually become a term of theological abuse ('Albrecht Ritschl und die Gegenwart', 21).

[23] Science is understood in the broader German sense of *Wissenschaft*, which carries a wider range of meanings in German than the English word. Generally it refers to any theoretical study or discipline which makes cognitive claims, although it can also be used of a systematic presentation of a subject in any discipline—it is often closer to the English word 'academic' than 'scientific'.

becomes clear in reading Herrmann, who was undoubtedly the most philosophically refined spokesman of the post-Ritschlian method (and whose system will be discussed in detail in Chapter 5), that, as Hasler points out, his
'attempt to solve all the possibilities for conflict between religion and natural
science by delineating the epistemological and scientific areas of compe-
tence had achieved a virtual canonical importance'.[24] Herrmann is indeed
the most consistent dualist of the post-Ritschlians[25] and for this very reason
he is of vital importance in the development of twentieth-century theology.

Another leading Ritschlian theologian, Julius Kaftan, Professor at Berlin,
remarked that a unified Ritschlian School 'expressive of the same theology'
existed only in the minds of its opponents.[26] Nevertheless, he went on, there
were 'essential points at which we are in agreement'. It was chiefly against
these points, rather than against Ritschl himself, that Troeltsch, as the most
consistent theorist of the History of Religion School, directed his theological
assault. These discussions provoked ever more vigorous and vitriolic attack
and counter-attack both from the post-Ritschlian theologians[27] and from
the positivist schools, with their theology of 'salvation facts' and utter
certainty.[28]

In his assaults on the dogmatic method, Troeltsch answered three leading
Ritschlian theologians: Julius Kaftan, who in his 'Die Selbständigkeit des
Christentums' had responded to Troeltsch's essay 'Die Selbständigkeit der
Religion';[29] Max Reischle,[30] who replied to Troeltsch's 'Über historische und
dogmatische Methode'[31] in 'Historische und dogmatische Methode in der
Theologie'; and Friedrich Traub, who responded more generally to

[24] Uli Hasler, *Die beherrschte Natur*, 294. Cf. Koch, 'Theologie unter den Bedingungen der
Moderne', esp. 1. For a clear statement of Herrmann's isolation of religion from the rest of reality see, for instance, *Gesammelte Aufsätze*, 256. See below, Ch. 5.

[25] Cf. Wagner, 'Aspekte der Rezeption Kantischer Metaphysik-Kritik'; Chapman, 'Theology
Within the Walls'.

[26] J. Kaftan, 'Die Selbständigkeit des Christentums', 378.

[27] Brief summaries of the debates can be found in G. Rupp, *Culture Protestantism*, 20–3. For a
discussion contemporary with Troeltsch see E. W. Mayer, 'Wesen der Religion'. Troeltsch
himself referred to the debates in *The Absoluteness* (A1901/23d), 30, 165 n., 168 n.4, 169 n.2.

[28] Cf. 'Christentum und Religionsgeschichte' (A1897/10a), 333. On Troeltsch's relationships
to the so-called 'positive' theologians see esp. the debate between Troeltsch and Theodor Kaftan. Cf. Th. Kaftan, *Ernst Tröltsch. Eine kritische Zeitstudie*; and *The Absoluteness* (A1901/23d), ET,
171. For a brief discussion of the relationship between Troeltsch and Ludwig Ihmels see Garrett
Paul, *'Religionswissenschaft'*, ch. 6, 191 ff. Cf. *The Absoluteness* (A1901/23d), ET, 33–6. Troeltsch
outlines his dissatisfaction with both the Ritschlian and the positive schools in a letter to Wernle
of 22 June 1898, in F. W. Graf (ed.), 'Ernst Troeltschs Briefe und Karten an Paul Wernle', 103.

[29] 'Die Selbständigkeit der Religion' (A1895/2; A1896/1 and 2).

[30] Max Reischle (1858–1905), *extraordinarius* in Gießen (1892–5); in Göttingen (1895–7);
ordinarius in Halle (1897–1905). Founder of the *Pfarrerverein* (1890). Troeltsch is also critical of
Reischle's elevation of the authority of the person of Jesus (letter to Wernle of 22 June 1898, in
Graf (ed.), 'Ernst Troeltschs Briefe und Karten an Paul Wernle', 104).

[31] 'Über historische und dogmatische Methode' (A1900/9a).

Troeltsch in 'Die religionsgeschichtliche Methode und die systematische Theologie: Eine Auseinandersetzung mit Tröltschs theologischen Reform-programm'.

The Dogmatic Versus the Historical Method

The most important of these conflicts in Troeltsch's early years was with Julius Kaftan.[32] Troeltsch's animosity towards his 'erstwhile friend'[33] was exemplified most clearly in the astonishing walk-out from the 15 October 1896 Eisenach meeting of the Friends of the liberal newspaper *Die christliche Welt*. In response to Julius Kaftan, who had given a lecture on the doctrine of the Logos, Troeltsch leapt to his feet and replied 'Es wackelt alles'—'Every-thing is tottering'. He then left the room, slamming the door behind him.[34] Although in a letter to Bousset he describes his essay, 'Religion und Kirche'[35] 'as marking the real breach with Kaftan and probably also with Herrmann',[36] after the Eisenach meeting Troeltsch felt himself increasingly distant from the Ritschlians, both personally and theologically. Despite this break with the Ritschlians, however, he expressed no desire to establish his own opposing school and was content with what he termed (perhaps ironically) his 'theological isolation'.[37]

In distinction to Troeltsch, Julius Kaftan understood modern science to be characterized by an all-pervasive empiricism and thus as a 'gradual emancipa-tion from philosophy and, perhaps more importantly, from metaphysics'.[38]

[32] Julius Kaftan (1848–1926), born Nordschleswig; studied theology in Erlangen; *PD* in Leipzig (1873); Prof. of Systematic Theology at Basel; *extraordinarius* (1874); *ordinarius* (1881); and then Dorner's (and ultimately Schleiermacher's) successor as Professor of Apologetics and Philosophy of Religion in Berlin (1883). Troeltsch had briefly studied under him in 1885–6. Kaftan was, as Troeltsch wrote to Bousset on 6 November 1885, 'imposing, but in no way illumin-ating' (cited in Drescher, *Ernst Troeltsch*, ET, 17). Unlike Ritschl, he emphasized the importance of mystical experience (particularly of the 'highest good'), placing particular weight on Paul's experience on the road to Damascus. From 1904–25 he was a member of the *Oberkirchenrat*, and from 1919 was its vice-president, and in this capacity was very interested in the unification of practical and systematic theology. Cf. *NDB*, 11, 16 f. On Troeltsch's relationship with Kaftan see esp. Horst Renz, 'Eine unbekannte Preisarbeit über Lotze', 55, and Drescher, *Ernst Troeltsch*, ET, esp. 86–7.
[33] Kaftan had reviewed *Vernunft und Offenbarung* (A1891/3) very favourably in *TLZ* 17 (1892), cols. 208–12.
[34] This incident is reported in Walter Köhler, *Ernst Troeltsch*, 1. It affected Troeltsch emo-tionally, as he explained to Bousset (27 January 1897) (G1976/2), 36): 'I am in any case finished with Kaftan personally and want to have nothing more to do with him'. See also Drescher, *Ernst Troeltsch*, ET, 86–7, 362–3.
[35] 'Religion und Kirche' (A1895/1).   [36] *Briefe aus der Heidelberger Zeit* (G1976/2), 31 f.
[37] Letter from Troeltsch to Martin Rade cited in Rathje, *Die Welt des freien Protestantismus*, 106.
[38] 'Die Selbständigkeit des Christentums', 373. For Troeltsch's criticisms see 'Geschichte und Metaphysik' (A1898/2), 31. Herrmann took this still further.

Against the possibility of any natural or philosophical knowledge of Christianity, Kaftan considered theology to be wholly dependent upon a special means of knowing founded upon faith and scripture: theology therefore had to have its own epistemology. The 'true central task of Protestant dogmatics' for Kaftan thus consisted in:

setting forth the knowledge which accrues to faith from the appropriation of the revelation of God borne witness to by Scripture. In the fulfilment of this task dogmatics is wholly determined by Scripture and ecclesiastical confession . . . That its task should be thus and not otherwise understood is not only a theological but also an ecclesiastical necessity.[39]

This meant that the absoluteness of Christianity could not be guaranteed through any philosophy of history, but rather 'the roots of religion rested in inner personal life'[40] mediated through the Christian community.[41] Philosophies came and went, Kaftan contended, but Christianity remained the same and was guaranteed by an inner conviction.[42] For Kaftan, then, the criterion to be used for assessing the historical phenomenon of Christianity was not to be obtained using a metaphysical or historical method, but rather was reached solely by a revelation directly mediated to the individual. Thus, according to Kaftan, Troeltsch had quite failed to see that there was a special way of conceiving of religious phenomena, which was itself rooted solely in faith in the absoluteness of the revelation of Jesus Christ. Thus Kaftan argued that 'whoever maintains the independence of Christianity also confesses the absolute truth of the Christian faith'.[43] Any other method of trying to secure the absoluteness of Christianity was like 'children who speak loudly in a dark room to drive away their fear'.[44]

Troeltsch, however, countered this tendency to guarantee the absoluteness of Christianity on an epistemology which rested upon a direct individual revelation. In his essay 'Geschichte und Metaphysik' he criticized Kaftan for what he considered to be his refusal to pursue the logic of his own thought:

To see all that is non-Christian as the result of sin is merely a product of theology and reflection, especially of the need to localize salvation firmly in the Church. To naïve religion this idea is quite alien . . . History of religion is no mere apologetic tool to show the peculiarity of Christianity, but rather treats all the great founders and leaders the same.[45]

Where Kaftan saw other religions as mere formal analogues, Troeltsch

---

[39] Julius Kaftan, *Dogmatik*, 104.
[40] Kaftan, 'Die Selbständigkeit des Christentums', 378 f.   [41] Cf. ibid., 380.
[42] Cf. ibid., 382.   [43] Ibid., 387.   [44] Ibid., 388.
[45] 'Geschichte und Metaphysik' (A1898/2), 8.

maintained that 'in reality these other religions have no idea that they are postulates ... Reality does not show the analogy of postulate and fulfilment, but only related religious attitudes to life'.[46] Although Troeltsch conceded that the 'dogmatic method' was consistent,[47] he nevertheless held that it could not presume to be scientific, since it depended on something which was simply an impossibility:[48] according to Troeltsch, there were no possible circumstances when the human being had the ability to perceive absolute truth from an absolute standpoint. Later, in his book *The Absoluteness of Christianity and the History of Religion*, Troeltsch over and over again stressed that 'to wish to possess the absolute in an absolute way at a particular point in history is a delusion'.[49]

The Charge of Hegelianism

Kaftan found Troeltsch's emphasis on reaching a knowledge of the truth through the study of history, at least as expounded in 'Die Selbständigkeit der Religion', to be a latent Hegelianism: the Christ-principle, Kaftan felt, had been separated from the historical Christ-event, which meant that the historical Jesus was no longer of much significance. If, as Troeltsch claimed, history could not be the source of divine knowledge, then the theologian was forced to look elsewhere for sources of truth, which was, according to Kaftan, Hegelianism by any other name. Against this, Kaftan asserted that Christianity depended on revelation alone.

Even though Troeltsch acknowledged that he had separated the person of Christ from the Christian principle in his essay on 'Geschichte und Metaphysik', he nevertheless claimed that this was directed first and foremost against a biblicism that restricted Christianity entirely to the New Testament.[50] This essay, however, he later came to realize could be construed as being 'strongly Hegelian',[51] and he decided against its inclusion in the second volume of his collected works. Nevertheless, although there is much talk of principles and absolutes, the absolute is never actually *identified* with any particular rational principle: its full realization, even in this more Hegelian phase, was left to the future, and it always depends on concrete history for its

[46] 'Geschichte und Metaphysik' (A1898/2), 8.
[47] Ibid., 10; 'Über historische und dogmatische Methode' (A1900/9a), 745; ET, 25.
[48] Troeltsch considers Ihmels to be making much the same mistake (*The Absoluteness* (A1901/23d), ET, 34): '[Supernatural certainty] seems unattainable to me because the relative, historical, and limited character of the history of Christian development has been established, in my view, by proofs whose validity cannot be diminished by the abstract impossibility of the denial of miracle or by the postulates of religious orientation'.
[49] *The Absoluteness* (A1901/23d), ET, 122.
[50] 'Geschichte und Metaphysik' (A1898/2), 61, 63.
[51] Cf. *The Absoluteness* (A1901/23d), ET, 168 n.4.

content.[52] For Troeltsch, the 'principle' of Christianity was not an abstract idea stemming from a metaphysics of the absolute, but rather something that could be known as a living power only in the course of history itself.

By upholding the impossibility of dogmatic knowledge, Troeltsch was directly opposing the method adopted by the Ritschlians. In this context, another of Troeltsch's opponents, Friedrich Traub, asserted:

It has to remain true that systematic theology pursues its own tasks . . . Indeed I am even of the opinion that the scientific character of systematic theology consists precisely in this: that it pursues a distinctive epistemology which is determined by the character of its object.[53]

On this view, the empirical study of history could say nothing whatsoever about such an object, which by definition had to remain beyond all criticism and scientific investigation: the knowledge acquired through faith was thus clearly distinguished from that acquired through history.

Against such an understanding of theological knowledge, Troeltsch maintained that theological truth was 'one and the same truth which is reached from different angles and in different relations to the other elements of the spiritual life'.[54] Rather than an epistemological dualism, Troeltsch clamoured after 'the retrieval of the unity of the spiritual life' (as was noted by Gustav Ecke in his lengthy discussion of Ritschl's successors[55]). He made this quest for a unity of truth and method most explicit in his lengthiest criticism of the dogmatic method, *The Absoluteness*.[56] Here he claimed that the dogmatic method was nothing less than a complete perversion of Christianity since it attempted to separate certain individual facts in history from any possibility of analogy: this implied a Christian epistemology[57] which depended on the 'dogmatic isolation of Christianity from its connections with its environment'.[58] Thus in speaking of what he called systems of exclusive naturalism he says: 'The demand for "absoluteness" is satisfied when Christianity has been traced to an immediate divine causality . . .

---

[52] In *The Absoluteness* (A1901/23d), ET, 104, 170 n.5, Troeltsch is careful to make a clear distinction between his own system and that of Hegel. Against Pannenberg's view (in 'Redemptive Event and History'), there is no evidence that Troeltsch ever divorced principle from person.

[53] Friedrich Traub, 'Die religionsgeschichtliche Methode und systematische Theologie', 340.

[54] 'Christentum und Religionsgeschichte' (A1897/10a), 349.

[55] Ecke, *Die theologische Schule Albrecht Ritschls*, i. 124.

[56] This book *Die Absolutheit* (A1901/23) originated in a famous lecture given at a meeting of the *Freunde der christlichen Welt* at Mühlacker on 3 October 1901. It was first published in 1902. The second edition, of 1912 (A1901/23b), contains a number of major alterations which have been analysed by Sarah Coakley (in *Christ without Absolutes*, ch. 2).

[57] *The Absoluteness* (A1901/23d), ET, 81; cf. 'Über historische und dogmatische Methode' (A1900/9a), 740.

[58] *The Absoluteness* (A1901/23d), ET, 32.

Absoluteness here consists of miracle. It is the absoluteness of a Christian Sunday causality in antithesis to the relativity and mediacy of a non-Christian weekday causality.'[59]

In a somewhat over-rhetorical book review of 1901, Troeltsch called the method of the Ritschlians 'a grotesque piece of theological scholasticism' of which the aim was to remove 'the critical historical method and any analogy with universal human events, and to erect a new theological history, which is not history but dogma'.[60] Similarly, in criticizing Max Reischle, Troeltsch remarked that 'we are back in the eighteenth century again with the problem of miracles, and we will have to start all over again'.[61] Although even in his earliest works Troeltsch felt the possibility of perceiving supernatural events in history to be a 'dangerous experiment',[62] he made his clearest statement of what he called the 'historical' method in the essay, 'Über historische und dogmatische Methode in der Theologie',[63] which was written as a response to Friedrich Niebergall,[64] a pupil of Julius Kaftan. Here Troeltsch gives a concise summary of the principles guiding the historical method in contrast to the theological or 'dogmatic' method of his opponents, which is perhaps his most well-known contribution to theology.[65]

The three principles were as follows: first, all religious tradition had to be open to criticism.[66] Secondly, what happened in times past had to be explicable in terms of normal everyday experience, which meant that 'Jewish and Christian history are analogous to all other history'.[67] (This was the principle

---

[59] *The Absoluteness* (A1901/23d), ET, 21; cf. *Glaubenslehre* (F1925/2), 36; ET, 37.

[60] Review of Steinbeck (A1901/11), col. 712.

[61] Review of Reischle (A1904/9), col. 616; cf. review of Lipsius (A1905/2), col. 209.

[62] 'Die Selbständigkeit der Religion' (A1895/2), 373.

[63] The importance of this essay has been noted by various commentators. Van Harvey, for instance, opens his long discussion of history and faith with a presentation of Troeltsch's method as the definitive statement of the historical approach (*The Historian and the Believer*, 14–19). See also Runzo, *Reason, Relativism and God*; Coakley, *Christ without Absolutes*, 24 ff.; Pannenberg, 'Toward a Theology of the History of Religions'. Similarly Ittel (in 'Die Hauptgedanken der "religionsgeschichtlichen Schule"', 62) sees the common conviction of the History of Religion School to rest in their shared appropriation of Troeltsch's method of probability, analogy, and reciprocity. As has been shown in the previous chapter, this is rather misleading.

[64] Troeltsch and Niebergall had long been adversaries. During his brief spell as *extraordinarius* in Bonn, from 1892–4, Troeltsch had developed the ideas which were later published as 'Die christliche Weltanschauung' (A1894/1) as a refresher course for Rhineland preachers, in whose journal Niebergall's essay, 'Über die Absolutheit des Christentums' was published. Niebergall later moved to Heidelberg as a *Privatdozent* in the winter semester of 1903–4. Cf. F. W. Graf, 'Profile: Spuren in Bonn'.

[65] For other discussions of similar themes see, for example, 'Über historische und dogmatische Methode' (A1900/9a); 'Christentum und Religionsgeschichte' (A1897/10a); *The Absoluteness* (A1901/23d), ET, 32.

[66] Cf. 'Christentum und Religionsgeschichte' (A1897/10a), 336; 'Geschichte und Metaphysik' (A1898/2), 6.

[67] 'Über historische und dogmatische Methode' (A1900/9a), 732; ET, 14.

of the fundamental similarity of all historical occurrences ('analogy').)
Thirdly, the phenomenon of religion, although irreducible to all other phenomena, could only be investigated in so far as it was correlated with the rest
of historical and spiritual life.[68] Indeed, 'once it is applied to biblical scholarship and Church History, [the historical method] is a leaven that transforms
everything and which finally destroys all previous methods'.[69] This meant,
Troeltsch later wrote, that the 'entanglement of Christianity in the universal
context of the history of religion with all its analogies and real connections,
and in the currents of ordinary practical and intellectual life, places it completely in the historical process'.[70] Indeed, Christianity could not rely on special 'theological methods of research and proof'.[71]

Against the dogmatic method, Troeltsch sees his own method as preferable, since, rather than building upon the isolated value judgement of a small
community, a unified view of reality is able to build upon the whole of the
tradition and make use of the whole of learning. On Troeltsch's conception,
theology could no longer look down on the rest of learning from its unshakable position as queen of the sciences, but was to be brought before the bar
of universal criticism, since only if theology was open to criticism could it
hope to maintain its status in the modern world. A haughty disregard for the
rest of learning would threaten its very existence: it would become little
more than a picturesque relic of a time long since past. Its supernatural
explanations would no longer seem tenable in the light of the success of
alternative explanations of reality which required no irrational surrender of
the intellect. In short, theological truth could not depend upon the isolation
of a dogmatic 'fact' since 'the modern idea of history . . . knows no concept
of a universal principle'.[72]

HARNACK AND THE HISTORICAL METHOD

The greatest of the post-Ritschlians, the church historian Adolf von
Harnack,[73] who was, according to Troeltsch, 'more or less symbolic of the

---

[68] Ibid., 731–3; ET, 13–15.

[69] Ibid., 730; ET, 12. In his article 'Wesen des Christentums', in *RGG*[1], Johannes Wendland
made the similar claim that 'we need no other method than that which is used in the human sciences . . . The hard facts of history are the objective moment which stands behind our subjectivity. Only history will reveal the essence of religion' (cols. 1967–73).

[70] 'Rückblick' (A1909/18a), 214; ET, 71. See also Troeltsch's letter to Wernle, 4 April 1897 (in
Graf (ed.), 'Ernst Troeltschs Briefe und Karten an Paul Wernle', 100), where he gives a concise
summary of his own programme as free of theological and doctrinaire 'schemata'.

[71] 'Zur Frage' (A1909/31a), 766; ET, 43.   [72] *The Absoluteness* (A1901/23d), ET, 64.

[73] Adolf von Harnack (1851–1930), PD (1874) and Prof. in Church History in Leipzig (1876);
Prof. in Gießen (1879); Prof. in Marburg (1886); Prof. in Berlin (1888); 1905–21 also director of

historicizing trend in theology',[74] provides perhaps the clearest example of such an isolationist method.[75] For Harnack, it was taken for granted at the outset of research that certain elements in the Christian and Jewish religions were beyond comparison. As Troeltsch put it:

> [These historians,] with such a mighty researcher as Harnack at their head, treat those points of history given prominence by the religious value-judgement very differently from the rest of history. Thus they make those high points into objective religious authorities and designate their effects as perceived by religious experience as the foundation of redemption amongst unredeemed humanity.[76]

Although, according to Troeltsch, with Harnack 'biblicism is ready to flow into the history of religion',[77] he nevertheless held back and clung to the 'dogmatic method',[78] thus trying to show what was 'distinctive in the origins of Christianity'.[79] Indeed the very idea that Christianity was of the same species as other religions and could be compared with them on an equal basis was quite out of the question. Such a method is well summarized by Harnack's pupil Ernst von Dobschütz:[80]

> Is it right to describe Christianity on Gentile soil essentially as an enthusiastic movement in which ecstatic experiences of all sorts played a leading role, in which the spirit manifested itself in all kinds of remarkable phenomena? Such a description characterizes it as one of the many religious movements of its time, without doing justice to its singularity . . . In our attempt to put ourselves entirely back into the ancient time, we must gradually come to the point where we are no longer struck by what the Christianity of those days had in common with the religiosity of its time, but by what distinguished it . . . Only then shall we be justified in speaking of a truly historical history-of-religion view of things.[81]

In his important and influential discussion of the function of the theological faculty in the modern university, Harnack makes his method of

---

the Prussian State Library. On Harnack see Agnes von Zahn-Harnack, *Adolf von Harnack*; F. Smend, *Adolf von Harnack. Verzeichnis seiner Schriften bis 1930*; J. C. O'Neill, *The Bible's Authority*, ch. 17; Kurt Nowak, 'Bürgerliche Bildungsreligion?'.

[74] 'Was heißt' (A1903/18a), 386; ET, 124.

[75] Both Troeltsch and Bousset recognized Harnack's contribution to the study of the history of Christianity. He 'broke ground by showing its continuity with Hellenistic culture' (Bousset, 'Die Religionsgeschichte und das neue Testament', 266).

[76] 'Rückblick' (A1909/18a), 205 n.7; ET, 63 n.4.   [77] Ibid., 209; ET, 66.

[78] Harnack's reticence about adopting a thoroughgoing historical method is emphasized in a rather bitter letter of 26 October 1908 from Greßmann to Gunkel: 'Nobody would expect him to slip on the black ice of the history of religion—but one might expect him to have some understanding for the new problems' (cited in Klatt, *Hermann Gunkel*, 44).

[79] Review of Dorner (A1901/12), 266.

[80] Ernst von Dobschütz (1870–1934), PD (1893) and Prof. of NT (1898) in Jena; Prof. in Strasbourg (1904); Prof. in Breslau (1910); Prof. in Halle (1913).

[81] Ernst von Dobschütz, *Probleme des apostolischen Zeitalters*, 78.

theological isolation even more apparent: theology did not require the study of the history of religion, he contended, for the simple reason that in knowing the one true religion the Christian was presented with the paradigm for all religions: 'We desire that the theological faculties should remain for the study of the Christian religion, because, in its pure state, Christianity is not *a* religion alongside the others, but is *the* religion . . . Some forms of Christian piety, especially the highest, just do not have parallels.'[82] The theology faculty thus remained solely concerned with the study of the Christian religion: knowledge of other religions could add nothing to the knowledge of Christianity as the true religion. Thus, according to Harnack, history of religion, as the study of the *natural* phenomenon of religion, had no business in the study of theology except perhaps to reveal those aspects of Christianity which remained trapped in nature and which could be dispensed with, thereby allowing it to be continually purified. Thus, as A. W. Hunzinger put it in a Ritschlian critique of the History of Religion School: 'The history of religion method serves theology by pointing to the real basis of faith, so that everything ethnic, secondary, and merely human is removed in order to concentrate on the kernel and the essence of the basis of salvation.'[83]

THE ESSENCE OF CHRISTIANITY

Troeltsch's debate with Harnack led him into a lively theological discussion of the 'essence' or 'nature' of Christianity, a subject which had occupied many thinkers in the nineteenth century at least from the time of Schleiermacher's influential discussion in his *Kurze Darstellung*.[84] Although many Ritschlians produced their own discussions of the essence of Christianity in the last years of the nineteenth century,[85] at the start of the twentieth century it was Harnack's influential set of lectures[86] that had reawakened

---

[82] 'Die Aufgabe der theologischen Fakultäten', 172. Cf. Rade, 'Religionsgeschichte', cols. 2183 f.

[83] A. W. Hunzinger, *Die religionsgeschichtliche Methode*, 35. A similar critique of the overdeterministic method of the History of Religion School is offered by John K. Riches in *A Century of New Testament Study*, ch. 3.

[84] See *Kurze Darstellung*, esp. §§74, 84. Troeltsch gives a brief outline of the history of the debates in the nineteenth century in 'Prinzip' (A1913/18), col. 1843, and he discusses the relationship between his own concept of essence and Schleiermacher's in *Glaubenslehre* (F1925/2), §1. 9. On the history of the term 'Wesen des Christentums' see esp. Hans Wagenhammer, *Das Wesen des Christentums*.

[85] Julius Kaftan, *Das Wesen*; Reischle, *Die Frage nach dem Wesen der Religion*; Wobbermin, *Zwei akademische Vorlesungen* and *Das Wesen des Christentums*; Bousset, *What is Religion?* On this see W. A. Brown, *The Essence of Christianity*, 223–87.

[86] Harnack, *Wesen des Christentums*; ET, *What is Christianity?*

interest in the subject and provoked a number of responses.[87] According to Harnack, once the abiding and true had been secured then the historian would be able to assume 'the royal function of a judge, for in order to decide what of the past shall continue and what must be done away with, or transformed, the historian must judge like a king'.[88] In his history of dogmatics Harnack had arrived at a relatively simple criterion for making historical judgements. Indeed, as he suggested in *Das Wesen des Christentums*, the Gospel message could be reduced to two straightforward themes: that God was the Father, and that the human soul was of infinite value.[89] It was in this Gospel message, which Harnack summarized as 'eternal life in the midst of time',[90] that Jesus revealed absolute religion itself: history was thus weighed against a particular viewpoint which had been given directly by Jesus, before any historical investigation.

Thus, although Harnack had ostensibly constructed his monumental *History of Dogma* on scientific historical grounds, his methodological contention that 'theology is dependent on innumerable factors, above all the spirit of the times'[91] was seriously called into question by his prior isolation of the Gospel message, what he called the 'essence of Christianity', as the criterion for the assessment of dogma. Thus he could write: 'An essence of Christianity has been constructed, out of which (as out of a Pandora's box) all doctrines have been formed, have been extracted and have been legitimated as Christian.'[92] Such a legitimation of dogma rested ultimately, according to Harnack, on the 'plain and simple' truths embodied in the personality of Jesus,[93] which in turn were grounded in that 'disposition which the Father of Jesus Christ awakens in human hearts through the Gospel'.[94]

Troeltsch's criticism of what he regards as Harnack's over-simplistic isolation of the essence of Christianity[95] shares much with that of Alfred Loisy,[96] whom Troeltsch regarded as 'one of the finest and most noble of the

[87] A discussion of the debates surrounding Harnack can be found in Wendland, 'Wesen des Christentums'; and Mayer, 'Wesen der Religion'.

[88] Harnack, 'Über die Sicherheit und die Grenzen geschichtlicher Erkenntnis', 7.

[89] *What is Christianity?*, 8. Although Troeltsch is at times highly critical of this immensely influential work, he also praised it as a work of apologetics for those people who stood outside the official structures of the Church and who were 'confused and distrustful of official theology' ('Was heißt' (A1903/18a), 439; ET, 168).

[90] *What is Christianity?*, 8.   [91] *History of Dogma*, 9; *Dogmengeschichte*, 12.

[92] *History of Dogma*, 9; *Dogmengeschichte*, 13.

[93] *History of Dogma*, 59; *Dogmengeschichte*, 69.   [94] *History of Dogma*, 896.

[95] 'Was heißt' (A1903/18a). On the different editions of this essay see Stephen Sykes, 'Ernst Troeltsch and Christianity's Essence'.

[96] See also Troeltsch's letter of 4 April 1908 to von Hügel in *Briefe an Friedrich von Hügel* (G1974/1), 87–9. Von Hügel mediated many of Troeltsch's works to various Catholic Modernists, including Tyrrell. Cf. Barmann, *The Modernist Crisis*, 167.

personalities of the modernists'.[97] However, Troeltsch parts company with
Loisy in his belief that it was equally deficient to locate the essence of Christianity in the Church.[98] This was little more, he maintained, than a 'remnant
of unhistorical catholic-dogmatic thought'.[99] For Troeltsch, Christianity
could not be identified with any one of its forms,[100] and similarly the study of
history could never show whether one form was closer to essential Christianity than any other.[101] According to Troeltsch, the conception of Christianity's essence was thus:

not merely an abstraction from the manifestations, but at the same time a criticism
of these manifestations, and this criticism is not merely an evaluation of that which is
not yet complete in terms of the driving ideal, but a discrimination between that
which corresponds to the essence and that which is contrary to it[102]

Troeltsch agreed with Harnack that the theologian was called upon to judge
history, but this could not be achieved simply by isolating a tiny snippet of
the whole spectrum of Christianity. Instead the theological task was to show
'what has been, so that its significance and meaning for human life as a
whole can be evaluated'.[103] This called for a philosophical assessment of
the history of religion which was based upon, 'but not exhausted by, the real
history of religion'.[104]

Earlier, in his lengthy essay on history and metaphysics, Troeltsch had
already adopted a similar method. Having shown the overwhelming importance of the historical method, he then emphasized the need for philosophy,
in order to obtain some sort of criterion, to prove the absoluteness of
Christianity:

We cannot presuppose or prove that Christianity is something totally different from
the non-Christian religions. We therefore have to assess the place and the truth of
Christianity on the basis of the whole manifestation of religion. That is nothing other
than philosophy of religion.[105]

Indeed he regarded this as the real continuation of Ritschl's work, which lay,
he contended, 'in the ever truer understanding of the real historical development of religion and of Christianity, which will lead to a philosophy of

[97] *Glaubenslehre* (F1925/2), 27; ET, 30.   [98] Cf. 'Der Modernismus' (A1909/7a), 59 f.
[99] 'Was heißt' (A1903/18a), 398; ET, 134. On Troeltsch's reception of Loisy's *L'Évangile et
L'Église* see Hans Rollmann, 'Troeltsch, von Hügel and Modernism', 41, 44–6. Cf. *Briefe an
Friedrich von Hügel* (G1974/1), 63–9. Troeltsch also discussed Catholic Modernism in 'Der Modernismus' (A1909/7a); *Die Trennung* (A1907/2), esp. 76 f.; and 'Katholizismus und Reformismus' (A1908/1).
[100] *Glaubenslehre* (F1925/2), §2. 2.   [101] Cf. *The Absoluteness* (A1901/23d), ET, 66.
[102] 'Was heißt' (A1903/18a), 407; ET, 141.
[103] Ibid., 408; ET, 143. On this see Hans Frei, 'The Relation of Faith and History in the
Thought of Ernst Troeltsch', esp. 59.
[104] 'Religionsphilosophie' (A1904/7), 143.
[105] 'Geschichte und Metaphysik' (A1898/2), 25.

religion which will clarify the presuppositions and yield a clear presentation of the Christian faith'.[106]

THE PHILOSOPHY OF THE HISTORY OF RELIGION[107]

The need to make some sort of philosophical appraisal of the history of religion was thus maintained by Troeltsch from the very outset of his career: indeed the significance of the philosophy of history in his constructive thought cannot be overestimated. As early as 1894 he talks about its importance: it was in the philosophy of history, he claimed, that the distinctive modern tasks of theology were located: 'Only in recent times has it become necessary to secure the abiding and true in human life using a philosophy of history against the apparently unbroken stream of happening.'[108] In short, he maintained, the modern period, which had seen the collapse of the all-embracing supernatural systems of the Middle Ages, had become 'the era of the philosophy of history.'[109]

In much of his earlier work Troeltsch sets about the philosophical appraisal and evaluation of the concrete phenomenon of religion investigated by the historical method. According to Troeltsch, there was no other method possible, since religion could not be isolated by a spontaneous value judgement nor by some special mode of perception, but could be investigated only as it appeared in concrete history: thus he claimed, against the Ritschlians, that 'the truth content of religion must be assessed in its historical movement and peculiarity'.[110] Those who felt that the absolute could be perceived directly, or who believed Christianity was *sui generis*, were, he contended, guilty of a dogmatic isolation of Christianity which was little more than an implicit use of the philosophy of history, 'which stood behind all theological systems'.[111] In *The Absoluteness*, Troeltsch thus countered any rigid distinction between revelation and reason by claiming that to 'aim the pistol of the either/or at a person is typical of the dogmatic method, while a contextual consideration of both/and is characteristic of the historical'.[112] Later in the same book he makes a similar point: 'The problem faced by the modern approach to history is not that of making an either/or choice between relativism and absolutism, but of how to combine the two.'[113]

---

[106] 'Geschichte und Metaphysik' (A1898/2), 67.

[107] On this see also Garrett Paul, 'Religionswissenschaft', ch. 4; H. R. Niebuhr, 'Ernst Troeltsch's Philosophy of Religion'; Ogletree, *Christian Faith and History*, ch. 2; Apfelbacher, *Frömmigkeit und Wissenschaft*, ch. 5, pt. C; Wyman, *The Concept of Glaubenslehre*, 36 ff.

[108] 'Die christliche Weltanschauung' (A1894/1a), 300.   [109] Ibid.

[110] 'Die Selbständigkeit der Religion' (A1895/2), 370.

[111] 'Die christliche Weltanschauung' (A1894/1a), 301.

[112] *The Absoluteness* (A1901/23d), 35.   [113] Ibid., 90.

Troeltsch thus developed a philosophy of history in order to discriminate the 'value difference' between the higher and lower stages of religion.[114] The problem of the development of religion was thus central: How could modern Christianity be said to be more developed than primitive expressions of religion?[115] Answering this question, according to Troeltsch, meant that the 'central science for us in the philosophy of religion is the determination of the essence and meaning of Christianity through the use of the philosophy of history'.[116] This method 'aims to establish the levels of development within history using the historical method, and presupposes a fundamental analysis of the religious consciousness under the viewpoint of the normative'.[117] Instead of deriving the criterion of truth through some seemingly arbitrary dogmatic isolation, Troeltsch thus attempted to derive a criterion from what he called a 'universal standpoint', which meant moving beyond the study of history to the 'philosophy of the history of religion'.[118] In this way, concrete historical religion is brought into contact with the normative, with what *ought* to be, or, as will become clear below, with the goal of development. Thus Troeltsch claimed:

The investigation moves here into the fundamental questions of the philosophy of history, which has to decide about the nature and meaning of the concept of development . . . The specific problem arising here for the science of religion is then the question about the goal of religious development.[119]

This leads on naturally to the question addressed in the fourth and fifth chapters of *The Absoluteness*:

Does the historical way of thinking include the positive acknowledgement of Christianity as the highest realm of religious life and thought that has validity for us?[120]

TROELTSCH AND THE TRUTH OF RELIGION

This attempt to obtain theological criteria by using philosophy inevitably led Troeltsch into a conflict with the second fundamental tenet of Ritschlianism: the loathing for metaphysics. Thus, against a supernatural principle for judging history, Troeltsch affirmed the need for a method for assessing history which recognized the 'simple, abiding, and true in historical development on the basis of a belief in the rationality of human history'. Indeed, he went on, the 'dangers [of the historical method] could only be

[114] 'Religionsphilosophie' (A1904/7), 143. [115] *RPH*, 16.
[116] 'Zur Frage' (A1909/31a), 767; ET, 44. [117] 'Religionsphilosophie' (A1904/7), 143.
[118] *The Absoluteness* (A1901/23d), ET, 65.
[119] 'Wesen der Religion' (A1906/5b), 49; ET, 117.
[120] *The Absoluteness* (A1901/23d), ET, 107; cf. review of Kaftan (A1912/8), col. 727.

overcome through a metaphysics of history'.[121] Later, in an article on the principle of religion for *RGG*[1],[122] Troeltsch clarified his ideas on this Christian principle or 'power' still further. Through the whole complex of religion, he claimed, there was a 'driving force or power'[123] behind any outward or inward manifestation, which could, however, never be perceived apart from the manifestation of real religion. Equating principle with 'essence', Troeltsch sees it 'always as a universal concept of a specifically historical kind, which formulates a totality for the purpose of presenting in this universal also the formulation of the factually developing driving power of the whole'.[124] Similarly, in his lectures on *Glaubenslehre*, Troeltsch saw the religious 'principle' as expressive of 'the whole religious position . . . and deriving from the universal method of contemporary psychological thought. It has the task of bringing the hugely diverse appearances to a single formula, which amounts to the unified root and the driving force of the whole phenomenon'.[125] For Troeltsch, then, the formulation of the principle of religion *required* concrete historical religion and was meaningless without the prior analysis of the history of religion. Thus in 'Die Selbständigkeit der Religion' Troeltsch claimed that the 'criterion grows in and with history itself'.[126]

In his presentation of the principle of Christianity, Troeltsch repeatedly denied that he was a Hegelian: he did not claim a metaphysics of the absolute, but rather sought a metaphysics of history.[127] The goals and values of history could not be imposed from above or by prior judgement, but rather were reached only through the analysis of history itself.[128] This is most clearly stated in *The Absoluteness*:

The modern understanding of history knows no evolutionary development in which an actual law-regulated universal principle produces values that are universally authentic. It knows, finally, no absolute realization of such a universal principle within the context of history where as a matter of fact, only phenomena

[121] 'Geschichte und Metaphysik' (A1898/2), 68; cf. 65.

[122] 'Prinzip' (A1913/18), col. 1844.

[123] Ibid., col. 1842; cf. 'Geschichte und Metaphysik' (A1898/2), 56.

[124] 'Prinzip' (A1913/18), col. 1843.   [125] *Glaubenslehre* (F1925/2), §5. 2.

[126] 'Geschichte und Metaphysik' (A1898/2), 78; cf. 'Die Selbständigkeit der Religion' (A1901/23d). In *The Absoluteness* (A1901/23d), ET, esp. 28, Troeltsch admits that in some of his earlier works he had failed to distinguish adequately between the empirical study of history, which could not make use of universals, and the philosophy of history, where universal categories were to be applied to empirical history.

[127] Cf. 'Geschichte und Metaphysik' (A1898/2), 41, 45, 46; 'Die Selbständigkeit der Religion' (A1895/2), 361; 'Die christliche Weltanschauung' (A1894/1a), 262; *The Absoluteness* (A1901/23d), ET, ch. 2, esp. 77.

[128] Like other commentators, G. von Schlippe (in *Die Absolutheit des Christentums bei Ernst Troeltsch*, 51f.) and Garrett Paul (in *'Religionswissenschaft'*, 149) probably overestimate Troeltsch's Hegelianism.

that are uniquely defined and thus possess individual character are brought forth at any given point.[129]

In order to evaluate the phenomenon of Christianity, Troeltsch claimed that the theologian did not need to resort to the exclusive supernaturalism of the orthodox, or the value-judgement dogmatic method of the Ritschlians, or the Hegelian metaphysics of the absolute. Instead, he went on, 'simple normative value is something distinct from exclusively supernatural revelation and likewise from absolute fulfilment of the principle of religion'.[130] Thus, even though the historical method leads to an inevitable relativization of religious phenomena as they become objects of human history,[131] it is nevertheless still possible for human beings to recognize movement towards the realization of absolute goals. The choice facing the theologian was thus not the either/or of naïve prejudice or anarchistic scepticism. Rather, Troeltsch claimed: 'the only course that remains is the kind of scientific enquiry in which humans strive as best they can to comprehend the empirical, historical reality and to acquire norms from history by conscientious comparison and reflection'.[132]

THE RESPONSIBILITY OF THE THEOLOGIAN

It was at this point that Troeltsch recognized the responsibility involved in the study of history. Nothing could be arbitrarily isolated from history, and yet there was still a need to reach norms for practical living. Thus he wrote in 1908 on Catholicism and reform:

Human beings must learn that in the arena of the religious life there is no absolute miracle which represents the truth supernaturally at *one* particular point or in *one* particular institution, but rather every person and every era must conquer faith for itself with its own calculations and with its own dangers, relying on the powers of history alone.[133]

Thus relativism, although an unavoidable aspect of modernity, did not

---

[129] *The Absoluteness* (A1901/23d), ET, 67. For this reason Troeltsch regards the Hegelianism which was still prevalent in certain quarters, for example in August Dorner's '*Volksmetaphysik*', as implausible, and later he claimed that Dorner's 'Christ-principle' was 'simply an abomination for my historical realism' (Review of Dorner (A1917/4), col. 87). Cf. August Dorner, *Grundriß der Religionsphilosophie*. The impact of Dilthey within the historical sciences indicated most clearly the end of the Hegelian hegemony. On the eclipse of Hegelianism see esp. Herbert Schnädelbach, *Philosophy in Germany, 1831–1933*, ch. 2.

[130] *The Absoluteness* (A1901/23d), ET, 57.

[131] Troeltsch made this point as early as 1897 ('Christentum und Religionsgeschichte' (A1897/10a), 353).

[132] *The Absoluteness* (A1901/23d), ET, 105.

[133] 'Katholizismus und Reformismus' (A1908/1), col. 26.

necessarily deprive Christianity of its absolute basis. Indeed, according to Troeltsch, it was 'only the misguided habits of thought of rational or super-natural dogmatics [that] surround the word "relative" with all the terrors of the uncertain, the unstable and the purposeless'.[134] Or, as he put it more pro-saically, the threat of relativism was overestimated.[135] Thus Troeltsch claimed: 'Only superficial acquaintance with God [can] estrange people from God, and only a superficial understanding of history [can] lead people to believe that religion must fade away because of the apparent contradic-tions of its different types of absoluteness.'[136] In all this, Troeltsch thus went to great lengths to stress the constructive possibilities latent in historical relativism.

Troeltsch began his defence of these possibilities from the beginnings of his career. Thus in many of his early works, and most particularly in *The Absoluteness*, he delineates the task of theology, distinguishing it from that of the social sciences. Theology alone, he claimed, maintained a vision of absoluteness. Thus, what is of chief importance is:

the victory of the highest values and the incorporation of all reality into their frame of reference. Determinative at every point, therefore, is ethically-oriented religious faith that includes the idea of an end, and this is something no scientific imagination can give. The assurance thus provided by faith need fear none of the effects of histor-ical relativism.[137]

This understanding of history as always in relation to a divinely inspired end had been introduced by Troeltsch in his earliest works: the challenge for the historian of religion was to see history as the place of God's dealings with human beings,[138] or as the arena where the majesty of God would be revealed.[139] This required a faith in the possibility of 'the absolute and the eternal in the endless stream of becoming and finitude'.[140] Faith, on Troeltsch's account, was thus not something isolated from history, but rather: 'Ideals derive from and are effective only in history but they are made effective only through *faith*, and in the last analysis can only be grounded in faith . . . History and the formation of ideals are not separate, but are directed to one another'.[141]

[134] *The Absoluteness* (A1901/23d), ET, 86.
[135] 'Über historische und dogmatische Methode' (A1900/9a), 747; ET, 27; cf. 'Die Selb-ständigkeit der Religion' (A1896/2), 217; *The Absoluteness* (A1901/23d), ET, 29. Coakley (in *Christ without Absolutes*, 26) is correct to emphasize the limited character of Troeltsch's so-called relativism, at least in this early period.
[136] *The Absoluteness* (A1901/23d), ET, 158.   [137] Ibid., ET, 94.
[138] 'Christentum und Religionsgeschichte' (A1897/10a), 341.
[139] 'Über historische und dogmatische Methode' (A1900/9a), 739; ET, 20.
[140] 'Die christliche Weltanschauung' (A1894/1a), 311.
[141] 'Geschichte und Metaphysik' (A1898/2), 32 f.; cf. 45.

Thus from the beginning Troeltsch was clear that the affirmation of an absolute was the sole preserve of religion, and could never be supplied by any immanent values which emerged from history. History was concerned with the partial and the relative and could never reveal the absolute in its fullness:[142] instead religion alone supplied 'the purpose of development'[143] and without it there could only ever be a 'history of culture'.[144] Thus Troeltsch held the goal of history to rest in the reconciliation of nature and spirit, as higher ('spiritual') ends shaped and guided nature and historical, social, and political particularities.[145]

In the early period of his writing Troeltsch characterized the individual human being (somewhat dualistically) as a creature in which nature and spirit were forever 'in opposition',[146] but in which the two sides were nevertheless always seeking after reconciliation. Thus, Troeltsch claimed, by mastering the world of nature and history, the human being would be released from oppression by forces beyond his or her control. Indeed, the history of religion was the 'history of escape from dependence, from natural strivings, for communion with God and for freedom of the spirit over the world, and from the mere factuality of existence'.[147] It was here that the 'unconditioned worth of the inner person' achieved full recognition.[148] Such escape is, however, highly reminiscent of post-Ritschlian theology and perhaps indicates a tension in Troeltsch's work. Thus he could write in 1897:

History of religion is the process of salvation as the divine majesty and love leads human beings out of the conditions of creation which ensnare them in need, pain, struggle, and sin, back to God.[149]

However, many of Troeltsch's early works move in the opposite direction to such an escapist theology, affirming the importance of the reconciliation of nature and spirit *within* the concrete historical realm. For instance, in *The Absoluteness* he could write:

within the individual and non-recurrent, there is something universally valid—or something connected with the universally valid—which makes itself known at the

---

[142] Cf. 'Die christliche Weltanschauung' (A1894/1a), 316.   [143] Ibid.

[144] 'Die Selbständigkeit der Religion' (A1896/1), 80. Cf. 'Christentum und Religions-geschichte' (A1897/10a), 341.

[145] 'Die christliche Weltanschauung' (A1894/1a), 320 f.

[146] 'Die Selbständigkeit der Religion' (A1896/2), 190. Throughout his career Troeltsch continued to emphasize the inevitable tension which characterized the human being, and with which all 'genuine theology' had to deal (review of Dorner (A1917/4), col. 87). His solutions, however, gradually became rather more tentative.

[147] 'Christentum und Religionsgeschichte' (A1897/10a), 342.

[148] *The Absoluteness* (A1901/23d), ET, 100. Cf. 'Die Selbständigkeit der Religion' (A1896/2), 194; cf. (A1896/1), 78.

[149] 'Christentum und Religionsgeschichte' (A1897/10a), 342; cf. 'Geschichte und Meta-physik' (A1898/2), 38; *The Absoluteness* (A1901/23d), ET, 112.

same time. The problem is to hold these two together in the right relation . . . The Enlightenment conception [of the universally valid] stood closer to the basic urgings of the human ethos and perceived the main tendencies of human history perhaps more correctly than the modern study of history with its concern for the microscopic . . . The problem is to define the scope of the relative and individual with ever increasing exactness and to understand with ever increasing comprehensiveness the universally valid that works teleologically in history. Then we will see that the relative contains an indication of the unconditional. In the relative we will find a token of the absolute that transcends history.[150]

Although there are admittedly strong Hegelian currents in such a vision, which (at least explicitly) disappear from his later works, this reconciliation between the absolute and the relative is one of the most persistent themes in Troeltsch's theology.

THE ABSOLUTE AND THE FUTURE

Later in his career Troeltsch became more cautious about asserting the possibility of full reconciliation in the present, moving away from the kind of teleological conception of history (the 'unfolding of divine reason')[151] which is frequently alluded to in his early works. At the same time, however, he did not usually resort to otherworldly redemption as the place of reconciliation. Although he emphasized the future dimension of the absolute,[152] such an absolute always *impinged* on concrete history. Indeed in his later works, as will be shown in Chapter 7, Troeltsch goes to great lengths to stress the ethical implications of all religion.

The emphasis on the future dimension of absoluteness can be seen in some passages from *The Absoluteness* where the absolute functions as 'the goal, characterized by a boundlessness and other-worldliness that transcend all history'.[153] Total reconciliation, Troeltsch claimed, was impossible; instead the absolute was to provide the motivation for historical construction. Historical norms could never be absolute, Troeltsch insisted, but were

---

[150] *The Absoluteness* (A1901/23d), ET, 106.

[151] 'Die Selbständigkeit der Religion' (A1896/1), 76.

[152] It is difficult to detect sharp breaks in Troeltsch's theology. There are shifts of emphasis and different concerns, yet central themes persist throughout his work. The future dimension of the absolute is certainly not ignored in Troeltsch's earlier writings. Thus in an essay on history and metaphysics he asserted that 'redemption is a deed of the future not of the past'. Similarly in an essay on Christianity and the history of religion of 1897 he maintains that it is only the 'future which holds the key in its fullness . . . [The ends of religion] concern the future, not the contemporary confessional confusion' ('Christentum und Religionsgeschichte' (A1897/10a), 350, 359).

[153] *The Absoluteness* (A1901/23d), ET, 147.

instead 'a situationally informed striving toward a future goal, a goal that is not yet completely realized and has not yet become absolute'.[154] Similarly, Troeltsch wrote in 1903:

What is really important is the push to the future, the elevation of the Christian ideal not as a patching up and improvement of what already exists, but an ever new order of life, standing in opposition to the natural drives of life, but based on the religious concept rooted in Christ.[155]

In a lecture Troeltsch maintained that the absolute was 'a unity which rests in a goal, not in history',[156] but which nevertheless functions to relativize all present value constructions. Similarly Troeltsch wrote in an essay on the philosopher Rickert, that in looking to the future 'we find a constant corrective for our own value constructions; that is we supplement and broaden our own existence (which is inclined to become constricted) and we dissolve all naïve attempts to isolate and absolutize that which is given'.[157] The centre of Troeltsch's system was thus a future vision which inspired the present but which could never be realized in its fullness, except 'perchance the soul return to the divine spirit'.[158]

According to Troeltsch, then, all knowledge and all human achievements were only provisional when measured against ultimate truth—or, in Kantian terms, against that (unrealizable) goal of knowledge of things-in-themselves, an idea which will be discussed in Chapter 6. Such an approach to truth, as lying out ahead, meant that human beings were to make a continued attempt to approximate to the goal, to absolute truth, which at the same time served to make them ever more aware of the limitations of their attainment of truth. 'This is,' Troeltsch maintained in *The Absoluteness*, 'enough to provide us with the sense of the absolute which we need and which we can attain'.[159] Troeltsch thus accepted that any vision of unity which understood reality as a whole, and which functioned as that absolute yardstick against which all partial perspectives could be measured, could be known only tentatively in trust or faith from the finite perspective of the human being. The absolute thus functioned as the spur to constant criticism, yet in itself was the unknowable object of hope and longing.

Only religion, Troeltsch held, could provide a hope that the end of the process would be reached; yet, paradoxically, as long as human beings were separated from this goal through their finitude, it was an end that could never be reached, except, that is, at the end of time. In a book review of one of his contemporary critics, the Lutheran confessionalist Theodor

---

[154] Ibid., 90.   [155] Review of Weinel (A1903/23), col. 2992.

[156] *Glaubenslehre* (F1925/2), 89; ET, 78.

[157] 'Moderne Geschichtsphilosophie' (A1903/4a), 701; ET, 296.   [158] Ibid., 712; ET, 305.

[159] *The Absoluteness* (A1901/23d), ET, 129; cf. 'Grundprobleme' (A1902/4a), 671.

Kaftan, Troeltsch gave what is perhaps his clearest summary of his concept of absoluteness:

The absolute is with God; all human truth is relative, but in one way or another connected to the absolute. We live within approximate values, and thereby overcome the distinction between relative and absolute ... My theology lives from the absolute which is contained in approximations to it. I see no other possibility to achieve a religious standpoint, and therefore it is preferable to me than confessional Catholicism or Lutheranism.[160]

Human knowledge was directed towards a gradual approximation to a hidden and unknown absolute which could only be affirmed in an act of faith. And yet, Troeltsch held, only this faith in a higher goal, a transcendent end beyond any absolutizations of merely finite ends, could liberate the human being from bondage to history, an imprisonment in what Weber called the 'iron cage'[161] of immanence, or what Troeltsch himself called 'the prison of ever-increasing dissatisfaction'.[162]

When such a method was applied to the Christian tradition itself it could have far-reaching consequences. Indeed the very task of 'defining the essence was to shape it afresh'.[163] As Troeltsch remarked in another essay on the essence of Christianity, the relevance of the study of the history of religion for theology was that it should be able 'to influence religion itself. Religion, like every other sphere of culture, needs to be harmonized and adjusted with the rest of life, and it can only in this way learn to separate kernel and husk and to bring the kernel into ever new and fruitful relationships with other areas of life'.[164] To search for the essence of Christianity was at one and the same time to attempt to refine and to renew the tradition, so that it might conform ever more to its absolute truth. Everything was thus

[160] Review of Kaftan (A1912/8), col. 728.
[161] The concept of the iron cage is used by Max Weber to indicate the oppressive character of purely instrumental 'rationality' upon modern human beings. Cf. Max Weber, *GASS*, 412: 'The key question is ... to oppose the machine mentality and to keep a part of humanity free from such fragmentation of the soul, from ultimate domination by the bureaucratic form of life'. See also L. Scaff, *Fleeing the Iron Cage*.
[162] 'Christentum und Religionsgeschichte' (A1897/10a), 347.
[163] 'Was heißt' (A1903/18a), 431; ET, 163. Yasukata (in *Systematic Theologian*, esp. pp. xxii, 21 ff.) bases his interpretation of Troeltsch on this idea of shaping Christianity afresh. He points to a modification Troeltsch made for the second edition of *The Absoluteness*, where he speaks of his task as that of the '*Gestaltung* of the Christian world of ideas which corresponds with the contemporary world' (*Die Absolutheit* (A1901/23b), p. viii). Although Yasukata is unjustifiably critical of Troeltsch's 'spiritualism' and thus ignores the vital importance of history in Troeltsch's thought (e.g. 65 f.), he is correct in emphasizing the importance of the constructive and critical tasks of the theologian.
[164] 'Wesen der Religion' (A1906/5b), 468; ET, 93; cf. 'Christentum und Religionsgeschichte' (A1897/10a), 359.

directed to the 'further cultivation of Christianity'.[165] History of religion was therefore not necessarily destructive to religion,[166] even though it might mean that what had often been regarded as outside the mainstream was rather closer to essential religion than had hitherto been considered to be the case: indeed, all that had been produced out of 'apathy and banality, passion and short-sightedness, stupidity and malice, indifference and mere worldly cleverness' would be removed from religion.[167] Thus Troeltsch claimed (somewhat contentiously) that it was 'immediately obvious' that Kierkegaard and Tolstoy stood closer to the preaching of Jesus than did any ecclesiastical dogmatics.[168]

The Task of Glaubenslehre

The task of dogmatics, or *Glaubenslehre* was thus not the 'combination of a group of ready-formulated propositions, but rather the attempt to develop new formulations appropriate to the present—a rejuvenation'.[169] Revelation was thus, according to Troeltsch, not something complete, but rather 'was in process. In the place of the mechanical concept of revelation,' he went on, 'is the dynamic'.[170] Similarly, he claimed, God's 'peculiar manifestation rests not in being, but in becoming; thus not in nature, as something static, but in history'.[171] This meant that any attempt to express the essence of religion was always relative to the constraints of the present, which would make it, to some extent at least, a 'compromise between good and evil',[172] since truth in its fullness could only be grasped in the future, at the end time.[173]

---

[165] *The Absoluteness* (A1901/23d), ET, 163.

[166] 'The Dogmatics' (A1913/2), 3; 'Die Dogmatik' (A1913/2a), 502.

[167] 'Was heißt' (A1903/18a), 410; ET, 144.

[168] Troeltsch comments that Tolstoy's Christianity was 'the radical early Christian ideal, shorn of its apocalyptic elements, which also refuses the aid of modern technical rationalism' (*Die Soziallehren* (A1912/2), 847 f.; ET, 728 f.). Gertrud von le Fort (in *Hälfte des Lebens*, 89) comments on Troeltsch's fondness for Tolstoy's form of Christianity. See also 'Was heißt' (A1903/18a), 406; ET, 140; cf. 'Die theologische und religiöse Lage' (A1903/16a), 14 f.; 'Grundprobleme' (A1902/4a), 600.

[169] 'Prinzip' (A1913/18), col. 1844.

[170] *Glaubenslehre* (F1925/2), §3. 4. Troeltsch had understood revelation in terms of a dynamic process from at least as early as 'Die Selbständigkeit der Religion' ((A1896/1), 105).

[171] *Glaubenslehre* (F1925/2), §12. 2.

[172] 'Was heißt' (A1903/18a), 410; ET, 144.

[173] 'Die Dogmatik' (A1913/2a), 500. Troeltsch did not include this statement about the future in the English version of this essay ('The Dogmatics' (A1913/2)).

The Ideal Concept and the Decision of Faith

Following Max Weber, Troeltsch describes the historical 'essence', which is extracted from the totality of history and yet animates history, as an 'ideal concept'.[174] Although it is derived from history using the ordinary means of historical investigation, it could nevertheless, according to Troeltsch, be given a constructive function:

A positive evaluation [of the past] will mean confidence in the ability of the ideas to persist, to be purified and to be strengthened, which means that the phenomena themselves are to be regarded in the light of the future.[175]

For Troeltsch, then, the ideal concept was given the task of helping the theologian attempt to establish a new combination or synthesis of 'the gains of the past and the living present, by taking from history the ideal contents of the values of life and energetically referring whatever attests itself to our judgement as important to the idea of ultimate values'.[176] Similarly, he claimed, the formulation of the ideal concept was 'nothing more than a formulation of the Christian idea in a manner corresponding to the present, associated with earlier formulations in laying bare the force for growth, but immediately allowing the latter to shoot up into new leaves and blossoms'.[177]

Troeltsch thus understood the ideal concept to be no mere value-neutral tool of research,[178] but rather as something which, although always constructively linked with present-day values, was orientated towards the future: 'In this formulation [of the religious principle] biblical and historical theology make way for systematic theology'.[179] The principle thereby became the new authority for Christianity, which had once been located in the Bible or in the Church.[180] However unlike the Bible or the Church, it was not something that merely presented itself authoritatively to the observer, but was rather something that required an active construction on the part of the observer, and it thus contained a 'strong subjective element'.[181] This implies a heavy emphasis on the creative and constructive abilities of the human being, who is thereby called upon to *create* a sense of meaning or purpose from concrete history.[182]

Indeed what should not be underestimated in Troeltsch's work is the personal decision of the human being in formulating the ideal concept. Since absoluteness could not be guaranteed by a return to any form of

---

[174] 'Was heißt' (A1903/18a), §5.   [175] Ibid., 424 f.; ET, 157.
[176] 'Moderne Geschichtsphilosophie' (A1903/4a), 709; ET, 303.
[177] 'Was heißt' (A1903/18a), 431; ET, 162.
[178] Cf. Weber, *The Methodology of the Social Sciences*.
[179] 'Prinzip' (A1913/18), col. 1843.
[180] Cf. *Glaubenslehre* (F1925/2), §1. 2.   [181] 'Prinzip' (A1913/18), col. 1843.
[182] Cf. 'Die Selbständigkeit der Religion' (A1896/1), 78 f.

supernaturalism, the human being had a part to play in shaping reality in accord with absolute ends. This meant, according to Troeltsch, that 'everything converges on the matter of present decision in the great world struggle'.[183] Ultimately, then, all authority depended upon 'personal conviction' and the 'modern principle of autonomy'.[184] Indeed, Troeltsch wrote in *The Absoluteness*, there could be 'no other way to obtain a criterion that will enable us to choose among competing values. It is, in short, a personally ethically oriented religious conviction acquired by comparison and evaluation'.[185] The determination of the highest values in Christianity was thus accomplished by a personal decision where 'space and time were overcome in the judgement itself'.[186]

Here Troeltsch emphasized the moment of action as the living idea was brought out of history and animated in the present.[187] It was the 'synthesis of history and the future which in the last analysis can only be fully sure of continuity in personal, subjective certainty because it is conscious of having grown out of living and deeply comprehended history itself'.[188] In this way, the future, that which ought to be, was combined with the past in the present moment of decision. Thus Troeltsch wrote:

The new formulation of the principle leads to a new submersion, a deepening into the fullness and breadth and continuity with the historically given, which is at once a re-evaluation of the consequences: that is, the adaptation to the present and future.[189]

Past and present were thereby brought together by 'personally seizing the necessary, rational content of reality and of the historical process in its

---

[183] *The Absoluteness* (A1901/23d), ET, 121; cf. 'Was heißt' (A1903/18a), 411; ET, 145; *Glaubenslehre* (F1925/2), 39; ET, 39. Many interpreters have placed great emphasis on Troeltsch's concept of decision. See, for instance, Benckert, 'Der Begriff der Entscheidung bei Ernst Troeltsch', 426 f.; Little, 'Ernst Troeltsch and the Scope of Historicism', 356; Wyman, *The Concept of Glaubenslehre*, esp. 79 ff. Troeltsch continued to affirm the importance of the individual judgement in reaching an ideal concept throughout his career. See *Der Historismus und seine Probleme* (A1922/22), 165 ff.

[184] *Glaubenslehre* (F1925/2), §6. 3, 38 f.; ET, 39; cf. 'Moderne Geschichtsphilosophie' (A1903/4a), 710, 712, 717; ET, 303, 305, 309.

[185] *The Absoluteness* (A1901/23d), ET, 94; cf. 90; *Glaubenslehre* (F1925/2), §2. 5, 37; ET, 38.

[186] 'Was heißt' (A1903/18a), 430; ET, 161.

[187] Ibid., 448; ET, 176; cf. *Glaubenslehre* (F1925/2), 130–1; ET, 114–15.

[188] 'Was heißt' (A1903/18a), 448; ET, 176.

[189] 'Prinzip' (A1913/18), col. 1843. As Robert Morgan has pointed out (in 'Troeltsch and the Dialectical Theology', esp. 61), there are obvious parallels here with dialectical theology as well as with Kierkegaard. Drescher (in 'Entwicklungsdenken und Glaubensentscheidung') concludes that Troeltsch never allowed for a complete identification between the naïve faith in the absolute and the absolute himself. Gogarten, on the other hand, believed the absolute to be present in its fullness in the moment of decision (102). Troeltsch's 'leap of faith' (*Der Historismus und seine Probleme* (A1922/22), 179, 312) can neither prove nor guarantee anything. See also Perkins, 'Explicating Christian Faith', 4–14. Perkins's conclusion, however, that Troeltsch was a 'harbinger of contemporary existentialism' (93) seems highly implausible.

present form, and aligning oneself through correct intuition with the creative course of world teleology'.[190]

Troeltsch recognized that his solution was inevitably subjective since, he felt, it was a 'logical circle' to derive that which ought to be from that which has been.[191] Nevertheless subjectivity could not be evaded, but rather required 'insight'.[192] Indeed it was better 'not to try to deny [subjectivity] but rather to recognize it freely and openly'.[193] Although all authority was ultimately rooted in the deciding individual, this did not mean that the individual itself became absolute. Instead any decision was made in the full knowledge that the perception of the absolute was always limited by the 'short-sightedness and sinfulness' of all human beings.[194] It was thus from a position of utter humility, rather than a position of power, that the human subject acknowledged that 'Christ comes to us through history to create a new life even in us'.[195]

This recognition of the ultimate relativity of all religion led inevitably, according to Troeltsch, to the idea of tolerance, to the 'subordination of doctrinal incompatibility beneath the unity of feeling and atmosphere'.[196] The recognition that all shared in a common humanity striving towards an absolute, yet one which none could possess in its fullness, was, Troeltsch believed, the sort of Catholicism espoused by Dante, which was quite different from 'the narrow and bellicose confessionalism of later Europe. In truth he stood far closer to the supra-confessional strivings towards a unity of spirit and faith and which once again enliven the torn and exhausted humanity of today'.[197] Consequently, according to Troeltsch, the subjectivism involved in the very definition of the essence of Christianity could 'have a unifying effect'.[198] All history, all aspects of the tradition, are thus seen by Troeltsch as resources with which the human being sets about the creative attempt to understand the nature of the goal to which history is moving. Since no one understanding is absolute, then no fanaticism is justified: instead tolerance will be the mark of the new transformation of Christianity.[199]

There are obvious dangers in a method which places such a responsibility

---

[190] 'Was heißt' (A1903/18a), 435; ET, 166.   [191] 'Historiography' (A1913/35), 722.
[192] Ibid.   [193] 'Was heißt' (A1903/18a), 436; ET, 167.
[194] Ibid., 437 f.; ET, 168.   [195] Ibid.   [196] Ibid., 438; ET, 169.
[197] *Der Berg der Läuterung* (A1921/11), 7.
[198] 'Was heißt' (A1903/18a), 439; ET, 169. The ecumenical potential of Troeltsch's theology has been recognized by Karl-Ernst Apfelbacher (in *Frömmigkeit und Wissenschaft*, esp. 242–51). Instead of seeing subjectivity as based on a recognition of human relativity, he interprets it as a form of mystical apprehension of the divine. Such an interpretation, however, underplays the importance of concrete history for Troeltsch, displaying 'more of the strategic theological intentions of Apfelbacher himself, than the real concept in Troeltsch's work' (H. Ruddies, 'Mystische Theologie', 105; cf. Wyman, review of Apfelbacher). Sarah Coakley has also been keen to emphasize the importance of Troeltsch's subjectivism in ecumenical dialogue, over and against the rigid intellectualism of much dogmatics (*Christ Without Absolutes*, 196).
[199] Cf. *The Absoluteness* (A1901/23d), ET, 121, 127, 135, 136, 160.

on the individual: indeed, Troeltsch admitted, 'death is possible in a system of danger'.[200] And yet, in the current situation, there appeared to him to be a future for Christianity. Thus he wrote in his lectures on *Glaubenslehre*:

Something fully new can only develop when there are shown to be religious powers which are stronger than those of Christianity. These are nowhere to be found: Christianity has not been surpassed.[201]

This meant that for Troeltsch the religious principle was 'far from being exhausted. It continues to be effective so long as it is not overcome by any stronger powers'.[202] Thus, although admitting that the long-term 'future might have worries of its own',[203] and even that his method might prove to be 'the gate which has shut out the roots of Christianity',[204] he nevertheless affirmed that 'Christianity is the only stable religious capital we possess, and a new religion exists only in books. Where religion is really alive, it requires nothing new, merely a transformation. We are not afraid for the future of Christianity'.[205] Thus, for Troeltsch, it was possible to say in faith that 'Christianity is affirmed when one has the Father of Jesus Christ in one's daily struggles and labours, hopes and sufferings, when one is armed with the strength of the Christian Spirit for the great decision to be taken in the world and for the victory of all the eternal, personal values of the soul'.[206]

THE ABSOLUTE AND THE VOCATION OF THE THEOLOGIAN

In these various attempts to secure the absoluteness of Christianity, Troeltsch clarified his understanding of theology. Instead of being a separate scientific discipline alongside the others, theology was that calling which sought to ground reality as a whole in a higher meaning, in an absolute end, to which all human life and action were relative. As will be shown in the discussion of Troeltsch's conception of ethics in Chapters 6 and 7, in the same way that Weber was able to outline the distinctiveness of the vocations of

---

[200] 'Was heißt' (A1903/18a), 439; ET, 169; cf. *Glaubenslehre* (F1925/2), 94; ET, 82.
[201] *Glaubenslehre* (F1925/2), 49; ET, 47.   [202] 'Prinzip' (A1913/18), col. 1844.
[203] 'Glaube und Geschichte' (A1908/6a), col. 1456; ET, 144. Troeltsch recognized this in a letter to Harnack of 23 March 1900 ((G1978/1), in Apfelbacher, *Frömmigkeit und Wissenschaft*, 98). Troeltsch never denies the possibility that there will be new ice ages and that human beings might even climb back up the trees (*Glaubenslehre* (F1925/2), 324; ET, 258).
[204] Letter to Harnack (G1978/1), in Apfelbacher, *Frömmigkeit und Wissenschaft*, 59.
[205] *Glaubenslehre* (F1925/2), 37; ET, 38. Even in 1922 Troeltsch continued to recognize that Christianity remained an abiding power. Although he admitted that perhaps his own system had moved away from any recognizable orthodoxy, he nevertheless believed that it stemmed from Christianity ('Ein Apfel von Baume Kierkegaards' (A1921/5), ET, 314 f.).
[206] 'Was heißt' (A1903/18a), 440; ET, 170.

science and politics, Troeltsch gave a vision of theology as something which overcame the incomplete and partial visions of science and politics: theology was thus the *vocation* of those who sought to ground reality in an absolute which provided the hope for a world otherwise hopelessly fragmented and in the process of ever-increasing fragmentation.

Although the absolute functioned as a goal to which the Christian could only ever approximate, this did not mean that the theologian was denied the responsibility for constructive synthesis in the present. Indeed an absolute which served to limit the claims of any ethical and theological construction meant that the relativities of history could be accorded their proper place. Human ethical achievements were thus to be seen for what they were— frail and feeble efforts to approximate to an absolute. On this model, the critical perception of the present possibilities for the Christian religion, together with an equally thorough and critical understanding of the enduring resources of the past, combined to give theology a new foundation based on a critical realism inspired and animated by a faith in a hoped-for absolute. Theology thus did not concern itself with Utopias, but relied upon an understanding of history and society in order to determine the constructive possibilities for the absolute to gain expression in the present. The study of the realities of history thus had profound ethical consequences.

In distinction to the Ritschlians, as well as many of his fellow-members of the History of Religion School, Troeltsch held that for theology to continue as a credible academic discipline alongside the others and for religion to continue to exert a potent ethical and social force there could be no withdrawal into what he regarded as the escapism of a self-authenticating theological epistemology. Such escapism was founded on what he considered to be the scientifically unjustifiable assertion of the possession of an (absolute) truth which could stand up to no critical test. In distinction, Troeltsch moved towards a more comprehensive theory of religion than that adopted by many of his colleagues, one which attempted to balance the primordial experience of religion in the individual with its realization in history: only in such a way could Christianity retain its unified vision of Church and society.

The arguments between the Ritschlians and Troeltsch often moved in the direction of epistemology. The sorts of claims to a special knowledge or for metaphysics needed justifying. It comes as little surprise, then, that much theological debate in the early years of the twentieth century was carried on in the guise of philosophy. An understanding of philosophy seemed almost as important as a knowledge of scripture or dogmatics: theologians had to be philosophers. The next three chapters present a detailed discussion of how the claims made by the different schools of theology found philosophical expression. It will become clear that the philosophical debates had a very familiar and very theological shape.

4

Kant, Materialism, and Theology

This chapter considers how the disputes which dominated the theological arena, and which have been discussed in the previous chapters, were mirrored in the philosophical debates with which many theologians were occupied in the first decades of the twentieth century. The burning questions were similar: To what extent was religion *sui generis* and thus not reducible to any other sphere? To what extent did it share its epistemology with other forms of knowledge? Answers to these questions took many theologians into deep and often confused philosophical debate. This chapter outlines the context which made theological engagement with philosophy so pressing. The specific philosophical debates between theologians, together with their ethical consequences, will be discussed more fully in the two subsequent chapters.

MATERIALISM AND ITS THREATS

The theological appropriation of philosophy, and especially Kantianism, by the post-Ritschlian generation of theologians from all schools was spurred on, at least in part, by the task of countering the widespread popularity of materialism and monism at the turn of the twentieth century. Theologians were forced to tackle the pressing question of how the human spirit and the domain of freedom could survive the assault from naturalistic determinism. By 1900 materialistic or naturalistic philosophy had taken on a quasi-religious form, finding its leading prophet not in a theologian or philosopher but in the eminent zoologist Ernst Haeckel,[1] whose

[1] Ernst Haeckel (1834–1919) was born in Potsdam and after studying medicine turned to zoology, becoming Director of the Zoological Institute at Jena in 1862 and Prof. of Biology there in 1865, where he remained until the end of his career. He published many scientific works which helped popularize Darwinian ideas (particularly the *General Morphology*). *Die Welträtsel* was one of his first forays into philosophy, although his *Der Monismus als Band zwischen Religion und Wissenschaft* had earlier sparked off a vigorous debate with theologians. In 1906 came the foundation of the *Deutsche Monistenbund* with Haeckel as the first President. This was a quasi-religious organization propagating a naturalistic world-view which proved highly popular up to the Second World War. A one-sided history of the *Deutsche Monistenbund*, which

Die Weltr ätsel became one of the best-selling philosophical books of all time.[2]
Haeckel presents a monistic philosophy in opposition to what he regarded as
the fallacious dualistic philosophies of Christianity and Kantianism. Kant's
practical philosophy is seen not as an essential counterpart to the theoretical
(or scientific), but as sullying the latter's crystalline ('monistic') purity. Thus
Haeckel wrote:

[T]he 'dogmatic Kant' superimposed on this true crystal palace of *pure* reason the glit-
tering, ideal castle in the air of *practical* reason, in which three imposing church-naves
were designed for the accommodation of those great mystic divinities [i.e. the postulates of pure practical reason]. When they had been put out at the front door by
rational knowledge they returned by the back door under the guidance of irrational
faith. The cupola of his great cathedral of faith was crowned by Kant with his curious
idol, the famous 'categorical imperative'.[3]

Haeckel saw the 'back to Kant' movement, which will be explained in detail
below, as the last-ditch battle for a dualism which, on his view, had been
dealt the final blow by the 'monistic cosmology based on the law of substance';[4] substance being defined as 'the fundamental law of the constancy of
matter and force'.[5] In turn, according to Haeckel, freedom of the will had
been rendered futile by the science of evolution, which had 'made it clear
that the same eternal iron laws that rule in the inorganic world are valid, too,
in the organic and moral world'.[6] Indeed Haeckel went further, seeing freedom as a religious self-deception based on the error of the dualism of soul
and body, by means of which the Christian religion denied the importance
and neglected the study of nature.[7] According to Haeckel, progress in
science meant that the old

idealistic dualism was breaking up with all its mystic and anthropistic [*sic*] dogmas;
but upon the vast fields of ruins rises, majestic and brilliant, the new sun of our realistic monism, which reveals to us the wonderful temple of nature in all its beauty. In

views it chiefly as a precursor of National Socialism, is given by Daniel Gasman in *The Scientific
Origins of National Socialism: Social Darwinism in Ernst Haeckel and the German Monist League*. The
Bund, however, was more often associated with freethinking liberals (F. Tönnies was an original member) than with the racial theorists of the 'third religious force' (the *Gottgläubiger*) of the
Nazi era. It was at a meeting of the *Monistenbund* in 1910 that Arthur Drews gave his famous lecture 'Hat Jesus gelebt?'. A more hagiographic treatment of Haeckel is given by Wilhelm
Boelsche in *Haeckel, His Life and Work*.
   [2] Over ten thousand copies of the library edition were sold within a few months of publication. A popular edition was soon prepared, which was to sell over half a million copies up to
1933. By 1906 there were already fourteen translations, including an English edition.
   [3] *The Riddle of the Universe*, 123.   [4] Ibid.   [5] Ibid., 134.   [6] Ibid., 123.
   [7] Haeckel is especially critical of Christianity's denial of the importance of cleanliness, which
was such a significant feature of the more 'monistic' Hindu and 'Mohammedan' religions.
Much of *Die Weltr ätsel* (esp. ch. 17) is a vigorous attack on Christianity and the hypocrisy of
the Christian nations. In particular, Haeckel is extremely vehement in his opposition to
Catholicism.

the sincere cult of 'the true, the good and the beautiful', which is the heart of our new monistic religion, we find ample compensation for the anthropistic ideals of 'God, freedom and immortality' which we have lost.[8]

Instead of a return to Kant, Haeckel called for a return to Goethe, who had given the '"philosophy of unity" a perfect poetic expression'.[9]

Although Haeckel's system clearly lacks philosophical rigour, his achievement and influence cannot be denied and he undoubtedly answered a specific need of the Germany of his time: an eminent scientist had shown that science could answer all the questions of religion and give a meaning to the world which did not rest on outmoded superstition. Although he was easy to criticize philosophically,[10] theologically,[11] and historically,[12] his central theme of the relationship between science and religion demanded a serious response. Philosophical critics failed to observe that it was not so much as a philosopher that Haeckel was read, but as a prophet inaugurating a new religion of nature.[13] Indeed, in the words of his disciple Heinrich Schmidt, he was 'the greatest theologian the world has ever seen'.[14] It was thus in the sphere of religion, which relied on presuppositions and concepts which

---

[8] *The Riddle of the Universe*, 135. It is not accidental that Haeckel chooses Kant's postulates as the 'anthropistic' ideals. Kant's was the 'best type' of contradictory dualism.

[9] Ibid.

[10] Within two years of its publication many eminent philosophers had responded to *Die Welträtsel*, pointing to its simplistic understanding of the history of philosophy. A typical criticism is offered by Oswald Külpe in *Die Philosophie der Gegenwart in Deutschland*, 34–47. Friedrich Paulsen, one of the leading Kant scholars of the period, ridiculed the book: 'I have read the book with burning shame about the condition of the general and philosophical education of our people. It is painful that such a book was possible, that it could have been written, edited, sold, read, pondered, and believed by a people who possess a Kant, a Goethe and a Schopenhauer' ('Haeckel als Philosoph', 36). Another rapid response from a Kantian was the polemical essay by Erich Adickes, *Kant Contra Haeckel*.

[11] Rudolf Eucken (in *Geistige Strömungen der Gegenwart*, 170–91) gave an elegant critique of monism, something which, when taken to its logical conclusions, 'could have no place for the concept of truth upon which science depends' (190 f.). Instead, he points out, monism has maintained the old 'Ideals of the Good and True' in contrast to its stated method. 'Is there not then', he asks, 'an even sharper dualism, materialist in world-view and Idealist in action? We have here a new example of the old adage, that the human being often achieves the opposite of what is intended' (191). On the theological debate with Haeckel see esp. Boelsche, *Haeckel, His Life and Work*, 305 ff. Haeckel received no fewer that five thousand letters relating directly to *Die Welträtsel*. The most violent theological critic was the Halle church historian Friedrich Loofs (1858–1928), in his short book entitled *Anti-Haeckel*.

[12] In particular his portrayal of Christianity lacks critical rigour and makes use of any available hostile theory, paying scant regard to developments in biblical studies. See, for example, *The Riddle of the Universe*, 109–17.

[13] Something of Haeckel's legacy survives in the continuing influence of Rudolf Steiner. See esp. *Haeckel, die Welträtsel und die Theosophie*.

[14] Heinrich Schmidt, 'Ernst Haeckel als Theolog', cited in Gasman, *The Scientific Origins of National Socialism*, 15.

were not open to empirical investigation and scientific research, that the threat posed by naturalism and materialism was especially serious.

Troeltsch's Criticism of Haeckel[15]

From the beginnings of his career Troeltsch was aware of the need to assert the independence of the spiritual world against such attacks from the monists. In so doing he entered directly into the debate with Haeckel's 'Gospel of monism', responding to *Der Monismus als Band zwischen Religion und Wissenschaft* in the long essay 'Die christliche Weltanschauung und ihre wissenschaftlichen Gegenströmungen',[16] as well as providing a fairly lengthy exposition of Haeckel in *Die christliche Welt* in 1900.[17] Against the materialism of the age, Troeltsch asserts the need for a philosophical system 'worth its salt' which 'recognizes the portrayal of the spirit before nature, where the seemingly so dead and deadly mechanical rigidity of the facts of nature embodies the warm and restless life of the spirit'.[18]

Christian theology, according to Troeltsch, required a philosophy which allowed for an independent realm of the spirit which 'makes room for religion to breathe'.[19] The doctrine of evolution, he claimed, could never fulfil this role, since, although it 'had taken the place of what had previously been divine', it lacked any conception of absolute truth.[20] Thus Troeltsch asserted in several places that every claim to religion 'expresses . . . the stimulus of an objective world of the spirit'.[21] This realm of the spirit in turn became for Troeltsch the subject for the philosophy of history, a history which was continually in conflict with naturalism.[22] Indeed this friction between spirit and nature was, according to Troeltsch, 'the universal human problem',[23] and as such could not be evaded in the simplistic solutions of monism. The fight against Haeckel was nothing less than a fight for the spirit, which Troeltsch confidently felt he would win, since what he called Christian 'personalism' 'played havoc with every system of thoroughgoing rationalism',[24] 'whose

---

[15] On Troeltsch and Haeckel see Shinichi Sato, 'Ernst Troeltsch und Ernst Haeckel'.

[16] (A1893/2 and A1894/1); reprinted as 'Die christliche Weltanschauung und ihre Gegenströmungen' (A1894/1a). See esp. 241, 264.

[17] 'Ernst Haeckel als Philosoph' (A1900/4 and 5). For other discussions specifically of Haeckel see Troeltsch's brief reviews of works on Haeckel by Nippold (A1901/13); Hönigswald (A1901/16); and Menzi (A1902/6).

[18] 'Die christliche Weltanschauung' (A1894/1a), 247.   [19] Ibid., 248.   [20] Ibid., 236.

[21] *The Absoluteness* (A1901/23d), ET, 139; cf. 'Religionswissenschaft und Theologie des 18. Jahrhunderts' (A1903/21), 46.

[22] *Der Historismus und seine Probleme* (A1922/22), 11.

[23] 'Die christliche Weltanschauung' (A1894/1a), 320. Elsewhere Troeltsch regarded the 'fundamental problem' of all philosophy as that of setting limits to both unbridled rationalism and unbridled empiricism (*EPH*, 7).

[24] 'Contingency' (A1910/20a), 88.

fanatics were only content when everything was dissolved in a unified whole where the personality was as nothing'.[25] Because Haeckel had failed to recognize the importance of the spiritual dimension, Troeltsch boldly asserted that his 'philosophy belongs to the gigantic ephemeral success of triviality which keeps returning but which is always dissolved by future triviality'.[26] In short, according to Troeltsch, all such developments in their different ways threatened human autonomy itself.[27]

Alongside these popular expressions of monism, there were other philosophical movements which shared an equal animosity towards the spirit and consequently towards religion. The empiricism which had emerged in the Enlightenment had grown during the nineteenth century into a fully-fledged *Weltanschauung* which challenged the very existence of the human spirit and with it the possibility of human autonomy and creativity. To Troeltsch it appeared to have grown ever more radical, merely attempting to amass and collect data, yet never subjecting them to any set of universal laws. On a popular level, what developed from empiricism was a widespread belief in the all-embracing efficacy of science which, according to Troeltsch, never moved further than a 'universally plausible utilitarianism'.[28] This led to a mechanical explanation for every detail of life, even though this 'collided with every aspect of actual life and was quite ridiculous to the profound thinker'.[29] This was most obvious in the positivist philosophies of Ernst Mach and Richard Avenarius, who considered all epistemology as merely the ever more precise description of observable phenomena; there could, however, be no unification of phenomena within a wider whole.[30]

Troeltsch was highly critical of Mach's principle of 'empirio-Kritizismus',[31] his 'modern equivalent of nominalism', since, he contended, 'to have overcome every rational concept of truth, every necessity and universal', was a 'degrading error'.[32] Rather than organizing the data presented to the consciousness, the human spirit was held captive by the very conditions of nature: there was consequently no space left for human autonomy. Faced with such a threat, there was a grave need for the theologian to reassert the values of human freedom against the complete mechanization of

---

[25] *EPH*, 5.   [26] 'Die Kirche im Leben der Gegenwart' (A1911/8a), 98.

[27] Cf. 'Ethik und Kapitalismus' (A1905/6), col. 321; *Der Historismus und seine Probleme* (A1922/22), 721.

[28] 'Das Wesen des modernen Geistes' (1907/8b), 323; ET, 259.   [29] Ibid., ET, 260.

[30] On Ernst Mach and positivism see esp. A. Giddens, 'Positivism and its Critics'; and Habermas, *Knowledge and Human Interests*, 71–90. For a theological critique by one of Troeltsch's contemporaries see G. Wobbermin, *Theologie und Metaphysik*.

[31] It is this principle of 'empirio-Kritizismus' that is the chief object of Wobbermin's attack in *Theologie und Metaphysik*.

[32] Review of Wlassak (A1917/24), col. 468.

life: empiricism had thus grown to threaten the very foundations of autonomy. Rather than remaining central as a creative force responsible for
organizing the data presented to the consciousness, the human spirit was
held captive by the conditions of nature. Thereby the Kantian centrality of
the transcendental ego was destroyed, as the human being became just
another animal determined by the omnipresent laws of causality.

What had to be maintained if theology was to survive, according to
Troeltsch, was a world 'distinct from scientific and social-utilitarian morals,
which summoned up otherworldly and superhuman powers in its unfolding
of the imagination and in its direction to what is beyond the senses'.[33] For
Troeltsch, this amounted to the task of showing how the 'dominion of the
spirit and of spiritual purposes in the universe could be maintained without
a denial of natural scientific knowledge'.[34] Similarly, he sought the 'autonomy of reason against all mere physical and psychological causality and
against all merely pragmatic relativism'.[35]

In his 1897 response to the Göttingen materialistic philosopher J. Bau-
mann,[36] whose theory 'of the emptiness of the spirit', he remarked, mirrored
'the actual emptying of the spiritual life',[37] Troeltsch asserted the need for
the realm of the spirit to prevent a descent into materialism. Empiricism, if
accepted in its pure form untempered by rationalism, would result in nothing less than 'spiritual suicide'[38] since there was no longer any space for the
spirit. Against such a view Troeltsch commenced his 'fight against disbelief
in the spirit',[39] boldly proclaiming that 'whoever has confidence in the realm
of the spirit is never far from the kingdom of God'.[40] The contemporary task
of theology was thus fundamentally apologetic and it was entrusted with
'reawakening interest in the imagination, the heart, and the soul'[41] amongst
an intellectual class which considered itself 'definitively freed' from thought
of the inner person.

The task of apologetics in the face of these massive assaults on spiritual life
thus proved ever more pressing. In response to such threats, according to
Troeltsch, religious people had to 'seek an eternal world of the spirit . . . in
spite of all parties, in spite of the overwhelming mass of power-hungry and
fanatical theologians and in spite of all power politicians and pan-
Germans'.[42] Against 'the soul-destroying superstition of the present, where

---

[33] 'Die Kirche im Leben der Gegenwart' (A1911/8a), 104.
[34] 'Religionswissenschaft und Theologie des 18. Jahrhunderts' (A1903/21), 46.
[35] 'Zur Frage' (A1909/31a), 763; ET, 40.
[36] 'Moderner Halbmaterialismus' (A1897/3 and 6).
[37] Ibid. (A1897/6), col. 161.
[38] Review of Günther (A1916/22), col. 488; cf. 'Der Deismus' (A1898/20a), 464 ff.
[39] 'Moderner Halbmaterialismus' (A1897/6), col. 161 f.   [40] Ibid., col. 162.
[41] Ibid., col. 161.   [42] 'Die Religion im deutschen Staate' (A1913/37a), 89 f.

spiritual life is seen merely as a reflection of social relations and class-based interests', Troeltsch (commenting on Dante) saw the need to assert the 'independence of the spirit':[43] the theologian had to stand firm with steadfast resolve against 'all ambition and demagogic rhetoric'.[44]

When theology was seen as part of the wider picture, according to Troeltsch, it required philosophy, since 'as soon as one moves towards the whole, one is no longer within an individual discipline but one is philoso-phizing'.[45] Indeed a return to philosophy meant a revolution in theology 'which would throw overboard the old doctrine of the radical corruption of everything natural and unchristian'.[46] Much of Troeltsch's work was thus concerned with philosophy of religion understood in the widest sense. Just as theology and religion could not be isolated in the attempt to rejuvenate a dead past, so they could not rest content with the assertion of a separate real-ity exempt from scientific criticism, without losing their own credibility and with it their relevance. The refuge in otherworldly 'asceticism', however tempting, would render theology ethically and socially impotent.

THE LEGACY OF GERMAN IDEALISM

In his search for what he called a 'middle path'[47] between nature and spirit, Troeltsch felt that he shared the fundamental objective of the philosophy of German Idealism, where, he claimed, the specifically modern problems 'of the relation of spirit and nature, together with the problem of epistemol-ogy, which, from the side of the spirit, is rational and constructive in form, and from the side of the object, is empirical and analytic . . . entered the fore-ground'.[48] Where some (like the materialists) had denied the realm of the spirit altogether, and others (like Spinoza) positioned the two spheres in a monistic equilibrium which could not account for contingency and change, what could not be denied in a realistic solution was that fundamental dis-tinction between nature and spirit 'which was the key to all philosophical thought'.[49] The force of German Idealism was thus primarily directed against the unfettered individualism of the Anglo-French Enlightenment, which had been characterized by 'dogmatism, empiricism, common sense and scepticism, utilitarian and individualistic-atomistic ethics, as well as by a subjective-critical conception of history, a mechanistic-atomistic view of nature, and the dominating influence of naturalism in all aspects of

[43] *Der Berg der Läuterung* (A1921/11), 11.
[44] 'Die Religion im deutschen Staate' (A1913/37a), 90.   [45] *EPH*, 27.
[46] 'Protestantisches Christentum' (A1906/4), 371.   [47] *EPH*, 6.
[48] 'Der deutsche Idealismus' (A1900/12a), 543.
[49] *RPH*, 52; cf. *Glaubenslehre* (F1925/2), 174.

thought'.[50] The disintegrating 'spirit of the Enlightenment could be overcome',[51] however, in the synthesis between the empirical and the rational
offered in the 'mediating position'[52] of a revitalized idealism.

Troeltsch thus understood German Idealism as a 'criticism of knowledge
. . . a universally valid ethics of universal rational values . . . a genetic-
objective view of history and organic-dynamic concept of nature which
orders the whole of nature under the spiritual purposes of the universe'.[53]
Idealism would thereby help ensure the 'overpowering impression of the
productive power of the consciousness, the liberation from materialism and
psychogenesis'.[54] Similarly it would help free the '*Weltanschauung* from
intellectual deterministic deduction' making room for 'the rationally necessary goals of the "personality" . . . On the last analysis . . . the *Weltanschauung*
is determined in the personal act of freedom . . . The value of the personality
does not rest in material intellectual culture but in the absolute value of the
personality'.[55] It was for this reason that Troeltsch regarded the 'great line of
thought derived both from Locke and the Scottish philosophy of common
sense, and from Leibniz and Lessing' as 'deepening and expanding the ideas
of the Enlightenment beyond measure'.[56]

In his defence of the human spirit, Troeltsch continued in the tradition of
Ritschl, who had earlier attempted an apologetic defence of the spirit against
the materialists and positivists of his own day.[57] Whatever his failings in
countering such threats, Ritschl nevertheless recognized the overwhelming
importance of tackling the problems posed by materialism and positivism.
At the heart of his *magnum opus, Justification and Reconciliation*, is the attempt
to show that the 'Christian view of the world and of life is opposed both to
that produced by materialism and to those views which are presented in
monistic idealism'.[58] A similar intention is displayed in his *Instruction in the
Christian Faith*:

How can man, recognising himself as a part of the world and at the same time capable of spiritual personality, attain to that dominion over the world, as opposed to
limitation by it, which this capability gives him the right to claim?[59]

---

[50] 'Der deutsche Idealismus' (A1900/12a), 532.   [51] Ibid., 544.   [52] *EPH*, 6.
[53] 'Der deutsche Idealismus' (A1900/12a), 533.   [54] Ibid., 547.
[55] 'Der deutsche Idealismus' (A1900/12a), 544 f.
[56] 'Protestantisches Christentum' (A1906/4), 434.
    [57] Albrecht Ritschl, *JR* iii. 209 ff., 229 ff. See esp. 209: the scientific character of materialism is
limited because 'it can only see chance as the moving force of the ultimate causes of the world'.
    [58] *JR* i. 24. This was an area in which Troeltsch shared something with Ritschl, who had a
'religious and ethical aversion to everything that smacked of pantheism and monism' ('Die theologische und religiöse Lage' (A1903/16a), 13). On Ritschl's rejection of materialism see
H. Timm, *Theorie und Praxis*, 99; and J. Wendland, *Albrecht Ritschl und seine Schüler*, 17 ff.
    [59] 'Instruction', 224.

However, it is also clear that Ritschl tended not towards a unification of knowledge in a systematic presentation of the sciences, but rather towards a dualism, which paved the way for the more consistent dualism of the post-Ritschlians, especially Wilhelm Herrmann's, that will be discussed in detail in the next chapter.

Against the threat of materialism, then, theology had to continue to maintain the independence of religion, but at least for Troeltsch it would be misguided to separate it off completely from the rest of reality. He thus addressed the question of whether religion was 'nothing more than a collection of many parallel, different sides',[60] of whether it was 'only a combination of other conditions, or whether it had its own independent essence like logical thought, ethical judgement, or aesthetic appreciation; that is, whether it is secondary or primary'.[61] In answering this question Troeltsch pointed to Schleiermacher's 'theory of feeling as up till today the correct solution which only needs working out'.[62] In 'working out' Schleiermacher's Romantic theory, however, he subjected it to a far more thoroughgoing philosophical treatment, as will be shown in Chapter 6.

'BACK TO KANT'

In the next two chapters it will become clear that many theological debates were disguised as competing interpretations of Kant. Indeed theological adaptations of Kant were used not merely to defend Christianity from its 'cultured despisers', but also, as the conflicts between Troeltsch and Herrmann and between Troeltsch, Otto, and Bousset reveal, to defend competing theological systems within the world of theology itself. Kant had thus unwittingly become a great polemicist for the most diverse theological systems. In the process, Kant's own ideas were often contorted beyond all recognition.

In this revitalization of Kant theology was not alone, since Kant had, according to the Heidelberg philosopher Wilhelm Windelband, 'influenced many scholars who were not professional philosophers. [His] position affected almost every aspect of German learning at some level of theoretical justification'.[63] Despite the tremendous growth in the biological and psychological sciences, 'sciences which Kant hardly knew',[64] Troeltsch similarly recognized the great wealth of apologetic resources in Kant's thought,[65]

---

[60] 'Die Selbständigkeit der Religion' (A1895/2), 371.
[61] 'Religionsphilosophie' (A1904/7), 151.   [62] Ibid., 155.
[63] Windelband, Präludien, i. 4.
[64] Troeltsch, 'Das neunzehnte Jahrhundert' (A1913/36a), 630.
[65] He recognized this as early as 1895 in 'Die Selbständigkeit der Religion' (A1895/2), 433.

viewing the 'back to Kant' movement as nothing less than the renewed awareness of 'the burning issue' of 'the problem of freedom, which was continually in conflict with the principle of the conservation of energy'.[66] Once again, the revival of Kant's fortunes at the end of the nineteenth century, usually seen as beginning with Otto Liebmann's plea (in his *Kant und die Epigonen*) for a return to Kant's philosophy,[67] was inspired by the attempt to counter the dominant materialism of the scientific world-view.[68]

More generally, after the long period of Hegelian dominance,[69] there had been a marked revival in Kant's fortunes in theology, owing much to Ritschl, for whom Kant was the 'first to perceive the supreme importance for ethics of the "Kingdom of God" as an association of men bound together by virtue',[70] after what he saw as the Lutheran Reformation's one-sided concentration on religion at the expense of ethics.[71] It was Kant, according to Ritschl, who had maintained the practical sphere of freedom over and against all naturalistic world views: after Ritschl it was this 'practical' strand of Kant's thought that was to have lasting influence in theology.

In praising Kant, Georg Wobbermin,[72] Troeltsch's successor at Heidelberg, went even further than Ritschl, pointing to Kant's rediscovery of the

---

[66] 'Das neunzehnte Jahrhundert' (A1913/36a), 630.

[67] Discussion of Kant had never entirely disappeared during the nineteenth century, as is clearly shown in the detailed study by Klaus Christian Köhnke, *Entstehung und Aufstieg des Neukantianismus*. On Liebmann see esp. 211–32. Köhnke provides a statistical analysis based on lectures and seminars given at German universities to show how neo-Kantianism separated from positivism and in turn developed into the distinctive schools of Marburg and Baden. The earlier studies by Hans-Ludwig Ollig (*Der Neukantianismus*) and, in English, by Thomas E. Willey (*Back to Kant*) both rely on an earlier generation of scholarship, especially the influential wartime book by G. Lehmann (*Die deutsche Philosophie der Gegenwart*) which fails to point to the importance of the social and political background of the development of neo-Kantianism during the Bismarck era, exemplified particularly by the debate between the crude economic materialism of the Social Democrats and the less materialist socialism of the Marburg neo-Kantians.

[68] For a brief history of the development of and the reaction to materialism see Schnädelbach, *Philosophy in Germany*, ch. 3. The most important reaction to the 'physiological' interpretations of Kant (perhaps best exemplified by Helmholtz) was F. A. Lange's *magnum opus*, *Geschichte des Materialismus*, published from 1866 onwards. The rise of 'scientism' is admirably charted by John Theodore Merz, *A History of European Thought in the Nineteenth Century*, vol. iii.

[69] Hegelianism was still prevalent in August Dorner's '*Volksmetaphysik*' (in *Grundriß der Religionsphilosophie*). See above p. 63 n.129.

[70] *JR* iii. 11. Cf. *JR* i. 390.

[71] Cf. *JR* i. 390. For Ritschl's attitude to Kant see Max Reischle, 'Kant und die Theologie der Gegenwart', 371.

[72] Georg Wobbermin (1869–1943), born Stettin; *PD* in Systematic Theology in Berlin (1898); Prof. in Marburg (1906); Prof. in Breslau (1907); Troeltsch's successor in Heidelberg (1915); Prof. in Göttingen (1922); Prof. in Berlin (1935). Like his teacher Julius Kaftan, he emphasized the importance of religious experience in distinction to Ritschl. Through his career Wobbermin became increasingly interested in psychology of religion, translating William James's Gifford

self-conscious personality as the most significant event since the Reformation, and which made him the philosopher of Protestantism *par excellence*.[73] It was primarily this redefinition of the problem of freedom and the importance of the personality that led all manner of philosophers and theologians to see Kant as the 'philosopher of Protestantism', a term coined by Friedrich Paulsen in an influential study of 1899.[74] In short, as Troeltsch remarked, 'Kant did for philosophy what Luther did for religion'.[75] This overwhelming influence of Kant at the beginning of the twentieth century was later remembered by Barth, who claimed to have learnt at Berne that 'all God's ways begin with Kant and if possible must end there'.[76]

In the early years of the twentieth century Troeltsch saw his own contributions to philosophy as in many ways continuing in this Kantian tradition. While recognizing that German Idealism was essentially a unified phenomenon, he was nevertheless willing to concede that some forms were better equipped for the contemporary tasks of philosophy than others. Thus, although he regarded Hegel as having reached a synthesis between the rational and the empirical in his doctrine of the dialectic, he nevertheless thought his actual system had resulted in a 'petrification in an all-pervasive rationalism'.[77] Unlike Hegel, however, Troeltsch held that Kant had retained a doctrine of 'real freedom', which was 'closer to the realities of life than Hegel's unification of reason'.[78]

Troeltsch considered himself as following in the footsteps of Kant, whose more open system was far more capable of explaining the 'multifarious character of reason'[79] and able to account for both empirical science and history. Troeltsch thus regarded Kant as both the father of idealism and the founder of true criticism.[80] Although he was not afraid occasionally to borrow from elsewhere in the great breadth of German Idealism, Troeltsch saw himself as

---

Lecture (*Varieties of Religious Experience* (1904)) into German (*Die religiöse Erfahrung in ihrer Mannigfaltigkeit* (1907)). He pioneered the 'religionspsychologischer Zirkel'—the dynamic interaction between the religious experience of the believer and the historical and traditional aspects of belief—which culminated in his *Systematische Theologie nach religionspsychologischer Methode*. For an assessment see esp. F. W. Schmidt (ed.), *Luther, Kant, Schleiermacher in ihrer Bedeutung für den Protestantismus*; Günter Irle, 'Theologie als Wissenschaft bei Georg Wobbermin', esp. 144 ff. For a thorough discussion of Wobbermin's theology and philosophy see Matthias Wolfes, *Protestantische Theologie und Moderne Welt*, esp. 251–406.

[73] Georg Wobbermin, *Theologie und Metaphysik*, 9.

[74] Friedrich Paulsen, *Kant, Der Philosoph des Glaubens*. Even the racial theorist H. S. Chamberlain (in *Immanuel Kant*) regarded Kant as the philosopher of Protestantism.

[75] Review of Paulsen (A1900/1), col. 158.

[76] Cited in Eberhard Busch, *Karl Barth*, 34.

[77] Review of Lasson (A1917/1), col. 16 f.

[78] Ibid., col. 17. Cf. review of Marck (A1918/18), col. 259; review of Dorner (A1905/10), col. 768.

[79] Review of Lasson (A1917/1), col. 17.   [80] *EPH*, 17.

continuing the great reconciling work of Kant which had set the agenda for the contemporary problems of philosophy:

The most influential (like Locke and Leibniz) maintained a belief in divine and spiritual purposes in the world, together with finite evil and imperfection as necessary concomitants of the finite world. The belief in spirit and the purposes of the spirit against the natural-scientific world-view was the meaning of the English doctrine of the coincidence of the moral with the physical ordering of the world and the Leibnizian doctrine of the best of all possible worlds. In their theories the thinking of the seventeenth and eighteenth centuries reached its conclusions and delivered its problems to the nineteenth. Kant's splendid solution set the agenda for the new battles over spirituality and the meaningfulness of the world, which have not yet been completed.[81]

This task of synthesis, which Troeltsch understood to be the basic thrust of idealist philosophy, and which characterized his own theological and philosophical purposes, was, he claimed, nothing less than the continuation of Kant's work in the present against the forces of unbridled individualism, which was the concomitant of radical empiricism.[82] Thus he wrote in 1907:

I do not believe that this problem has basically changed in the course of the development of idealism. The extraordinary power and the vast mass of the impersonal and of the subpersonal remain the same, whether the subject matter is a [Kantian] representation or a [Hegelian] thing-in-itself.[83]

The absolute idealism of Hegel and the critical idealism of Kant (though with a preference for the latter) were united in Troeltsch's quest for the integrated and creative human personality against the dominion of the impersonal. German Idealism was characterized by the search for a synthesis between the empiricist and rationalist strands of Enlightenment thought. It was 'without the coincidence of the creaturely and divine life process and therefore without the dialectic—the idea of Hegel, or—without determinism and pre-established harmony—the idea of Leibniz'.[84] Against the increasing segmentization of the distinctive spheres of life, each guided by its own immanent goal, Troeltsch sought a grounding for the whole of reality in a universality, in an absolute end, as all aspects of life were endowed with a sense of purpose. This was nothing less than the idealist task.

---

[81] 'Religionswissenschaft und Theologie des 18. Jahrhunderts' (A1903/21), 46 f.
[82] Cf. 'Der deutsche Idealismus' (A1900/12a), 534.
[83] [Kant bleibt im Ansatz ('Kant is the starting-point')] (A1907/13), 232 f.
[84] 'Zur Frage' (A1909/31a), 764; ET, 41.

Kant's Two-Hundredth Anniversary

The activities surrounding the centenary of his death in 1904[85] served to bring about even greater interest in Kant amongst theologians, with the Königsberg philosopher becoming the subject of numerous articles in theological journals and Church newspapers. As the Ritschlian, Max Reischle pointed out, this was with 'good reason, for in fact Kant's influence in theology and its development has been of great importance'.[86] In the same article Reischle goes on to ask whether this influence 'should remain in the perfect tense' or whether there is a sense in which it continues in the present, before concluding that, despite the number of modifications required to make Kant's system applicable for the present day, he was still of the utmost importance. Reischle thus confidently asserted that he stood on the same ground as Kant, a philosopher who had not left a great theory of God and world along the lines of Aristotle, but who had rather made philosophy into a

methodical labour. Kant did not want to teach a philosophy but a means of philosophizing. It thus depends less on picking up the actual results of his philosophy than on following in the footsteps of his method of working. In this connection in particular we are Kantians and are able to say that he is the magister of modern theology and that a *tenere magistrum* is possible even when one distances oneself from his results.[87]

From almost all quarters it was similarly observed that Kant was relevant for the contemporary tasks of philosophy:

The cry 'back to Kant' has now for many years been the almost universal cry in Germany. It is now felt that the absolutist and idealistic line of development of Kant's doctrines was not the true line for philosophy to take ... The cry, however, if it is not to be misleading, must be understood to mean—Begin where Kant began, examine again the facts, not in order simply to adopt, but in order to verify, and in Kant's own sense criticize, his distinction between things-in-themselves and Phenomena. Use that distinction solely as a lantern to the path.[88]

---

[85] Hans Vaihinger (in 'Das Kantjubiläum im Jahre 1904') gives an account of the almost religious acts of veneration ('Säkulierfeier') of the February 12 celebrations. No fewer than fifty-six special articles as well as six important German Festschriften (listed on pp. 146–50) appeared in the year 1904, 'a fact which goes to prove that Kant is still a power today' (105). In 'An die Freunde der Kantischen Philosophie: Bericht über die Begründung einer "Kantgesellschaft" und die Errichtung einer "Kantstiftung" zum hundertjährigen Todestag des Philosophen' he reports on the founding of the *Kant-Gesellschaft*. Particularly striking is the generosity of the donations to the *Kantstiftung*. The largest (one thousand marks each) were from Prof. Walter Simon, a councillor in Königsberg, and Baumeister F. Kuhnt, a Halle factory owner. This diversity among the friends of Kant continued: the 1912 list of the 400 members of the Society included the industrialist Werner von Siemens.

[86] Reischle, 'Kant und die Theologie der Gegenwart', 357.   [87] Ibid., 387 f.

[88] Shadworth H. Hodgson, 'The Centenary of Kant's Death', 181.

This notion of Kant as the foundation, and all philosophy as a mere embellishment and modification, characterizes German philosophical life at the start of the twentieth century.[89] As Wilhelm Windelband put it in a famous maxim: 'Kant verstehen heißt über ihn hinausgehen' ('To understand Kant means going out from him'.),[90] since 'after [Kant] there was essentially nothing new'.[91]

It was such a Kantian method that Troeltsch adopted as the foundation for his constructive theological and philosophical tasks. As he put it in his important St. Louis lecture of 1904:

The problem was put by him in a fundamental way, and his solutions need nothing more than modification and completion . . . The ideas of Hume and Leibniz must once more be brought into relation with the continuation of Kant's work, and the combination of the Anglo-Saxon sense for reality with the German sense for the speculative is still the task for the new century as well as for the century past.[92]

Similarly, in a short discussion article in the *ZThK* for 1907, Troeltsch emphasized the continued importance of Kant for theology. In answering the question, 'Wo bleibt Kant?', he asserted: 'Kant bleibt im Ansatz'.[93] Or, as he wrote in an essay on the philosophy of religion published in 1904: 'the Kantian answer remains in principle the right solution'.[94] The different ways in which this solution was put into effect by theologians are the subject of the next two chapters.

---

[89] The publication of many hitherto unavailable sources and the gradual appearance of the *Akademieausgabe* did, however, lead to a revival of biographical and philological interest in Kant himself. See, for example, Albert Schweitzer, *Die Religionsphilosophie Kant's* for a close philological study of the development between the great *Critique of Pure Reason* and the later work on religion.

[90] Windelband, *Präludien*, i. p. vi. This approach to Kant is also emphasized in his contribution to the *Kant-Studien Festheft*: 'Nach hundert Jahren'.

[91] Windelband, *Präludien*, ii. 100.

[92] 'Main Problems' (C1905/1), 288. This passage does not occur in 'Psychologie und Erkenntnistheorie' (A1905/7).

[93] [Kant bleibt im Ansatz] (1907/13), 231–3.

[94] Troeltsch, 'Religionsphilosophie' (A1904/7), 149.

5

Wilhelm Herrmann and the Philosophical
Isolation of Christianity

THE KANTIAN THREAT TO PROTESTANTISM

The previous chapter showed that the interpretation of Kant had become a vital aspect in the defence of Christianity against its materialist and monist opponents in the early years of the twentieth century. This chapter considers how Wilhelm Herrmann,[1] Professor of Systematic Theology in Marburg, and one of the most important and influential of the post-Ritschlian theologians,[2] developed a theological system on the basis of a form of Kantian epistemology. The philosophy of Kant provides the context in which Herrmann sought to justify his rigorous distinction between the realms of faith and science or learning. It was, however, not directly to Kant that Herrmann appealed, but rather he responded, at least in part, to the 'unity of method'[3] espoused by his Marburg colleague, the Jewish neo-Kantian

---

[1] Wilhelm Herrmann (1846–1922), PD in Halle (1875–9); Prof. of Systematic Theology in Marburg until his retirement (1879–1917). On Herrmann see esp. Peter Fischer-Appelt, *Metaphysik im Horizont der Theologie Wilhelm Herrmanns* (which contains a fairly complete bibliography); and Weinhardt, *Wilhelm Herrmanns Stellung in der Ritschlschen Schule* (which offers a detailed analysis of Herrmann's theological system (esp. pt. III)). On Herrmann's philosophical background see also Falk Wagner, 'Theologischer Neukantianismus. Wilhelm Herrmann'. Herrmann was a popular figure. It is interesting to note that on his arrival in Marburg in 1879 there were only 60 theology students, a figure which had increased to 176 by 1886 (the year of Harnack's appointment) and 241 by 1888.

[2] Herrmann Fischer (in 'Theologie des positiven und kritischen Paradoxes') points to the importance of a dualistic conception of reality (and thus the influence of Herrmann) in the theologies of Barth and Tillich. For the influence of Herrmann on Barth see also Simon Fisher, who (in *Revelatory Positivism?*, 123–69) provides a very useful account of Herrmann's theology in relation to Marburg neo-Kantianism and the development of Barth's theology. For the relationship between Herrmann and Bultmann see esp. Koch, 'Theologie unter den Bedingungen der Moderne'; Jensen, *Theologie zwischen Illusion und Restriktion*; Evang, *Rudolf Bultmann in seiner Frühzeit*. John Baillie (in *The Interpretation of Religion*, 30) points to the great influence of Herrmann on the 'two generations of English [sic] and American students who flocked to his classroom in Marburg'. He discusses Herrmann at length on pp. 291–8. Baillie himself had studied in Marburg, as had his fellow Scot H. R. Mackintosh. It was reported in the obituary notice by D. M. Baillie that Mackintosh kept a portrait of Herrmann on the wall of his study.

[3] For a vigorous defence of this view of Kant's so-called 'unity of method' see esp.

philosopher Hermann Cohen.[4] Crucial for this Marburg interpretation of
Kant was the basic premise that knowledge of the world could not be
acquired immediately through the senses but was the work of the subject,
who shaped the chaotic mass of sense-data in accordance with a priori laws
of reason: the causal world of nature was secondary to the primary structur-
ing role of the subject. This created obvious difficulties for Christian epistemology: if the subject was responsible for knowing, then this would
contravene the cardinal Protestant dogma of justification by faith. Knowledge would be a work of human beings.

Neo-Kantian epistemology thus created new demands for theology, since
if knowledge itself was a product of human effort then it appeared to
threaten the status of the directly revealed or freely given knowledge of
faith. Consequently if the Kantian premise was accepted then knowledge of
God had to be of a wholly different kind from that of the natural world:
knowledge about God could (self-evidently) never be the product of human
thought. A knowledge of God-in-himself, or at least of divine activity, which
could never be the product of human reason, had thus to be directly
acquired in a special judgement of faith independent of human synthesis. In
turn, if God were to exist objectively apart from human beings then he had
to be 'completely separate' from the world of nature. Thus, according to
Herrmann, unless we could think of God as 'wholly other', we would have
to 'give up the idea of God's distinctiveness from the world and with it religion itself'.[5] The 'natural world', the world of cause and effect, which was a
'work' in the sense that it depended on human labour, could never reveal
divine purpose. If there were to be a revelation of God untainted by human
sin, there had to be a special mode of perception, a direct knowledge of
things as they were in themselves; that is, an absolute knowledge of
absolutes. In short, divine revelation appeared to require divine epistemology. And in turn Herrmann was equally critical of attempts to reach a *natural*
knowledge of God through any system of metaphysics which claimed to
know God apart from a freely given revelation on his part. There was no

A. Lewkowitz, 'Die Religionsphilosophie des Neukantianismus', esp. 21; cf. H. R. Mackintosh,
'The Philosophical Presuppositions of Ritschlianism'.

[4] An excellent account in English of Marburg neo-Kantianism and its attitude to religion is
given in Fisher, *Revelatory Positivism*, chs. 1 and 2. On the relations of Herrmann's *Die Metaphysik
in der Theologie* to the philosophy of Cohen see esp. Jensen, *Theologie zwischen Illusion und
Restriktion*. Troeltsch was highly antagonistic towards the absolute 'canonical presuppositions
which are valid in Marburg rationalism', since they 'left no room for religion' (review of
Cohen (A1916/4), col. 62). In a lecture he claimed that science 'cannot crave for a complete
explanation unless it wants to be a new Pope with the same kind of infallibility' (*EPH*, 10). On
Herrmann's critique of Kant see Wagner 'Aspekte der Rezeption Kantischer Metaphysik-
Kritik', esp. 40 f.

[5] *SGT* ii. 27.

place for such knowledge in the post-Kantian universe: knowledge was either brought about through critical reason or by direct revelation.

Herrmann's theology can be understood as a clear response to Kant's perceived epistemological threat to Protestantism. His solution was remarkably straightforward: while accepting the validity of Kantian epistemology in the natural sciences, he held that it should restrict itself to its own domain, that of science or nature, and make no greater claims for itself. Religious epistemology was of a quite different kind, to which Kantian strictures just did not apply. For Herrmann, then, there was simply 'no way from the world of science to the world of faith'.[6] Again, there were good Protestant grounds for this distinction: above and beyond the scientific world was the world of faith where the individual was directly presented with a knowledge freely given by grace and unmediated by any activity ('works') on his or her own part. There were thus, according to Herrmann, two types of cognitive knowledge: the one, the (public) contingent knowledge acquired in the empirical sciences which was open to critical philosophical investigation, and the other the apodeictic or certain knowledge accessible only to the eye of faith. There could be no possibility of a natural knowledge of God, or a natural theology, when 'nature' itself was a construction of human reason.

'KANTIAN' DUALISM IN WILHELM HERRMANN'S THEOLOGY AND PHILOSOPHY

Religious knowledge thus seemed to Herrmann to require a move to a different mode of perception which could reach an immediate awareness of God. Only such an epistemology could provide a certain knowledge which could overcome the merely human activity of Kantian reason. Whereas scientific knowledge, according to Herrmann, could only ever of itself amount to a disunified 'chaotic manifold of things',[7] religious knowledge, with its absolute certainty, resulted in 'the completion of such a developed knowledge that reality is not a manifold for us but a unified power over our life'.[8] In such a knowledge all that was merely human was cast aside, and the world was given a 'wonderful unity'.[9] Such a unity, however, was acquired not within the world but in a mysterious world of faith.

In criticism of Troeltsch, Herrmann maintained that it was Kant himself who was originally responsible for the differentiation of science and religion,[10] a distinction for which 'Christianity and Protestantism should be most grateful'.[11] Indeed, Kant had 'freed that faith in which the human heart

---

[6] *SGT* i. 115.   [7] *SGT* i. 275.   [8] *SGT* i. 276.   [9] *SGT* i. 279.
[10] *SGT* i. 121.   [11] Herrmann, 'Die Lage und Aufgabe der evangelischen Dogmatik', 183.

finds peace from an unworthy dependence on science'.[12] The Kantian conception of science, Herrmann maintained, could never achieve an understanding of religious experience as scientific, since 'a science of supernatural reality . . . just does not exist'.[13] Science, concerned as it was purely with the explanation of the natural and human world, would find the notions of eternity or of the supernatural soul quite meaningless.[14] Indeed, according to Herrmann, even 'faith in God was quite untenable for science'.[15]

Herrmann frequently used the Bible to defend his epistemology. Thus, in emphasizing that God did not *cause* the world, but *created* it, the very first sentence of the Bible, he claimed, 'dug the grave for a science that held God to be provable'.[16] Similarly the authors of the New Testament had recognized that there was no question of a 'scientific proof' of religious knowledge or the truths of faith.[17] In short, a faith which was 'grounded in science would be a faith in the world, but not a faith in the supernatural God who raises human beings above the world'.[18] Not surprisingly Herrmann here cites John 16: 33: 'I have said this to you, that in me you may have peace. In the world you have tribulation; but be of good cheer, I have overcome the world.'

The threat to Protestantism, however, became more and more pressing in the face of the dominant all-embracing world-view of Herrmann's time. Vulgar materialism and monism, which have been discussed in the previous chapter, threatened to destroy the reality of faith and ethics altogether.[19] This meant that 'to the younger generation, the scientific justification of Christianity over and against the all-pervasive materialism of popular culture appeared to be more important than anything else'.[20] In his attempts to counter this threat, Herrmann made use of his distinctive epistemology, with its dualistic methodology.[21] Instead of seeing the materialistic view of science as the 'true' reality, he insisted that the 'scientific and the faithful world-views' were to be pursued 'alongside one another, without disturbing or destroying one another'.[22] In this way Christianity was removed from the sphere of theoretical understanding altogether and given its own different and 'special mode of inner perception'.[23] This was quite distinct from that of science, since 'science involves facts as they are interrelated', as they are ordered by laws, not as 'they affect our individual lives'.[24]

According to Herrmann, then, science, which was concerned not with

[12] *SGT* i. 106.   [13] Herrmann, 'Die Lage und Aufgabe', 183.   [14] *SGT* i. 114.
[15] *SGT* i. 250.   [16] *SGT* i. 258 f.   [17] *SGT* i. 116.   [18] *SGT* i. 120.
[19] Herrmann, 'Religion und Sozialdemokratie', 274, 279. On Herrmann's reaction to materialism see Herrmann Timm, *Theorie und Praxis*, 99; and Hasler, *Die beherrschte Natur*, 180 f.
[20] Timm, *Theorie und Praxis*, 99.
[21] On this see Wagner, 'Aspekte der Rezeption Kantischer Metaphysik-Kritik', esp. sect. III.
[22] *SGT* i. 108.   [23] *SGT* i. 289.   [24] *SGT* i. 249.

'absolute certainties, but with probabilities',[25] could never hope to reach the goal of secure knowledge.[26] Whereas science was thus directed towards a *provable* (*nachweisbar*) reality, religion was concerned with a reality which was beyond scientific proof. Religious certainty was something that could be directly experienced (*erlebbar*) in the individual.[27] Thus, according to Herrmann, religious conceptuality could never 'agree with knowledge about the provable real, since this is something which denies a universally valid knowledge from the outset. [Religious conceptuality] stems from an individual experience'.[28] In this way, by attempting to delineate the spheres of faith and science, Herrmann introduced a system of parallel realities which seems to reflect something of an underlying ontological dualism. Thus, on the one hand, there was that mode of being expressed by a natural or scientific reality which could only help to sustain life, but which could never reveal anything of true life[29] since everything it touched was 'dead'; on the other hand, there was the reality of faith, of 'life', which made manifest a higher realm of absolute or 'authentic' being.[30]

For Herrmann, although it was impossible to *prove* the reality of God, his reality could nevertheless be *asserted* on the basis of a direct experience of a higher reality. In such an experience the normal canons of scientific proof did not apply.[31] Thus, although it might appear that religion was in competition with science, 'in truth it was quite the opposite', since, according to Herrmann, religion was never concerned 'with the world, neither with the world as a whole or with particulars in the past or the future, but only with the inner vitality of the individual human being'.[32] Indeed, he claimed, religion was real 'only in the inner composure in which we differentiate ourselves from the law-governed . . . world of experience'.[33]

Rather than seeing any danger in this separation of religion from scientific proof, Herrmann felt that it liberated faith and clarified the point that 'what is to overcome the world cannot be derived from the world'.[34] In this way, he went on, religion was able 'to achieve such a position towards science that science does not crush it. With this in mind, however, it must not attempt to influence the scientific conception of the world. That was always a difficult course, and today it is exceedingly dangerous'.[35] In short, Herrmann remarked, 'science can achieve only one thing in the study of theology: it can show that in the sphere of knowledge which is

---

[25] Herrmann, review of Troeltsch, *Die Absolutheit des Christentums*, col. 332.

[26] *SGT* i. 121.   [27] *SGT* i. 249.

[28] 'Die Lage und Aufgabe der evangelischen Dogmatik', 197 f.

[29] *SGT* i. 287.   [30] Ibid.   [31] *SGT* i. 256.   [32] *SGT* ii. 105.

[33] *SGT* i. 289.   [34] Herrmann, *Die Gewißheit des Glaubens*, 7.

[35] *SGT* i. 259. Cf. review of Troeltsch, *Die Absolutheit des Christentums*, col. 331; and 'Die Religion und das Allgemeingültige', 229.

established through faith, there is not even the slightest trace [of science] to be found'.[36]

HERRMANN, RITSCHL, AND THE CRITIQUE OF METAPHYSICS[37]

In his criticisms of science as incapable of revealing anything other than a sham knowledge of the absolute Herrmann displays a similarity with Ritschl, who was equally vehement in his attacks on any claim to know God apart from revelation. Thus, for Ritschl, there could be no place for metaphysics in theology, since it would 'become a rival to the distinctive revelations found in Christ'.[38] Metaphysics, which claimed natural knowledge of the things of faith apart from direct revelation, was banished from the system. Under such a view there was no question of dialogue between naturalism and theology in a mutually comprehensible metaphysical discourse: religion survived merely as a distinct form of life immune from the threats of science. To know God through metaphysics was nothing other than a particular form of natural theology, which could no longer have any place in theology.

However, although Ritschl had denied metaphysics as a route to knowledge of God, he had nevertheless always allowed for the possibility of a *reconciliation* between the knowledge acquired through faith and that acquired through science.[39] Indeed, Herrmann contended, Ritschl had never 'completely separated religious knowledge from knowledge of the world and metaphysics'.[40] For Ritschl, nature did not constitute a lower reality from which the human was called to escape into the higher reality of faith, but rather, as has been shown above in Chapter 2, faith was combined with ethics in the conception of the kingdom of God.[41] Unlike Herrmann, Ritschl never lost sight of a unity between the two worlds, but merely aimed to show that this was possible only in Christian revelation and not in any metaphysical notion of the universal.[42]

The differences between Ritschl's and Herrmann's attacks on metaphysics can be clearly seen from a comparison between Ritschl's *Theologie und Metaphysik* of 1881 and Herrmann's *Die Metaphysik in der Theologie* of

---

[36] *Die Gewißheit*, 60.
[37] On Herrmann's conception of philosophy and metaphysics see esp. Peter Fischer-Appelt, *Metaphysik im Horizont der Theologie Wilhelm Herrmanns*.
[38] Robert Mackintosh, *Albrecht Ritschl and his School*, 252.
[39] On this see Wagner, 'Theologischer Neukantianismus', 258.
[40] Herrmann, *Gesammelte Aufsätze*, 256.   [41] Cf. *Instruction*, §§46 f.
[42] Ritschl, *Theologie und Metaphysik*, 182.

1876 (which may indeed have led Ritschl to write his own essay).[43] Ritschl's anti-metaphysical theology took the form of an attack on orthodox Lutheran natural theology aimed in particular at F. H. R. Frank (1827–94) of Erlangen and C. E. Luthardt (1823–1902) of Leipzig. Ritschl's somewhat confusing epistemology[44] appears to owe more to Melanchthon than Kant: faith itself was at the basis of any knowledge of God, which depended not on any metaphysics, but solely on the 'revelation through God's Son'.[45] Thus, following Luther in 'his resolve to break with the scholastic methodology',[46] and against his own theological opponents who claimed a natural knowledge of God 'apart from some real revelation on his part',[47] Ritschl asserted that knowledge exists only 'in its relationships and it is only in them that we can know the thing and only by them that we can name it'.[48] Thus for Ritschl there was no question that the knowledge acquired in science was any less 'real' than that acquired by faith.[49] For Ritschl, knowledge acquired in science and that acquired through faith were *different* but not exclusive.[50]

In the muddled epistemological sections of the third volume of *Justification and Reconciliation*[51] Ritschl points to H. Lotze as his philosophical mentor, maintaining a similar causal theory of perception: knowledge of the effects of a thing implied knowledge of the thing-in-itself. Thus Kant's restriction of knowledge merely to phenomena was apparently overcome[52] and the Kantian 'unknown = X' became for Ritschl the 'cause of its qualities operating upon us'.[53] According to Ritschl, then, God was not 'wholly other', but was known through his actions towards human beings,[54] which

---

[43] Herrmann's essay is reprinted in *SGT* i. 1–80. Both Michael Beintker (in *Die Gottesfrage in der Theologie Wilhelm Herrmanns*, 12) and Herrmann Timm (in *Theorie und Praxis*, 91–102) contend that Ritschl's interest in metaphysics was first aroused by the publication of Herrmann's essay.

[44] On Ritschl's epistemology see esp. James Richmond, *Ritschl: A Reappraisal*, ch. 2; and John Baillie, *The Interpretation of Religion*, 276–90.

[45] *Theologie und Metaphysik*, 192.   [46] Ibid., 209.   [47] Ibid., 180.   [48] Ibid., 184.

[49] Falk Wagner (in 'Aspekte der Rezeption Kantischer Metaphysik–Kritik', 36 f.) similarly concedes that although Ritschl may have had tendencies towards the sort of dualism developed by Herrmann, his governing conception of the kingdom of God prevented him from maintaining it with such rigour.

[50] Cf. Timm, *Theorie und Praxis*, 23.   [51] *JR* iii, esp. §3. 14–25.   [52] *JR* iii. 19 f.

[53] *JR* iii. 20. P. Wrezcionko (in *Die philosophischen Wurzeln der Theologie Albrecht Ritschls*, 143–98) and James Orr (in *Ritschlianism*) both emphasize the 'value judgement' Kantian character of Ritschl's thought. Orr's outline of the main characteristics of the term 'value judgement', however, has much more in common with the later Ritschlians than with Ritschl himself. In giving practical reason priority over theoretical reason, and in emphasizing the impossibility of any theoretical knowledge of God, they drew a much stronger distinction between religious and theoretical knowledge than Ritschl himself had made. Ritschl is critical of Kant precisely because of his ethicization of the Gospel and denial of the objective fact of justification. Cf. *JR* i. 429–58, esp. 452 f.; ET, 387–415.

[54] Cf. *Theologie und Metaphysik*, 194.

meant ultimately through the reconciliation effected by Christ. The character of such knowledge was not, however, categorically different from scientific knowledge (as it was for Herrmann): for Ritschl there was neither
unmediated knowledge of God nor of anything else. All knowledge of anything required a prior judgement on the part of the knower.

It is important to note, however, as Wendland observed, that Ritschl was
not primarily a philosophical thinker.[55] Similarly, according to Troeltsch, he
was 'satisfied at this point with a few *aperçus* and a firm declaration of will'.[56]
Like his hero Luther he used philosophy for his own (primarily theological)
purposes.[57] It was only after Ritschl that the concept of the 'value judgement' of faith received a full systematic treatment. This is clear in the first
part of Herrmann's book *Die Metaphysik in der Theologie*, where he already
acknowledges the absolute impossibility of any reconciliation between
the knowledge acquired in faith and that acquired by science. Indeed,
according to Fischer-Appelt, Herrmann 'saw the historical legacy of theology to rest in a mixture of religion and metaphysics, and demanded the
separation of religion and metaphysics as the critical exercise of theology'.[58]
Whereas for Ritschl the value judgement was a precursor to all knowledge,
it was transformed in Herrmann into something inward, and related to the
isolation of the knowledge acquired in Christianity from the remainder of
knowledge.[59]

---

[55] Wendland, *Albrecht Ritschl und seine Schüler*, 22.

[56] 'Rückblick' (A1909/18a), 217; ET, 73.

[57] Cf. Richmond, *Ritschl: A Reappraisal*, 26. Similarly, David Lotz, in his close analysis of
Ritschl's concept of freedom (in *Ritschl and Luther*, 144 ff.) suggests that it was a devious misrepresentation to see Ritschl as involved in the 'back to Kant' movement. Ritschl's idea of vocation seems to owe far more to Luther than to the autonomous ethical personality of Kant as
developed by Herrmann. Barth's insistence (in *Protestant Theology in the Nineteenth Century*, 391)
that Ritschl had ethicized the Gospel is misleading since for Ritschl the ethical aspect of the
kingdom of God required the religious. Any ethics was impossible without an (objective)
justification by Christ. It was precisely here, on Ritschl's view, that Kant was mistaken
(*Rechtfertigung und Versöhnung*, i. 429–58, esp. 452 f.; *JR*, i. 387–415). Far more important than
Kant in the development of Ritschl's thought were Luther and the Reformation, as has been
emphasized by David Lotz, *Ritschl and Luther*, esp. 144–53, and D. L. Mueller, *An Introduction to
the Theology of Albrecht Ritschl*.

[58] Peter Fischer-Appelt, *Metaphysik im Horizont der Theologie Wilhelm Herrmanns*, 12.

[59] Cf. Wagner, 'Aspekte der Rezeption Kantischer Metaphysik-Kritik', 39. Herrmann Timm
(in *Theorie und Praxis*, 24, 58) argues that Ritschl always maintained a conception of a
quasi-Hegelian universal where spiritual and natural phenomena were both aspects of the same
reality; Herrmann, however, had relocated this universal in the sphere of the ethical personality. Wagner (in 'Theologischer Neukantianismus', 258) goes still further and sees Herrmann
as radicalizing Ritschl's conception in removing any degree of worldliness from religion. Ethics
is no longer about realizing one's vocation in the world, but is focused on escape from this
world.

The Certainty of Faith

For Herrmann, this distinction between the knowledge of faith and the knowledge of science was placed at the heart of his religious epistemology: faith was a reality which every person had to experience for him- or herself, a reality which was thus 'bound up with the personal life of every individual'.[60] Consequently the sort of knowledge acquired in faith was 'obviously' of a different kind from that acquired in science, since it involved not the 'objectively real' 'but a reflection on what we experience for ourselves',[61] thus revealing an absolute 'knowledge of objects' as they were in themselves, unmediated by any human faculty.[62] In this internal experience there was an 'inner liberation' as the human being stood immediately before God.[63]

Although the experience of faith, according to Herrmann, could never be related to other people, 'it could also never be replaced by any higher claim to universality'.[64] Religious experience was self-authenticating, and thus 'the only answer that can be given to the question of how an object can be presumed to be real which cannot be proved to others, was simply saying "through religion"'.[65] The human being was given the courage to assert this, Herrmann maintained, because 'God lets us see this in the world we experience'.[66] For Herrmann, then, religion concerned a higher world experienced in the activity of living (*Lebensführung*), as the '"whence" which we must accept'.[67] It was this alone that gave meaning to the personality in self-reflection.[68] Nature, the object of the world of science, led to death, whereas the true life, which was to be found in the inner life of faith, led to 'self-denial',[69] or (more positively) 'a release from oneself to life'.[70]

THE BASIS OF HERRMANN'S ETHICS

It was at this point that Herrmann claimed that religion made contact with ethics. Yet ethics concerned this 'higher life' where, he claimed, 'we could enjoy ethical discourse with other persons'.[71] Ethics was thus conceived as a 'different mode of life which separates itself off from the natural'.[72] The

---

[60] *SGT* i. 252.
[61] *SGT* i. 290. Cf. 'Die Lage und Aufgabe der evangelischen Dogmatik', 180.
[62] *SGT* i. 121.   [63] *Ethik*, 93.
[64] Herrmann, 'Die Religion und das Allgemeingültige', 232.   [65] *SGT* ii. 232.
[66] Ibid. This form of unverifiable individualistic interpretation of knowledge has been criticized by Wagner as sanctioning a decisionism which is catastrophic for the ethical personality ('Aspekte der Rezeption Kantischer Metaphysik-Kritik', 38).
[67] *SGT* i. 107.   [68] *SGT* i. 297.   [69] *SGT* i. 118.   [70] *SGT* i. 293.
[71] *SGT* i. 118.   [72] *Ethik*, 37.

dualism of faith and nature could thus not be overcome in ethics but rather gave

shape to the spiritual life of all people who wanted to remain human and to work their way out of nature. As long as the animal state of the human species lasts, as long as we live in the flesh and nevertheless wish to tame this flesh, we move into the opposition between these two thoughts. The one thought corresponds to the goal after which we are striving, the other to the factual circumstances from which we rise.[73]

Religion thus provides the power to escape the condition of nature,[74] which inevitably conceals the ethical life.[75] Thus, according to Herrmann, whereas in nature 'everything is determined by its surroundings',[76] the 'experienced power which ethical value creates in us'[77] raises ethical life above nature.[78] In turn, joy is experienced when all the energies of the natural world are cast aside;[79] that is, when the previous life is 'overcome'[80] in 'faith in God, the real religion'.[81] This implies that the human being can only be said to be fully educated when 'people demand of us a new will that makes us free of all natural desires'.[82]

This power to escape the confines of nature, according to Herrmann, emanates from the lips of Jesus, who speaks to us in the inner experience 'in which we are truly alive' and in which we are given ethical power.[83] The 'impression' (*Eindruck*)[84] of the intense personality of Jesus creates in us a 'certainty that a loving will is the omnipotent ground of all being and that we are called through him to an eternal goodness, to a blessed life in ethical freedom'.[85] For the Christian, then, according to Herrmann, there is a 'joy in the pure trust of being grasped by the God revealed to us in Christ, and in these circumstances what else can a living being do in the world apart from serve from the heart in a spirit of self-denial'.[86] In turn, Herrmann goes on, the ethical power emanating from Jesus 'which makes the strains of life worthwhile' can be shared by everyone on the basis of this inner experience.[87]

JESUS AND HISTORY

It is in such an inner experience, according to Herrmann, that a direct impression of Jesus becomes possible, despite all the relativities revealed by

---

[73] Herrmann, 'Religion und Sozialdemokratie', 281   [74] *SGT* i. 277.

[75] *SGT* i. 118.   [76] *SGT* i. 271.   [77] *SGT* i. 279.   [78] *SGT* i. 271.

[79] *SGT* i. 279.   [80] *Ethik*, 75.   [81] *SGT* i. 279.   [82] *Ethik*, 38.

[83] *SGT* i. 279. For a discussion of Herrmann's Christology in relation to later developments in Christology see esp. W. Grieve, *Der Grund des Glaubens*; and Robinson, *Das Problem des heiligen Geistes*, 81 ff.

[84] *SGT* i. 122.   [85] Ibid.   [86] *SGT* i. 279.   [87] *SGT* i. 122.

historical research. Indeed historical research, because it is forever trapped in the natural world, can reveal nothing of true religion. Just as the 'authentic "historical" (*geschichtlich*) fact' of Jesus is not to be found in his ethical teaching or in his understanding of the kingdom of God but in his personal 'impression' which creates a 'life history' in the individual, so 'real' or authentic experience is that direct self-authenticating experience of being in communion with God.[88] On Herrmann's view, then, all personal doubts are overcome in the appropriation of a revelation[89] which is gained neither from the Bible nor from the Church but solely from a direct 'experience' (*Erlebnis*).[90]

For Christians, according to Herrmann, the New Testament could be understood only in so far as 'we are wrapped up in the spiritual picture of Jesus and when we experience the historical fact given directly to us'.[91] The Christian knowledge of Jesus is thus not something open to the canons of historical or scientific reason,[92] since knowledge of 'Jesus as saviour' is not a work of a priori structures of human reason, but rather it is freely 'given' in faith.[93] Indeed, according to Herrmann, 'everything that was fully clear in the moment of religious experience becomes inconceivable as soon as we submit it to the canons of provable reality'.[94] Herrmann went still further, however, in seeking to establish religious *certainty* on the basis of this direct mode of apprehension through faith. Since the forgiveness of sins was a *religious* experience it could never have the 'definite character of the facts given to the senses'. It had instead to 'be won afresh each time'.[95] The basis of faith thus had to be 'grasped in the same independent fashion by learned or unlearned, by each for himself'.[96]

---

[88] Troeltsch, however, considered this distinction to be little more than a deceptive play on words: 'Today one calls every possible kind of thing historical [*geschichtlich*] and a fact [*Tatsache*] which is not and should not be: rather it is the reverse because it is a miracle affirmed through faith' ('Über historische und dogmatische Methode' (A1900/9a), 741; ET, 21). On this see also J. Wendland, 'Wesen des Christentums', col. 1968: 'We need no other method than that used in the human sciences [*Geisteswissenschaften*] . . . The hard facts of history are the objective moment which stands behind our subjectivity. What the essence of Christianity is, only history will yield'. For Herrmann, the very idea of a science of the spirit [*Geist*] was anathema.

[89] *SGT* i. 280.

[90] *SGT* i. 254. There are obvious points of contact between Herrmann's theology, particularly his concept of *Erlebnis*, and Wilhelm Dilthey's *Lebensphilosophie*. See esp. Peter Fischer-Appelt, *Metaphysik im Horizont der Theologie Wilhelm Herrmanns*, 158 ff.; Michael Beintker, *Die Gottesfrage in der Theologie Wilhelm Herrmanns*, 35 ff.; and John Leland Mebust, 'Wilhelm Dilthey's Philosophy of History'.

[91] *Ethik*, 100; cf. 'Religion und Sozialdemokratie', 282. In a letter to Paul Wernle of 16 March 1904 (cited in Graf (ed.), 'Ernst Troeltschs Briefe und Karten an Paul Wernle', 117) Troeltsch is critical of Herrmann's attempt to establish the basis of truth in the person of Jesus: 'The person of Jesus gives strength and life to truth, but does not establish truth. Once it is represented, truth is established simply on its own basis'.

[92] *SGT* i. 107.   [93] *Ethik*, 99 f.   [94] *Ethik*, 131.   [95] *Ethik*, 131.

[96] Herrmann, *The Communion of the Christian with God*, 76.

Herrmann's subjective understanding of religion led him to criticize the members of the History of Religion School, who, he claimed, had 'no clear conception of religion' and had thus failed to understand the nature of the phenomenon they were studying.[97] A historical view would never be adequate, since religion can only be grasped in so far as 'we participate in it'. A truly non-partisan study of religion was thus quite impossible, according to Herrmann, since 'nobody can have a conception of the reality of religion which is divorced from his position towards it'.[98] There could thus be no 'historical lesson to be learnt in what the kingdom of God meant for Jesus'.[99] Similarly, Herrmann claimed, 'if we see in holy writ the revelation of God finally breaking in overwhelmingly in the person of Jesus, we need have nothing to fear from historical science'.[100] Indeed if there was to be genuine salvation in Christ this implied an experience where the ordinary canons of scientific and historical reason were displaced in an 'overpowering fact',[101] or the 'undeniable factuality' of 'the power of the inner life of Jesus'.[102] It was this fact alone that gave authority to 'make us free' in our ethical lives,[103] offering the human being the power to 'tame his desires in accordance with the unconditional validity of the law'.[104]

HISTORY AND ETHICS

According to Herrmann, since religion is concerned with a higher life which is different from the ordinary historical life, it cannot supply ethical goals,[105] but rather 'empowers'[106] ethics. It is at this point, however, that Herrmann seeks to connect religion with activity in the world (even though the epistemological presuppositions upon which he makes the connection are not clear). Indeed faith in God is understood by Herrmann as 'a special expression of ethical conviction', where love of God is conceivable only at one and the same time as love of neighbour.[107] The community of free spirits in the 'union of wills'[108] becomes 'the eternal goal', and 'the exercise of love' becomes 'the untiring task. In turn, whoever clearly sees this begins to be inwardly alive'.[109] For Herrmann, this meant that the ultimate goal of all Christian theology was 'the building up of the Christian community; and if Christianity serves and furthers the natural powers of society, so also Christian theology will not retard the development of scientific knowledge of the world'.[110] Since the higher religious reality and the reality which was the

---

[97] *SGT* i. 287. On this see Weinhardt, *Wilhelm Herrmanns Stellung*, 86–105.
[98] *SGT* i. 283 f.   [99] *Ethik*, 102.   [100] *SGT* i. 263.   [101] *Ethik*, 121 ff.
[102] *SGT* i. 297.   [103] *Ethik*, 121 ff.   [104] *SGT* i. 268.   [105] *SGT* i. 294.
[106] *Ethik*, 137.   [107] *SGT* i. 274.   [108] Ibid.   [109] *SGT* i. 253.
[110] *Die Gewißheit des Glaubens*, 58.

product of human reason were unrelated, this meant that, for Herrmann, the ethical could only be 'purely formal'.[111] True religion was to be found not in the ethical transformation of nature, but in a complete release, a *Weltflucht*,[112] from a natural world which 'oppressed us' and 'finally destroyed us'.[113] Herrmann's system thus resulted in the very opposite of a vocational ethic. Spirit and nature, which in Kant and the idealist tradition in general are two parts of a single system of philosophy, are in Herrmann's thought completely separated: indeed, he claimed, the notion of spirit is for nature simply 'nonsense'.[114]

In such a system nothing in nature could be other than ethically neutral;[115] similarly no political party (even the Social Democrats)[116] could be said to be unethical or unchristian.[117] Taking this view to its extreme, Herrmann asserted that war was 'neither Christian nor unchristian, neither ethical nor unethical'; instead it was merely 'the inevitable expression in a particular set of historical circumstances of human nature which developed in particular cultural surroundings into a political life'.[118] Thus personal communion with God and true ethical freedom could never be completely realized in time.[119]

Nevertheless, Herrmann contended, it was still the case that 'we have to be able to remain Christians in cultural life. If we do not do this then the product of culture will be corruption'.[120] However, although Herrmann felt it necessary to maintain a link with a historical community for as long as the human being was imprisoned in the natural body, such a community was always striving to raise itself out of its natural surroundings to exchange natural human life 'for something higher',[121] namely the true 'ethical intercourse between human beings'.[122] Indeed if the corruption of culture was so overwhelming it might prove the case that the best option for the furtherance of the ethical goal was 'to withdraw from the temptations of such a society', whilst at the same time striving 'to better the circumstances as far as we can'.[123] This would allow the circumstances to be realized which would make it possible for the Christian to escape from the clutches of culture and history. In such an escape, 'in the devotion of the heart to justice and good, we are made aware of another reality . . . wherein we are removed from the sphere of utter loneliness'.[124] For Herrmann, then, the final realization of ethics was in a complete escape from nature and history in the triumph of a community experiencing authentic existence in the community of love.

---

[111] *Ethik*, 35.   [112] *Ethik*, 178.   [113] *SGT* i. 310.

[114] Wagner, 'Aspekte der Rezeption Kantischer Metaphysik-Kritik', 40.   [115] *Ethik*, 205.

[116] Cf. 'Religion und Sozialdemokratie', 260. Only when they claimed to be more than merely an economic interest group, when materialism became a world-view, did the Social Democrats pose a threat to religion and ethics (265).

[117] *Ethik*, 209.   [118] *Ethik*, 221.   [119] *Ethik*, 233.   [120] *Ethik*, 198.

[121] *Ethik*, 182.   [122] *Ethik*, 197.   [123] *Ethik*, 198.   [124] *SGT* i. 310.

CRITICS OF HERRMANN

Not surprisingly Herrmann's thought, which seemed to some to threaten the very basis of a historical faith and which appeared to remove religion from the public domain altogether, was subjected to a barrage of criticism. Many critics considered Herrmann's dualist epistemology to be an evasion of the fundamental problems of philosophy. Indeed the urgency of the apologetic task, particularly after Haeckel, meant that Ritschl's and Herrmann's vigorous separation of theology from metaphysics had to be called into question. The reasons for this were obvious: according to Johannes Wendland, although 'the independence of religion was correctly asserted against all philosophy, it thereby succeeded in isolating itself and was no longer able to enter into a fruitful interaction with the rest of culture'. Thus, quite against their own intentions, Ritschl and Herrmann had made religion 'something less real and less grounded in worldly science'.[125]

Georg Wobbermin: Theology and Metaphysics

Similarly, in an early attack on Herrmann's dualism of faith from one who had also been nurtured by Ritschlian theology (and a work which is at the same time one of the best theological apologetics against materialism), Georg Wobbermin asserted that only by entering into scientific debate could religion retain a vital role in the modern world and defend itself from its competitors and detractors. Thus he uttered the battle-cry: 'theology without metaphysics is impossible',[126] a phrase that was echoed by many others.[127] What was demanded of theology, according to Wobbermin, was, above all, that the 'unity of the spiritual life be not torn apart',[128] which meant a return to the study of its epistemological basis in connection with the wider world of learning.[129] His own discussion emerged from an assessment of empirical psychology, but he developed this into a criticism of what he regarded as all forms of positivism. Empirical psychology, he contended, could alone never hope to answer the truth questions of religion; it could amass data and could categorize and classify types of religious experience, but it could never hope to secure religious faith. For this, the empirical method, which was 'of such great merit' (and which had been developed

---

[125] Wendland, *Albrecht Ritschl und seine Schüler*, 25.

[126] Georg Wobbermin, *Theologie und Metaphysik*. 27.

[127] Cf. Ernst Troeltsch (review of Marshall (A1903/10), col. 1017): 'I believe it is a vain effort to exclude metaphysics from religion, which in its essence is the primitive form of metaphysics'; and Rudolf Otto: 'There can be no religion without metaphysics' ('Jakob Fries' Religionsphilosophie', 150; ET, 91).

[128] Wobbermin, *Theologie und Metaphysik*, 11.   [129] Ibid., 15.

particularly in the USA by William James), had to be 'expanded by critical epistemological thought using transcendental psychological procedures'.[130]

The absolute distinction between faith and knowledge implied by Herrmann's 'revelatory positivism'[131] was artificial and could serve no apologetic task.[132] Instead, theology had to return to the study of its epistemological basis, which meant a decisive metaphysical turn,[133] or what Wobbermin called a 'definite orientation towards a total view of the world and an integrated attitude towards life. More precisely such an orientation points beyond the entirety of what is immediately given to us, beyond, that is, the world that is determined empirically'.[134] According to Wobbermin, the scientific study of the empirical sciences, and particularly psychology,[135] in which he had thoroughly immersed himself, could never establish the truth of religion. The empirical method, which was admittedly 'of such great merit', had thus to be 'expanded by critical epistemological thought using transcendental psychological procedures'.[136]

Similarly Troeltsch, although regarding William James[137] as of the 'utmost freshness and originality',[138] and Wundt as 'providing a scientific presupposition for the possibility and the discussion of the specifically religious',[139] saw empirical psychology as merely the 'entrance gate to epistemology'.[140] He remarked in a lecture: 'the fact that we have an idea says nothing about whether it is true . . . Truth or non-truth is no longer a psychological question'.[141] Thus for both Wobbermin and Troeltsch mere pragmatism was no substitute for epistemology,[142] since 'complete

[130] Wobbermin, *Aufgabe und Bedeutung der Religionspsychologie*, 7 f.

[131] Religion, for Herrmann, seemed to demand what Robinson called a 'revitalized empiricism' (James M. Robinson, *Das Problem des heiligen Geistes bei Wilhelm Herrmann*, 30), which could easily lead to a 'revelatory positivism' (*Offenbarungspositivismus*). This term was originally used by Bonhoeffer as a criticism of Barth's theology. It has since enjoyed a 'privileged status in theological polemic' (Simon Fisher, *Revelatory Positivism*, 306; cf. 334).

[132] Wobbermin, *Theologie und Metaphysik*, 4.   [133] Ibid., 15.

[134] Wobbermin, *Monismus und Monotheismus*, 118.

[135] Psychology was becoming an increasingly important subject in the first years of the twentieth century, particularly after the publication of Wundt's *Völkerpsychologie. Eine Untersuchung der Entwicklungsgesetze von Sprache, Mythus und Sitte*, from 1905–9. Perhaps the most significant section in relation to religion was 'Die Tabugebote', reprinted in Carsten Colpe (ed.), *Die Diskussion um das 'Heilige'*. Rudolf Otto pointed to the importance of Wundt in 'Mythus und Religion in Wundt's *Völkerpsychologie*'. Almond (in 'Rudolf Otto: Life and Work', 313) sees this essay, together with his extensive travels in Africa and India, as pivotal in the formulation of Otto's ideas on the holy.

[136] Wobbermin, *Aufgabe und Bedeutung der Religionspsychologie*, 7 f.

[137] See esp. 'Empiricism and Platonism' (A1912/6). Cf. Troeltsch's review of James' *Varieties*, (A1904/13).

[138] *EPH*, 4.   [139] Troeltsch, review of Lipsius (A1901/2), col. 72.

[140] 'Main Problems' (C1905/1) 281; *Psychologie und Erkenntnistheorie* (A1905/7), 34.

[141] Troeltsch, *RPH*, 49.

[142] Others, notably G. Vorbordt, asserted that pragmatism would help overcome the

relativism results where there is merely psychology and no criterion of the validity of religion, since there is neither supernatural revelation nor rational criteria and necessity'.[143] Without epistemology, psychology was a 'purely provisional description and analysis of the phenomena',[144] or a 'highly indefinite, relative description which piles up various characteristics'.[145] The question of 'ultimate truth or highest reality' moved beyond mere empirical analysis to the problem of epistemology.[146] In short, according to Troeltsch: 'Epistemology is not possible unless we previously have psychology, and psychology is not possible unless we first have epistemology'.[147]

According to Wobbermin, although Ritschl recognized the vital importance of epistemology (which was, he claimed, his real achievement),[148] he had gone too far in discounting any contact with metaphysics, and had 'thrown out the baby with the bathwater'.[149] There was always the need for non-dogmatic reflection about the transcendent, which Ritschl's theology as well as that of Herrmann after him had disallowed from the outset. In the contemporary fight against radical positivists like Mach (whom Wobbermin christened 'the new Lucretius'[150]), what mattered above all was that the truths of religion might attain a universal validity outside their purely religious context. Indeed with this question of universal validity (*Allgemeingültigkeit*) theology 'stands or falls'.[151] Thus, over and above empirical analysis, the question of 'ultimate truth or highest reality' belonged intimately to the study of religion.[152]

Ritschlian Critics

Others, more directly influenced by Ritschl, also began to see the deficiencies of Ritschl's and Herrmann's attempts to separate theology and metaphysics. Max Reischle claimed, for instance, that:

Systematic theology had once more to search for an understanding of the thought forms of our time as these are mirrored in philosophy. Indeed it must do more than this: It must *submerse itself in philosophical labour*; for it is only possible to gain a scientific understanding of the Christian faith, its foundations and its content,

'perpetual oscillation between subjectivism and rationalism' ('Religionspsychologie als Methode und Objekt der Dogmatik', 61).

[143] Troeltsch, review of Hébert (A1907/12), col. 1907.
[144] Troeltsch, 'Empiricism and Platonism' (A1912/6), 421.
[145] Ibid., 413. Cf. Otto Scheel, 'Die moderne Religionspsychologie'.
[146] Wobbermin, *Aufgabe und Bedeutung der Religionspsychologie*, 15.   [147] *EPH*, 30.
[148] Wobbermin, *Theologie und Metaphysik*, 19.   [149] Ibid., 30.
[150] Ibid., 59. According to the canons of their positivism, all that was possible was an ever more precise description of observable phenomena.
[151] *Theologie und Metaphysik*, 57.
[152] Wobbermin, *Aufgabe und Bedeutung der Religionspsychologie*, 15.

in the context of the methodical research into the whole of intellectual life and its essential functions.[153]

More importantly, Julius Kaftan sought to confront the modern world on its own terms, thoroughly immersing himself in philosophical and scientific literature. Indeed, according to James Orr, he was 'distinguished from the other members of the [Ritschlian] school by the earnestness of his attempts to find a means of adjustment between faith and theoretic knowledge which may avoid the appearance of collision between them'.[154] Thus, however strong the theological disagreements between Julius Kaftan and Ernst Troeltsch, they both sought reconciliation between faith and science. Against Ritschl's denial of metaphysics, Kaftan asserted that the Christian faith was

the true knowledge of the First Cause and of the final purpose of all things . . . it offers just what philosophy has sought as the highest knowledge, or as the solution to the enigma of the world . . . The task is no other than that of proving that the knowledge supplied by Christianity as the First Cause and final purpose of all things is true.[155]

Indeed, according to Kaftan, 'evangelical faith and empirical science belong together in a unified conception and are shown to be necessary members of a greater whole which is the personal spirit'.[156]

Religion, Kaftan felt, required a greater foundation than the subjective assurance of the individual mind. Like Troeltsch, he did not accept Herrmann's fundamental dualism of all thought, but rather sought its unity. Religion thus spoke not of a *parallel* reality, but of one and the same reality as that discussed by the sciences. Thus, in an obituary, Arthur Titius wrote that for Kaftan '[e]vangelical faith and empirical science belong together in a unified conception and are shown to be necessary members of a greater whole which is the personal spirit'.[157] Religion and science were thus not regarded as separate realities but as distinct modes of representing the one greater reality. And also, like Troeltsch, Kaftan saw Kant as profoundly important for this unified perception of reality.[158]

Ernst Troeltsch's Criticism of Herrmann

Against Herrmann's rigorous division of reality into two, Troeltsch sought after a reconciliation between all aspects of reality, arguing that it was

---

[153] Max Reischle, 'Kant und die Theologie der Gegenwart', 388.

[154] James Orr, *Ritschlianism*, esp. 58 ff., here 59. See also Wobbermin, *Theologie und Metaphysik*, 32 ff.

[155] Julius Kaftan, *The Truth of the Christian Religion*, ii. 4 f.

[156] A. Titius, 'Julius Kaftan', 18.   [157] Ibid.

[158] Significantly Kaftan's inaugural lecture (*Die religionsphilosophische Anschauung Kants*) at

impossible fully to separate one sphere from another.[159] For Troeltsch, that
meant there was always some degree of reciprocity between science and
religion. Indeed it was Troeltsch's retention of a unified vision that led Herrmann to regard him as 'the most reactionary and conservative of us all'.[160]
However, for Troeltsch, to assume that science was limited to the virtual
positivist method of cause and effect was an unnecessary (and, he contended, an un-Kantian) constraint placed on the meaning of science. A
broader conception of the nature of science, which Troeltsch maintained,
allowed religion to be assessed by scientific and rational means of investigation. Thus he wrote:

I contest the universal applicability of the causal view, in the sense of a closed system
of necessary causes and effects, as far as historical phenomena and the entire compass
of human events are concerned.[161]

Troeltsch did not see Kant as restricting 'science' to the sphere of the exact
sciences, and as removing all other aspects of reality to the sphere of (irrational) value judgements, but rather saw science as a 'striving for order
between all objects'.[162] Kant's theory, he claimed, was a 'theory of reason in
all its a priori functions; it is a Platonism without Plato's metaphysics',[163] and
not a mere account of the natural scientific method. Indeed, according to
Troeltsch, Kant's theory was concerned more with a unification than a division of reality. As will be shown in the next chapter, he thus placed great
weight on the second and third Critiques. Consequently human ethical
activity, human history, as well as human religion, were as open to scientific
investigation as anything else:

Kant placed the study of religion in the sphere of universal history, and brought the
highest ascertainable values of moral philosophy, aesthetics, and philosophy of
religion into the closest relationship with the results and problems of his natural
philosophy.[164]

According to Troeltsch, rather than seeking to create an epistemological
dualism, Kant was motivated by the desire to *overcome* the contradiction
between the empirical causality of the exact sciences and the intelligible

Basel was on Kant's use for apologetic. In 1904 Kaftan gave the official Berlin lecture, *Kant, der
Philosoph des Protestantismus*, to celebrate the centenary of Kant's death, and in 1917 he produced a systematic philosophy of religion: *Philosophie des Protestantismus: Eine Apologetik des
evangelischen Glaubens*.

[159] In *Against False Apologetics*, Brent Sockness discusses the different approaches to apologetics of Troeltsch and Herrmann. The fundamental distinction, he convincingly suggests, was
over their understanding of the relationship between religion and science. See esp. chs. 6–8.

[160] *SGT* i. 258.   [161] *The Absoluteness* (A1901/23d), ET, 31.

[162] *Die wissenschaftliche Lage* (A1900/7), 45 f.   [163] 'Kant' (A1914/15), 656.

[164] 'Die wissenschaftliche Lage' (A1900/7), 46. Herrmann is critical of such a view. See, for
instance, his review of Otto Pfleiderer's *Die Ritschl'sche Theologie*, col. 383.

freedom which was required for meaningful action. Troeltsch also pointed to the ethical problems of Herrmann's dualism. 'On the one hand,' he remarked, in a review of half a century of theology, 'he allows full validity to the enormous world in its mechanical causal nexus of events, and leaves it alone, and then allows the religious person simply a religious and ethical autonomy which is based on the experience of God's holiness and love in the picture of Jesus'.[165] For Troeltsch, religion had to allow for what he called an 'interpenetration' of the worlds of spirit and nature.

It is no surprise, however, that Troeltsch's most fundamental criticism of Herrmann, whose system he characterized as the 'realization of ethical autonomy through trust in Jesus',[166] is of the ethical implications of the epistemological isolation of Christianity.[167] He considered this to be little more than a dogmatic isolation. Herrmann had thus become, according to Troeltsch, 'quite the hard dogmatician and apologist, who maintains the value of Christianity at the expense of denying the value of everything unchristian'.[168] Indeed, in identifying the formal ethical will with the 'revelation' of Jesus Christ, Herrmann had made the material content of ethics indeterminate.[169]

In criticizing Herrmann, however, Troeltsch is at one and the same time engaged in developing his own conception of ethics. In the lengthy essay 'Grundprobleme der Ethik' he consequently expresses his gratitude to Herrmann for having given him the opportunity to expound his own ethical system.[170] Thus, against Herrmann's understanding, Troeltsch contended that Christianity had always required an immanent cultural ('material') expression: there was thus a dynamic relationship between the formal and the material, between spirit and nature. For Troeltsch, Christianity could not rest content with a world of faith unsullied by the ethical compromises of material history. According to Troeltsch, this relationship between formal and material was completely ignored by Herrmann, who, in denying anything but a purely formal content to Christian ethics, had rendered the cultural sphere something ethically indifferent.[171] For Troeltsch, however, the

---

[165] 'Rückblick' (A1909/18a) 219; ET 74. Cf. 'Grundprobleme der Ethik' (A1902/4a), 552–672. Wilhelm Bousset regarded Herrmann's theology as a vain attempt at a 'theology of mediation, which denies from the outset an adequate scientific knowledge in matters of religion and Christianity' ('Anwendung', 428).

[166] 'Grundprobleme der Ethik' (A1902/4a), 590.

[167] On the relationship between Troeltsch's and Herrmann's ethics see esp. Walter Wiesenberg, 'Das Verhältnis von Formal- und Materialethik'; H. Diehl, 'Herrmann und Troeltsch'; W. Pannenberg, 'Die Begründung der Ethik bei Ernst Troeltsch'.

[168] 'Grundprobleme der Ethik' (A1902/4a), 647.

[169] Troeltsch here offers the same criticism he makes of Kant, whose formal ethical a priori, he claims, could not be realized in practice ('Grundprobleme der Ethik' (A1902/4a), 623. Cf. *Christian Thought* (E1923/7), 47).

[170] 'Grundprobleme der Ethik' (A1902/4a), 672.   [171] Ibid., 592 f.

ethical personality was no mere isolated individual in direct communion with God, but was always an embodied person in a particular social context.

According to Troeltsch, the precursors of Herrmann's ethics were clear: 'All in all,' he remarked, 'it is Lutheran ethics translated into the spirit of Kant'.[172] Later, in *Die Soziallehren*, Troeltsch compares Herrmann's system with Luther's understanding of the natural conditions of life. For them both, the practice of the Christian ethics of love of neighbour took place in a world untouched by nature:

> Just as Luther regarded the class guild, agrarian and absolutist form of life as a condition which was permanently demanded by nature, as conditions which determined the outward form of life compatible with Christianity, so (in Herrmann's *Ethik*) an unlimited mobile shaping of these things, including the modern militaristic, capitalistic, and scientific and aesthetic civilisation, is regarded as the 'form' of the natural life which is to be inspired by faith . . . Everywhere any possibility of an inner opposition between the natural forms of the ethic of civilisation (*Kulturethik*) and the spirit of love (whose radical and other-worldly aims ought to fill them) has been entirely forgotten, and Luther's conflicts around this problem are simply regarded as 'Catholic relics' . . . In catholicism Nature and Grace are different in degree; in Protestantism they finally divide as form and content.[173]

Troeltsch's second problem with Herrmann's ethics is in his identification of the formal Kantian categorical imperative with the ethic of Jesus. Thus, although Troeltsch agreed with Herrmann that autonomy was of great importance in Jesus's ethic of love, he nevertheless felt that the infinite value of the soul was not the primary motivation behind Jesus's command to love, which was derived instead from the priority of the love of God.[174] Jesus's ethic was thus not primarily humanitarian, but was instead God-centred:[175] there was no room for any other motive besides love of God, which was an objective good which always stood in tension with the world. This was indeed the goal to which everything else stood in a relationship of 'vital becoming' in the active surrender to this highest possible end.

For Troeltsch, as will be shown in greater detail in Chapter 7, modern Protestantism had to recognize the tension between the command to love God and the sanctification of the world for God: the goals of the world were always in conflict with the highest good, however ethical they might appear. Nevertheless, Troeltsch held, at the same time the Christian had a responsibility to try and secure as close a correspondence between the two as possible, even though full reconciliation would never be realized. Thus the 'quintessence' of Jesus's ethic did not rest merely in the *form* of the moral

---

[172] 'Grundprobleme der Ethik' (A1902/4a), 603.
[173] *Die Soziallehren* (A1912/2) 502 n.227; ET, 848 n.227.
[174] 'Grundprobleme der Ethik' (A1902/4a), 630 ff.
[175] Cf. *Christian Thought* (E1923/7), 55.

law, but also in its *material content*. Such content, however, could not be taken for granted but was something which would only be realized in the interaction of the form and content in the constant effort to move towards the highest good, the love of God himself.[176]

In distinction to Herrmann, Troeltsch regarded culture as that sphere where formal ethical demands were to be realized in practice. God therefore 'grants to the work of the human being the task of building up a community of persons which sanctifies secular goals and makes them subservient to his overall purpose'.[177] Nature and 'history' did not stand in a necessary opposition to God, but were rather to be seen as domains which could grow to reflect God's purposes as human beings lived their lives ethically. Herrmann's view was quite different from this: since the ethical was given no material content, there could be no scope for its active realization in the world. Indeed the only function Herrmann gave to nature and history was as necessary conditions determining human life: one could only practise Christian ethics in so far as one 'held back' from this society or natural world.[178]

CONCLUSION

If these criticisms of Herrmann's thought are accepted, then it would appear that he has completely transformed Ritschl's careful balance between religion and ethics. Religion, in Herrmann, appears to have retreated into its own sphere: it may be the 'true' sphere, but it is hard to know how it is connected with the remainder of human life, since community, ethics, and history seem to have been ruled out of court.[179] In the face of the massive scientific and technological edifice of modern society, there seemed to Herrmann to be no place left for religion other than 'in the corner'.[180] Theology thus became a theology *intra muros*, centred in on itself,[181] and unable to fulfil its public role. It was, in James Robinson's words, a 'monotonous postlude which accompanies the unchurching of the masses'.[182] In such a

---

[176] Cf. 'Grundprobleme der Ethik' (A1902/4a), 638 f.
[177] Ibid., 637; ET, 44.   [178] Cf. Ibid., 599.
[179] Johannes Wendland had observed as early as 1889 that the desire for epistemological security in response to Kantian relativism led to a complete isolation of religion from the rest of life. Theology had retreated 'into its own special sphere where it was able to achieve a great deal', but in so doing it had cut itself off from scientific reality. Although it had developed its own method 'with scant regard to the rest of science' it still expected 'recognition for itself' (*Albrecht Ritschl und seine Schüler*, 29). Cf. Horst Stephan, 'Albrecht Ritschl und die Gegenwart', 35.
[180] D. Schellong, *Bürgertum und christliche Religion*, 89.
[181] Cf. Chapman, 'Theology Within the Walls: Wilhelm Herrmann's Religious Reality', 80–4.
[182] James M. Robinson, *Das Problem des heiligen Geistes bei Wilhelm Herrmann*, 67.

situation theology would grow increasingly irrelevant as it moved outside the public domain.

Although Herrmann's system provides an elegant attempt to circumvent Kantian epistemology, without denying its truth for the scientific sphere, it nevertheless gives rise to more questions than answers. Theology, in pushing religion beyond the limits of communicability, appears to have rendered itself scientifically irrelevant and apologetically useless.[183] A theology which was to retain its relevance and public role could not retreat into its own corner, but instead had to advance into the public domain by seeking a unified conception of reality, and relocating theology in the picture of 'the whole', without succumbing to the enticements of ontological dualism, or more *real* realities. Indeed, this was the real issue between Troeltsch and Herrmann.[184] The latter, however, was not alone in creating an epistemology of ethical escape and apologetic irrelevance. Members of the History of Religion School could be equally inclined towards a privatized religion, as the next chapter demonstrates.

---

[183] On this see W. Pannenberg, 'Kontingenz und Naturgesetz', 35: 'theological statements are irrelevant not merely for the work of the natural scientist, but also for the world-view of the modern human being, oriented as this is around the results of the scientist'.

[184] Cf. Sockness, *Against False Apologetics*, 205: 'At virtually every turn and amidst all the variations of expression, the predominant and overarching subject of contention between the two great "liberals" concerned the proper character of a viable apologetic in the modern theological situation.'

6

Struggles over Epistemology: The Religious A Priori

This chapter surveys the use of Kantian thought in theology which took hold with the revived interest in things Kantian following the centenary of 1904. The principal theme is that of the elusive notion of a 'religious a priori', which dominated philosophical debate by theologians in the first decades of the twentieth century.[1] Much of the concern for the adoption of this terminology was apologetic, since a specifically religious a priori would function as a defence against philosophical reductionism. As Troeltsch remarked: 'either origin of religion out of the psychological illusion of positivism . . . or the foundation of religion in an a priori of consciousness'.[2] However, the concern was not merely apologetic. Inner theological debates about the nature of religious epistemology and thus about the possibility of the reconciliation of all thought were also subsumed in what appeared a somewhat technical debate. Thus E. W. Mayer exclaimed in 1912: 'The "religious a priori"!! It is astonishing how the programme which is embodied by this catchphrase has captivated the theological youth of today'.[3] He could quite understand such fascination, however, since 'the programme points not merely to Ernst Troeltsch, but also to a great shadow, the "armoured shadow" of Kant, as Treitschke liked to call him'.[4] Thus, in a sense, the religious a priori 'carried the whole of the philosophy of religion'.[5]

As will be shown, there was profound disagreement on what the religious a priori implied epistemologically: for some, it was nothing less than an 'attempt to form a substitute for a natural theology',[6] whereas for others it was merely a preliminary delineation of the phenomenon of religion prior to epistemological evaluation. Such confusion meant that it soon became an 'ambiguous catch-phrase'[7] or a 'very cloudy notion'.[8] Herrmann found such a confusion in the work of Troeltsch:

---

[1] Rudolf Köhler (in *Der Begriff Apriori*) lists some sixty-two items in his bibliography. For a good account in English see John Baillie, *The Interpretation of Religion*, 235–55.
[2] Troeltsch, review of Breysig (A1906/13), 688.
[3] E. W. Mayer, 'Über den gegenwärtigen Stand', 59.   [4] Ibid., 60.
[5] Köhler, *Der Begriff Apriori*, 2.   [6] Walter Bodenstein, *Neige des Historismus*, 30.
[7] Wilhelm Mundle, 'Das religiöse Apriori', 428.
[8] Traub, 'Zur Frage des religiösen Apriori', 181.

Whoever wishes to express experience, on the one hand, and the idea or the principle on the other, expresses two conflicting conceptions of religion. Whoever wishes to represent them both together achieves a confusing wordplay which is today exemplified by the phrase 'a priori of religion' which Troeltsch proposes.[9]

Rudolf Otto, although continuing to use the expression, was well aware of its shortcomings, regarding it as a 'not particularly fortunate expression which is beset with misunderstandings'.[10] Despite this lack of clarity, however, what is evident is that the religious a priori was intended as the application of a modified Kantianism for the purposes both of theological apologetics and inner theological debate.

THE CONCEPT OF THE A PRIORI

For Kant, a priori concepts were the conditions without which the apodeictic certainty of the empirical sciences would not be possible, for 'only by means of these fundamental concepts can appearances belong to knowledge or even to our consciousness and thus to ourselves'.[11] They were those concepts without which no object could be thought, but were not themselves derived from experience: 'on the contrary,' Kant remarked, 'they have to confer upon appearances their conformity to law, and so to make experience possible'.[12] Without an a priori concept no object could be thought, since all 'appearances necessarily agree with this formal condition of sensibility, since only through it can they appear, that is, be empirically intuited and given'.[13] However, unless the a priori concept was applied to experience it remained a purely logical form. Thus Kant suggested: 'We must be able to show how pure concepts can be applicable to appearances'.[14] The categories of pure reason required transcendental schemata if they were to be applied to sensibility.[15] As Troeltsch put it in an article on Kant: a priori concepts had to do with empirical data alone and 'if employed apart from and beyond them [they] remain altogether empty—a use of them which results in a futile metaphysical hypostasis, such as was fabricated by Plato, and, in a more cautious and covert manner, by Leibniz'.[16]

For Kant, philosophical problems arose when knowledge was sought in

⁹ Hermann, 'Wilhelm Herrmann über Ernst Troeltsch', 233.

¹⁰ JFR, 34; ET, 19. (References have been given to the English translation, *The Philosophy of Religion based on Kant and Fries*, although all translations are my own and have made use of the 'Author's Notes on the Translation' prepared by Otto for the English translation and included as a flysheet in some copies and later reprinted in H.-W. Schütte, *Religion und Christentum*, 122–7).

¹¹ Immanuel Kant, *Critique of Pure Reason*, A125.   ¹² Ibid., A126.
¹³ Ibid., A93 = B125.   ¹⁴ Ibid., A138 = B177.   ¹⁵ Ibid., A147 = B187.
¹⁶ Troeltsch, 'Kant' (A1914/15), 655.

the realm of pure reason without application *in concreto*,[17] something which would lead to a necessary antinomy. For instance, the thesis of pure reason that 'the world has a beginning' enters into a necessary antinomy with the antithesis 'that the world has no beginning, and no limits in space' (the First Antinomy). It was, however, the Third Antinomy which was of special importance in ethics and the philosophy of religion. The lengthy thesis: 'Causality in accordance with the laws of nature is not the only causality from which the appearances of the world can one and all be derived. To explain these appearances it is necessary to assume that there is also another causality, that of freedom' was in opposition to the antithesis that 'There is no freedom; everything takes place solely in accordance with laws of nature'.[18]

In his *Critique of Practical Reason* Kant reaffirmed his interest in human freedom; that is, in a higher form of motivation than that of mere deterministic necessity. In the realm of practical reason (i.e. human action) as in pure reason there were regulative ideas (or postulates) which determined the nature of moral judgements, and conferred on them a universal logical character. What seemed to be lacking, however, was that *necessary* status of the categories of pure reason. There were merely parallel causalities, the one of human willing and the other of the rigid determinism of scientific judgement, but there was no bridge between the two and thus no solution to the Third Antinomy. It was this problem that Kant tackled, albeit only tentatively, in his *Critique of Judgement*, where he attempted to bring the world of cause and effect into harmony with the causality of freedom, a harmony introduced by the judging faculty of the human being as the world was shown to conform to patterns detected by the human being.

There were thus great theological resources in Kant's philosophy: first, although he may not have solved the problem of human freedom, he had at least recognized it as a problem and had not attempted to explain it away in a manner akin to Humean scepticism. Secondly, he provided the terminology for looking at the logical form of empirical and non-empirical judgements, and, finally, he offered a tentative solution to the problem of freedom and determinism. One of the reasons why the religious a priori became such a misunderstood term was that it was used both as a substitute for the tentative solution to the Third Antinomy mooted by Kant in his Third Critique, and, at the same time, the mere delineation or 'stabilization'[19] of the logical form of religion as a distinct form of life alongside the scientific, moral, and aesthetic.[20] The religious a priori thus became a distinctively religious form

[17] *Critique of Pure Reason*, A327 f. = B383 f. [18] Ibid., A444 = B472, A445 = B473.
[19] Cf. Mayer, 'Über den gegenwärtigen Stand', 60.
[20] Kant would himself never have countenanced such a claim. Troeltsch suggested that he had avoided introducing a specific religious a priori because he 'saw all the dangers of mysticism lurking in it' ('Main Problems' (C1905/1), 287; *Psychologie und Erkenntnistheorie* (A1905/7), 54).

of judgement, which would at the same time serve to unify freedom and determinism. There were therefore at least two distinct levels in the philosophical debate over the religious a priori, which, as will be shown, were often confused and misunderstood, not least by the proponents themselves.

ERNST TROELTSCH AND THE RELIGIOUS A PRIORI

Troeltsch, for instance, operates at both these levels: his primary concern was the 'critical regulation' of the 'uncultivated psychical life' which would confer on the amorphous 'religious feeling' a greater logical clarity which did not reduce it to some epiphenomenon.[21] His aim was to show 'whether the religious function of consciousness attains the character of the a priori'.[22] In this, Troeltsch considered himself to be following Kant, who, 'with the most fundamental coherence, undertook the analysis of consciousness in general, making it his fundamental proposition, and, under this allocation, religion was given a defined place in the economy of consciousness'.[23] Thus, he remarked, 'science of religion allows religion to exist as religion and regulates it according to its own a priori which permeates the great historical centres of revelation with ever greater clarity and undertakes the task of closely connecting it with the rest of reason'.[24] Such a delineation of religion in terms of a religious a priori provoked an immediate reaction from those influenced by Herrmann for whom there was room for either the 'a priori law of reason, *or* the living God of religion',[25] but never a combination of the two, since for them Kantian epistemology was applicable only to the sphere of science. Thus the 'special means of knowing . . . where the experience of subjective certainty nevertheless has the character of objective necessity'[26] was replaced 'with a rational proof'.[27] In short, Friedrich Traub remarked: 'We deny an intellectual, rational a priori based on compelling grounds. It contradicts the essence of religion which is always irrational'.[28]

To counter these charges that he had rationalized religion, Troeltsch wrote 'Zur Frage des religiösen Apriori',[29] as a vigorous defence of the irrational content of religion, where he sought to affirm the need for a 'deed of

---

[21] 'Main Problems' (C1905/1), 288; *Psychologie und Erkenntnistheorie* (A1905/7), 54 f.
[22] *RPH*, 51.   [23] 'Religionsphilosophie' (A1904/7), 143.
[24] 'Main Problems' (C1905/1), 287; *Psychologie und Erkenntnistheorie* (A1905/7), 53.
[25] R. J. Jelke, 'Das religiöse Apriori', 48.   [26] Ibid., 54.
[27] Traub, 'Zur Frage des religiösen Apriori', 185.   [28] Ibid., 187.
[29] This essay was written specifically in response to Paul Spieß, 'Zur Frage des religiösen Apriori'. Similar charges came from many others. Cf. K. Dunkmann, *Religionsphilosophie*, 13; G. Ritzert, 'Die Religionsphilosophie Ernst Troeltschs', 13; Wobbermin, *Aufgabe und Bedeutung der Religionspsychologie*, 7 f.: 'The decision of the religious value judgement in the question of faith cannot be translated into rational universality or be replaced by such'; and Pannenberg,

the will', an irrational decision to accept the validity of the religious a priori.[30] Indeed, in the last resort, a *deed* was responsible for all knowledge.[31] It was in the act that doubt was overcome rather than by any religious or rational means of proof. Such an act was nothing less than 'a decision about the value of our very being'.[32] By suggesting his system relied on a decision of faith, Troeltsch thus sought to make himself more Protestant than his opponents, while at the same time showing that with his method one could pursue a legitimate apologetics which remained untainted by natural theology.

For Troeltsch, however, the delineation of a religious a priori could never *prove* the existence of the religious object, since 'if we want a scientific proof of God then we are back with theories that Kant destroyed'.[33] Similarly it could not take on the hard and fast character of the categories of pure reason, but would be 'obliged unceasingly to correct itself, and contain open spaces',[34] since, in the realm of human freedom there was no 'ready system of categorical forms, but only developing forms and approximations'.[35] The religious a priori, which Troeltsch defined as that form of judgement *sub specie aeternitatis*,[36] was necessarily subject to human error and illusion: 'The true and rational reality to be attained by thought is always in conjunction with the untrue reality, the psychological, that containing illusion and error'.[37] Thus 'the two realities, which the critical system must recognise at its very foundation, continue in strife with each other'.[38] In introducing the notion of 'openness' Troeltsch aimed to make Kant's categories 'fit life, not to abolish them altogether and put the chaos of reality into their place'.[39]

The Solution to the Third Antinomy

From the delineation of the religious form of judgement Troeltsch moved on to the attempt to overcome the parallelism of the Third Antinomy,

---

'Toward a Theology of the History of Religions', 100 n.47: 'If religious experience were grounded in an *a priori* capacity of the human spirit, then it [i.e. religious experience] would be a creature of this capacity'.

[30] Troeltsch 'Zur Frage des religiösen Apriori', 761.   [31] *EPH*, 41.   [32] *RPH*, 63.

[33] *RPH*, 54.

[34] 'Main Problems' (C1905/1), 280; *Psychologie und Erkenntnistheorie* (A1905/7), 32.

[35] *RPH*, 53.

[36] It is not true, as Ansgar Paus (in *Religiöser Erkenntnisgrund*, 135) and Garrett Paul (in '*Religionswissenschaft*', 103) maintain that Troeltsch gave no content to the specific form of the religious judgement, although admittedly it was vague and imprecise.

[37] 'Contingency' (A1910/20a), 89.

[38] 'Main Problems' (C1905/1), 281; *Psychologie und Erkenntnistheorie* (A1905/7), 32 f.

[39] 'Empiricism and Platonism' (A1912/6), 422. Cf. H. R. Niebuhr, 'Ernst Troeltsch's Philosophy of Religion', 269.

seeing the religious a priori as 'carrying' the other a prioris, conferring on them a sense of unity. Just as Kant, in the *Critique of Judgement*,[40] had provided a basis for overcoming the antinomy practically by reading a teleological purpose into nature, so the religious a priori became a 'unity of spirit against the flowing stream of life',[41] whereby both causalities were seen as part of one greater absolute reality. Without the perception of the absolute, everything remained in flux:

When we connect matter and spirit to one another in the theoretical functions, when we unite that which is diffuse, we can only do this because we have experienced this unity in the religious consciousness.[42]

By introducing unity into the Kantian parallelism, the religious a priori became the 'tacit immanent presupposition of all value functions'.[43] The very conception of a unified reality itself became a religious viewpoint as the religious a priori 'connected divine and human reason',[44] and the 'supersensuous had the effect of permeating the natural phenomenal life of the soul'.[45] As Rudolf Otto put it:

In so far as the pure capacity for knowledge in Kant is preconscious and subconscious, and all perceptions of unity, meaning and value rise from the depth of the mind which itself lies far below the level of the senses and of the understanding, Kant also knows the 'ground of the soul'.[46]

Troeltsch modified Kant by claiming to overcome the Third Antinomy, as the 'intelligible ego', the initiator of willed action, interacted with the world of cause and effect:

Within the phenomenal ego by a creative act of the intelligible ego in it, the personality should be formed and developed as a realisation of the autonomous reason, so that the intelligible issues from the phenomenal, the rational from the psychological, the former elaborates and shapes the latter, and between both, a relation of regular interaction, but not of causal constraint, takes place.[47]

Thus, according to Troeltsch, it was in meaningful action, in praxis, that the human will overcame the Third Antinomy. There could be no proofs for this interaction except in the decision of the will to accept the meaningful

---

[40] See esp. pt. ii, §23. 434 ff. (page numbers according to the first edition of 1790): 'Only in man, and only in him as the individual being to whom the moral law applies, do we find unconditional legislation in respect of ends. This legislation, therefore, is what alone qualifies him to be a final end to which entire nature is teleologically subordinated' (453 f.)
[41] Karl Bornhausen, 'Das religiöse Apriori', 194.   [42] *RPH*, 60.   [43] Ibid.
[44] Ruth Schlesinger, 'Probleme eines religiösen Apriori', 42.
[45] 'Main Problems' (C1905/1), 285; *Psychologie und Erkenntnistheorie* (A1905/7), 47.
[46] Rudolf Otto, *Mysticism East and West*, 245.
[47] 'Main Problems' (C1905/1), 284; *Psychologie und Erkenntnistheorie* (A1905/7), 40.

organization of consciousness, the possibility of purposeful behaviour, to accept 'something unconditioned . . . in every act of thought'.[48] Ultimately, however, such a solution, however much it might be couched in philosophical language, rested on an 'ethical decision of the will . . . Only this can conquer scepticism'.[49] For Troeltsch, this was at the heart of religion: 'Kant had himself often enough practically felt this, and spoke of freedom as an experience of communion with the supersensuous as a possible but unprovable affair.'[50] Troeltsch's solution was ably summarized by Wilhelm Mundle, one of his early commentators:

Through our thought we search for the depths of being in nature and history; through our will we grasp the elevated heights of the ethical ought. Through our imagination we know ourselves to be carried into a realm where the conflict between is and ought, idea and reality, is overcome, but this realm is only a dream, an illusion, which cannot last—only through religious faith can we succeed in really solving the conflict.[51]

Troeltsch thus sees in Kant the basis for that 'religious longing to be free over and against naturalist determinism',[52] where the worlds of nature and freedom 'belong together', not out of necessity, but in 'the synthesis of natural conditions with value or meaning or freedom',[53] as 'the human personality rose out of oppressive forces'.[54]

The A Priori as the Goal of History

Having provided the basis for the interaction of the phenomenal and the intelligible egos, Troeltsch then moved on to the application of the religious a priori to concrete historical religion, to the question of how the religious a priori, as the assertion of the 'final valid goal', was to be realized in history.[55] As he makes clear in his extended essay 'Das Historische in Kants Religionsphilosophie',[56] the basis was again provided by Kant. Against the dominant interpretation of Kant of the Marburg School, Troeltsch aimed to show how 'from Kant's basic viewpoint, a doctrine of the principles of historical research and the epistemological value of history can be attained'.[57] In short:

[48] Troeltsch, 'Die Selbständigkeit der Religion' (A1895/2), 431.
[49] Troeltsch, review of Nelson (A1913/12), col. 342.
[50] 'Main Problems' (C1905/1), 283; *Psychologie und Erkenntnistheorie* (A1905/7), 38.
[51] Mundle, 'Das religiöse Apriori', 470.
[52] Troeltsch, 'Christentum und Religionsgeschichte' (A1897/10a), 332.
[53] Troeltsch, *Der Historismus und seine Probleme* (A1922/22), 40.   [54] Ibid., 51.
[55] Troeltsch, 'Logos und Mythos' (A1913/8a), 831; ET, 67.
[56] Troeltsch, 'Das Historische' (A1904/4a), 21–154.
[57] Troeltsch, review of Medicus and Lask (A1903/6), col. 245.

The more philosophical thinkers of the present give up the tendency to achieve a one-sided world-view of natural laws and see . . . the contents and values of the spiritual as at least as important for the formation of the total view, so the philosophical treatment of history, as the sphere of values, will become all the more important.[58]

Troeltsch emphasizes the regulative character of reason for historical religion, something which is 'deeply rooted in Kant's thought, in his philosophy of history, in his political-judicial as well as in his scientific-rational convictions, in his idea of vocation in a century of progress'.[59] For Kant, all tradition, however sacred, was to be subjected to rational criticism in the public domain, something which did not threaten religion but which 'gives us freedom, peace, and confidence',[60] as human beings gradually approach absolute truth. Thus Troeltsch wrote:

The philosopher needs a connection with theology in order to make pure religion practical, and the theologian needs a connection with the philosophy of religion in order to make biblical theology scientific.[61]

Absolute truth would, however, never be reached since it is 'not only unknowable by man, but this kind of "truth" is absolutely impossible because of the vital, changing character of our world . . . where . . . there are increasingly new and vital attempts to construe the essential nature of reality which is ever in process of development'.[62] It was the duty of the contemporary theologian to move to an 'ever more approximate'[63] realization of the religious a priori in history, even though it could never be achieved in its fulness. Troeltsch thus saw himself as developing Lessing's dictum that 'the historical serves only as illustration, not as demonstration'.[64]

Despite this idea of approximation, however, empirical history was vital for any religion, since 'without a means of expression there is no community; without an organized community there is no durability and no power for life for the new religion'.[65] Here Troeltsch extends Kant's doctrine of schematization:

Religion is not a freely created product of the understanding but an expression of the fundamental laws of reason. It has rational necessity but is never an independent reality cut off from all sensibility and psychological intensity . . . It needs an

---

[58] Troeltsch, review of Medicus and Lask (A1903/6), col. 244 f.

[59] 'Das Historische' (A1904/4a), 60. Cf. 'Main Problems' (C1905/1), 287; *Psychologie und Erkenntnistheorie* (A1905/7), 52.

[60] Review of Mezger (A1913/24), col. 502.   [61] 'Das Historische' (A1904/4a), 63.

[62] 'The Dogmatics of the "Religionsgeschichtliche Schule"' (A1913/2), 17 f.; 'Die Dogmatik der religionsgeschichtlichen Schule' (A1913/2a), 516.

[63] 'Das Historische' (A1904/4a), 82.   [64] Ibid., 154.   [65] Ibid., 143.

anthropomorphic picture, or schematism of analogy, or sensory symbols through which it is first mediated, is given the power to motivate, is organized, and is lived.[66]

Consequently, according to Troeltsch, a religion 'within the limits of reason alone' was quite impossible, since all that the religious a priori could achieve was a 'purification of positive religions through a religion of reason' but never their replacement.[67] Thus even Kant's own doctrine of religion 'does not therefore look to an unconditional religion of reason, but rather to a transformation and approximation of the faith of the Church to the religion of reason, as this is demanded by the contemporary situation'.[68] Against those who charged him with setting up a rational religion[69] Troeltsch asserted: 'The religious *a priori* should serve only to establish the essential in empirical appearance, but without stripping off the appearance altogether, and from this point of the essential, to correct the intricacies and the narrowness, the errors and false combinations of the psychical situation'.[70] The human being could never fully grasp the rational a priori of religion, since all human efforts were subject to error: 'What will happen in a thousand years time nobody can know'.[71] In short:

We can never grasp the timeless in an abstract manner, for life is nowhere abstract. There is no idea of a religion which could be conceived without the historical, but there again there is nothing purely historical which is purely historical . . . The pursuit of the pure Idea, the rationalistic Ideal, is nonsense.[72]

This application of the religious a priori to history soon became the object of violent attack, since a conception of Christianity as capable of full realization only at some unknowable point lacked the epistemological security after which many clamoured. Troeltsch seemed to have been entranced by his own Kantian historicism, a historicism which his critics sought to overcome by adopting another very different form of Kantianism. Again, it was Kant who became an unlikely target and an unlikely weapon in the most violent theological polemics.

---

[66] Ibid., 140.
[67] Ibid., 130.   [68] Troeltsch, review of Kalweit (A1905/8), 169.
[69] D. C. MacIntosh, for instance (in 'Troeltsch's Theory of Religious Knowledge', 281), suggests that Troeltsch sought to reduce religion to its thoroughly rational form. For Troeltsch, however, there can be no such rational form except perhaps at the end of time.
[70] Troeltsch, 'Main Problems' (C1905/1), 286; *Psychologie und Erkenntnistheorie* (A1905/7), 48 (translation amended).
[71] Troeltsch, 'Das Historische' (A1904/4a), 153.
[72] Troeltsch, *Glaubenslehre* (F1925/2), 93; ET, 81.

RUDOLF OTTO, WILHELM BOUSSET, AND THE
RELIGIOUS A PRIORI: BACK TO FRIES[73]

Rudolf Otto

In the first years of the twentieth century it was Rudolf Otto[74] more than anybody else who sought to defend the religious dimension of human life from the onslaught of naturalism and materialism. In this he made use of his own version of the religious a priori. From as early as 1899, in the preface to his centenary edition of Schleiermacher's *Speeches*,[75] he recognized the need to respond to the threats to religion posed by 'l'homme machine' of the French Enlightenment; despite the great advances in science during the eighteenth century, he claimed, there was one dimension which had been neglected; namely, human piety.[76] Schleiermacher's contemporary relevance thus rested in his delineation of religion as its 'own free arena of human being'.[77] Alongside the principles of the 'Kantian catechism' of the first two Critiques ('What can we know?' and 'What should we do?') Schleiermacher had inserted a third; namely, 'What do we experience in the soul?' Against all interpretations that attempted to reduce Schleiermacher's theology to some form of 'eclecticism', Otto pointed to his originality in relocating 'piety' at the centre of human life.[78] This reassertion of the religious dimension of human life did not deny science but grounded it in an

unshakable certainty of the priority of the absolute value of the spiritual in the world, the conviction that the '*universum*', the totality of all being and happening, was neither ceaseless clockwork nor a meaningless collection and museum of chance and purposeless coexistence, but a unified, meaningful, and profound 'system', an eternal 'harmony' empowered by eternal high ideas, measured and designed in terms of eternal plans and directed towards eternal goals[79]

---

[73] On the background to Otto's theory of the religious a priori see esp. Ansgar Paus, *Religiöser Erkenntnisgrund*; R. F. Davidson, *Rudolf Otto's Interpretation of Religion*, 159–178; and William Julius Hälfter, 'The Religious A Priori', 172 ff. For more general discussions of Otto's philosophy of religion see esp. Philip C. Almond, 'Rudolf Otto and the Kantian Tradition'; and Theodor Siegfried, 'Theologie als Wissenschaft bei Rudolf Otto'.

[74] On Rudolf Otto (1869–1937) see R. Schinzer, 'Rudolf Otto—Entwurf einer Biographie'; R. Boeke, 'Rudolf Otto, Leben und Werk'; Jack S. Boozer, 'Rudolf Otto'; Philip C. Almond, 'Rudolf Otto: Life and Work'. The best introductions to Otto's thought remain Schütte, *Religion und Christentum in der Theologie Rudolf Ottos*, which contains a thorough bibliography, 143–57; and in English, R. F. Davidson, *Rudolf Otto's Interpretation of Religion*.

[75] F. D. E. Schleiermacher, *Über die Religion. Reden an die Gebildeten unter ihren Verächtern*.

[76] Otto, introd. to Schleiermacher, *Über die Religion*, pp. v f.

[77] Ibid., p. viii f.

[78] Cf. 'How Schleiermacher Rediscovered the Sensus Numinous'. This is a revised version of 'Wie Schleiermacher die Religion wiederentdeckte'.

[79] Otto, in Schleiermacher, *Über die Religion*, 173.

This sense of the unity of all things, which Schleiermacher had most clearly perceived, became a characteristic feature of Otto's own theology.[80] In short, he remarked:

> Schleiermacher not only rediscovered the *sensus numinis* in a vague and general way but he opened for his age a new door to old and forgotten ideas: to divine marvel instead of supernaturalistic miracle, to living revelation instead of instilled doctrine, to the manifestation of the divinely infinite in event, person, and history, and especially to a new understanding and valuation of biblical history as divine revelation. Without falling back again into the trammels of a primitive supernaturalism he prepared the way to a rediscovery not only of religion but of Christian religion and to a new interpretation of Christian religion, which was better and more modern than the old orthodox or rationalistic theology could give.[81]

The emphasis on the spiritual dimension as both an independent and a necessary sphere of human life is at the centre of Otto's *Naturalistische und religiöse Weltansicht*, which offers a thorough discussion of materialism and its impact on the religious world-view.[82] This book attempts to counter materialism not with quasi-scientific proofs, but rather by seeking to show that a proper understanding of the natural sciences leads to the 'fresh revelation of the depth of things . . . the increased recognition that our knowledge is only leading us towards mystery'.[83] Against Darwinism, with its emphasis on 'explanation',[84] Otto asserts the importance of the mysterious, of the feeling of 'dependence', a term borrowed from the 'profound insight' of Schleiermacher.[85] Otto concludes by affirming the autonomy of the spirit, that mysterious power which activates itself in nature. No amount of knowledge in the natural sciences, he claims, could ever 'rob it of its freedom and independence'.[86]

Otto's book is thus a defence of the depths of feeling which rest beyond the limits of naturalistic explanation.[87]

---

[80] It is interesting to note that Otto asserts the primacy of the suprarational from at least as early as the time of this new edition of Schleiermacher's *Reden*, but possibly even from his doctoral thesis on Luther and the Holy Spirit (as maintained by Hans- Walter Schütte, *Religion und Christentum in der Theologie Rudolf Ottos*, esp. 12).

[81] 'How Schleiermacher Rediscovered the Sensus Numinous', 77.

[82] There is also a clear apologetic intent in many of his later works, particularly *Das Heilige*. On this see Hans-Walter Schütte (*Religion und Christentum in der Theologie Rudolf Ottos*, esp. 3) who emphazises the continuity of Otto's apologetic intentions.

[83] Otto, *Naturalism and Religion*, 275. Cf. Schleiermacher, *Über die Religion*, 181.

[84] *Naturalism and Religion*, 46 f.   [85] Ibid., 41.   [86] Ibid., 276.

[87] In *JFR*, 222; ET, 124, Otto emphasizes the centrality of the concept of mystery in Fries' philosophy: 'The doctrine of the necessary mysteries of religion seems to me one of the finest and most delicate in Fries' philosophy'. Cf. Schütte, *Religion und Christentum*, 33: 'Rudolf Otto as a theologian was never satisfied with purely rational thought, as it might at first appear on a superficial reading. It is no accident that the concept of the mysterium is central even in his early work on "Naturalism and Religion".' The background to Otto's

This world of feeling is for us the meaning of all existence. The more we plunge ourselves into it, the deeper are the intricacies and mysteries it reveals. At every point
underivable and unintelligible in terms of physiological processes, it reveals itself from
stage to stage as more deeply and wholly unique in its relations, interactions, and
processes, and grows farther and farther beyond the laboured and insufficient schemes
and formulae under which science desires to range all psychical phenomena.[88]

Otto considered his work as apologetics, not because religion had to go
on the defensive before the challenge of science (since, for him, science
implied a religious viewpoint), but rather, he claimed:

Our undertaking only becomes defensive and critical because, not from caprice or
godlessness, but, as we shall see, from an inherent necessity, the natural sciences, in
association with other convictions and aims, tend readily to unite into a distinctive
and independent system of world-interpretation, which if it were valid and sufficient,
would drive the religious view into difficulties, or make it impossible. This independent system is Naturalism, and against its attacks the religious conception of the world
has to stand on the defensive.[89]

J. F. Fries and the Religious A Priori

For Rudolf Otto, as for Troeltsch, it was the concept of the religious a priori
that functioned as a solution to 'the absolute mystery' at the heart of the
Christian Gospel: the dualism of freedom and determinism. He makes this
clear in an early work on the life of Jesus where, reflecting on his healing
ministry, he remarks:

Perhaps Christ's gift of healing which seems so mysterious to us, was 'only' a development of capabilities slumbering in human nature in general. The prime instance of
the effective influence of a psychical agent upon a physical reality is the power of the
will to move the body: a spiritual cause producing a mechanical result. This is an
absolute mystery; and were it not so common it would still be recognised as such.[90]

Otto could not countenance the isolation of religion from science in the
Herrmann school, but instead sought to overcome what he regarded as
dualism:

Instead of a simple parallelism, the conviction gains ground that nature and natural
processes are inadequate appearances, an incomplete picture of true things
conditioned by a limited comprehension . . . [an] inadequate image of the true world,

---

thought, particularly the influence of Schleiermacher, is discussed by Almond in 'Rudolf Otto:
The Context of His Thought'. For Bousset too 'trembling fear' was at the heart of all real
religion' (*What is Religion?*, 22), and even Troeltsch saw 'the sense of mystery as the soul of all
religion' ('Religionsphilosophie' (A1904/7), 155 f.).

[88] Otto, *Naturalism and Religion*, 326.   [89] Ibid., 5 f.
[90] Otto, *Life and Ministry of Jesus*, 33.

which is a world free from natural law, from mathematics and mechanics, a world of the mind, of minds, a 'realm of grace', a world of God.[91]

Similarly for Wilhelm Bousset[92] there was a need to show, against the shallowness of modern science, that the depths of reality could be expressed only in a religious world-view:

In today's society the will to reflect on the ultimate truths of life has largely disappeared, if we exclude those areas where dogma and authority rule. And in its place so much else has become vital: a one-sided stress on economic-group or class interest, grabbing the rewards of the day . . . added to this is a one-sided aestheticism which lacks seriousness and which, like the butterfly, sucks now from one flower and now from the next, continually clamouring after something new.[93]

Both Bousset and Otto set about the apologetic task of showing a world beyond that of cause and effect, which displayed a higher unity.

Like Troeltsch, they considered themselves to be adapting Kant, but claimed no originality for their modifications, seeing themselves as following in the footsteps of 'the genius'[94] J. F. Fries (1773–1843), whom Otto saw as attempting a philosophical refinement of Schleiermacher but in the process deepening him almost beyond recognition:[95]

In reality it is not so much what unites Fries with Schleiermacher as what separates them that makes Fries of particular interest in the study of religion. Even where they agree he is quite original and a closer look shows him to be more comprehensive, profound, and plausible.[96]

Or, as Bousset put it in a moment of adulation:

I would very much like to add my personal confession that I have not come across many human beings who have so touched the heart and mind as J. F. Fries. In him there is at once clear and sober understanding, heroic enthusiasm, and ethical duty; fine humanity in the sense of Schiller is there along with an open-mindedness for the new realism which flowed into German life from the natural sciences, technology, and political life; he combines a proud inner certainty with a sacrificial enthusiasm for all the great questions of the nation, an austere reserve with extraordinarily sensitive personal love; and above all this shines a bright light of piety which unifies all clarity of thought, depths of conscience, and formidable ethical power.[97]

It was Fries who 'stood in the midst of a new spiritual spring which was bestowed on Germany'.[98] In short, 'it was a wonderful time when Fries

[91] JFR, 55; ET, 42.
[92] On Bousset's appropriation of Friesianism see esp. Verheule, *Wilhelm Bousset*, 390 ff. Schütte (*Religion und Christentum in der Theologie Rudolf Ottos*, esp. 41) sees Bousset as completing a 'polemical turn against the History of Religion School'.
[93] Bousset, foreword to *Julius und Evagoras*, p. xviii.   [94] JFR, 42; ET, 29.
[95] JFR, 50; ET, 35.   [96] JFR, 31; ET, 15.   [97] 'Anwendung', 487.
[98] Bousset, foreword to *Julius und Evagoras*, p. xvii.

wrote; it was the daybreak of the ascent of national freedom' when a *tabula rasa* was made of the past.[99]

In this call for a return to Friesian epistemology Otto shared much with his Göttingen colleague Leonard Nelson, who saw Fries' epistemology as 'the most important philosophical labour from the appearance of the Kantian writings up till the present day'.[100] In turn Otto regarded Nelson as leaving a great 'impression on contemporary "epistemology" and perhaps even creating a new epoch'.[101] As Nelson himself pointed out, Wilhelm Bousset had read his work 'with great interest . . . and it would seem with great understanding . . . If this interest persists I do not think it will be very difficult to bring him over to our point of view. That would be a valuable acquisition'.[102]

There was a flurry of interest in Fries in the first decade of the twentieth century, with new editions of the most important works,[103] together with the refounding of the *Abhandlungen der Fries'schen Schule*,[104] which, Bousset claimed, might 'really mean his resurrection to new life and to a powerful influence'.[105] Although Fries appeared to offer 'great bowls of the golden fruit'[106] of epistemological security in the face of the massive threats posed by the modern world, his importance had been tragically overlooked.[107] Thus, Otto mused:

Perhaps, if the choice had fallen on him [as Berlin Professor, instead of Hegel], there would have been a Friesian instead of a Hegelian period. For the location, influence and circumstances contributed a great deal to spread that School's influence'.[108]

Otto was at one with Troeltsch in delineating the distinctiveness of the phenomenon of religion, but was not content to remain merely with the realm of appearances, since for 'the religious person, this is no matter of indifference'.[109] Religion seemed to require an epistemology which allowed

---

[99] Bousset, foreword to *Julius und Evagoras*, p. xxxi.

[100] L. Nelson, *Über das sogenannten Erkenntnisproblem*, 725.

[101] Otto, review of Nelson, col. 475. Karl Bornhausen, on the other hand, criticized Nelson for rejuvenating the confusion between the a posteriori psychological knowledge and the a priori realm of pure reason. His book merely served to confuse Kantian teaching and belonged 'to one of those unsatisfactory writings; writings where one is never quite certain that one has correctly understood the author' ('Wider den Neofriesianismus in der Theologie', 374).

[102] Letter from Nelson to Otto, in Schütte, *Religion und Christentum in der Theologie Rudolf Ottos*, 126 f., here 127.

[103] Bousset himself prepared a new edition of Fries' philosophical novel, *Julius und Evagoras*. Most influential was probably Nelson's edition of Fries' popular work, *Wissen, Glaube und Ahndung*.

[104] Cf. Bousset, 'Anwendung', 422 f.

[105] Bousset, foreword to *Julius und Evagoras*, p. xxxviii.   [106] Ibid., p. xviii.

[107] Ibid., p. xi.   [108] *JFR*, 41; ET, 26. Cf. Bousset, foreword to *Julius und Evagoras*, p. xii.

[109] *JFR*, 35; ET, 19.

for direct access to things-in-themselves. According to Otto, it was Fries' 'improvement' to Kant's philosophy that allowed for this direct apprehension of things-in-themselves.[110] This was seen by Otto as the true inheritance of the Kantian tradition, and thus, according to Bousset, Fries was 'one of the most faithful pupils of Kant throughout his life; and however much he altered and developed him, he did all this in the spirit of Kantian criticism'.[111]

For Fries, the world of appearances which was determined by the spatio-temporal form of apprehension would 'gradually dwindle into nothing' leaving the realm of spirit and of freedom.[112] Rather than being mere forms of possible experience, as they were for Kant, the a prioris became objects of a possible cognition (*Erkenntnis*) founded on reason's self-confidence, a confidence which no scepticism could shake.[113] Reason was thus endowed with its own form of knowledge which rested on 'obscure and deep feelings of truth'.[114] Behind the world of appearances the human being was thus granted access to an 'imperishable understanding of the essence of things'.[115] Thus, for Fries, the religious a priori was 'the same *a priori* with which we guarantee the reality of a tree, of a headache, of certainty and of God'.[116] Such perception was patently not of the same kind as that perception of objects in the natural world, but was, according to Otto, nevertheless real:

Whoever sees a landscape through a mist does not cognise absolutely nothing—he is not dreaming and it is no *fata morgana* that he beholds; he cognises the landscape itself, and his cognition (*Erkenntnis*) has validity, albeit conditioned. And if he knows further what mist is, and how this affects his vision, so he also cognises the fact of his limitations and can escape these limitations when he can imagine what traits are absent from the perfect knowledge (viz. greyness and haziness) even if he cannot himself positively supply the additions.[117]

Bousset could similarly affirm that 'in the spiritual possession of this higher idea of reason we have the courage to speak of this whole world of nature: you are only an appearance of a deeper reality'. In short, he goes on, 'there is no more powerful weapon against the a priori of naturalism'.[118]

On this view, the misty access to the realm of things-in-themselves overcame the Third Antinomy as a fact 'known of Reason' yet 'incapable of

---

[110] *JFR*, 35; ET, 19.   [111] Bousset, foreword to *Julius und Evagoras*, p. vi.
[112] *JFR*, 41; ET, 26.   [113] *JFR*, 115; ET, 51 f.
[114] *JFR*, 120; ET, 58 f. There is something implausible about E. Lessing's judgement that Otto had rectified Troeltsch's emphasis on the primacy of knowledge in religion ('Die Bedeutung des religiösen Apriori', 355).
[115] *JFR*, 66 f.; ET, 127.
[116] *JFR*, 35; ET, 19. Cf. Bousset, foreword to *Julius und Evagoras*, p. xxiv.
[117] *JFR*, 128; ET, 67.   [118] Bousset, foreword to *Julius und Evagoras*, p. xxv.

proof',[119] where the spatio-temporal world was transcended.[120] This form of knowing (*cognoscere*)[121] had absolutely nothing in common with knowledge (*scientia*) limited by space and time, but was rather conferred by '"pure apperception", by the I-consciousness which guarantees the spiritual substance as distinct from the material'.[122] It was a 'sentiment and obscure conception' or *Ahndung*[123] (a mode of knowledge guaranteed by feeling (*Gefühl*)), a 'cognizance in an unconceptional [*sic*] or preconceptional [*sic*] way ... apart from sensual or conceptual cognizances', and thus a mode of apprehension quite distinct also from faith (*Glaube*), which abandons all witnesses of the senses and scientific knowledge (*Wissen*)'.[124] Thus, according to Otto:

Feeling gives a third manner of cognition alongside knowledge and faith which combines the two and brings them to a unity. Under the power of the dark feelings of the beautiful and the sublime in all its forms in natural and spiritual life we understand immediately the eternal in the temporal and the temporal as an appearance of the eternal.[125]

The a prioris were no longer mere forms but could be experienced in a manner akin to aesthetic feeling; they were, as it were, 'schematised' in the secret places of the mind where 'eternal reality broke through the veil of temporality'.[126]

According to Otto, Fries' philosophy had profound implications for the contemporary tasks of the philosophy of religion: no longer was it to be conceived as a supernatural form of physics conferring proofs for theological

---

[119] *JFR*, 132; ET, 68. For Otto's conception of the religious proof of the religious a priori, see Gotthart Nygren, 'Die Religionsphilosophie Rudolf Ottos', esp. 96. Cf. Bousset 'Anwendung', 476: 'We recognize that our sensual organization pulls a veil across the ultimate and deepest reality which we are never in a position to remove. But we can at least recognize that a veil lies across the object of our knowledge and indirectly perceive the deeper reality, that we are made conscious of the boundaries and limitations of our cognitions according to our understanding and then again sublimated in thought'.

[120] *JFR*, 140 f.; ET, 81 f.

[121] Cf. Otto's notes on the English translation, in Schütte, *Religion und Christentum in der Theologie Rudolf Ottos*, 125.

[122] *JFR*, 144; ET, 85.

[123] This is a rather archaic form of the modern German word '*Ahnung*'. This latter word is used throughout *JFR*. In *Das Heilige*, however, Otto reverts to Fries' '*Ahndung*'.

[124] Otto remarks that *Ahnung* is 'not so much "man's deepest longing and need" as a *Gefühl* ... It comes very near to what I have described in the Idea of the Holy as "divination"' (notes on the English translation in Schütte, *Religion und Christentum in der Theologie Rudolf Ottos*, 124 f.).

[125] *JFR*, 159; ET, 100 f.

[126] *JFR*, 152; ET, 93. On Otto's use of 'schemata' see esp. John P. Reeder, 'The Relation of the Moral and the Numinous in Otto's Notion of the Holy'; and Davidson, *Rudolf Otto's Interpretation of Religion*, 188. The latter is particularly critical of Otto's failure adequately to differentiate between the highest good and the holy, which at times both seem to function as the a priori basis of religion.

knowledge in a manner equivalent to that of the natural sciences, but rather it was a science of the outworkings of the eternal in the temporal, as they were dimly perceived in the cognition of feeling.[127] There was thus an immediate perception of the unity of all things, which created 'a feeling of peculiar satisfaction', of the unity of the human being and God.[128] In Fries, all that was lacking, according to Otto, was an adequate application of philosophy to historical religion, which manifested itself in a variety of forms as different from one another as the 'human being is from the tortoise',[129] yet, as de Wette brilliantly showed, he nevertheless provided the resources for such an application. How and where the highest forms of religion express themselves was determined by the 'free judging power of feeling', which in turn was 'only possible after the philosophy of religion has provided the basis and the guiding threads for the whole undertaking'.[130]

Fries' philosophy continued to provide the basis for Otto's later influential work, *Das Heilige*, and for his comparative studies of religion. Indeed throughout the whole of his career Otto characterized the essence of religion as an 'immediate feeling'[131] or the apprehension of the 'numinous' (that 'immediate, underivable judgement of pure recognition that follows a premise that defies exposition and springs directly from an irreducible experience of the truth').[132] Thus, whether Otto was talking of the recognition of 'the holy' as an a priori category (as in *Das Heilige*) or of the epistemological security of the unity of all a priori categories (as in *JFR*), his theory identified, albeit mysteriously,[133] the numinous, the thing-in-itself, with the natural

---

[127] *JFR*, 159; ET, 101. Cf. *Mysticism East and West*, 244–7.   [128] *JFR*, 230; ET, 133.

[129] *JFR*, 240; ET, 146.   [130] *JFR*, 240; ET, 146.

[131] Cf. *Gottheit und Gottheiten der Arier*, 4: 'religion is that disposition of the mind characterized through feelings of a peculiar sort, which have analogies to feelings in other arenas and continually combine with them in many ways, but which are nevertheless qualitatively different and cannot be derived from the others'.

[132] *The Idea of the Holy*, ET, 187. The picture of Christ presented in *The Kingdom of God and the Son of Man* is similarly dominated by the 'numinous nimbus' (164) which surrounds the historical figure. This marks the breaking in of the eschatological realm to the present, the subsequent ecclesiastical allegorizations of which are mere trivializations (375 f.). It is interesting to note that the picture of Christ in *Life and Ministry of Jesus* of 1902 was already imbued with 'the faculty of divination of particularly gifted natures' (33). The heroic qualities of Christ in the earlier work (84) are transformed into the charismatic and numinous qualities in the latter. The continuity of purpose is emphasized by Philip C. Almond, 'Rudolf Otto and the Kantian tradition', esp. 52–5. Otto expressed his continuing commitment to Friesianism in 1923 in a conversation with R. F. Davidson (*Rudolf Otto's Interpretation of Religion*, 134 n.2). Søren Holm, however (in 'Apriori und Urphänomen bei Rudolf Otto'), emphasizes the discontinuity between the conceptions of the a priori in *JFR* and *Das Heilige*.

[133] Cf. Troeltsch's review of *Das Heilige*, 'Zur Religionsphilosophie' (1918/21), 75: 'Otto confirms my thesis that modern philosophy of religion and theology stand much closer in their scientific thought to spirituality than to objective theology, the word and authority of Luther, or the natural religion of the Enlightenment'.

character of objects and not merely as a form of possible perception. The double-sided character of reality to which Kant gave expression in the Third Antinomy is overcome in the experienced unity of all that exists in the knowledge guaranteed by dark feeling or *Ahnung*.

The A Priori and the Historical Method: Wilhelm Bousset's Response to Troeltsch

Wilhelm Bousset, in his attempt to answer the question of 'how, in the midst of a comparative and all-embracing conception of history, norms and a normative conception of reality could be found',[134] developed ideas that had been merely hinted at by Otto:

> We are once again searching for the 'religious *a priori*' from all directions. Supernaturalism and the historical method (*Historismus*) refuse to renounce a criterion and a principle for truth in religion. History of religion becomes a Leviathan. But how will it succeed in moving from a mere description of religions to being a science of religion, if it is nothing other than a history of religion? . . . Indeed, how can it even be a history of religion unless it already possesses a principle, even if only dimly seen, according to which one selects, not to say classifies, the historical subject matter.[135]

For Bousset, the historical sciences, which treated the history of religion in the same manner as any other phenomenon, thrust theology into a great dilemma: on the one hand, the acceptance of a thoroughgoing historical method 'liberated more and more from special Christian presuppositions' by such scholars as Wrede and Wellhausen had created a 'feeling of insecurity' which, when taken to its extreme by materialists like Kautsky and monists like Arthur Drews, could lead to a 'denial of the historicity of Jesus and the dissolution of Christianity into a complex of historical religious connections'. On the other hand, however, the practical systematic 'theology of mediation' of the Ritschlian School had 'in principle denied an adequate scientific knowledge in matters of religion and Christianity and replaced it with a practical-religious value judgement'.[136]

Bousset sought a way out of this dilemma which would 'free us from the consequences of a strong conservatism and respect for the products of history on the one side, and the tired scepticism where everything is dissolved in relativism on the other'.[137] Neither Herrmann's evasion of history nor Troeltsch's relativist historicism offered satisfactory answers; instead

---

[134] 'Anwendung', 429.   [135] *JFR*, 32; ET, 17.

[136] 'Anwendung', 427 f. Cf. Davidson, *Rudolf Otto's Interpretation of Religion*, 92 f.: The quest for the religious a priori, the numinous, was nothing short of the 'urge to escape the impotence and profaneness of finite human existence'.

[137] Foreword to *Julius und Evagoras*, p. xxv.

Bousset sought a third position which offered a 'universal a priori element'[138] as 'a secure foundation against modern empiricism and evolutionism'.[139] Bousset thus viewed Troeltsch, with his teleological historical philosophy of religion which allowed only for approximations to the truth but never for a full perception of the truth, as unable to provide that sense of epistemological security demanded by the absolute claims of religion.[140] He thus demanded a return to 'universally rational elements in what we call religion' with the same epistemological status as the principle of causality in the natural sciences.[141] Thus, against Troeltsch's interpretation of Lessing's maxim, 'the historical serves only for illustration, never for demonstration', Bousset sought an a priori not in the unknowable future or goal of history, but in the knowable present, since 'history cannot reveal the last meaning of life'.[142]

The basis for such a solution had been provided by Fries, 'who up till now has been little more than a name to the younger generation of theologians',[143] and, although 'it might seem a strange enterprise to recommend to theology the return to a half-dead philosophy and a half-forgotten name',[144] Bousset nevertheless saw him as deepening the 'deepest thought of the *Critique of Judgement* . . . by bridging the gap between the eternal and the finite in feelings which belong necessarily to our being'.[145] Thus in *Ahnung* religion became alive as eternity was grasped in history.[146] In short, Bousset maintains: 'If one wants to indicate the service that Fries has had or could have for theology, then one can say that the separation between theoretical and practical reason is overcome and religious ideas are shown to be a necessary part of one undivided reason'.[147] It was consequently in the sphere of the philosophy of history that 'Fries' philosophy can be used for the service of today's people'.[148]

For Bousset, the flux of development into which Troeltsch had plunged religion became an intolerable accommodation to the growing edifice of historical (and consequently relative) knowledge, which could serve only to mask the absolute truth of religion. A historical a priori could only ever lead to 'historicism (*Historizismus*) and empirical psychologism'.[149] Thus Bousset asserts:

To answer the question of the a priori of religion in human spiritual life is at the same time a justification of religion; and with all this we find ourselves in the arena of pure

---

[138] 'Anwendung', 431.
[139] Letter from Bousset to Otto of 3 December 1916, in Schütte, *Religion und Christentum in der Theologie Rudolf Ottos*, 127 f., here 127.
[140] 'Anwendung', 471.   [141] Ibid., 432 f.
[142] Foreword to *Julius und Evagoras*, p. xxv.   [143] 'Anwendung', 420. Cf. 488, 422.
[144] Ibid., 427.   [145] Ibid., 481 f. Cf. foreword to *Julius und Evagoras*, p. xxvii.
[146] 'Anwendung', 486.   [147] Ibid., 472.
[148] Foreword to *Julius und Evagoras*, p. xxv.   [149] 'Anwendung', 433.

philosophical investigation, whereby all pure empirical-historical elements must ultimately be excluded.[150]

The possibility of a direct access to a reality beyond 'everything historical and everything individual' offered a 'storm-free arena' which would overcome the uncertainties of Troeltsch's theology, which, Bousset claimed, 'has not completed the return to Kant's rational method strongly enough and which has exchanged the rationalism of Kant for strong historical-empirical elements'.[151] Thus Bousset offered a very different view of Kant's contribution to theology: instead of locating the religious a priori as the goal to which history was proceeding as it gradually conformed more and more to its rational core and which served to limit all human attempts to realize absolute religion, Bousset dislocated the a priori from this teleological basis. He saw the a priori of religion not as the goal, but as the unification of the future with the present in the atemporal realm of direct apprehension of the thing-in-itself. Thus, although Bousset agreed with Troeltsch that the historical could never embody the rational, he removed the teleological basis of this statement, thus devaluing the historical as a necessary factor in any religion. Bousset instead created a 'storm-free arena' for direct apprehension of absolute truth.[152]

This direct apprehension of the absolute was not, however, to be equated with the 'pathological' response of mysticism whereby the individual was granted a direct knowledge of God.[153] Rather, a mysterious unity felt within ourselves, and not any mystical unity sensed within the spatio-temporal world, led to the moment of religious certitude. Fries' philosophy thus provided the 'deepest foundation for reality by directing us with all our questions to ourselves and to research the laws of our spiritual being. It teaches: look to yourself and nowhere else, where you will find the fundament of your being'.[154] Thus, Bousset goes on, 'the miraculous in the deeper sense of the word, the miracle of the individual spiritual life, still exists for us',[155] and the depths of the individual human soul become the very heart of 'the Gospel [which] proclaims [a] God who in the first instance seeks and desires the individual human soul'.[156] In short, Bousset concluded: 'These researches lead man to the depths of his own being and demand this of him: affirm the depths of your own life'.[157]

---

[150] 'Anwendung', 435f.   [151] Ibid., 436.   [152] Ibid.

[153] Thus 'against the turbulent character of Anglo-American Christianity', Bousset asserts that he holds fast to 'Ritschl's battle against all mysticism . . . which is a task taken over by Herrmann, and which, indeed, is his greatest service to religion' ('Anwendung', 487).

[154] Foreword to *Julius und Evagoras*, p. xx.   [155] Bousset, *What is Religion?*, 287.

[156] Bousset, *Unser Gottesglaube*, 20.

[157] 'Anwendung', 479. Cf. Foreword to *Julius und Evagoras*, p. xix.

In a lecture on the meaning of the historical Jesus for faith, Bousset applied his Friesian method to Christology, where he suggested that 'if history is taken seriously and sustainedly, then it shows that it leads beyond itself, and compels us to search for another basis outside of it, and that is—in Reason'.[158] He later remarked: 'as soon as mankind has reached the highest stage of prophetic religion which strives after universalism, reason raises its head in religion'.[159] Consequently, the Friesian 'storm-free arena' could answer even the most radical historical criticism. Thus, Bousset claimed, 'if science were to pronounce the most extreme verdict that Jesus had not existed, faith cannot be lost as it touches us with its eternal basis; the Gospel picture of Jesus nevertheless remains, even though it is merely great poetry, the poetry of eternally symbolic meaning'.[160] The Jesus of history became the 'highest symbol of an eternal world'[161] but could never be equated with that world. In short, 'the great religious personality does not only create symbols of faith, but himself becomes a symbol for the community of faith'.[162] Under the power of such symbols the 'inconceivable' naked truths of reason were clothed with temporal symbols. Thus, just as the concept of causality was used for thousands of years before it was ever conceptualized, so in religion the religious a priori was for a long time hidden beneath primitive symbolic forms. The symbol made the rational kernel alive, it 'gives the skeleton flesh and blood', but it could never fully reveal this kernel, which could be known only in the immediacy of feeling in the cognition of *Ahnung*.[163]

The Clash between Fries and Kant

Even though he claimed to be 'not remotely personally hurt'[164] by Bousset's discussion of the religious a priori, Troeltsch was disappointed that his friend should have gone so readily into print, without even a discussion of the matter beforehand. Although he recognized that 'many difficulties continue to lurk in my still unfinished investigations',[165] Troeltsch defended the rational character of his system in response to Bousset's charge of historicism, asserting that 'however anti-intellectual the decision is, it is no act of chance or mere taste; rather it introduces the feeling of objective necessity into all subjectivity'.[166]

[158] Bousset, *Die Bedeutung der Person Jesu für den Glauben*, 10.
[159] Bousset, 'Religion und Theologie', 33.
[160] Bousset, *Die Bedeutung der Person Jesu*, 17.   [161] Ibid., 14.   [162] Ibid., 16.
[163] 'Anwendung', 479 f.
[164] Troeltsch, letter to Bousset of 14 December 1909, in 'Briefe aus der Heidelberger Zeit an Wilhelm Bousset' (G1976/2), 45 f.
[165] Troeltsch, letter to Bousset (G1976/2), 45 f.
[166] Troeltsch, 'Logos und Mythos' (A1913/8a), 821.

Ultimately, however, Troeltsch could not agree with Bousset:

I cannot leave history, as I cannot find the courage to affirm decisively a dim rationalism. I've obviously thought further about this matter but without being compelled to give up my interest in history and psychology.[167]

Although recognizing that Bousset's rationalism moved beyond the vagaries of history, and while admitting that he found it 'quite exciting,' Troeltsch nevertheless remarked that 'along with this the Christian character of religion is lost'.[168] Indeed he claims that it was nothing more than

passing chance that rational truths are united with the person of Jesus, and thus the difficulties of historical research into this object are allowed to fall . . . [T]his is nothing more than the crystallization of a religion of reason out of traditional Christianity, and the loss of all media, piety, cult, imagination, and feeling for the concrete and historical . . . If one does not feed a religion of reason with impressions from concrete life and banishes it to the universally valid, one ends up with a formalism, and one gets universal laws in place of a living Godhead. That, however, is an inversion of actual religion.[169]

Troeltsch openly conceded that he had not succeeded in clearly uniting the streams of the historical and the rational. Instead he tended 'strongly towards an anti-rationalistic affirmation of life, with which the rationalistic currents of my thought can only be united with the greatest difficulty. I have up till now held back from this position. I believe I can no longer achieve a philosophical or theological theory which will solve the difficulties of the situation'.[170] Although he may not have been able to offer any neat alternative to Bousset's Friesianism, Troeltsch at least recognized that Bousset failed to do justice to the historical vitalities of the Christian religion.

Bousset's 'storm-free' solution to the problems of faith and history provoked bitter reaction from other theologians, chiefly because what had begun as a useful apologetic device had become, in Bousset, a device to overcome history, which had profound dogmatic implications for a historical religion. Probably the most vitriolic debate ever to have occupied the pages of the *Zeitschrift für Theologie und Kirche* was that provoked by Bousset's review of Otto in the *Theologischer Rundschau*. It was initiated by Troeltsch's student Karl Bornhausen,[171] who criticized Otto and Bousset for their attempts to repristinate Fries. 'Our culture', he remarked, 'is too bland for

---

[167] Troeltsch, letter to Bousset (G1976/2), 45 f.   [168] Ibid., 46.   [169] Ibid.
[170] Ibid.
[171] Karl Bornhausen (1882–1940), from 1911 *PD* and from 1916 Prof. at Marburg; from 1919 Prof. at Breslau; from 1933 Prof. at Frankfurt am Main. Bornhausen played a vital role in the relationships between American and German theologians before the First World War. He was an active and often vituperative participant in many theological debates. After the First World War he became increasingly attracted by *völkisch* ideology, joining the *NSDAP* in 1932. See esp. Manfred Marquardt, 'Karl Bornhausen'.

heroes'.[172] Despite its claims to be returning to a corrected form of Kantianism, Otto's system was, according to Bornhausen, a form of empiricism which destroyed the purity of Kant's reason.[173] Indeed the Friesian position no longer deserved the name of Kantianism, since 'if one correctly grasps the Kantian a priori position, then the worthlessness of such a world of being for human reason is made apparent'.[174]

In another discussion article of the same year Bornhausen compared Troeltsch and Otto, remarking that 'for Troeltsch the noumenal is still other, whereas for Otto it has become identified with the natural character of things'.[175] He went on to, claim that, although 'Otto might appear to have created the unity of the a priori, he had in fact destroyed religion by giving it purely psychological foundations'.[176] Thus the transcendental question 'is a question as to the form of knowledge—how is it possible? The psychological [or in Friesian terms, the anthropological] question is a question as to the content of knowledge—of what does it consist?'[177] This was, according to Bornhausen, a grave confusion of Kantianism: the importance of the Kantian categories rested not in the realm of things-in-themselves, but in the limitations they gave to human thought. The idea that they could be grounded psychologically was quite anathema to Kant, and in reality was 'a naïve repetition of the realism of the empiricists which lessened none of their errors'.[178] In a bold statement, Bornhausen claimed that Otto's attempt to get behind the idea to a misty perception of the thing-in-itself 'smashed idealism in the face'.[179]

Bornhausen's greatest criticism, however, was reserved for Bousset's separation of reason from history, which would, he claimed, mean that religion would 'lose contact with ethics'.[180] A religion located purely in the individual's soul seemed to lose its connection with the historical world and thus with ethical activity. Indeed, in a provocative statement, Bornhausen went as far as accusing Bousset of mysticism, since cognition divorced from any interest in the historical realm 'would hover in the air'.[181] In short, he maintained, 'the human being is not given psychologically but is revealed historically'.[182] Instead of a vague feeling of psychological security, Bornhausen

[172] Bornhausen, 'Wider den Neofriesianismus', 345.   [173] Ibid., 353.
[174] Ibid., 356.   [175] Bornhausen, 'Das religiöse Apriori', 201.   [176] Ibid.
[177] Bornhausen, 'Wider den Neofriesianismus', 364.   [178] Ibid., 366.
[179] Ibid., 367. Cf. 'Das religiöse Apriori', 202. In reviewing Otto's *Das Heilige*, in 1918, Troeltsch made an identical criticism. Otto's mistake was his belief that 'strong norms' could be obtained from experience alone. Such a theory 'leads back to Hume . . . The pure psychological and anthropological has little or nothing to do with the Kantian doctrine of the critical *a priori*, that is, with inner necessity and validity' ('Zur Religionsphilosophie' (A1918/21), 70). Such a philosophy might mean that the 'labyrinth of metaphysics' could be avoided, but was essentially 'the formal elevation of the philosophy of religion and the theology of rationalism' (74).
[180] Bornhausen, 'Wider den Neofriesianismus', 387.   [181] Ibid., 397.
[182] Bornhausen, 'Das religiöse Apriori', 204.

searched for a stream which flows from the divine, which alone could ground ethical behaviour and give shape to history.[183] He thus asserted that:

the speculative tasks of religion at present are without doubt in the cautious development of the philosophy of history . . . The rational character of religion is not to be clarified psychologically but rather psychology and history are to be evaluated epistemologically on the basis of the Kantian a priori: this is the contemporary task for a systematic theology which makes use of philosophy.[184]

In conclusion, he went on: 'Psychologism, neo-Friesianism comes too late; time has moved on. The next great decisive battle for philosophy and religion will be fought on the ground of the philosophy of history.'[185]

Bousset's reply to Bornhausen,[186] which must count as one of the most vituperative articles ever to have been published in a theological journal, began by accusing him of a failure to read Fries and of 'massive polemics rather than a concerted attempt to understand the opponent'.[187] Attempting to show that he had a far greater understanding of the primary sources, Bousset built up a complicated argument around a misunderstood possessive pronoun which, whatever its justification, did little to counter Bornhausen's case.[188] All that Bousset was prepared to concede was that the psychological method was not Kant's, but there was no question of rejecting Fries until his opponent came up with something better. Thus Bousset concluded:

It is very seldom that I have come across such a critical writing as Bornhausen's 'Wider den Neofriesianismus,' which has done so little justice to its opponent, and which swarms with such numerous and basic misunderstandings, especially when the conditions for understanding had been so clearly given by like-minded researches. Bornhausen's ability to study strange currents of thought, which he has already proved elsewhere, allows us to hope that he might make good the blunders of his polemic, which might then give us the opportunity for a discussion which might actually further the debate.[189]

Not unreasonably, the editors of the *Zeitschrift für Theologie und Kirche* gave Bornhausen, who was evidently deeply hurt by the assault from such a senior figure, the opportunity to respond to Bousset's accusations:

Professor Bousset has personally laid bare his heart and soul in the defence of neo-Friesianism given here. Only seldom in the course of his discussion does he lose my lesser person from his sight.[190]

---

[183] Bornhausen, 'Wider den Neofriesianismus', 404 f.
[184] Bornhausen, 'Das religiöse Apriori', 205.
[185] Bornhausen, 'Wider den Neofriesianismus', 405.
[186] Wilhelm Bousset, 'In Sachen des Neofriesianismus, i. Wider unsern Kritiker'.
[187] Ibid., 145.   [188] Ibid., 149.   [189] Ibid., 159.
[190] Bornhausen, 'Duplik des Kritikers', 159.

However, Bornhausen found it difficult to comprehend the personal offence taken by Bousset: his article was merely intended as one of a series which entered into constructive debate with another thinker. Bousset, who intended to bring the matter to close, had admittedly succeeded, but only by default, since there was now no possibility that any constructive debate could continue. With an air of pathos, Bornhausen once again entered into discussion with Bousset, but asked, 'Have we chosen the best place for a battle?'

He again criticized the psychological method:

Whoever searches for pure a priori knowledge with a psychological or anthropological beginning; whoever believes he can ... thus possess the 'true being of things', the things-in-themselves, sees nothing more than spectres by the clear light of day. He has failed to understand Kant and does not have the right to dress himself up with this name.[191]

Fries' words might be very close to Kant, Bornhausen went on, but 'his thoughts are very distant'.[192] Indeed, he was far closer to English empiricism than to Kant himself. Bornhausen continued by asserting the need to return to a genuine Kantianism, to the 'simplicity and security' of Kantian cognition by which alone the 'freedom of the living spirit can be won; to make the self-consciousness of man, with his creative strivings for knowledge, the basis of our culture is the immediate task of systematic theology. Thus I had the duty to begin with the Kantian critical concept of knowledge in my attack on Fries and thus I have the right also to finish with it'.[193] The importance of Kant rested in his critical method, which defined human limitations but also allowed for a continual criticism of the past and thus a progress to a better understanding of the rational basis of all things. Bousset's 'storm-free arena', with its immediate cognition of such a rational basis, robbed humanity of the chance of this (admittedly stormy) progress. Thus Bornhausen concluded:

'Begone with this idle talk of orthodoxy and dogmatics'. Was Galileo orthodox when he saw that the earth went around the sun? And just as the earth orbits the sun, so the world of appearances revolves around human reason. In this pithy innocence and greatness the law of Kantian critical knowledge stands before us. To make this in future into the common possession of mankind is the task which neo-Friesianism has not been able to obscure.[194]

There are few debates in theological journals which provoke a written apology from the editors; however, Wilhelm Herrmann and Martin Rade felt compelled to respond to Bousset's vitriol. They were critical not of neo-Friesianism *per se*, but of the sort of neo-Friesianism which accused

---

[191] Ibid., 165.   [192] Ibid., 164.   [193] Ibid., 165.   [194] Ibid.

Bornhausen of ignorance and misunderstanding. Thus they state: 'Whoever "methodically" misunderstands will not be able to dismiss the charge of not being scientific for very long'.[195] They then went on to suggest that perhaps the philosophical press was the best place for debate on the relative merits of Kant and Fries. With this the discussion was brought to a close.

HISTORY AND ETHICS

The last two chapters have shown that in German theology in the first two decades of the twentieth century Kant's philosophy functioned as a screen behind which profound theological debates were fought out. Three points emerge which are of importance for the survival of theological ethics in the face of the development of the historical method: first, it is clear that under the threat of naturalism and materialism theology was forced to respond with a rigorous defence of the scientific credibility of religion and of its own methods. Kant's philosophy, with its abundance of possible theological applications, was a natural apologetic resource. Secondly, however, it is also clear that Kant could provide the weaponry for the most diverse dogmatic interpretations of Christianity. Kantianism was used not merely to defend religion but also, by those who followed Herrmann, to isolate it from science, and thus to relegate it to apologetic impotence and scientific incredulity. Finally, even amongst those who borrowed Kant's terminology for the defence of religion against naturalism there was dogmatic conflict: a modified form of Kantianism even suggested to some, notably Bousset, the possibility of an escape from historical relativism. This too had severe ethical consequences.

Troeltsch's teleological religious a priori, which appeared to many to be closely 'bound up with the destiny of an epoch' long since past,[196] seems on closer analysis, however, to be a genuine search for reconciliation between spirit and nature, and thus it continues to allow for the ethical transformation of the historical world. His combination of realism and optimism, where there can be no easy solutions within history, no immediate perception of absolute truth, but where nevertheless there is always the hope that history might be moving to its goal, perhaps better reflects the continued need not to escape or to evade but to transform history; that is, to discipline it ethically. For Troeltsch, it is the dare to accept the meaningfulness of history that ultimately provides the justification for religion. Human life is not to be denied in a deeper life of faith, but is given hope as the goal of history,

[195] Hermann and Rade, 'In Sachen des Neofriesianismus, iii. Nachwort der Redaktion', 165.
[196] Ruth Schlesinger, *Probleme eines religiösen Apriori*, 72.

the 'religious a priori', empowering the human being to shape a future which will gradually resemble a picture of reality viewed *sub specie aeternitatis*. Such hope, however, does not usurp the realism that recognizes that no present construct, however sacred and however profound, can ever be completely identified with the absolute. As he wrote in his review of Theodor Kaftan: 'the absolute is with God, all human truth is relative. All we can have is approximation'.[197] The next chapter shows in detail how Troeltsch developed this theme into a fully-fledged ethical theology, as he sought to put historical flesh on his philosophy of religion and history.

---

[197] Review of Kaftan (A1912/8), col. 728.

7

Re-Establishing the Unified Vision: Troeltsch's Ethical Theology

'DEVOTION TO THE FACTS'

It should by now be clear that Troeltsch was concerned first and foremost with the unification of all aspects of reality: in particular religion was not to be separated from history, but had to gain concrete expression in the real world. As has already been suggested in the course of this book, one of the key problems confronting theologians in the rapidly changing social and economic conditions at the turn of the twentieth century was that of social integration within the ethical constraints of the modern world. The weaknesses noted in both Herrmann's theological dualism and Bousset's direct apprehension of the eternal are fundamentally ethical: for them both, the reality of the historical world is of a quite different kind from that of the religious world. Consequently ethical transformation becomes at the very least questionable. For Troeltsch, and for others who sought to maintain a unified vision of reality in the face of both theological and antichristian opposition, however, there was a continued need to reassert the possibility of Christian transformation of the historical world. Only then would Christianity become a potent ethical force.

The Christian religion had therefore to be clear about the historical conditions within which it was working. Part of the task of theology was thus to describe the modern world and in turn what differentiated this world from the past. Only after this descriptive task could the construction be attempted: the broader social and political context thus determined the possibilities for theological action. Theology could therefore neither clamour for the impossible nor invent its facts. Indeed, if the *facts* of the modern world were ignored, constructive theology would be confined to the realms of the impossible, and religion would be discarded on the dustheap of irrelevance. In many ways, this was what Troeltsch regarded as the major fault of those who sought a distinctive theological epistemology.

Theology could only provide a realistic unified vision for the modern world once the phenomenon of modernity with its constraints and possibilities was understood. The theologian was thus forced into economic, social, and political analysis. Such 'untheological' tasks provided the factual basis for the theological response to modernity. Reality was thus not an invention of religion but functioned as a constraint. Consequently without some form of assessment of its limitations religion would be deprived of any *possibility* for action and thus robbed of its chance to change and reshape the world. On this model, the preliminary task of theology was thus essentially historical and descriptive: yet this was not the 'historical theology' which formed the subject matter for Schleiermacher's theologian. Rather than an account of the historical state of the Church and its doctrines, it was an account of the prevailing social and cultural conditions within which theology had to work. A *realistic* theology thus required a thorough submersion in the modern world, and only then could there be criticism and construction in terms of higher ends.

Troeltsch was paradigmatic among theologians concerned with theological analysis of modernity, seeking theological responses to what he called the 'great fact' of the modern world. Thus he asked, in an important programmatic essay written in 1907: 'what are the characteristic fundamental currents of the modern world?'[1] And in another essay written in the same year he claimed:

An epoch that truly understands itself . . . can act with respect to itself only if it furthers what is great and recognizes the dangers of this task . . . Nothing is left but to adapt ourselves to the given, which from all appearances is very far from exhausting its vital powers, and, to repeat this principle, devotedly to further the elements of greatness and to counteract the dangers with ever vigilant self-criticism.[2]

Although he engaged in an extraordinary range of studies which embraced many different academic disciplines, and although much of his work was unsystematic, sometimes highly polemical, and often ephemeral, it would be wrong to assume that his work lacks unifying threads.[3] His overriding interest, which permeates nearly all his published work and unpublished lectures, is in the theological, philosophical, and ethical response to modernity and the concomitant breakdown of what he regarded as the unified

---

[1] 'Autonomie und Rationalismus' (A1907/11), col. 199.

[2] 'Das Wesen des modernen Geistes' (A1907/8b), 337; ET, 272.

[3] Although Troeltsch expressed his desire to write a systematic theology and a philosophy of religion on a number of occasions (*Briefe an Friedrich von Hügel, 1901–1923* (G1974/1), 63, 93; *The Absoluteness* (A1901/23d), ET, 43), his failure to produce a systematic theology or philosophy creates a problem for interpreters and has recently been dubbed the 'Troeltsch–problem' by Yasukata (*Systematic Theologian*, p. xiii). Although the task is difficult, I would agree with H. R. Niebuhr, who, in his doctoral dissertation, wrote that 'to collect and systematize, as best we can, is the best possible way of understanding [Troeltsch's] thought as a whole' ('Ernst Troeltsch's Philosophy of Religion', 11).

conception of Church and society which had undergirded earlier stages of European history. Thus as late as 1921 he wrote that it is only a thorough 'devotion to objects, to firm truth, exact observation, and gallant achievement . . . [that] allows a personality to develop'.[4]

On occasion Troeltsch offered relatively succinct accounts of his theological programme, which provide a useful point of departure.[5] Thus in 1907 he wrote:

The theologian, whose concerns are the formation of ethical and religious ideas for the present, finds himself confronted with one great fact: that the 'modern world' has created new foundations and presuppositions by which it is differentiated from the ecclesiastically unified period of European culture. If his theology is to apply to the modern human being, and if it is to be expressed using the presuppositions of its own time, then his chief task is to clarify the nature of this transformation [of the world], with its lasting achievements, and to construct his ethical and religious thought upon it. Both of these conditions will be the case when the labourer himself is convinced of the truth and the necessity of that fundamental change [which characterizes the modern world].[6]

Of primary importance for Troeltsch was thus the analysis of the modern world and the recognition of its irreversibility. Later in the same essay he went on to contrast the present with the past:

Instead of authority and humble self-abnegation [there is] a reliance on individual conviction and personal devotion. But individual conviction and personal devotion do not yield a rational body of thought which is everywhere identical, but merely an individual and subjective attitude to what has been handed down. [Theology requires] criticism of the tradition, the balancing of religious ideas with the rest of life which is ever changing, as well as its inclusion in a broader perspective with new practical and theoretical problems and a wider comparison with other religions and free metaphysical speculations. [This leads to the recognition] that there are many possibilities in the different positions and also to the rejection of what is no longer compatible with advances in knowledge. Certain aspects of foreign religions, together with other elements of culture, are forged with religion . . . However, in such a task, the point of departure always remains in the given constitution of the mind, in the religion that has been handed down to us which cannot be denied or replaced, altered or conserved. What characterizes all this is still the striving forward from what is given to obtain the most comprehensive knowledge possible of the whole sphere of religion and ultimately to take a position towards this in an irrational spontaneous value judgement. If this analysis of the powers of history leads to a strong affirmation of Christianity or shows its decisive importance, it is against the

---

[4] *Der Berg der Läuterung* (A1921/11), 13.

[5] e.g. 'Meine Bücher' (A1921/29b), 11; ET, 371–2; review of Günther, *Die Grundlagen der Religionsphilosophie Troeltschs* (A1916/22), cols. 448–50; review of Theodor Kaftan, *Ernst Tröltsch. Eine kritische Zeitstudie* (A1912/8), cols. 724–8.

[6] 'Autonomie und Rationalismus' (A1907/11), col. 199.

whole spirit of the modern era. Autonomy can be very revolutionary but also very conservative. [Such conservatism] is justified in respect of religion if in fact the eth- ical and religious powers of Christianity have this decisive importance, and if the modern world has brought forth no greater revelation of life. If it is affirmed [that there is no greater revelation] then theology will be understood as something which forms the religious idea out of the historical material whatever else might appear alongside[7]

Any application of the theological tradition thus had to work within the con- straints of modernity, and most crucially its discovery of human autonomy.

Troeltsch clearly distinguished the different strands of opposition to his thought, and in doing so offered a partial explanation of the circumstances of his own thought. In another essay, written in 1916 as a review of one of his early commentators, W. Günther, he once more outlined his own pro- gramme, again emphasizing his 'devotion' to the facts:

There is then nothing left but to work from the concretely given, to ask how an increasing and ever-expanding knowledge of the religious world allows us to assert the basic currents of our religious world, and to ask how far these basic currents are theoretically and practically related to the modern world. This is not the question of an absolute logical truth, but rather the question as to the possibility of maintaining the root of western religion, and the possibility of further development out of this root, in order to tackle the problems of the current situation.[8]

He went on to suggest that all aspects of his work were guided by the attempt 'to connect the positive factual to the inner logic of development, or better, to a divine ground of life, and bring the mere continuation of the trad- itional substance of life into a universal context; that is, into our theoretical and practical picture of life. That is what is basic in my position . . . My theory might have its failings, but the intention is correct.'[9] On the basis of his sociological, philosophical, and historical analysis of reality, Troeltsch thus claims to be setting about attempting a further development of religion in frank interaction with the forces of the modern world. He made this clear in another systematic essay, written in 1917 as a review of a book by Johannes Wendland on social ethics. For Christianity to retain its relevance, he claimed, 'the contents of our real life had to some extent to be capable of Christian evaluation. This is demanded if we are not to withdraw from the world like the radical Christians or to erect a new centre for the orientation of life like the non- or the antiChristians.'[10] A theology which was not to succumb to unrealistic or Utopian tasks, or to escape from the world, was thus forced to understand the character of contemporary reality, thereby exposing its constructive possibilities. Troeltsch thus considered a thoroughgoing

---

[7] Ibid., col. 209 f.   [8] Review of Günther (A1916/22), col. 450.
[9] Ibid.   [10] Review of Wendland (A1917/12), col. 297.

analysis of historical, economic, and social conditions to be vital if Christianity was to remain a potent force in the modern world, since 'many ethical decisions are only possible after the facts have been laid bare, and this laying bare of the facts is an infinitely arduous task'.[11] This *Feststellung der Tatsachen* could indeed have provided the motto for much of Troeltsch's descriptive work, and especially *Die Soziallehren*.

THE *EVANGELISCHER SOZIAL KONGREß*

Troeltsch was thus convinced that for the constructive task of a practical Christian ethics the theologian required a firm grounding in objectivity. This led him to a positive evaluation of the work of the *Evangelischer Sozial Kongreß* (*ESK*), which had adopted the task of 'investigating impartially the social conditions of our people, to measure them against the moral demands of the Gospels, and to make this latter more fruitful and effective for economic life today'.[12] In particular, Troeltsch had a high regard for its Secretary from 1891, Paul Göhre,[13] who collaborated with Max Weber in much of his early empirical work and whose researches had led to the collapse of the 'old tradition of Lutheran Ethics'.[14] Troeltsch regarded '[the] development of thought towards a free Protestantism gradually turning its attention to ethics rather than to dogma, that can be traced in the reports [of the *ESK*], [as] extremely instructive and attractive'.[15] In the very same note in *Die Soziallehren*, however, Troeltsch laments the lack of seriousness with which these sociological findings had been treated by theologians: 'Where', he asks, 'at the present day, do we find a really penetrating social ethics?' Instead of focusing purely on the moral absolutes of the Sermon on the Mount, contemporary Christian ethics, in Troeltsch's view, had to be brought into contact with the rough and ready of historical reality. This did not destroy religion, he claimed, but rather paved the way for its practical development in the future. In short, to seek escape in the medieval or to accept false explanations of modernity was an evasion of the responsibility of the theologian.

In criticizing Gottfried Traub's[16] attitude towards Christian social ethics

---

[11] 'Ethik und Kapitalismus' (A1905/6), col. 323.

[12] Statement of aims (cited in H. Liebersohn, *Religion and Industrial Society*, 11). For a brief history of the *ESK* see W. R. Ward, *Theology, Sociology and Politics*.

[13] On the work of Max Weber for the *ESK* see esp. Aldenhoff, 'Max Weber and the Evangelical Social Congress'. Göhre had produced an influential study of factory life: *Drei Monate Fabrikarbeiter und Handwerksbursche*.

[14] *Die Soziallehren* (A1912/2), 591 n.291; ET, 568.   [15] Ibid., 593 n.294; ET, 568.

[16] On Traub's theology see G. Hübinger, *Kulturprotestantismus und Politik*, 68–71; and S. Sato 'Ernst Troeltsch und die soziale Frage'.

(which he felt lacked any clear understanding of what was actually possible) Troeltsch makes his own position clear: 'Many ethical decisions are possible only after the facts have been established, and this establishing of the facts is an infinitely arduous task.'[17] He was thus convinced that for the constructive task of theology, and most particularly for the discipline of practical Christian ethics, the theologian was required to have a firm grounding in 'objectivity' or 'factuality':

Only an exact knowledge of sociological, as well as both micro- and macro-economic, literature of the present can provide the basis for our undertaking. Something merely based on the fulness of the heart and the good conscience, or something based merely on local or personal observations, can have nothing to contribute. Our humanistically and theologically educated clerics and intellectuals normally understand absolutely nothing of these things.[18]

It is not so much Traub's theology that Troeltsch calls into question, as his failure adequately to recognize the *facts*. Thus, Troeltsch claimed, his overoptimistic faith in the possibilities of education failed to account for the realities of human selfishness and the pursuit of power.[19]

In this concern for the practical and the ethical dimension of theology against the rigid dogmatic systems which had dominated theology in the past, Troeltsch claimed to be following Schleiermacher, who, he suggested, had 'founded his theology on his ethics; that is, on his philosophy of history and of the spirit'. This, as Troeltsch maintained at the beginning of his career, 'is exactly what I am attempting in my essays'.[20] Similarly, he maintained in 1905, 'the great chief tasks of contemporary Christianity rest first and foremost in the sphere of ethics, which stands up against new challenges not merely from economics and political life, but also from art and science'.[21] For Troeltsch, then, there was a primacy of the ethical, established on the basis of the positive and the practical, in any attempt to create a theology relevant for the modern world.[22]

---

[17] 'Ethik und Kapitalismus' (A1905/6), col. 323.

[18] Ibid., col. 322 f.; cf. 'Die christliche Weltanschauung und ihre Gegenströmungen' (A1894/1a), 291.

[19] 'Ethik und Kapitalismus' (A1905/6), col. 325 f. On this point see esp. Sato, 'Ernst Troeltsch und die soziale Frage'.

[20] 'Geschichte und Metaphysik' (A1898/2), 8. Cf. W. Wyman, *The Concept of Glaubenslehre*.

[21] 'Ethik und Kapitalismus' (A1905/6), col. 322.

[22] Troeltsch gave remarkably little thought to the precise role of the Church in the solution to the problems engendered in the Enlightenment. The few attempts (for example, in *Die Trennung von Staat und Kirche* (A1907/2), ET, 116) he did make (which he humbly considered 'would be a solution appropriate to the nation of Kant and Goethe') were most often mere restatements of the problem: 'the ideal of one truth . . . and the plurality of subjective convictions of truth would continue to coexist'.

UNDERSTANDING THE CONSTRAINTS OF THE PAST

Before setting out on any theological construction, the theologian, on Troeltsch's account, had to understand the phenomenon of modernity as thoroughly as possible by undertaking an investigation of the 'new foundations and presuppositions by which it is essentially differentiated from the ecclesiastical-unified period of European culture'.[23] Troeltsch's characterization of modernity can thus only be fully understood in relation to his analysis of earlier periods of European culture, and in particular to his understanding of the unified conception of the State and Church of the Middle Ages and of the territorial Churches of the Reformation. By comparing the modern period with the past, Troeltsch aimed to establish its distinctive characteristics. At the same time he sought to show how the religious ideal embodied by the Christian Church in its distinctive relationships with broader culture might gain concrete expression under the constraining conditions of modernity.[24]

Just as the contemporary task of Christian theology involved making some form of compromise with the constraints imposed by modernity, so in the past the ideals of Christianity had been forced to compromise with the prevailing conditions of the world. As the Christian vision of the highest good came into contact with the values of the world, there was always a 'mediation' between the two.[25] Indeed without some fusion between the forces of religion and the cultural environment of the day faith itself would always be relegated to the sidelines.[26]

When this is taken into account Troeltsch's 'favourite book',[27] *Die Soziallehren*, can be understood primarily as preparing the objective 'sociological' or factual basis for the constructive theological task. The book has, however, often been seen in isolation from Troeltsch's broader theological concerns, even though it stands in continuity with interests that had been first displayed as early as 1895.[28] Thus Troeltsch wrote to his friend Friedrich von Hügel that it was 'a preparation for my actual task which will be a philosophy of religion and an ethics, from which a systematic theology and a Christian ethics will follow'.[29] It was thus not merely an aside, a rather accidental sortie into sociology, but had a vital function within Troeltsch's *theological* system, as he makes clear in the foreword:

[23] Troeltsch, 'Autonomie und Rationalismus' (A1907/11), col. 199.
[24] Cf. 'Grundprobleme der Ethik' (A1902/4a), 554 ff.
[25] Ibid. A similar method was adopted by Richard Niebuhr in *Christ and Culture*, though with markedly different conclusions.
[26] Cf. *Die Soziallehren* (A1912/2), 27; ET, 45.
[27] Letter to Paul Siebeck, 18 January 1914, cited in H.-G. Drescher, *Ernst Troeltsch*, ET, 408.
[28] Cf. 'Religion und Kirche' (A1895/1a), 146–82.
[29] *Briefe an Friedrich von Hügel* (G1974/1), 93.

All this research, however, was only intended to serve the purpose of solving the systematic problem, in order to think through and to formulate the world of Christian thought and life in frank relation to the modern world.[30]

Furthermore, the book's emergence as an attempt to review a 'miserable book'[31] on social ethics by M. V. Nathusius,[32] and its original publication in the *Archiv für Sozialwissenschaft*, emphasize the constructive ethical designs behind the work.[33]

The method adopted in *Die Soziallehren* had, to some extent at least, already been displayed by Troeltsch in his doctoral dissertation on Melanchthon and Gerhard: only by looking at these figures without inherited Lutheran preconceptions would it ever be possible to reach a genuine understanding of the 'coexistence of secular education and religious truth'.[34] Theology was not something that could be divorced from culture, and which required a special mode of apprehension, but was rather merely one ingredient of culture alongside the others, and it had to be investigated using the most acute historical sense. In turn, it would become clear that the study of religious ideas was absolutely crucial for any proper understanding of history.[35] To understand the history of theology, according to Troeltsch, was to look at how it had related with the prevailing culture; this would serve as a prelude to looking at how it might relate with culture in the future.[36] As Troeltsch put it in *The Absoluteness of Christianity*, the synthesis of tradition with the powers of the present was what it was to write 'authentic history' for the sake of the future.[37]

THE HISTORY OF CHRISTIANITY

At the very outset of Christianity, Troeltsch maintained in a lecture, 'the tension between [the highest values] and those of culture first arose out of eschatological expectation'[38] as the failure of the Parousia forced some degree of compromise with the world. This was manifested in the two characteristic strands of early Catholicism with, on the one hand, its ideal of the

[30] *Die Soziallehren* (A1912/2), p. vii; ET, 19.

[31] 'Meine Bücher' (A1921/29b), 11; ET, 372. Cf. *Die Soziallehren* (A1912/2), 950 n.510; ET, 809.

[32] *Die Mitarbeit der Kirche an der Lösung der sozialen Frage.*

[33] I have analysed the theological role of *Die Soziallehren* in 'Polytheism and Personality', esp. 3–5. Part of its complexity stems from its intellectual context. On the writing of *Die Soziallehren*, see H.-G. Drescher, 'Zur Entstehung von Troeltschs "Soziallehren"'; and F. W. Graf, '"endlich grosse Bücher schreiben". Marginalien zur Werkgeschichte der "Soziallehren"'.

[34] *Vernunft und Offenbarung* (A1891/3), 3.   [35] 'Meine Bücher' (A1921/29b), 5; ET, 367.

[36] *Vernunft und Offenbarung* (A1891/3), 3.   [37] *The Absoluteness* (A1901/23d), ET, 87.

[38] PCE, lecture, 50. Cf. *Die Soziallehren* (A1912/2), 34 f.; ET, 51 f.

common life and its concomitant world-denying asceticism, and, on the other hand, the view that saw the whole of the world as a divine creation permeated by its own natural law.[39] Indeed the

fiction of a Christian natural law, which makes it possible to regard State and society as though both were ordered by one Christian law, will be the means through which it will become possible to speak of a Christian unity of civilization at all, and it is this alone which makes it possible to believe in such. The Christian law also provides the daughter churches of western Catholicism, i.e. Lutheranism and Calvinism, with the means for regarding themselves as a Christian unity of civilization (*Einheitskultur*).[40]

By making extensive use of this concept of natural law, Troeltsch eventually came to delineate three great compromises, syntheses, or unified visions of Christianity and culture in its pre-modern forms.[41] Each of these stood in marked contrast to the contemporary world, which at least in part was characterized by its differences from the visions of unity achieved in earlier periods:

Augustine

Although Troeltsch readily admitted that he had failed to deal adequately with Augustine in *Die Soziallehren*, he later sought to remedy this deficiency with a short book in which he investigated what he called the 'first great culture ethic'[42] of the Christian era. According to Troeltsch, Augustine's system was fundamentally dualistic, and reflected 'the tensions between irrationalism and the transcendence of the Christian spirit in metaphysics, ethics, and aesthetics, and the rationalistic-universalistic, immanent spirit of stoicism and neo-Platonism which unfolds itself in stages'.[43] The tensions between irrationalism and rationalism and between individualism and universalism, Troeltsch maintained, reflected the problem of all unified visions, and remained at the centre of the contemporary task.[44] The history of the Christian ethos is thus:

on the one hand . . . the sanctification of the self for God by the practice of detachment from everything which disturbs inward communion with God, and by the exercise of everything which inwardly binds the soul to God's will, and, on the other hand, the demand for neighbourly love, which overcomes all the tension and harshness of the struggle for existence in God . . . This is an ideal which requires a new world if it is to be fully realized; it was this new world order that Jesus proclaimed in his message of the kingdom of God. But it is an ideal which cannot be realized within

---

[39] *Die Soziallehren* (A1912/2), 152–7, esp. 155; ET, 145–50, esp. 149; cf. 'Grundprobleme der Ethik' (A1902/4a), 554 ff.
[40] *Die Soziallehren* (A1912/2), 173; ET, 160.   [41] *Augustin* (A1915/6a), 173.
[42] Ibid., 47.   [43] Ibid., 157.   [44] Ibid., 173.

this world apart from compromise. Therefore the history of the Christian ethos becomes the story of a constantly renewed search for this compromise, and of fresh opposition to this spirit of compromise.[45]

Because Augustine maintained a distinction between the highest good and any concrete embodiment of this good, he 'laid the foundations for all formulations of religious ethics, even for the present'.[46] Troeltsch repeated this point in a pamphlet on the social philosophy of Christianity published shortly before his death:

Just as theology found a connection between the natural wisdom of the world and the Christ-God by means of the Logos, so too social ethics and reconciliation with the world found it in natural law and a natural law of ethics. It is a compromise. There is always the expectation of the *Civitas Dei*, of the heavenly Jerusalem, and the world remains a kingdom of sin and darkness. Yet within this world reason, which is seen both as natural and at the same time as stemming from God, is present as a remnant of the heavenly paradise.[47]

In his historical studies of the Christian social ethos, Troeltsch was therefore attempting more than a mere presentation of the various forms in which the Christian ethos had been historically displayed. At the same time he sought to provide resources for the development of the ethos in the future:

The world should be reworked until it resembles the holiness of God . . . The Christian view of the world is this: an absolute divine value stands against the world . . . There is obviously a contradiction between God and the world, but still this world is to be connected with the highest purpose . . . Christianity thus fluctuates between these two poles of identification with culture and acosmism throughout its entire history.[48]

Medieval Catholicism

This second form of synthesis between Christianity and culture is far more fully treated by Troeltsch in the second chapter of *Die Soziallehren* and is characterized by its virtual conflation of the natural and supernatural. The remnant of dualism in Augustine is almost completely overcome,[49] which results in a unified vision of all aspects of reality. Although there is a lack of clarity in Troeltsch's understanding of a 'unified culture',[50] he does at least give some passing definitions of a society in which there was an all-embracing vision of truth and in which Church and State were at one. The role played by religion in such a situation was best characterized by the

---

[45] *Die Soziallehren* (A1912/2), 973; ET, 999 f. [46] *Augustin* (A1915/6a), 173.
[47] *Die Sozialphilosophie des Christentums* (A1922/27), 9. [48] PCE, 49 f.
[49] *Augustin* (A1915/6a), 158.
[50] On this see Ulrich Köpf, 'Die Idee der "Einheitskultur"', esp. 103 f.

Church model, that religious organization of which all people were members by virtue of their birth:

> With the supernatural idea of the Church which regards the Church as a divine foundation, endowed with a truth absolutely authoritative . . . there was constituted the absolute conception of truth, which implied unity, unchangeable character, universality, and infallibility of the Church in the heart of the organization upon which it is based.[51]

Nevertheless, despite this all-embracing unity, there were always strands, in particular the 'safety-valve'[52] of monasticism, which aimed to represent the Christian ideal in its purity and which stood in marked contrast with the values of everyday society which were based on natural law.[53]

Luther–Calvin: the Protestant Compromise[54]

Although Troeltsch was well aware of the significant changes wrought in the Reformation, he nevertheless saw it as something inherently medieval.[55] Religious organization, he claimed, was still characterized by the Church model, which could equally be applied to the Church which emerged from the Hildebrandine reforms as to the territorially limited Churches of the Reformation:

> In Catholicism this idea was achieved through dogma and tradition, through the hierarchy and the sacraments, and from the fundamental impulse it developed into the world-dominating system which was finally forced to inscribe upon its banner its principle of compulsion, in direct opposition to its original principles.
>
> In Protestantism this central fact was the word of the Scriptures . . . The conception of the Church as the organ of salvation, divinely instituted, required once for all a truth which should be firmly established, clearly defined, equally binding upon all, and this conception of truth required the absolute authority of the Bible . . . The Protestant extension of the Incarnation in the Bible corresponds to the Catholic extension of the Incarnation in the priesthood.[56]

Indeed, the Reformation had not fundamentally challenged the medieval

---

[51] *Die Soziallehren* (A1912/2), ET, 487.   [52] Ibid., 179; ET, 201

[53] Ibid., 257 ff.; ET, 237 ff.; 'Grundprobleme der Ethik' (A1902/4a), 654; 'Ethik und Kapitalismus' (A1905/6), col. 321; *PCE*, dictation, 20, lecture, 51.

[54] Cf. *Die Soziallehren* (A1912/2), 506 f.; ET, 510 f.; 'Grundprobleme der Ethik' (A1902/4a), 556 ff., 654; 'Ethik und Kapitalismus' (A1905/6), col. 321.

[55] Cf. 'Die Aufklärung' (A1897/14a), 338. Troeltsch (following Dilthey, in 'The Interpretation and Analysis of Man', 12) held the contentious view that the modern world began with the Enlightenment from the outset of his career, as is clear from his doctoral thesis *Vernunft und Offenbarung* (A1891/3), esp. 44 f. By implication this put into doubt Luther's immediate applicability to the modern world.

[56] *Die Soziallehren* (A1912/2), 462, 463; ET, 485, 487.

cultural synthesis: all aspects of reality were connected within an all-encompassing system, and similarly scope for individual action was limited by the emphasis on obedience to the duties of one's worldly calling (even that of the hangman),[57] and by the persistence of the guild system. Similarly, the dogmatic systems of the Reformation and of orthodoxy were still firmly lodged in the Aristotelian systems of the Middle Ages. Thus, far from being the first triumph of individual liberty, the Reformation had not fundamentally challenged the medieval *corpus christianum*, but had merely boosted the claims of the civil authorities. Indeed it became the duty of the Christian State to suppress heresies:

> Luther and the jurists of Wittenberg . . . adopted this policy [of coercion] deliberately, of their own free will, without, however, giving up the theory that the Church ought to exercise her influence solely on spiritual lines. It was a form of self-deception which is possible to men who believe that they are in possession of absolute truth, and who are therefore honestly convinced that it is right to claim from the political authorities toleration for the truth, but no toleration for falsehood. It is not the Church, as such, which punishes the rebels, and gets rid of them by violent methods, but the ideal created by the Church of the universal dominion of the only saving truth over society, the absolute objective conception of truth, and the universal idea of a Christian society supported by it.[58]

Troeltsch's description of the Church was thus in part sociological—the Church took on a particular form, and was protected by a particular system of coercive authority in all the Protestant states—and yet it was also characterized theologically, in terms of a particular understanding of exclusiveness, absoluteness, and truth.

The Breakdown of Unified Culture

Despite the persistence of the medieval Church model, Troeltsch nevertheless regarded the division of western Christendom at the Reformation as (somewhat ironically) the first major stage in the breakdown of a unified culture, since if there was more than one claim on absolute truth it of necessity led to a redefinition of the medieval Catholic synthesis.[59] Even though the dogmatic systems of the Reformation clung to the scholastic legacy of the Middle Ages, their very plurality weakened the dominion of an all-embracing cultural synthesis, thereby paving the way for a modern conception of truth.

At the same time the development of the radical religious sects led to competing claims on the absolute truth *within* a single culture, and, despite

---

[57] PCE, lecture, 53.   [58] *Die Soziallehren* (A1912/2), 472; ET, 493 f.
[59] Cf. *Die Trennung von Staat und Kirche* (A1907/2), 8 ff.

brutal repression, a number of sectarian movements emerged, each claiming to represent the absolute truths of Christianity.[60] This again was bound to affect the claims to universality inherent in the Church model, and had a profound impact on the main confessional churches.[61] Thus, alongside the Church, according to Troeltsch, there developed

the sects, [which] are comparatively small groups; they aspire after personal inward perfection, and they aim at a direct personal fellowship between the members of each group. From the very beginning they are forced to organize themselves in small groups, and to renounce the idea of dominating the world. Their attitude towards the world, the State, and the society may be indifferent, tolerant, or hostile, since they have no desire to control or incorporate these forms of social life; on the contrary, they tend to avoid them; their aim is usually either to tolerate their presence alongside their own body, or even to replace these institutions by their own society.[62]

This meant that, although each sect claimed an absoluteness and maintained an ethical purity within its own boundaries, the mere fact of plurality forced an element of toleration. Though the rest of the world might be destined for the outer darkness, its sheer existence forced some degree of recognition. Thus, according to Troeltsch, the coexistence of more than one sect thereby came to be of crucial importance for the development of the modern world. Membership of the sect, though requiring total commitment, was *voluntary*, a fact which led to a weakening of the claims of the Church as a universal religious system within each territory and into which one was born. Thus, however absolute the claims of sectarian religion, allegiance was ultimately a matter of choice, which led to a *de facto* if not *de jure* separation of religion from government. Tolerance of diversity, however limited, could not coexist with a Church defined on the medieval model. In short, Troeltsch claimed in a lengthy essay on Protestant Christianity and modernity, 'the victory of the baptist ideal [i.e. voluntarism and conversionism] marked the end of the medieval'.[63]

Moving on to discuss later developments, Troeltsch regarded the English Civil War, with its unprecedented increase in religious diversity and sectarianism, as in some senses marking the end of the wars of religion and the 'departure point for the modern world'.[64] The example of the Levellers, together with other experiments in communal living in the seventeenth century, in particular, 'unintentionally planted the roots of liberalism'.[65] Thus the coexistence of the various independent and congregationalist groups created a demand for tolerance, which, after the repression of the Clarendon

[60] Cf. *Die Soziallehren* (A1912/2), 794 ff.; ET, 691 ff.   [61] Ibid. 827; ET, 714.

[62] *Die Soziallehren* (A1912/2), 362; ET, 331.

[63] 'Protestantisches Christentum und Kirche in der Neuzeit' (A1906/4), 371.

[64] Ibid., 367.   [65] Ibid., 365; cf. *Die Soziallehren* (A1912/2), 821; ET, 710.

Code, was later enshrined in the (admittedly limited) constitutional guarantees of the settlement of William and Mary.[66] In this settlement, according to Troeltsch, the example of independency was once again of special importance in that, instead of a vision of a unified society where everything functioned in terms of an organic whole, there was within the sect itself a recognition of diversity of religious practice as fundamental for society.

On this historical basis Troeltsch was able to date the beginnings of the modern period, with its separation of Church and State and the emphasis on the autonomous individual, at least symbolically, to the Glorious Revolution of 1688 and the Act of Toleration of 1689.[67] In short, he maintained, 'the dissolution of the confessional-absolutist State begins with the English revolution'.[68] With the overthrow of James II, the State had become in some degree 'neutral towards the Churches', a fact which marked the final break with the dominant 'idea of a medieval culture which saw the State and the Church as two harmonious organs of Christian society or as the *corpus christianum*'.[69]

The development of competing sects within the one realm, and limited degree of toleration afforded them, created what Troeltsch called a 'polymorphous' conception of truth,[70] out of which emerged the Enlightenment in the seventeenth century, a period which also saw the beginning of the end of the universal polities of the Middle Ages.[71] In turn, the idea of toleration led to a conception of the State as guardian of 'the ethical idea of human rights', which served to 'militate against confessionalism and its wars'.[72] Similarly the influence of Hobbes helped at once to destroy medieval theories of the foundations of the State and to bring about the separation of the divine law and (a rationally based) natural law.[73] This emphasis on the independence of natural law ensured that relationships between individuals were no longer determined by their obedience to a predefined and divinely sanctioned role, but, at least to some extent, by the decisions of the individuals themselves.[74] Such principles, Troeltsch held, achieved their most excellent summary in the American constitution.[75] When all these developments

---

[66] Cf. 'Protestantisches Christentum' (A1906/4), 365.

[67] Cf. Mark D. Chapman, 'Concepts of the Voluntary Church', esp. 43 f.

[68] *Der Historismus und seine Probleme* (A1922/22), 763.

[69] 'Protestantisches Christentum' (A1906/4), 391.

[70] *Die Soziallehren* (A1912/2), 970 f.; ET, 997 f. On this see also Wilhelm Schenk, 'Ernst Troeltsch's Conception of History', 26.

[71] *Die Soziallehren* (A1912/2), 857 f.; ET, 739; cf. 'Die englischen Moralisten' (A1903/24a), 387; 'Grundprobleme der Ethik' (A1902/4a), 561.

[72] 'Protestantisches Christentum' (A1906/4), 385.   [73] Ibid., 395.

[74] Cf. 'Die englischen Moralisten' (A1903/24a), 376.

[75] Cf. 'Protestantisches Christentum' (A1906/4), 367; *Die Trennung von Staat und Kirche* (A1907/2), 29 f.; review of White (A1913/11), col. 273; *Der Berg der Läuterung* (1921/11), 20.

were taken into consideration it became quite clear, as Troeltsch remarked in a lecture, that 'there is no compulsory truth any longer; rather all share in it. Nobody sees the Antichrist in Catholicism any more. The Protestants have achieved union . . . Even the Salvation Army enjoys rights and recognition'.[76] The Enlightenment, with its emphasis on autonomy and human rights, thus became the foundation for the modern world.

THE CHARACTERISTICS OF THE ENLIGHTENMENT

Troeltsch did not dismiss the Enlightenment as an exercise in the folly of placing all one's trust in human reason, but instead understood it as a process of critical communication in which everything was open to public debate.[77] According to Troeltsch, it was this critical process, coupled with the reluctance to submit to the religious and political authority of the past, that marked the decisive beginning of the modern period and which introduced the problems with which contemporary theology had still to deal. In the third edition of the *Realencyclopädie für protestantische Theologie und Kirche*, Troeltsch contributed a lengthy article on the Enlightenment,[78] where, with typical hyperbole, he claimed:

the Enlightenment marks the beginning and the foundation of the characteristically modern period of European culture and history in distinction from the hitherto prevalent culture which was dominated by the Church and theology . . . It is in no sense purely or even predominantly a scientific movement, but is a complete reorientation of culture in all spheres of life.[79]

The Enlightenment was defined in opposition to the ecclesiastically dominated unified culture of the Middle Ages, and through its process of criticism of heteronomous forms of authority it 'unleashed forces which had hitherto been imprisoned in supernatural forms of tradition'.[80] Consequently, for Troeltsch, the Enlightenment had placed in sharp relief the dilemma of modernity: the liberation of the individual was its greatest achievement, yet nevertheless individuals had still to find meaning for their existence and to find 'unity and peace' in the 'critical insecurity . . . of the many contradictions of historical reality'.[81]

Troeltsch's understanding of the Enlightenment stresses its liberative

---

[76] *Glaubenslehre* (F1925/2), 15; ET, 20–1.

[77] On this understanding of the Enlightenment see my essay, 'Why the Enlightenment Project Doesn't have to Fail'.

[78] Troeltsch, 'Aufklärung' (A1897/14 and 14a). On Troeltsch as enlightened theologian see Trutz Rendtorff, 'Theologische Orientierung im Prozeß der Aufklärung'.

[79] 'Die Aufklärung' (A1897/14a), 338 f.

[80] Ibid., 340.   [81] *Briefe an von Hügel* (G1974/1), 65 f.

qualities, and, unlike many other theological characterizations (right up to the present day), where it is viewed as fundamentally anti-religious,[82] he sees the Enlightenment itself as at least in part a religiously inspired process of liberation.[83] Troeltsch here is being true to many of the Enlightenment thinkers themselves, who frequently saw their engagement in public criticism as a process of religious emancipation. For instance, the Tübingen theologian and statesman Ludwig Timotheus Spittler (1752–1810) wrote, in 1782, that 'on the whole we have achieved an extraordinary amount through this revolution of the last thirty years, and it will probably one day be characterized as one of the most radiant periods of the history of the Lutheran church'.[84]

According to Troeltsch, the main features of Enlightenment thought were: empiricism and the rise of the scientific method; individualism; rationalism; and individual autonomy, each of which is considered below.

Empiricism and the Rise of the Scientific Method

Troeltsch held that the 'ecclesiastical-confessional culture' of the Middle Ages had been finally destroyed as 'the individual's critical faculties' were liberated and 'no longer tied down by supernaturalism'.[85] Similarly, although theology had continued to fight against it, 'science was no longer to be corrected by dogma'.[86] These ideas, which can be seen to emerge in the breakdown of the supernaturally based medieval system, and which culminate in the ideas of the autonomous individual and the universal application of the principle of criticism, formed the fundamental tenets of the thought of the Enlightenment, marking the beginning of the modern period in contrast to the church-dominated culture of the past.[87] Although there were hints of the spirit of the Enlightenment present in earlier periods, it was only in the Enlightenment itself that 'the new anti-supernaturalist foundation for theology and the science of religion as well as for the natural sciences' had

---

[82] See, for example, the recent accounts by Colin Gunton: *Enlightenment and Alienation*; and *The One, The Three and The Many*.

[83] Ritschl too had seen the Enlightenment as a 'stage in the development of Christianity' (lectures on Theologische Moral given in 1882, cited in Helga Kuhlmann, *Die theologische Ethik Albrecht Ritschls*, 179).

[84] Cited in Walter Sparn, 'Vernünftiges Christentum'. On this point see also R. Vierhaus, 'Aufklärung als Emanzipationsprozeß', 3–8; and Horst Möller, *Vernunft und Kritik. Deutsche Aufklärung im 17. und 18. Jahrhundert*. For general accounts see H.-U. Wehler, *Deutsche Sozialgeschichte*, esp. 278–327; and James J. Sheehan, *German History 1770–1866*, pt. I.

[85] Review of Gastrow (A1906/7), col. 146.   [86] *Glaubenslehre* (F1925/2), 62; ET, 57.

[87] Cf. 'Die Aufklärung' (A1897/14a), 338.

been laid.[88] There was, in short, a trust in the senses at the expense of super-natural authority or revelation.[89]

Individualism

The concomitant of this reliance on the senses was, according to Troeltsch, the 'liberation of the individual'. Indeed 'the reliance of the individual upon itself . . . against what remains of the world of authority' was the lasting achievement of the Enlightenment and marked the beginning of the end of the old order, soon becoming the 'formula of the modern world'.[90] The Enlightenment was suspicious of all tradition and thus attempted to remove the semblance of divinity from the past 'by annihilating the supernatural forms of tradition and unleashing powers which had previously been subju-gated'.[91] In short, according to Troeltsch, 'the eighteenth century is anti-supernaturalist and destroys the authority of divine and superhuman truths and criteria. Along with this it led to the emancipation of the individual, who had previously been bound up in divine authority'.[92] For Troeltsch, then, the achievement of the Enlightenment was clear: it had created the conditions for the human being, in Kant's words, to 'come of age'.[93]

Another aspect of such individualism was also manifested in an individu-alization of religion, which began to be characterized no longer by adher-ence to a rigid orthodoxy but by enthusiasm and feeling. Indeed, according to Troeltsch, such 'irrational' manifestations were of vital importance in any attempt to interpret modern religiosity, even if they had often been ignored.[94] In Germany the impact of pietism could not be disregarded. Like the Enlightenment, it was 'no mere episode which has been superseded, but marked a lasting reorientation of Protestantism in contrast to its Reforma-tion and orthodox forms'.[95]

Rationalism

At the same time as the Enlightenment was concerned to liberate the indi-vidual from the bondage to tradition, there was another equally important

[88] 'Geschichte und Metaphysik' (A1898/2), 40.

[89] 'Die englischen Moralisten' (1903/24a), 409 ff.

[90] 'Autonomie und Rationalismus' (A1907/11), col. 200. Becker (in *Neuzeitliche Subjektivität*) regards 'subjectivity' as the index of the modern epoch, and uses it to present his interpretation of Troeltsch. In doing so he does not place sufficient weight on the rooting of such subjectivity in absolute ends.

[91] 'Die Aufklärung' (A1897/14a), 340.   [92] Review of Gastrow (A1906/7), col. 145.

[93] Kant, 'What is Enlightenment?', 3.

[94] 'Die Selbständigkeit der Religion' (A1895/2), 402.

[95] Review of Horst Stephan (A1909/5), col. 245.

but opposed development, which Troeltsch characterized as the 'immanent explanation of the world using universally valid means of knowledge . . . a rational ordering of life in the service of universal practical purposes'.[96] Troeltsch sees this as most clearly displayed by Kant, who, having affirmed the liberation of the individual from tutelage to supernatural authority, also regarded the motto of the Enlightenment as 'Have courage to use your reason!'[97] Thus, despite the tendencies towards individualism and autonomy, the Enlightenment still maintained a sense of firm order, of the capacities of the human being to shape his or her life around rational ends.

This sense of order, of the meaningfulness and rationality of all reality, had previously been guaranteed by Christianity; its all-embracing vision was able to balance the competing claims between individuality and universality in the synthesis which characterized the medieval world-view. Such a static world-view had, however, been destroyed in the Enlightenment emphasis on the critical capacity of human beings: rational meaning could no longer be conferred on the individual from outside, since life was no longer seen as *heteronomously* structured; instead meaning came from within, as the individual shaped reality *autonomously* around rational ends. This situation created enormous problems, since it appeared to separate each human being from any higher order in which to ground this universality. In Kant's words:

Reason [is] man's release from the womb of nature, an alteration of the condition which is honourable, to be sure, but also fraught with danger. For nature had now driven him from the safe and harmless state of childhood—a garden, as it were, which looked after his needs without any trouble on his part—into the wide world, where so many cares, troubles, and unforeseen ills awaited him . . . It would not permit him to return to that crude and simple state from which it had driven him to begin with.[98]

With the Enlightenment there was thus a loss of innocence, which could never be regained, which set the boundaries within which any theological construction had to work. In short, according to Troeltsch, the Enlightenment had 'sowed the seeds of all the problems of the modern world'.[99]

Autonomy as the Mark of the Modern World

The most important change accomplished during the Enlightenment was thus, according to Troeltsch, the 'discovery' of the autonomous self-legislating individual. Although this may indeed have been merely the

[96] 'Die Aufklärung' (A1897/14a), 339. In *EPH* Troeltsch traces the history of these competing strands of Enlightenment thought (13 ff.).

[97] Kant, 'What is Enlightenment?', 3.

[98] Kant, 'Conjectural Beginning of Human History', 59.

[99] Review of Gastrow (A1906/7), col. 145.

'invention' of the Enlightenment, as some modern critics have claimed,[100] it was also, at least for Troeltsch, its crowning achievement.[101] Autonomy simply could not be supplanted by any supernatural theological system. Consequently, far from seeing the Enlightenment as a project that necessarily had to fail, Troeltsch regarded it as something which had replaced the previous unified culture once and for all, and which constrained all intellectual and moral activity.

In his description of the contemporary tasks of theology, Troeltsch's strongest emphasis is on the notion of autonomy as constituting the single most important feature of the modern world. Yet autonomy, the human ability for self-legislation unencumbered by the tutelage of the past, was not, according to Troeltsch, something inherently destructive. Indeed it could serve to reveal ends which could be affirmed as the highest and of decisive importance. Such ends, however, could not be *proved* and ultimately had to be accepted in an 'irrational' decision, but nevertheless they could be critically weighed by the individual in the constructive attempt to confer the highest possible meaning on the world under the present conditions of reality. The modern world could once again be given shape, not by denying the resources of the past, but by using them critically for the renewal and reformation of the tradition in order to express unity and meaning in the present. Any such solution would in turn always be open to criticism.

THE SYNTHESIS FOR THE PRESENT

Having thus looked at the origins of modernity in relation to the unified world-views of the Middle Ages and at the specific intellectual currents of the Enlightenment, Troeltsch devoted a great deal of energy to outlining the various modifications which these currents had undergone in the modern world. This was to serve his overall purpose of delineating the constraining conditions of the present day. His historical work thus prepares the ground for 'a new Christian ethic'[102] which might provide for the 'spiritual-ethical mastery of this present situation'.[103] A return to the unified world-views of the Catholic or the Lutheran Middle Ages was, he held, a delusion, since the modern world had created new conditions for Christianity. In his own efforts to provide a solution to these problems of modernity, then, Troeltsch was driven by the urge towards the integration of the individual within an all-embracing social whole, which he believed had also characterized

---

[100] This is the (now famous) understanding of the Enlightenment project held by Alastair MacIntyre in *After Virtue*, 58 f.

[101] Cf. 'Autonomie und Rationalismus' (A1907/11), col. 201 f.

[102] *Die Soziallehren* (A1912/2), 975; ET, 1002.   [103] Ibid., 977; ET, 1003.

Christianity in its medieval and Reformation forms, but which seemed to him to be impossible simply to reproduce in the circumstances of the contemporary world: 'The time of the unified Church with its unique claim to salvation, its unified spiritual life, and its all-embracing dogma has its greatness. Yet this era is definitively past'.[104] Nevertheless, he contended, although the 'idea of a society inspired by a uniform world-view is undoubtedly medieval, it is still a vital problem that has not yet been solved'.[105] Troeltsch sought after what he called a 'new and more all-embracing compromise'.[106] Only such a compromise, Troeltsch contended, could provide the modern world with anything like religious hope.

In order to establish a form of Christianity which could remain a vital ethical force, but one which did not ensnare the autonomous individual in medieval forms of authority, the modern theologian was thus called upon to confront the modern world on its own terms. Indeed there could be no going back on the Enlightenment without profoundly dangerous repercussions:[107]

The ideal which characterized antiquity and the Middle Ages—the thought of a unified culture filled with the religious spirit—is for the time being in the distant blue horizons of the past. Its renewal on the soil of free spiritual agreement is something which the wearisome individualism of the present will long for in ever greater degrees, but which for the moment is likewise in the distant blue horizons of the future.[108]

Nevertheless, the search for a new synthesis was 'still a vital problem which has not yet been solved. There cannot be a real social coherence at all without the unity of the world-view'.[109]

Any attempt to reach a new synthesis would have to move beyond the historical compromises of the past by forging new syntheses with the most ethical powers of modern culture. Thus, Troeltsch wrote in *Die Soziallehren*:

In the modern world Christian social teachings are in an infinitely difficult situation. On the one hand, Christianity is no longer completely ecclesiastical, and yet it seeks free spirituality and adaptability of the Church without the compelling guarantees of ecclesiasticism; while, on the other hand, in spite of its position based on subjective conviction and freedom, and vital ethical verification, Christianity cannot bear a

---

[104] 'Schleiermacher und die Kirche' (A1910/16), 35.
[105] *Die Soziallehren* (A1912/2), 470 n.214; ET, 492 n.214.
[106] 'Protestantisches Christentum' (A1906/4), 371.
[107] In a review of Hirsch ((A1923/1), col. 23) Troeltsch is deeply critical of the 'crass impossibility' of his critique of the Enlightenment: 'Somebody who recognizes the infinite complexity and the real contradictions of life and the spiritual mixture of modern nations, just has nothing to say to those who make these generalizations'.
[108] Troeltsch, 'Protestantisches Christentum' (A1906/4), 451.
[109] *Die Soziallehren* (A1912/2), 470 n.214; ET, 833 n.214.

radical lack of culture, the confines of the conventicle, or the social reform of the sects which is bound up with a literal understanding of the Gospel. It is neither Church nor sect, and has neither the concrete sanctity of the institution, nor the radical connection with the Bible . . . but it is a free union between like-minded people which is equally remote from both Church and sect.[110]

In such a way, Troeltsch held, the Church could begin to help instil the modern world with absolute meaning: indeed without such an acceptance of something higher as an ultimate motivation for action the fragmented world would rob the individual of his or her individuality and thus of the lasting gains of modernity. The modern world presented fundamentally new conditions within which any ethical compromise had to take place. Troeltsch's conception of ethics thus emphasizes the creation of a contemporary synthesis out of the powers revealed in the past. Although such a synthesis must always be less than ideal,[111] the central task remained the same:

Just as the old Christian ethic was a compromise, a synthesis, so today every order of our ethical concepts and evaluations is also seen under the dominant viewpoint of the highest value of the personality united in God and the brotherly love existing in God . . . The old problem confronts us again, and we have to make a new synthesis, the best that is possible; it is the synthesis that is valid for the present.[112]

The central methodological feature emerging from *Die Soziallehren* and displayed elsewhere in his work is thus of significance for Troeltsch's whole theological enterprise: knowledge of the interaction between the Christian ethos and sociological forms yields the picture of the factual conditions upon which the constructive task of ethical renewal can build.

This need for a synthesis for the present day based on a faith in the future but requiring a constructive use of the past provides a leitmotiv in Troeltsch's work. Indeed he never ceased to believe in the possibility of a single unifying principle or 'absolute' appropriate for the modern world: 'the human being is longing after simple, absolute, and universally valid laws, which can never be found in technological progress or positivism, but only in religion'.[113] At the end of his career Troeltsch reaffirmed that such a synthesis required 'a creative act . . . of those who refuse to be lulled to sleep or to be destroyed, but who maintain in each present the task of such a combination according to the measure of their strengths and their capacities'.[114] A picture of how such construction was achieved in the past could yield vital information

---

[110] *Die Soziallehren* (A1912/2), 424 f.; ET, 381. For Troeltsch's views on Church reform at the beginnings of the Weimar Republic see esp. 'Religiöser Subjektivismus' (A1919/41), 699.

[111] Cf. *Die Soziallehren* (A1912/2), 977; ET, 1003.

[112] 'Grundprobleme der Ethik' (A1902/4a), 663.

[113] 'Christentum und Religionsgeschichte' (A1897/10a), 361.

[114] *Der Historismus und seine Probleme* (A1922/22), 771 f.

about how it is to be achieved in the present. Christianity is not thereby relativized but is made aware of the possibilities and the limitations of its scope for action. This is perhaps brought out most clearly in the concluding words of *Die Soziallehren*:

There is no absolute ethical transformation of material or human nature; so current and future Christian ethics will be adapted to the situation and *will pursue only what is possible*... This is the cause of that ceaseless tension which drives the human onwards yet it also gives the sense that the ethical work will never be completed... The final ends of all humanity are hidden within [our heavenly Father's] hands.[115]

From what can be ascertained from the rather vague closing pages of *Die Soziallehren*, as well as from the many asides in that work and elsewhere, it is clear that Troeltsch saw modern Christian political and social thought as something which was 'in an infinitely difficult situation'. The problem facing contemporary Christians was how to ensure the 'free spirituality and adaptability of the Church' without succumbing to the 'binding guarantees of ecclesiasticism'. Similarly there was a need for its position to be 'based on subjective conviction and freedom... Christianity cannot bear a radical lack of culture'.[116]

The sociological appraisal of the history of the Christian ethos thus had a significant function within Troeltsch's theology, at least as he sought to look at the relevance of the Church for the future. Thus he remarks that the 'central life of the Church type is being permeated with the vital energies of the sect and of mysticism... In the mutual interpenetration of the three chief sociological categories, which must be united with a structure which will reconcile them all, lie its future tasks'.[117] In this Troeltsch saw himself as following Schleiermacher, for whom, at least on his own interpretation, the 'dogmatic content of religion could never be independent of the sociological'.[118] Elsewhere he maintained that within the sociological and political understanding of the Church there had to be room for the various levels of subjective religious experience, which Troeltsch called 'mysticism',[119] to penetrate the communal structures of the Church.

From these hints it is clear that Troeltsch understood the contemporary Church, at least where it was not merely attempting to reinstate what he

[115] *Die Soziallehren* (A1912/2), 986; ET, 1013 (my emphasis).   [116] Ibid., 424; ET, 381.

[117] Ibid., 982; ET, 1009. The only clear expositions of Troeltsch's comprehensive union of Church, sect, and mysticism are found in this essay and 'Religiöser Individualismus und die Kirche' (C1911/2b). Cf. also *Die Soziallehren* (A1912/2), 424 f.; ET, 381. Trutz Rendtorff (in '"Meine eigene Theologie ist spiritualistisch"', esp. 189 ff.) draws out some implications of Troeltsch's understanding of mysticism for the form of the Church. Cf. 'Die Kirche im Leben der Gegenwart' (A1911/8a), esp. 105 f.; 'Die Zukunftsmöglichkeiten des Christentums im Verhältnis zur modernen Philosophie' (A1911/1a).

[118] 'Schleiermacher und die Kirche' (A1910/16), 27.

[119] 'Die Kirche im Leben der Gegenwart' (A1911/8a), 107 f.

regarded as an impossible medieval synthesis, as something akin to an association of like-minded individuals freely consenting to certain forms of
authority: it was a 'voluntary church'.[120] It thus contained certain characteristics of the sect, but at the same time it could not deny individuality by relying on a rigidly exclusive and supernatural authority. Troeltsch's analysis of
history is thus vitally related to the ecclesiological dimension of his constructive task. His task was in creating a new 'comprehensive union' of the
powers of the sect, the universality of the Church, and the depths of mysticism in an all-embracing synthesis for the future.[121] How he attempted this
in response to the countercurrents of the modern world is the subject of the
final chapter.

[120] Cf. Mark D. Chapman, 'Concepts of the Voluntary Church'.
[121] 'Die Kirche im Leben der Gegenwart' (A1911/8a), 107 f.

8

Troeltsch's Constructive Ethics

THE VOCATION OF THEOLOGY

This chapter discusses Ernst Troeltsch's attempt to realize his ethical theology in the context of an increasingly fragmented and dismembered society. Against the sectarian tendencies of the escapist epistemology adopted by both Herrmann and the neo-Friesians—and, by the end of his career, many others besides—he retained what I have termed a 'public theology', whereby theology, and the religion it sought to regulate, were not to be separated off from the rest of reality. The central question facing him was this: How was it possible to re-establish a unified vision in which religion was placed at the heart of ethical life, but which did not at the same time deny the lasting gains of modernity?[1] Beginning with an account of Troeltsch's perception of modernity—his analysis of the constraints within which the theologian was forced to work—this chapter focuses on the threats to his project which emerged towards the end of his life, particularly during and immediately after the First World War. Finally, Troeltsch's project is compared with that of Max Weber:[2] the contrasts reveal much about the specific function or 'vocation' of theology in the modern world.[3]

What will become clear is that Troeltsch continued to hold a faith in a future that allowed history to be guided by a higher authority capable of

---

[1] Cf. *PCE*, lecture, 54.

[2] Troeltsch and Weber had a close intellectual and personal relationship. I have discussed this at length in 'Polytheism and Personality'. See also F. W. Graf 'Max Weber und die protestantische Theologie seiner Zeit' and 'Friendship between Experts: Notes on Weber and Troeltsch'. On Weber's ethics see Ulrich Barth, 'Ethische Aspekte der Kapitalismus-Deutung Max Webers'. According to Barth, Weber's characterization of human existence is determined by antinomy and by a reduction of reason to pure calculation. Although Weber clamoured for a vision of absolute ethics which made space for emotion, there seemed little possibility for such a union with the machine mentality of the modern understanding of reason.

[3] See his lectures 'Wissenschaft als Beruf' in *GAW* and 'Politik als Beruf' in *GPS*. On the lengthy debate around these lectures see P. Lassman and I. Velody (eds.), *Max Weber's 'Science as a Vocation'*. Several of the important texts are translated in this volume. Troeltsch contributed to this debate in 'Die Revolution in den Wissenschaft' (A1921/28a). On the relationship between Weber's and Troeltsch's ethics see my essay, 'Polytheism and Personality', esp. 9–15.

providing reasons and meanings for autonomous ethical activity. Unlike so many of his colleagues and contemporaries he did not evade his responsibility to keep alive a vision of the unity of reality and the possibility of its ethical transformation: he never sought escape into the past or into an alternative religious reality but instead trod the infinitely more difficult path which affirmed the possibility of Christianity *within* the apparent chaos of the present. Christianity was public or it was nothing. For Troeltsch, then, religion was neither mystical escape nor esoteric knowledge, but practical theodicy: a coherent answer to the incoherence of the present and, perhaps more importantly, an answer which could be put into practice and shape ethics. For this reason, Troeltsch maintained, theology was one of the most 'interesting, most exciting, and most revolutionary of the disciplines'.[4]

THE CONSTRAINTS OF MODERNITY

In his deeply pessimistic 1903 review of 'the coldest and most desolate time that the Church, theology, and the science of religion has yet experienced',[5] Troeltsch pointed to the difficulties of the task which theology encountered in the modern world. The contemporary situation, he claimed, was marked by an increasing domination of materialism, which itself was characterized by a 'loss of all freedom, all life and spontaneity ... a hotly sought after entry into a world of mere necessity which barred the world of creative freedom and new life'.[6] In such a world, he went on, a religion which asserted an independent realm of the spirit appeared to many to be nothing more than an 'abstraction of savages'.[7]

Similarly in his 1907 essay on the essence of the modern spirit Troeltsch outlined the 'abstract depersonalized rationalism, coupled with the principle of might is right[8] which seemed to typify so many of the struggles of the modern world. This, when combined with a 'universally plausible utilitarianism',[9] led to ever-increasing fragmentation, where life was seen as 'merely the fight for survival, inequality, and the triumph of force'.[10] The modern world had thereby succeeded in 'destroying the old religious ties with great thoroughness', but it had 'not produced any genuinely new force'.[11] Similarly, demographic changes created their own problems, as he made clear in a lecture on practical christian ethics:

---

[4] 'Meine Bücher' (A1921/29b), 4; ET, 366.
[5] 'Die theologische und religiöse Lage' (A1903/16a), 3.   [6] Ibid., 10.   [7] Ibid.
[8] 'Das Wesen des modernen Geistes' (A1907/8b), 310 f.; ET, 249.
[9] Ibid., 323; ET, 259.   [10] Ibid., 312; ET, 250.
[11] Ibid., 329; ET, 264.

Our contemporary problems are not deeper or more profound, but are simply different. Where once twelve million people lived, now over sixty million people want to live. All problems have to depart from this fact, not of progress, but of the increase of the masses, which complicates all questions of existence and, along with these, those of ethics.[12]

In response to such threats, Troeltsch contended, there was a continued need for theologians to reaffirm the primacy of the spirit and make room for human freedom, by picking out 'the deepest and strongest religious forces [which were] to be found in Christianity' and bringing them into 'free fusion with elements of modern life', such as was achieved 'by the poets and thinkers of German Idealism'. For Troeltsch, 'no other future development is thinkable than that both adjust to each other and learn to stimulate each other instead of attacking one another'.[13] Only in this manner could the theologian help elevate 'the person out of the mere conditions of nature to a union with God'.[14]

For Troeltsch, the major problems of the modern world emerged from the attempt to find some form of social integration in a situation marked by social dislocation and individualism. Indeed he saw the primary theological task as that of establishing an ethical basis and discipline for the individual which did not at the same time deny individuality or subsume it in some destructive universal. The modern world had thus brought with it a grave ethical dilemma. What had begun as a 'liberation and an elevation' could very quickly become a 'burden and a confusion'[15] as the human being became an isolated individual undefined by its relation to a wider whole. Although the power to criticize had freed the human being from the bonds of supernaturalism, it had failed to provide any new authorities. In response, Troeltsch claimed that:

a genuine Christian love and a sense of the value of the personality demanded expression along the following lines: a fundamental breach with the individualistic social order which has developed over the last two centuries; the devotion not merely of individuals but of everybody to the whole; the creation of a just and efficient means for an adequate natural existence as the basis for the development of spiritual values.[16]

Troeltsch was thus embarking on a theological quest to redeem modernity from meaninglessness and fragmentation by bringing to it a vision of wholeness, unity, and meaning rooted in Christianity, which 'alone takes the soul from the diversity and confusion of the world up to truth'.[17] To see

---

[12] *PCE*, dictation, 16.   [13] 'Das Wesen des modernen Geistes' (A1907/8b), 329; ET, 265.
[14] Ibid.   [15] *Der Historismus und seine Probleme* (A1922/22), 10.
[16] Troeltsch, *Die Soziallehren* (A1912/2), 844; ET, 726.
[17] 'Die Selbständigkeit der Religion' (A1896/2), 212.

individuality as such a 'deadly poison that kills culture' would be to 'despair of the fundamental demand of morality'. There was thus always the duty 'to discipline it ethically and thus to transfigure the natural powers of individualism'.[18] He therefore felt that the development of individualism 'which, as liberalism, democracy, and capitalism, profoundly determines the cultural formations of modernity' was nevertheless 'one of the greatest historical problems which had scarcely been solved'.[19] With the liberation of the individual the modern world had achieved enormous progress, but, at the same time:

something has to be conceived along with it, which binds the individual and provides laws for communal living . . . The individual is only freed from the external, earthly, and otherworldly authority because it contains within itself an inner law, the free thought and the free recognition of the value of humanity . . . Autonomy is the great human right and the most inspired confession of the modern world.[20]

Troeltsch's quest was thus to provide a grounding for such autonomy not by relocating the individual in the heteronomy of supernaturalism and medievalism but in modern analogies to absolute structures which did not deny his or her individuality.[21] Thus he asked: How could a 'balance between the achievement of individualism and the need for universality and firm order be achieved?'[22] As he put it in *Die Soziallehren*:

Today one knows or senses all too clearly how complicated problems of our common life and culture converge in these great questions [of the relationship to the world]. With the arrival of the modern giant states which permeate even the smallest details of life, and with the emergence of the nature of the capitalist system of social order, the ideal has actually become different.[23]

In this search for a unity and authority which did not deny the Enlightenment principle of the autonomous individual, Troeltsch shared much with many of the leading social theorists of his time in their reaction to the ahistorical thought of the rationalists and empiricists of the eighteenth century: 'It must not be overlooked,' he remarked in 1913, 'that the whole sociological reaction to the eighteenth century continues and still defines today's problem of how to balance the achievement of individualism with the need for universality and firm order'.[24] As he wrote in *Die Soziallehren*:

---

[18] 'Das Wesen des modernen Geistes' (A1907/8b), 335; ET, 271. On this point see the important programmatic essay by F. W. Graf, 'Religion und Individualität'. Graf sees Troeltsch's theology and philosophy of religion as resting on the 'connection of the freedom of the individual subject with the transcendental grounds of that freedom' (229).
[19] Review of Přibram (A1913/28), col. 596.
[20] 'Autonomie und Rationalismus' (A1907/11), col. 201 f.
[21] Cf. 'Das neunzehnte Jahrhundert' (A1913/36a), 649.
[22] 'Die Restaurationsepoche' (A1913/38a), 613.
[23] *Die Soziallehren* (A1912/2), 843 f.; ET, 726.
[24] 'Die Restaurationsepoche' (A1913/38a), 613.

There cannot be a real social coherence at all without the unity of the world-view, and it is good for us to remember that, in opposition to the modern world with its anarchy which has a disintegrating influence on society, two so fundamentally different thinkers as the Romantic Novalis, and the sober empiricist Auguste Comte deliberately look back to the Middle Ages as the classic epoch of social unity based on the unity of ideas. At present we have the example of the Social Democrats.[25]

According to Troeltsch, the ultimate dilemma of the modern world was to be characterized thus: the individual sought authority, yet could find no satisfactory authority which did not contradict the principle of autonomy. How was it possible, he asked, to achieve a unified conception of the 'rational-universal and the individual-factual currents of reality', to conceive, at one and the same time, 'the rational-deductive and the irrational-original'?[26] Or more simply: 'What am I to do with my hard-earned freedom? No art and no science can decipher this ultimate problem, but rather, all they can do is to let us merely glimpse a higher harmony now and then.'[27] In other words: How was autonomy to be regulated in accord with realizable higher ends?

The task, then, which Troeltsch saw at the 'heart of religion',[28] was to structure autonomous individuality through the perception of a unifying whole,[29] disciplining it with a new authority,[30] which nevertheless remained an 'authority of freedom'.[31] He did not consider autonomy to be an aimless and amoral individualism, an 'unbounded anarchy',[32] but instead saw it as rooted in an intersubjective authority which did not deny human freedom.[33] In this manner, the problem of freedom became 'bound up with the problem of responsibility'.[34] This was, in theological terms, nothing less than human participation in divine creativity, as autonomy and theonomy became one in divine love.[35]

---

[25] *Die Soziallehren* (A1912/2), 473 n.215; ET, 835 n.215.

[26] Review of Maria Raich (A1906/15), 681 f.   [27] *PCE*, lecture, 54.

[28] 'Christentum und Religionsgeschichte' (A1897/10a), 351.

[29] 'Die Restaurationsepoche' (A1913/38a), 614. Cf. *Der Historismus und seine Probleme* (A1922/22), 5.

[30] 'Die Restaurationsepoche' (A1913/38a), 614.

[31] The phrase is Trutz Rendtorff's. See 'The Modern Age as a Chapter in the History of Christianity', 499: 'Theological thought should be guided by the "authority of freedom", which was shaped by the historical profile of Christianity in this world. Consciousness of this freedom has given birth to the modern age, but, as we can now clearly see, it has also made us aware of its limits, which call for theology to view the modern age as a chapter within the history of Christianity'.

[32] 'Autonomie und Rationalismus' (A1907/11), col. 201 f.   [33] Ibid., col. 203.

[34] *Allgemeine Ethik*, 29.

[35] *Glaubenslehre* (F1925/2), sect. 14. 3; cf. 'Christentum und Religionsgeschichte' (A1897/10a), 343.

The Challenge of Capitalism

According to Troeltsch this task was rendered still more difficult by the increasingly 'rational' form of capitalism, which had emerged after the Enlightenment, becoming 'an organic constituent of modern existence which flowed into every pore of our being',[36] and which attempted 'to reconstruct the whole of our existence according to economic laws'.[37] Where once the guilds had organized the professions, and where once the son followed on from the father in a predetermined calling, the mechanization of work meant that 'where there had previously been professions ordained by God, there was now merely work in order to exist'.[38] Just as the scientific world-view was dominated by an all-pervasive materialism which threatened to stifle human creativity, so in the economic sphere the worker's sense of personal involvement was destroyed as the human being was reduced to the level of a mere machine.

Capitalism's main effect led to the abuse of power as well as increased alienation and anonymity.[39] Indeed Troeltsch recognized that 'the acquisition of technology which appeared for some to be an enormous progress was, for others, an unbearable mechanization of life'.[40] The Enlightenment principle of humanity, with its optimistic estimation of the natural endowments of the human being, had apparently reached its term in the 'inequalities of life . . . It thus evokes the opposition of an entirely different conception of nature which sees it merely as the fight for survival, inequality, and the triumph of force'.[41] Capitalism posed equally grave challenges to religion. It too threatened to stifle human freedom and creativity and to reduce the human being to little more than an economic unit.

Aristocratic Individualism

Alongside capitalism and materialism there was, according to Troeltsch, the parallel development of 'aristocratic individualism'; 'a resigned wisdom that everywhere seeks and honours greatness but which accepts the unfathomable and unpredictable variety of human life as a dark fate'.[42] The rise of such unbridled individualism meant that it was not clear where any higher unity, which had hitherto ordered the whole of life, could be found.[43] Similarly it was

---

[36] 'Ethik und Kapitalismus' (A1905/6), col. 321.
[37] 'Das Wesen des modernen Geistes' (A1907/8b), 309, ET, 248; cf. 'Ethik und Kapitalismus' (A1905/6), col. 321.
[38] PCE, lecture, 54.
[39] Cf. 'Das Wesen des modernen Geistes' (A1907/8b), 310; ET, 249.   [40] EPH, lecture, 7.
[41] 'Das Wesen des modernen Geistes' (A1907/8b), 312; ET, 250.   [42] Ibid., 318; ET, 255.
[43] Cf. 'Grundprobleme der Ethik' (A1902/4a), 561–5.

not clear what sort of 'objectivity' could be given to ethical behaviour, since there was such a great gulf between facts and values: nothing in nature seemed to imply any higher end. The institutions which had previously ordered society, and which had been seen as ordained by God, had become little more than practical expedients for the future development of the human race.[44]

This again posed a great threat to religion, since there could be no question of any higher motivation. Instead everything was determined by what Troeltsch called 'a metaphysics of immanence where the sensual was identified with the spiritual and the finite with the infinite'.[45] Although this 'gospel of beauty' evidently moved beyond the materialistic denials of the human spirit, it merely replaced this with an inner-worldly good of pure aesthetic pleasure.[46] Indeed, Troeltsch lamented, amongst German *belles-lettres* it was difficult to recognize Germany as any longer a Christian nation;[47] it appeared instead to be under the influence of France, 'that European country most broken with Christianity'.[48]

The artistic view of life was, however, 'by no means favourably disposed towards the other fundamental elements of the modern world'. Although the ethical implications of a refined aestheticism were often negative and egoistic, nevertheless, Troeltsch held, 'the ways were constantly being prepared for mystical and religious ideas'.[49] Although there was an artistic recognition of human creativity, what appeared lacking, according to Troeltsch, were higher ends around which to orientate such activity: the artists were merely 'virtuosi, who need something external to develop their individuality, but, lacking this, fall into the void'.[50] Without higher goals, according to Troeltsch, there could be no lasting morality. Thus a genuine morality was entrusted with the task of 'lifting human existence to the level of a higher necessity, to eternity'.[51] In short, this meant a 'faith in a purpose and meaning for life . . . which keeps on crying out for religion'.[52]

MAX WEBER'S ETHICS OF RESPONSIBILITY

In many ways, Weber's sociology is a secular counterpart to Troeltsch's theology. He too analysed a situation in which all values seemed to have been relativized and in which there could be 'no scientifically demonstrable

---

[44] Ibid., 656; cf. *Allgemeine Ethik*, lecture, 6 ff.

[45] 'Das Wesen des modernen Geistes' (A1907/8b), 320; ET, 257.

[46] Cf. 'Die christliche Weltanschauung' (A1894/1a), esp. 250 ff.; 'Religionsphilosophie' (A1904/7), 118.   [47] 'Die Religion im deutschen Staate' (A1913/37a), 74.

[48] Ibid., 73.   [49] 'Das Wesen des modernen Geistes' (A1907/8b), 321; ET, 258.

[50] 'Die Kirche im Leben der Gegenwart' (A1911/8a), 99.

[51] 'Das Wesen des modernen Geistes' (A1907/8b), 326 f.; ET, 262.   [52] Ibid., 327; ET, 263.

ideals'.[53] In the modern capitalistic world, he maintained, there could be no 'external expression of a style of life based upon an ultimate, finished, and demonstrable unity of the personality'.[54] For Weber, as for Troeltsch, there had been profound and permanent changes which brought the human predicament into ever sharper focus. In particular, the overriding Christian ethic of neighbourliness had broken down in the changes in the relationships between individuals in the modern world:

In the past it was possible to regulate ethically the relationship between master and slave precisely because the relations were personal. But it is not possible, at least not in the same sense and with the same success, to regulate the relations between the ever-changing lenders and the ever-changing debtors between whom there are no personal relations.[55]

The theodicies of religion could thus no longer coexist with a scientific assessment of a reality which in itself was devoid of all absolute meaning. For Weber, this created a fundamental tension:

Wherever rational empirical cognition has systematically completed the disenchantment [lit. demagification] of the world and its transformation into a causal mechanism, there re-emerge definitively the tensions with the claims of the ethical postulate that the world is a divinely ordained ethically *meaningful* concern. From the empirical and ultimately the *mathematically* oriented conception of the world develops the fundamental denial of every way of looking at the world which asks after the meaning of inner-worldly events.[56]

Thus, just as primitive polytheism declined and was replaced by a religious rationalization in the all-explaining theodicy of monotheism,[57] so, as the world grew increasingly disenchanted, monotheism collapsed and was replaced by a demythologized polytheism, a breakdown of any system of all-embracing values. The world could not reveal order since 'every empirical study of the facts, as the old Mill observed, leads to a recognition of a polytheism'.[58] For Weber, as for Troeltsch, the world in itself could display no absolute order: there could be no natural knowledge of any *Weltanschauung* or set of absolute values.

Instead, the human being had a responsibility to create order for him- or

[53] *GASS*, 420. Cf. Herring, 'Max Weber und Ernst Troeltsch', 419.
[54] Weber, *Die Protestantische Ethik*, 269 f.   [55] *GARS*, 544.
[56] *GARS*, 564. On this point see esp. Tenbruck ('The Problem of the Thematic Unity in the works of Max Weber') who emphasizes the point that, for Weber, religion is not so much cognition as theodicy, a rationalization to overcome the meaninglessness of reality (338 ff.). As the influence of religion declines, so there is a quest for a new 'ethical unification of action' (345). To make sense of reality in an age when the world had been demagicalized (disenchanted) required a recognition of the responsibility for the creation of that cultural web which is reality.
[57] Cf. *GARS*, 537: 'Religious interpretations of the world and the ethics of religions created by intellectuals were strongly exposed to the imperative of consistency'.   [58] *GAW*, 507.

herself by ordering reality, which in itself was value-neutral, in terms of 'concepts and judgements [which] are not empirical reality and do not copy it'.[59] The insistence that order and meaning were introduced into reality (the basic tenet of Baden neo-Kantianism), and were not to be 'read off' from the facts, meant that meaningful reality was ultimately a matter of the individual will:

> The destiny of a cultural epoch that has eaten of the tree of knowledge is to have to know that we cannot discern the *meaning* of world events from the results of even the most thorough investigation, but we must be in a position to *create* it. *Weltanschauungen* can never be the product of advances in empirical knowledge, and thus the highest ideals which motivate us the strongest can only take effect in conflict with other ideals which are just as sacred to others as ours are to us.[60]

The most frightening prospect for values rested not so much in this recognition of the value-neutrality, ethical indifference, or even the ultimate polytheism of reality, but in the human evasion of the responsibility for the creation of value: relativism could not be allowed to become a value in itself. The quest for a utilitarian comfort was at odds with the human destiny 'consciously to take a position towards the world and to give it a meaning'.[61] The deadly enemy of *all* values was the voluntary evasion of the 'unbreachable conflict, as between "God" and the "devil", between which there can be no relativizations and compromises'.[62] Another 'unavoidable fruit of the tree of knowledge', was 'to know these contradictions and to be able to see that every single important action and, to top it all, life itself as a whole, if it is not to slide by like a natural event, but is to be lived *consciously*, means a chain of ultimate decisions, through which the soul, as in Plato, chooses—that is the meaning of its action and its existence'.[63] In an age when 'we must create our

[59] *GAW*, 213.   [60] *GAW*, 154.
[61] *GAW*, 180. Cf. 'Die deutschen Landarbeiter', 80 f.: 'We do not engage in social policy in order to create human happiness . . . We want to protect and sustain that which appears most valuable in people: self-responsibility'. See also *GPS* 24, where Weber points to the weaknesses of 'flabby eudaemonism'.   [62] *GAW*, 507.
[63] *GAW*, 107. W. Hennis (*Essays in Reconstruction*, 21–104) emphasizes the importance of freedom as the dominant value in Weber's thought. The central question was this: 'What does this order, this type of social relationship imply for the *human type* to which it sets limits or opens up chances?' (59 f.). Consequently Weber was vitally interested in the problem of the effects of the social order on humankind. Each of the life orders implied the possibility for a certain type of personality to develop. Determining all action was the question of fate. Hennis points to the *anethisch* character of the contemporary world, a world which no longer allows for ethical interpretation. Weber's theme is to present the possibility for a life to be lived in an ethically interpretable manner under the prevailing conditions, and in this way to stand outside these conditions as they threaten to dominate. Lawrence A. Scaff (*Fleeing the Iron Cage*, 103) also emphasizes the ethical importance of Weber's methodology, of the continual need to give an account of the ultimate meaning of conduct. Cf. Weber, *GASS*, 412: 'The key question is . . . to oppose the machine mentality and to keep a part of humanity free from such fragmentation of the soul, from ultimate domination by the bureaucratic form of life'.

ideals from within our chests' such a choice, Weber contended, would not
prove easy. Indeed it was 'the stigma of our human dignity that the peace of
our souls cannot be as great as the peace of one who dreams of such a
paradise'.[64]

Weber shared with Troeltsch a belief in the importance of the objective
assessment of reality to bring us to an understanding of the 'reasons for its
having become thus and not otherwise, [which] gave rise to a position of
clarity as the necessary preliminary to any ethical choice'.[65] This is perhaps
most succinctly stated in Weber's incisive response to Gertrud Bäumer of
1916. Without a responsibility to reality, the purest of motives could have
disastrous results. Indeed a failure to recognize the constraints placed on
ethics by political reality, in Weber's view, was a sin against the Holy
Ghost.[66]

[The Gospels] stand in contradiction not just to war—which they do not especially
single out—but ultimately to each and every law of the social world in so far as these
involve a world of culture which is centred on the here and now, that is on beauty,
value, honour, and the greatness of the 'creature' . . . It is only within this system of
laws that the current 'demands of the day' have any relevance . . . The old sober
empiricist J. S. Mill said: empiricism alone will never arrive at the idea of *one* God—
at least, in my opinion, at the God of goodness, but at a *polytheism*. In fact whoever is in
the world (in a Christian sense) can never experience anything but a conflict between a
plethora of values . . . He has to *choose* when to serve one God and when another.[67]

Thus, for Weber, the human being, inescapably bound up with the irrationalities of reality, could no longer make a choice between conflicting
values based solely on the ethical absolutism of the Sermon on the Mount. If
historical and political reality were brought into consideration, the choice
rested between the greater and lesser evil, since 'the genius, or the demon,
of politics lives with the God of love'.[68] An ethic of responsibility forced a
compromise of the absolute—a Faustian pact with the devil.[69]

[64] *GASS*, 420.

[65] *GAW*, 170. Indeed this was the whole purpose of the study of 'culture' or that 'finite section
of the meaningless eternity of world events' which was analysed in the social sciences, as ideas
of value were related to one another, and related to one's own values (*GAW*, 180).

[66] *GPS*, 547.

[67] *GPS*, 145. On the subject of 'polytheism' see esp. Mommsen, *The Political and Social Theory
of Max Weber*. The characterization of the world as polytheistic is seen by Mommsen as the logical conclusion of the Enlightenment, where the individual was freed from the naïve hope in
rationality as a liberating factor and 'was confronted by just the multiplicity of competing forces
which people of earlier epochs not infrequently tried to explain in mythological terms' (144).

[68] *GPS*, 557.

[69] There was a lively debate during the First World War on the contemporary ethical significance of the Sermon on the Mount and of Hebrew prophecy. Cf. Bailey, 'Gott mit uns'. Against
the Jewish neo-Kantian Hermann Cohen, who saw the direct relevance of Hebrew prophecy,
Troeltsch regarded it as essentially Utopian and of little immediate application to the modern

Weber took up a similar theme in his influential Munich lecture on the vocation of learning, of 1918. Again he pleads for objectivity, for the impartial assessment of reality, against those 'professorial prophets' who introduced universalist speculation into the lecture theatre under the guise of scientific truth. This was a deception, since science could not reveal absolutes and could never answer the question, 'Which of the warring Gods are we to serve?'[70] The proper use of science, however, would at least ensure that the individual could arrive at a reasoned decision and thereby help him or her achieve a position of *clarity*.[71] Indeed, a clear world-view required a knowledge of the devil himself.[72] Nothing could prevent the ultimate decision, yet the necessary sacrifice of the intellect did not imply submission to falsehood.[73]

There were profound political implications in Weber's position: to obey the dictates of conscience to the exclusion of the demands of political reality could never satisfactorily describe the vocation of the politician. Indeed, by refusing to resist evil with force, the politician might make himself responsible for the increase of evil which resulted from his inaction. Absolutist ethics could have little role in the 'ethical irrationality of the world'.[74] Consequently, the mark of political maturity was the knowledge or the understanding of the conditions of life: although Weber recognized that absolutist ethics, the ethics of the sect, might provide the ultimate *motivation* for action, it was only possible to construct a coherent system for political action if all the *consequences* of behaviour were taken into account. Thus historical reality always tempered ethical activity: 'a successful politics, correctly understood' was 'the "art of the possible"'. Nevertheless, Weber claimed, it was 'no less

world ('Glaube und Ethos der hebräischen Propheten' (A1916/13a), 34–65). On this see Dietrich, *Cohen and Troeltsch*. Dietrich is, however, far too willing to locate Troeltsch in a 'Hegelian mind set' rather than in the First World War. See also Mark D. Chapman, 'Theology, Nationalism and the First World War' for an analysis of Otto Baumgarten's wartime discussion of the Sermon on the Mount.

[70] *GAW*, 605; cf. 608. On the circumstances of this lecture see Schuchter, 'Value-Neutrality and the Ethic of Responsibility', 113 ff.

[71] *GAW*, 607.

[72] Thus, according to Troeltsch, on the basis of his 'icy cold' assessment of factuality Weber escapes the excesses of dialectical and universalist history (*Der Historismus und seine Probleme* (A1922/22), 161). Troeltsch saw Weber's prime task as that of the 'clarification of social and political problems by pointing out the special character of western civilization' (*Der Historismus und seine Probleme* (A1922/22), 567; cf. 367, 565).

[73] Troeltsch again offers a profound insight into Weber's position: 'There are even those who believe he died of a broken heart because the youth movement ignored him. In truth, he sought to make clear to the world and to youth in particular that the world could only be rescued through clear insight into its historical situation and through a clear, calculated formation of ideals based on this insight, and not through fantasy and not through stupidity' (*Der Historismus und seine Probleme* (A1922/22), 160 n.73; cf. Mommsen, *Max Weber and German Politics*, 321).

[74] *GPS*, 553.

true that the possible is often reached only by striving towards the impossible that lies beyond it'.[75] Or, as he put it in a memorable phrase: '"ideas" have often determined the track (just like the pointsman) along which the action has been pushed by the dynamic of interests'.[76] For Weber, there was thus a point at which the conflict between absolutist ethics and political reality reached its limits. In full recognition of the facts, the politician had eventually to assert, in Luther's heroic terms, 'Here I stand, I can do no other.'[77]

TROELTSCH, WEBER, AND THE BREAKDOWN OF CULTURE

Towards the ends of their lives both Weber and Troeltsch became aware of the difficulties of irresponsible solutions which failed to give due regard to the practical possibilities of the situation. This became clearest in the ethical and political crisis of the beginnings of the Weimar Republic, which was accompanied by the frightening dilettantism of the anti-intellectual and 'anti-historicist'[78] reaction to the breakdown of Wilhelmine culture.[79] According to Troeltsch, their battle cry was:

Away with naturalism and the intellectualism that is almost identical with it, but also away with *Historismus* and the specialization and relativism of the fossilized knowledge-industry that is almost identical with it.[80]

Such a flight from this responsibility towards scientific objectivity into antihistoricist methods was admittedly, Troeltsch conceded, 'a strong spiritual power, but in all social aspects' it was 'helpless and indifferent'.[81] Troeltsch expressed this clearly in a letter to Eugen Diederichs[82] the leading publisher of the new movement:

---

[75] *GAW*, 514. Cf. Kollman, 'Eine Diagnose der Weimarer Republik', 309: 'Politics is also for Troeltsch the art of the possible—and almost every page of the *Spektatorbriefe* is filled with a critical realism'.   [76] *GARS*, 252.

[77] *GPS*, 559.

[78] On the 'anti-historical revolution' see esp. Nowak, 'Die "antihistoristische Revolution"', esp. 136.

[79] Indeed this brought about some degree of reconciliation between the two old friends. Cf. letter to Marianne Weber (cited in Graf, 'Max Weber und die protestantische Theologie seiner Zeit', 145): '[In] the last few years I have thought about him almost daily. I think I can detect that in the last decade he also experienced developments which brought our communal basis closer together'. Cf. Marianne Weber, *Max Weber*, 618.

[80] 'Die Revolution in der Wissenschaft' (A1921/28a), 655. For a general discussion of the intellectual situation of the Weimar Republic see esp. Barnouw, *Weimar Intellectuals and the Threat of Modernity*. On the youth movement see esp. Klemens von Klemperer, *German's New Conservatism*.

[81] *Die Sozialphilosophie* (A1922/27), 21; ET, 224.

[82] Eugen Diederichs (1867–1930) founded his publishing house in 1896 in Florence, moving in 1897 to Leipzig and in 1904 to Jena. As well as publishing fairy tales from around the world,

I admire your idealism—your untiring work for spiritual regeneration. Through your press you have moved in a new direction. Yet for such things there is no organization. That would require a new Church or religious order, a cultural Salvation Army. The realms of pure thought and the organization of literature have their limits. Social Democracy can only do this because it is a closed and dogmatic system like a Church. Everything else only has ideas to sow, and nobody has any hope that they will grow.[83]

With their escape into a realm of pure ideas untempered by history, both neo-Romanticism and the revolutionary alternative of political upheaval were quite futile.

Similarly for Weber, just as the politician required a certain detachment from the emotionalism of involvement in the economic struggle, so the scientist required a detachment from any quasi-religious or mystical experience:

The hunt after 'experience'—the most fashionable word of present-day Germany—can be seen in the most part to be a product of the increasing loss of strength inwardly to withstand the 'everyday', and that publicity which the individual seems compelled to give to his 'experience' can be seen as perhaps a loss of 'distance' and thus also of appropriate style and dignity.[84]

Similarly, although Troeltsch was willing to recognize that 'everywhere people are striving after freedom, originality, vitality, and a clear attachment to an ideal',[85] and thirsting for a *'Weltanschauung, and a living law'*[86] and 'unity',[87] he was nevertheless convinced, along with Weber, that they could not be allowed 'simply to push aside practical considerations with scorn and disgust'. 'What Weber says about [science]', Troeltsch went on, 'is clearly . . . the only truth'.[88]

The neo-Romantics of Stefan George's circle failed to address the question of how they were to influence the German people, which meant (as—Troeltsch remarked—Weber continually reminded them) that 'their new Romanticism will founder just like the old on the unshakable rocks of real social and economic relations'.[89] This failure to recognize the importance of praxis was analogous to the adoption of sectarianism, of an absolutist, yet impotent, ethic. 'One can either withdraw to the hermitage or to the idealistic conventicle', Troeltsch remarked, 'or one can connect men's faith with these real relationships. Writing books and Jeremiads is an unfruitful middle way'.[90]

he sponsored much radical and esoteric literature. On Diederichs see Gangolf Hübinger (ed.), *Versammlungsort moderner Geister*; and Irmgard Heidler, *Der Verleger Eugen Diederichs und seine Welt (1896–1930)*. On the religious policy of the press see Graf, 'Das Laboratorium der religiösen Moderne. Zur "Verlagsreligion" des Eugen Diederichs Verlags'; and Hübinger, 'Kulturkritik und Kulturpolitik'.

[83] Letter of Troeltsch to Diederichs cited in Hübinger, 'Kulturkritik und Kulturpolitik', 111.
[84] *GAW*, 519.   [85] Troeltsch, 'Die Revolution in der Wissenschaft' (A1921/28a), 656.
[86] Ibid., 669.   [87] Ibid., 655.   [88] Ibid., 673.   [89] Ibid.
[90] Ibid. For Weber's views on the ineffectiveness of the cultural alternatives to religion see esp. Weber, *GARS*, esp. 569.

The youth movement, it was true, had made the proponents of a thoroughgoing scientific method more aware of the need to justify their practices in the face of continued criticisms, yet nothing in their alternatives could legitimately claim scientific credibility. According to Troeltsch, just as Edmund Burke had written a highly revolutionary book against the revolution, so these attacks on the scientific method were just as revolutionary, yet they could achieve no restoration of the *ancien régime*, since 'the solid realm of economic-social relationships would remain'.[91]

The importance of the neo-Romantics, according to Troeltsch, did not rest in their constructive alternatives to the scientific perception of reality, but in making ever more apparent the problems of capitalism and of mass industrialization. Troeltsch shared their concerns: just as the modern idea of the State was 'in inner and essential contradiction to all Christian ideas', so, he went on, 'capitalism, or centralized concentrated industry, which entices everything and all creative freedom of movement into its sphere of influence, constitutes the most perfect contradiction to that peace, calm, structured existential security, and independence of the personality which is the presupposition of Christian ethics and the love of one's neighbour'.[92]

The capitalistic and bureaucratic threats to individuality were clearly recognized by those who strove to establish new communities which aimed to recreate the consensus of the Middle Ages. Yet, Troeltsch went on, books on Shakespeare and Dante were no substitute for realistic alternatives, since 'they both had the advantage of being part of a unified, formed, and homogeneous world'[93] which had now been superseded. It was not surprising that the obvious solution to the problems of capitalism should be in sectarian or mystical escape. Against this, however, Troeltsch affirmed a practical solution: 'We can create no new ideals; an abandonment of them altogether would be deadly; a pietistic attitude only comes into question for the few. So we must attempt some kind of balancing act.'[94] It was such a balancing act that Troeltsch attempted through his participation in the practical problems of postwar reconstruction.

RECONSTRUCTION

Both Weber and Troeltsch were profoundly concerned with the problem of reconstruction during the revolutionary period after the First World War; a period which, Troeltsch claimed, displayed

---

[91] 'Die Revolution in der Wissenschaft' (A1921/28a), 677.
[92] *Die Sozialphilosophie* (A1922/27), 29; ET, 230.
[93] 'Die Revolution in der Wissenschaft' (A1921/28a), 663.   [94] *Allgemeine Ethik*, 37.

historical lessons of the most frightful and amazing power. We theorize and categorize no longer under the protection of an order in which everything has its place, but in the midst of the storm of the reconstruction of the world, where every old word can be tested as to its practical value or impotence, where much that formerly appeared to be real or of value has become mere wordplay and paper. The ground underfoot is shaking and is dancing rings around the different possibilities for further development.[95]

In such an urgent situation the concern with objectivity led both Troeltsch and Weber into the sphere of practical politics.[96]

What was obvious to both Troeltsch and Weber was that political solutions which could match the gravity of the situation could not be created out of nothing, as Weber made clear in his address to Diederichs' first Lauenstein Conference of May 1917. It was of the utmost importance, he maintained, that 'the battle against materialism must derive its power from the sober facts of the day'.[97] Indeed, on his view, German political parties were too dominated by politicians of conscience (*Gesinnungspolitiker*) and consequently they were unable to offer constructive solutions to the problems of the present. Instead, Weber maintained, politics required a certain sense of ideological detachment, of 'distance' from the 'politics of the streets'.[98] An irresponsible approach to politics became most apparent in the Versailles peace treaty itself, which, according to Weber, was the gravest denial of economic and historical factuality and would lead to 'endless struggles'.[99]

An ethically responsible attitude towards politics was adopted by the *Deutsche Demokratische Partei* (DDP) of which both Weber and Troeltsch were early advocates. The DDP stood for a particular approach to politics which appealed to those primarily interested in the practical realization of a political programme which avoided the doctrinaire extremism (or idealism)

---

[95] Troeltsch, *Der Historismus und seine Probleme* (A1922/22), 6.

[96] Troeltsch had previously been actively involved in politics as a University of Heidelberg representative in the Baden Parliament in the years before the First World War (cf. Kollman, 'Eine Diagnose der Weimarer Republik', 293). On Troeltsch's political involvement see Rubanowice, *Crisis in Consciousness*, 99–130; H. Ruddies, 'Soziale Demokratie und freier Protestantismus'; Gustav Schmidt, *Deutscher Historismus*; Bernd Sösemann, 'Das "erneute Deutschland". Ernst Troeltschs politische Engagement im ersten Weltkrieg'. Weber was actively involved in the DDP but failed to secure nomination for Parliament. Disgusted with the petty powermongering, he resigned his membership, ostensibly over the commitment of the DDP to socialization, something he regarded as quite impractical in the situation. Cf. Mommsen, *Max Weber and German Politics*, 309 ff.

[97] *MWG*, 15/1, 706. On the circumstances of this conference see esp. Weber, *MWG* xv. 1, 701 ff.; Mommsen, *The Political and Social Theory of Max Weber*, 138; and Hennis, *Essays in Reconstruction*, 70.

[98] Weber, *GPS*, 287. Weber suggests that the modern entrepreneur can never achieve enough detachment from economic struggles to act as a rational politician (*GPS*, 274).

[99] *GPS*, 456.

of right and left, and where, according to Carl Petersen, 'practical work' was 'more important than programmatic'.[100] Similarly for Troeltsch, ideas and doctrines came from outside politics; conscience could never dictate which party one should support.[101] What was vital for the party was that its guiding ideas should be capable of practical realization. Thus Troeltsch remarked:

For my own part I had quite enough ideas for myself; for these I did not need a party. From a party I demanded realistic knowledge of the situation, ability to bring itself to government, and the average amount of human understanding needed to govern everyone and which one might expect from a party. Important politicians can have the ideas when they are carried forwards and protected in this way.[102]

Troeltsch took his practical responsibilities seriously and was elected to the Prussian State Assembly (*Landtag*) in 1919, becoming an under-secretary in the Ministry for Science, Art, and Education with a special responsibility for Church affairs.[103] He stood on a platform which sought to move away from the 'class domination of the revolutionary Left and the resurgence of *Junker* militarism from the Right'.[104] Any alternative to this middle ground, he felt, would 'be complete damnation', since 'the destruction of the [secular] centre threatens the constitution and the *Reich*'.[105] Although not a founder member of the *DDP*,[106] Troeltsch soon became actively involved in

---

[100] Carl Petersen (Friedrich Naumann's replacement as leader; cited in W. Stephan, *Aufstieg und Verfall der Linksliberalismus*, 142). Troeltsch first expressed this idea as early as 1904 in a speech to the *ESK* (Troeltsch, *Politische Ethik* (A1904/6)). It is interesting to note that he traces the development of these ideas to Weber (3). Liebersohn (in *Fate and Utopia in German Sociology*, ch. 3) interprets Troeltsch's attitude to politics on the basis of this lecture (which also forms the basis for his interpretation in *Religion and Industrial Society*) and consequently fails to see the importance of his practical political involvement after the First World War. Troeltsch is characterized by Liebersohn as a reluctant Culture Protestant rather than the active democrat that he became.

[101] At an earlier stage, however, Troeltsch did remark that 'one perhaps has the duty to vote liberal, even if one is not liberal oneself' (*Politische Ethik* (A1904/6), 43; ET, 209).

[102] Troeltsch, 'Kritik am System' (A1920/14), 215. This quotation was not included in the selection published in *Spektatorbriefe* (H1924/3).

[103] On Troeltsch's involvement in Church/State politics see esp. Wright, 'Ernst Troeltsch als parlamentarischer Unterstaatssekretär im Preußischen Ministerium für Wissenschaft, Kunst und Volksbildung'. Cf. Jacke, *Kirche Zwischen Monarchie und Republik*; and Nowak, *Evangelische Kirche und Weimarer Republik*. On the legacy of a *Volkskirche* in a democracy see Ruddies, 'Soziale Demokratie und freier Protestantismus', 165 ff. Troeltsch saw the Church as the basis for social integration, something which, according to Ruddies, was only realized after the Second World War (173).

[104] Poster from the 1919 Prussian *Landtag* election (Museum of Berlin collection).

[105] *Spektatorbriefe* (H1924/3), 143, 163.

[106] Cf. Ruddies, 'Soziale Demokratie und freier Protestantismus', 158. On the *DDP* and the failure of German liberalism see esp. W. Stephan, *Aufstieg und Verfall*; Neumann, *Die Parteien der Weimarer Republik*, 50 ff.; Jones, *German Liberalism*. Jones stresses the contingent factors in the demise of liberalism, against those who surveyed history from the point of view of a 'tyranny of hindsight' where all forces lead inexorably to 1933: 'The founding of the Weimar Republic

shaping the programme, particularly at the Second Party Congress held in December 1919, where his contributions to the debates on cultural policy reveal a marked continuity with his theology.[107] If a political party dogmatically reflected a *Weltanschauung*, he claimed, then this was nothing other than a doctrinaire dismissal of the facts which constrained the realization of ideals. This was particularly true of the *SPD* which, Troeltsch contended, had become a *Weltanschauungspartei* only in Germany.[108] Instead he claimed that only 'pure democracy' could solve the problem of reconstruction, as dogmas were compromised in the search for a practical solution to the exigencies of the time. There was 'no other way and no other help'.[109] Democracy had 'stepped fully outside the arena of pure doctrine and dogmatism, and stepped into the arena of pure practical necessity . . . It is *not the product of doctrine*, but is an *expression* of the real social situation which has been cloaked by war and destruction'.[110]

In his rejection of political absolutism Weber moves in a similar direction to Troeltsch. For Weber, the real world restricts the scope for political action; ideals thus remain vacuous unless they are capable of realization:

Democracy will reject *all* the slogans of the ideologues of whatever kind: whether it is 'organization' or 'free economy', 'communal provision' or 'nationalization'. The identification of a measure as 'socialist' or, on the contrary, as 'liberal' is neither a recommendation nor its opposite. For every sector of the economy the question must be one exclusively of the *actual* results: that is to say, how is it possible, on the one side, to improve the earnings prospects of the broad masses of the workers; and, on the other side, to make a greater abundance of provisions available to the population as a whole.[111]

marked the culmination of a revival of liberal forces that had begun under Naumann's nimbus at the beginning of the twentieth century and that set the stage for what the more progressive elements of Germany's liberal bourgeoisie regarded as a moment of unprecedented promise' (476). Cf. Dahrendorff, *Society and Democracy in Germany*, for an eloquent statement of Germany's *Sonderweg*; and Blackbourn and Eley, *The Peculiarities of German History*, for an opposing view.

[107] Cf. Kollman, 'Eine Diagnose der Weimarer Republik', 314 f.; Erdmann, *Die Weimarer Republik*, 246. Other theologians, notably Bousset and Martin Rade (cf. Ruddies, 'Soziale Demokratie und freier Protestantismus', 160), were also members of the *DDP*. For a brief account of Bousset's political involvement see Verheule, *Wilhelm Bousset*. During the First World War, Rudolf Otto had been a left-wing deputy for the National Liberals. Cf. Wright, 'Ernst Troeltsch als parlamentarischer Unterstaatssekretär', 189 n.

[108] Troeltsch's contributions to the second party Conference of 15 December 1919 are recorded in W. Stephan, *Aufstieg und Verfall*, 138 ff.

[109] *Spektatorbriefe* (H1924/3), 11.   [110] Ibid., 305 f., 307; Troeltsch's emphasis.

[111] Weber, *GPS*, 460. This mirrors Weber's early judgement on Friedrich Naumann's National Social Party, where he was deeply critical of its failure to recognize the facts with which any viable political party had to work: 'Politics is a hard business, and whoever wants to take responsibility upon himself to penetrate the spokes of the wheels of the political development of the fatherland must have strong nerves, and cannot be sentimental . . . Whoever wants to carry out earthly politics, however, must be free of all illusions and recognize one great fact: that of the uncontrollable ceaseless conflict of man with man' (*GAW*, 28 f.).

What unified politics was thus the need to recognize the practicalities of any solution, something which doctrinaire ideologues could never accept. Indeed, Weber remarked, 'a discussion with convinced socialists and revolutionaries is always an awkward thing. From my experience they can never be convinced'.[112] Rather than ideological warfare, the hallmark of the parliamentary system was *compromise*:

Nowadays, as in former times, it is once more compromise which prevails as the means to settle the economic conflicts of interest, especially those between employers and workers; here it is unavoidably the only final form of settlement, and so it belongs to the essential character of all really vigorous economic interest groups. Naturally it also prevails in parliamentary politics between the parties: an electoral compromise or a compromise over legislative proposals. The possibility of the latter, it should be restated, belongs to the most important advantages of a parliamentary system.[113]

Troeltsch in his ethical theology and Weber in his political solution, both conclude with the idea of a necessary compromise. Nevertheless there were important differences which remained between them.

TROELTSCH'S ETHICAL SOLUTION

Despite these material similarities in their approaches to ethics, Troeltsch felt himself to be moving beyond what he called Weber's 'heroic scepticism'[114] and was deeply critical of what he regarded as Weber's 'quite impossible' connection of facts and values.[115] According to Troeltsch, an emphasis on a series of ultimate decisions could never be sufficient to guarantee a political or ethical system;[116] thus alongside Weber's astonishing clarity lay an apparently arbitrary decisionism.[117] 'The most comprehensive and cautious knowledge of history is placed in the service of this single unprovable

---

[112] Weber, *MWG* 15/1, 633; cf. Nowak, 'Die "antihistoristische Revolution"', 167.

[113] Weber, *GPS*, 265. On Max Weber and politics see esp. Mommsen, *Max Weber and German Politics*; Beetham, *Max Weber and the Meaning of Modern Politics*. Mommsen has emphasized the anti-democratic and anti-liberal traits of Weber's thought, stressing his sympathy for a new Caesarism along Bismarckian lines (e.g. 330, 344, 353). Against this view Beetham plausibly points to the fact that Weber's regard for charismatic leadership was not an alternative to democratic institutions, but was a means for ensuring a unity against the disintegrating aspects of a party system. The national leader was no demagogue but merely provided a counterbalance to the compromises of parliament (esp. 237). Any leader was subject to dismissal by the will of the people in a plebiscite. Cf. Weber, *GPS*, 500: 'But now we have a situation where all constitutional proposals have degenerated into a blind faith in the infallibility and sovereignty of the majority—not of the people, but of parliamentarians . . . true democracy means not the helpless surrender to cliques, but a submission to a leader whom the people have elected themselves'. Cf. *GPS*, 544.   [114] *Der Historismus und seine Probleme* (A1922/22), 569; cf. 571.

[115] Ibid., 49.   [116] Ibid., 90.   [117] Cf. ibid., 569.

value which is formed only through the decision of the will'.[118] For Troeltsch, history itself was integral to the very perception of absolute values, and could never be wholly isolated from the sphere of individual values. What was lost in Weber's individualism, he claimed, was thus the 'real intrusion into the inner dynamic, tension and the rhythm of events, the interpenetration of being and value'.[119]

Thus, on the one hand, Weber's thought was characterized by an 'iron discipline' which avoided all personal attitudes and evaluations, whilst, on the other hand, there was a heroic affirmation of personal values.[120] Troeltsch saw this as no more than a Romantic escape from the factuality of history in the irrationality of decision. To adopt Weber's methodology was ultimately to deny the possibility for the realization of absolute values in history. This meant nothing less than the dislocation of any religious or ethical universal goal (*Gesamtziel*) from its rootedness in history, and ultimately the dissolution of the European ideal of humanity upon which the Weimar constitution was established.[121]

Towards the end of his career Troeltsch became ever more aware of the depth of the crisis of individualism, and in particular of the tendency of so many to reject history altogether as they moved towards Kierkegaard or the neo-paganism of the wilder extremes of the Diederichs press. According to Troeltsch, the quest for totality, for unity amidst the apparently so meaningless diversity of modern life, could not be satisfied by an escape into the individual, where eternity no longer had a point of contact with real history,[122] but required a thoroughgoing immersion in the factuality of historical existence.

There are strong hints of a practical solution to the problems of *Historismus*[123] towards the end of *Der Historismus und seine Probleme* and also

---

[118] Ibid., 161.   [119] Ibid., 568.   [120] Ibid., 569; cf. 571.

[121] In *Der Historismus und seine Probleme* ((A1922/22), esp. 571) Troeltsch regarded Weber as strongly dependent on Anglo-Saxon positivism and included discussion of Weber in a broader discussion of neo-Kantianism and of positivism. This is a misunderstanding of Weber (esp. *GARS*, 569), who was bitterly critical of the deification of the natural-scientific method. Cf. Herring, 'Max Weber und Ernst Troeltsch', 433: 'These and other utterances lead to the conclusion that Troeltsch failed to understand Max Weber in the depths of his thought'.

[122] See esp. Troeltsch, 'Ein Apfel vom Baume Kierkegaards' (A1921/5a). Cf. Graf, ' "Kierkegaards junge Herren" '. Troeltsch's often bitter critique of dialectical theology mirrors his earlier critique of Wilhelm Herrmann.

[123] For Troeltsch, *Historismus* does not normally carry the negative connotation of the English term 'historicism', and corresponds to the 'philosophical position which, on the grounds of the historically conditioned and variable nature of all cultural phenomena, rejects, indeed classifies as crude, all claims to absolute validity' (Schnädelbach, *Philosophy in Germany*, 35). Cf. G. Schmidt, *Deutscher Historismus*, 325 f. On the uses of the term 'Historismus' see Herbert Butterfield, *Man on His Past*, 137–41; Schnädelbach, *Philosophy in Germany*, esp. 35–65; Georg Iggers, *The German Conception of History*, ch. 1. *Historismus* is variously translated 'historicism' or

in *Christian Thought*, which Troeltsch regarded as 'containing the next volume of my *Historismus* book'.[124] Even though he famously recognized that there were 'no circumstances in which "humanity" as a unified historical object can be found',[125] he was still able to see such a relativism, even about human nature itself, as not completely unbridled and as not necessarily leading to scepticism. He became, in the words of the English student of comparative religion A. C. Bouquet, 'a kind of Einstein of the religious world'. Yet, as Bouquet pointed out, 'we are not left in the grip of a critical uncertainty'.[126] In *Der Historismus* Troeltsch welcomed Bouquet's analogy with Einstein, commenting that his 'relativity is no unbounded relativism . . . but is the absolute in the relative'. After all, he went on, 'Einstein is no sceptic'.[127] And it becomes clear that at the end of his life Troeltsch had begun to regard relativity as having virtues of its own.

Criticism, far from threatening the very survival of Christianity, could provide the basis for the task of ethical and religious construction. As he wrote in his programmatic essay of 1916:

In the course of events I discovered that the move from psychological analysis to the recognition of the nature of reality was more difficult than I had originally envisaged, and also that the problem of development was far more complicated. In spite of this I have maintained my basic starting-point: the conquering of the historical and the psychological through the acceptance of modern criticism.[128]

Throughout his life Troeltsch wrestled with a theological method which sought to incorporate the enlightened criticism of all tradition by ensuring that it retained a vision of higher ends: in this sense, then, he gave criticism a goal, offering the project of the Enlightenment, with its demolition of idols and ideologies, a new sense of constructive purpose and hope. 'In order to free ourselves from history and obtain sovereign dominion over it,' he wrote as late as 1922, 'we dive into the ocean of historical criticism and construction'.[129] Nothing which ignored the possibilities revealed in the study of historical reality could ever hope to achieve a lasting solution to the crisis of the present. According to Troeltsch:

'historism'. The latter (which I have sometimes used), although less common, is to be preferred, since it does not convey the pejorative sense of historicism. Moreover, on Troeltsch's sense of the term, where *Historismus* is contrasted with *Naturalismus*, the use of 'historicism', which is more frequently used to mean 'historical determinism' (and thus as an analogy with natural determinism), might be misleading. A combination of 'historism' and paraphrase was used by J. E. Anderson in his translation of Meinecke's *Die Entstehung des Historismus—Historism: The Rise of a New Historical Outlook*. This may be the best solution.

[124] Letter to Friedrich von Hügel, in *Ernst Troeltsch. Briefe an Friedrich von Hügel* (G1974/1), 148.   [125] *Der Historismus* (A1922/22), 706.
[126] A. C. Bouquet, *Is Christianity the Final Religion?*, 241.
[127] *Der Historismus* (A1922/22), 219.   [128] Review of Günther (A1916/22), col. 448.
[129] *Der Historismus* (A1922/22), 723.

a completely new modern theory which has no foundations in our system as it has developed and which has no support in the western metaphysics of two millennia, and also nothing that has been borrowed from the wisdom of the Far East or from foreign religions, will help us here. Our means of salvation must in essence have been prepared in our own blood.[130]

On Troeltsch's view, the problems of *Historismus* did not need over-coming,[131] but rather, the recognition of relativism became the necessary basis for any realistic theological construction for the future. History provided the 'arsenal of examples',[132] the 'picture-book of ethics'.[133] As was shown in the previous chapter, to reject history was to reject possibility altogether.

Troeltsch's solution to the problems of modernity, what he called his 'material philosophy of history',[134] rested in an ethical compromise which was practically orientated around the concrete possibilities of the contem-porary world. While sharing Weber's vision of the vital need for a socio-logical and historical appraisal of the concrete situation, he nevertheless emphasized, unlike Weber, the indispensability of a universal value within history which alone could provide the ethical basis for the future. Facts thus had to be reconciled with values in any viable solution:

Today, when there has been such a progressive differentiation of the whole of life, it is quite conceivable that religious and political-economic-social life have been sep-arated from one another, and that the solution to the resulting problems will be something profane and independent . . . This situation cannot be changed and should not surprise us. Enthusiasts, ideologues, and theoreticians must come to terms with this fact and must find a purely sociological solution to the whole problem.

On the other hand, it is also true that such enormous tasks cannot be solved with-out ethical renewal and profundity, without a sense for good and justice, without a willingness for sacrifice and solidarity, indeed without a position towards the world and towards life which rests on faith. It is this that is the second great task of the crit-ical world-historical moment in which Europe finds itself . . . This task is enough in

---

[130] *Die Sozialphilosophie* (A1922/27), 5; ET, 211.

[131] This is suggested by his widow's rather misleading title for his posthumous set of lectures. The German title is *Der Historismus und seine Überwindung* (E1923/7a). This book was first pub-lished in English as *Christian Thought: Its History and Applications* (E1923/7). On the circum-stances of Troeltsch's posthumously published lectures see Mark D. Chapman, 'The "Sad Story" of Ernst Troeltsch's Proposed British Lectures of 1923'.

[132] *Der Historismus und seine Probleme* (A1922/22), 156.   [133] Ibid., 357.

[134] Troeltsch's premature death prevented him from fully realizing his project. However, he presented it in outline at the end of *Der Historismus und seine Probleme* (A1922/22) and in *Chris-tian Thought* (E1923/7) as well as in the various late essays cited here. His 'formal logic of history' or metaphysics, which aimed to reconcile facts with values in a revitalization of Leibnizian monadology in the 'interpenetration of spirit and nature', is singularly unconvinc-ing, and required a practical expression for its full realization. Cf. *Der Historismus und seine Probleme* (A1922/22), esp. 209 ff.

itself to prevent religion from plunging into social-philosophical and political dilettantism . . . The spirit which is so aroused will come to the help of social and political reconstruction . . . For now, in the confusion of the present we need to look clearly at the tasks and problems without complicating them and to achieve what is possible by vocation and talent in a given situation and to succeed in every place in once again achieving contact and agreement. Otherwise the biblical myth of the tower of Babel . . . might become a symbol of a European Kingdom of the Giants which has neglected God. *Deus afflavit et dissipati sunt* [God blew and they were scattered].[135]

What Troeltsch affirms, in distinction to Weber, is that a dominant value is not merely imposed upon history, but emerges from *within* history. And it is this value alone, even though it might become secularized and de-Christianized, that allows for the survival of human freedom and the responsibility to shape reality. Indeed, for Troeltsch, the dominant value (albeit in a demythologized form) was that of Christian freedom and responsibility, of human participation in divine creativity. Although Weber shared a belief in the importance of freedom,[136] he saw no possibility for its universal realization; instead it became little more than the source of motivation for a few heroic individuals. For Troeltsch, however, it was at the very centre of the new world:

At the heart of all the current ideas about the League of Nations, the organization of the world, and the limitation of egoisms and the forces of destruction, there is an indestructible moral core, which we cannot in its essence reject, even if we are painfully aware, at the moment, of the difficulties and the abuse to which it is liable. We may see the difficulties and the abuse clearly; we may seek to overcome them, but what we cannot do and what we must not do, is to deny the ideal itself in its own essence, in its ethical significance, in its connection with the philosophy of history.[137]

Troeltsch was concerned with the control of national egoisms, not by creating new absolutist myths or by escaping history, but by limiting all claims to an absolute standpoint.

Troeltsch differed from Weber chiefly in his faith in the future, in his conviction that the Enlightenment ideal of *Menschentum* (humanity) might come to fruition in the constitutional settlement and the international guarantees of 1919. Indeed, for Troeltsch, the irrationality of reality could continue to be shaped rationally and ethically in the acceptance of the demythologized rational theodicy of the ideal of humanity. Weber, acutely aware of the tragedy of the situation, placed no such faith in rationality, or in the practical realization of the Enlightenment ideal.[138] For Troeltsch,

---

[135] *Die Sozialphilosophie* (A1922/27), 33 f.; ET, 233 f.

[136] Cf. Hennis, *Essays in Reconstruction*; and Scaff, *Fleeing the Iron Cage*.

[137] 'Naturrecht und Humanität' (A1922/23b), 25; ET: 220.

[138] Liebersohn has looked at the work of the leading German sociologists of the turn of the twentieth century. Correctly, he regards them as motivated by a Utopian vision, testing

however, the possibility of the human being to make decisions and thus to stand above the materialistic world rested on the concrete embodiment of the ideal of humanity. It was this alone that could allow for the survival of freedom. However, it could never be secured purely on sociological or scientific grounds, since reality in itself displayed a polytheism in its indifference to absolute values. For the ideal to gain a foothold in history, Troeltsch maintained, it required 'a position towards the world and towards life which rests on faith', a willing submission to the rational interpretation of reality, as facts were connected with values. Where sociology and history were ignored altogether in sectarian exclusivism or mystical escape or even in aristocratic individualism, and where there was no longer a faith that history could be shaped along rational ends, then the ideal of humanity could never hope to structure reality.

Weber and Troeltsch both perceived the vital importance of a factual appraisal of the realities of history as the basis for any practical solution to the problem of reconstruction for a future which recognized the fundamental changes of the modern world. Similarly, they both appreciated that the solutions of the neo-Romantics were at best an impractical delusion or at worst a dilettantist sham. Their paths thus converged in the face of the political and ethical tasks of the reconstruction. Yet, according to Troeltsch, Weber's recourse to individualism was a denial of the responsibility to ensure a historical embodiment of the 'indestructible moral core' of the European ideal of humanity which alone could provide the basis for an ethical reconstruction. Weber may have shared this ideal, but he did not see it as universally realizable. Unlike many of his contemporaries, then, Troeltsch did not crave a return to the social forms of the past, or an escape into mystic experience or the sectarian conventicle, but aimed rather to construct a universal value out of the gains of the past. Only by reaffirming the need for a shared universal founded on the historical tradition of the west—the European ideal of humanity—could the anti-historicist and anti-democratic solutions of the neo-mystics and the neo-Romantics be avoided in a practical solution for the future.

At the end of his career Troeltsch reaffirmed the vital importance of the attempt to shape the future through the creation of a new synthesis applicable to the modern world. He did not aim to found his religion on the acceptance of a religious hero or on mystical experience, but rather, his theology immersed itself in the study of history and in the realm of human possibilities. The greatest task of the present was thus 'to mould the new and the

---

'society's limits for the sake of an uncertain future' and thus as 'more realistic than any purely tragic perspective' (*Fate and Utopia in German Sociology*, 196). A Utopian vision which can be realized only by power and coercion rather than democracy and consensus, however, represents an even more tragic perspective.

deep sources of our spiritual life so as to form a unity to preserve us, or to reveal their meaning for the necessities of life'. This had to be 'a union of the richest traditions and the deepest regard for history, with living power and freshness'.[139] He never deviated from this task; indeed at the end of *Der Historismus und seine Probleme*, published only a few months before his death, Troeltsch reaffirmed his theological goal of shaping history afresh, of forming

a unity from the melting-pot of historicism . . . of creating a new sociological body for the ideological content, and to enliven the sociological body with a new and fresh spirituality, a new combination, adaptation, and reconstruction of the great historical powers. There is admittedly no way of proving how this act should be done. Rather, it is a creative act and a dare by those who believe in the future, of those who refuse to allow themselves to be lulled to sleep or to be destroyed, but who maintain in each present the task of such a combination according to the measure of their strengths and capacities. This is the task of thoughtful and courageous persons, not of sceptics and mystics, nor of rationalist fanatics . . . This task, which is either consciously or unconsciously present in every epoch, is especially pressing in the present. The idea of a construction means overcoming history through history and levelling the foundations for the new creation.[140]

Indeed, it was this recognition of the possibility of a new historical construction which allowed him to end his life on a note of hope.

In his late work Troeltsch can be seen as moving in a very Anglo-Saxon direction: a practical desire to limit egoisms amounts to an ethics of compromise as participants in a dialogue limit their claims to an absolute standpoint in the face of the other. Despite the metaphysical musings of parts of *Der Historismus*, which have rightly been subject to much criticism,[141] it is interesting to note that it is precisely this theme of compromise that is so prominent in Troeltsch's final work, *Christian Thought*. It is not some kind of irrational or escapist leap that forms Troeltsch's final solution, but instead a very provisional decision which can always be modified or reversed by proper debate. It is hardly accidental that he makes explicit use of a metaphor drawn from English practical politics:

Many of us in Germany regard 'compromise' as the lowest and most despicable means to which a thinker can resort. We are asked to recognize a radical disjunction

---

[139] *Der Berg der Läuterung* (A1921/11), 20.
[140] *Der Historismus und seine Probleme* (A1922/22), 771 f.
[141] Although Troeltsch would presumably have distanced himself from Gogarten's critique of *Der Historismus*, there is some truth in his judgement that, despite all claims to be staying in history, Troeltsch was escaping into some higher realm. See *Verhängnis und Hoffnung der Neuzeit*, esp. 113–17. A little more healthy pragmatism and trust in psychology could have stopped Troeltsch from adopting the somewhat implausible metaphysics of Malebranche and Leibniz. See Hintze, 'Troeltsch und die Probleme'.

here, and to choose either *for* or *against* . . . But twist and turn the matter as you will the fact remains that all intransigence breaks down in practice, and can only end in disaster.[142]

Troeltsch went on to suggest that in England the word 'compromise' carried fewer negative connotations than in Germany, since 'the principle of compromise is less undervalued' because of 'political experience and the influence of empirical systems'.[143] Thus, despite what he calls 'a natural distaste for a purely empirical philosophy', he nevertheless admits that he has 'found this a particularly attractive and instructive feature of your [i.e. English] literature'.[144] In *Christian Thought*, the metaphysics of *Der Historismus und seine Probleme* seems to have dissolved into a pragmatic compromise between the ideal and real which was to be realized in practical life. Thus, the best possible solution had to be a

compromise between naturalism and idealism, between the practical necessities of human life upon earth and the purposes and ideals of the life of the spirit . . . The history of Christianity itself is the most instructive in this connection. It is, in the long run, a tremendous, continuous compromise between the Utopian demands of the kingdom of God and the permanent conditions of our actual human life.[145]

Indeed, Troeltsch went on, 'it is only by keeping this ideal ever before our eyes that we can continue in hope for a better future in the midst of a cold and sinister world'.[146] The solution to the problems of historicism—if it can be considered a solution at all—is thus nothing more than a rough-and-ready compromise which trusts in a better future but which is not afraid of the present. This is a long way from dialectical escapism, but it might nevertheless be the most important contribution from the Anglo-Saxon tradition. As Troeltsch put it strikingly:

The task of damming and controlling is . . . essentially incapable of completion and essentially unending; and yet it is always soluble and practicable in each new case. A radical and absolute solution does not exist; there are only working, partial, synthetically uniting positions . . . In history itself there are only relative victories; and these relative victories themselves vary greatly in power and depth, according to time and circumstance.[147]

In the history of theology since the First World War, however, this readiness to compromise with history has seldom been praised. Instead the isolationist strand stemming from Herrmann has been most often dominant. Theology was isolated from a history identified with the meaningless

---

[142] *Christian Thought* (E1923/7), 164 f.   [143] Ibid., 166.   [144] Ibid.
[145] Ibid., 164, 165.
[146] Ibid., 167. For an application of this realism and relativism see my essay, 'A Theology for Europe'.   [147] *Christian Thought* (E1923/7), 128, 129.

slaughter of the fields of Flanders; it was consequently robbed of apologetic potential, except perhaps as a silent witness to the frailty of all human constructs. The alternatives to Troeltsch's theology which were to develop in the 1920s lost faith in the powers of history, and thereby succeeded in the sectarianization of theology, as contact with the wider world of learning was severed in a world-view inspired by faith. All theology was destined to be dogmatics. Similarly religion seemed to offer little hope for a reform of the present since all history was equally doomed to death and corruption. Instead one was obliged to find a more real reality in which to live as a Christian.[148] Although such a theology may have had its place as an alternative to the massive evils of the 1930s, the legacy of the 'anti-historicist revolution'[149] in theology was to create a more real reality of an eternal now which had little connection with secular reality.[150] Eternity seems to have little to say about ethical activity in the present. Historical reality was thus too often evaded in the pseudo-realities of religious or cultural escape, which all too easily led to barbarism and savagery.[151] Yet, where history could no longer be controlled, the irrationalities of reality itself or the arbitrariness of absolutes which ignored the constraints of history would soon ensnare the personality through their own dynamic, facts that became tragically clear in the German experience of the 1930s. Troeltsch's historical theology may not be satisfactory; yet the alternatives which have been discussed in the course of this book seem worse, robbed as they are of ethical potential. And from this it would not seem unreasonable to conclude that it may be better for the Christian religion to compromise than to be removed from history altogether.

---

[148]   There is a sense too in which Bousset's direct perception of eternity survived (albeit divested of its Friesian overtones) in Bultmann's accounts of authentic existence. Cf. Martin Evang, *Rudolf Bultmann in seiner Frühzeit*. His project of demythologization can perhaps best be seen as another attempt to grasp the rational kernel behind the historical form. The direct confrontation with 'the word' seems at least the dynamic equivalent of *Ahnung*. Again this seems to result in an evasion of history and consequently of ethics, and, ultimately, a denial of human responsibility.

[149]   Cf. Kurt Nowak, 'Die "antihistoristische Revolution"'.

[150]   Cf. Richard H. Roberts, 'Ideal and the Real in the Theology of Karl Barth'.

[151]   B. Croce, 'Antihistorismus', 460; cf. Nowak, 'Die "antihistoristische Revolution"', 171.

Bibliography

PRIMARY WORKS (UNPUBLISHED)

Allgemeine Ethik. Lectures on general ethics given at Heidelberg, winter semester 1911–12, edited by K.-E. Apfelbacher. Copy in possession of F. W. Graf.

Einführung in die Philosophie. Lectures on Introduction to Philosophy given at Heidelberg, winter semester 1911–12, prepared from the lecture notes of Gertrud von le Fort. Copy in possession of F. W. Graf.

Praktische christliche Ethik. Lectures on Practical Christian Ethics given at Heidelberg, winter semester 1911–12, prepared from the lecture notes of Gertrud von le Fort by Eleonore von la Chevallerie. Copy in possession of F. W. Graf. Significant portions of these lectures were dictated. Benckert (in *Ernst Troeltsch und das ethische Problem*, 110 ff.) quotes from the lectures *Ethik*, of summer term 1899, and *Praktische christliche Ethik*, of winter semesters 1907–8 and 1911–12. His Table of Contents helps clarify discrepancies between the paragraph numbers of the dictated sections and those of the von le Fort typescript. The dictated sections have been published recently, edited by Eleonore von la Chevallerie and F. W. Graf in *MdETG* vi. 129–74. References are to typescript.

Religionsphilosophie. Lectures on Philosophy of Religion given at Heidelberg, summer semester 1912, prepared from the lecture notes of Gertrud von le Fort by Eleonore von la Chevallerie. Copy in possession of F. W. Graf.

PRIMARY WORKS (PUBLISHED)

The following list of works by Troeltsch makes use of the chronological cataloguing scheme adopted by F. W. Graf and Hartmut Ruddies in *Ernst Troeltsch Bibliographie*:

A = works published during Troeltsch's lifetime
B = works by Troeltsch edited by other people
C = works recorded stenographically
D = co-authored works
E = posthumously published works
F = lectures
G = published letters
H = posthumous reprints

A1891/1a   'Thesen zur Erlangen der theologischen Lizentiatenwürde an der Georg-Augusts-Universität zu Göttingen 1888–1893', introd. Horst Renz, *TS*, i: 299–300.

A1891/3   *Vernunft und Offenbarung bei Johann Gerhard und Melanchthon. Untersuchung zur Geschichte der altprotestantischen Theologie* (Göttingen: Vandenhoeck and Ruprecht).

A1893/2 and 1894/1   'Die christliche Weltanschauung und die wissenschaftlichen Gegenströmungen', *ZThK* 3: 493–528, and *ZThK* 4: 167–231.

A1894/1a   'Die christliche Weltanschauung und ihre Gegenströmungen', *GS* ii: 227–327.

A1895/1   'Religion und Kirche', in *Preußische Jahrbücher*, 81: 215–49.

A1895/1a   'Religion und Kirche', *GS* ii: 146–82.

A1895/2   'Die Selbständigkeit der Religion, i and ii', *ZThK* 5: 361–436.

A1896/1   'Die Selbständigkeit der Religion, iii', *ZThK* 6: 71–110.

A1896/2   'Die Selbständigkeit der Religion, iv', *ZThK* 6: 167–218.

A1897/3   'Moderner Halbmaterialismus. Erste Hälfte', *CW* 11: 98–103.

A1897/6   'Moderner Halbmaterialismus. Zweite Hälfte', *CW* 11: 157–62.

A1897/10a   'Christentum und Religionsgeschichte', *GS* ii: 328–63. (A brief section is translated in *RH*, 77–86.)

A1897/14   'Aufklärung', in Albert Hauck (ed.), *Realencyclopädie für protestantische Theologie und Kirche*, 3rd edn. (Leipzig: J. C. Hinrichs'sche Buchhandlung), ii: 225–41.

A1897/14a   'Die Aufklärung', *GS* iv: 338–74.

A1898/2   'Geschichte und Metaphysik', *ZThK* 8: 1–69.

A1898/20a   'Deismus', *GS* iv: 429–87.

A1900/1   Review of Friedrich Paulsen, *Kant der Philosoph des Protestantismus* (1899), *DLZ* 21: cols. 157–61.

A1900/4 and 5   'Haeckel als Philosoph', *CW* 14: 152–9, 171–9.

A1900/7   *Die wissenschaftliche Lage und ihre Anforderungen an die Theologie* (Tübingen: J. C. B. Mohr (Paul Siebeck)).

A1900/9a   'Über historische und dogmatische Methode in der Theologie', *GS* ii: 729–53. ET, *RH*, 11–32.

A1900/12a   'Der deutsche Idealismus', *GS* iv: 532–87.

A1901/2   Review of F. R. Lipsius, *Die Vorfragen der systematischen Theologie* (1899), *DLZ* 22: cols. 72–3.

A1901/11   Review of Johannes Steinbeck, *Das Verhältnis von Theologie und Erkenntnistheorie* (1898), *DLZ* 22: cols. 710–12.

A1901/12   Review of A. D. Dorner, *Grundriß der Dogmengeschichte* (1899), *GgA* 163: 265–75.

A1901/13   Review of F. Nippold, *Kollegiales Sendschreiben an Ernst Haeckel* (1901), *CW* 15: col. 492.

A1901/16   Review of R. Hönigswald, *Ernst Haeckel der monistische Philosoph* (1900), *CW* 15: cols. 1020–1.

A1901/23   *Die Absolutheit des Christentums und die Religionsgeschichte* (Tübingen: J. C. B. Mohr (Paul Siebeck), 1902).

A1901/23b   *Die Absolutheit des Christentums und die Religionsgeschichte*, 2nd edn. (Tübingen: J. C. B. Mohr, 1912).

A1901/23d   *Die Absolutheit des Christentums und die Religionsgeschichte*, 3rd edn. (Tübingen: J. C. B. Mohr, 1929). ET: *The Absoluteness of Christianity and the History of Religions*, tr. David Reid (London: SCM, 1972).

A1902/4a 'Grundprobleme der Ethik', *GS* ii: 552–672. ET of brief section in *The Unitarian Universalist Christian*, 34/1–2 (1974), 38–45.

A1902/6 Review of Th. Menzi, *Ernst Haeckels Welträtsel oder der Neomaterialismus* (1901), *CW* 16: cols. 499–500.

A1902/13 'Theologie und Religionswissenschaft des 19. Jahrhunderts', in *Jahrbuch des Freien Deutschen Hochstifts* (Frankfurt am Main: Knauer), 91–120.

A1903/4a 'Moderne Geschichtsphilosophie', *GS* ii: 673–728. ET, *RH*, 273–320.

A1903/6 Review of F. Paulsen, *Immanuel Kant* (1898), *Historische Zeitschrift*, 48: 497–500.

A1903/10 Review of Newton H. Marshall, *Die gegenwärtigen Richtungen der Religionsphilosophie in England und ihre erkenntnistheoretischen Grundlagen* (1902), *DLZ* 24: cols. 1017–18.

A1903/16a 'Die theologische und religiöse Lage der Gegenwart', *GS* ii: 1–21.

A1903/18a 'Was heißt, "Wesen des Christentums"?', *GS* ii: 386–451. ET, *MP*, 124–79.

A1903/21 'Religionswissenschaft und Theologie des 18. Jahrhunderts', *Preußische Jahrbücher*, 114: 30–56.

A1903/23 Review of H. Weinel, *Jesus im neunzehnten Jahrhundert* (1903), *DLZ* 24: cols. 2990–3.

A1903/24a 'Die englischen Moralisten des 17. und 18. Jahrhunderts', *GS* iv: 374–429.

A1904/4a 'Das Historische in Kants Religionsphilosophie. Zugleich ein Beitrag zu den Untersuchungen über Kants Philosophie der Geschichte', in Hans Vaihinger and Bruno Bauch (eds.), *Zu Kants Gedächtnis. Zwölf Festgaben zu seinem 100-jährigen Todestage* (Berlin: Reuther und Reichard).

A1904/6 *Politische Ethik und Christentum* (Göttingen: Vandenhoeck and Ruprecht). ET, *RH*, 173–209.

A1904/7 'Religionsphilosophie', in Wilhelm Windelband (ed.), *Die Philosophie im Beginn des zwanzigsten Jahrhunderts*, Festschrift for Kuno Fischer (Heidelberg: Carl Winter), 104–62.

A1904/8 Review of Paul Natorp, *Platos Ideenlehre* (1903), *CW* 18: cols. 834–5.

A1904/9 Review of Max Reischle, *Theologie und Religionsgeschichte* (1904), *TLZ* 29: cols. 613–17.

A1904/13 Review of William James, *The Varieties of Religious Experience* (1902), *DLZ* 25: cols. 3021–7.

A1905/1 Review of Morris Jastrow jun., *The Study of Religion* (1901), *DLZ* 26: cols. 12–14.

A1905/2   Review of F. H. Lipsius, *Kritik der theologischen Erkenntnis* (1904), *DLZ* 26: cols. 206–10.

A1905/6   'Ethik und Kapitalismus'. Review article on Gottfried Traub, *Grundzüge einer Sozialethik* (1904), *CW* 19: cols. 320–6.

A1905/7   *Psychologie und Erkenntnistheorie in der Religionswissenschaft. Eine Untersuchung über die Bedeutung der Kantischen Religionslehre für die heutige Religionswissenschaft* (Tübingen: J. C. B. Mohr). Expanded German version of 'Main Problems' (C1905/1).

A1905/8   Review of Paul Kalweit, *Kants Stellung zur Kirche* (1904), *Historische Zeitschrift*, 58: 127–8.

A1905/10   Review of A. Dorner, *Grundriß der Religionsphilosophie* (1903), *GgA* 167: cols. 761–72.

A1906/4   'Protestantisches Christentum und Kirche in der Neuzeit', in Paul Hinneberg (ed.), *Die Kultur der Gegenwart* (Berlin and Leipzig: Teubner), 1/4: 431–755.

A1906/5b   'Wesen der Religion und Religionswissenschaft', *GS* ii: 452–99. ET, *MP*, 82–123.

A1906/7   Review of P. Gastrow, *Joh. Salomo Semler in seiner Bedeutung für Theologie* (1905), L. Zscharnack, *Lessing und Semler* (1905), and Gottwald Karo, *Johann Salomo Semler* (1905), *TLZ* 31: cols. 146–9.

A1906/13   Review of Kurt Breysig, *Die Entstehung des Gottesgedankens und der Heilbringer* (1905), *GgA* 168: 688–98.

A1906/15   Review of Maria Raich, *Fichte* (1905), *GgA* 168: 680–2.

A1907/2   *Die Trennung von Staat und Kirche, der staatliche Religionsunterricht und die theologischen Fakultäten* (Tübingen: J. C. B. Mohr (Paul Siebeck)). ET of small sections, *RH*, 109–20.

A1907/8b   'Das Wesen des modernen Geistes', *GS* iv: 297–338. ET, *RH*, 237–72.

A1907/11   'Autonomie und Rationalismus in der modernen Welt', *Internationale Wochenschrift für Wissenschaft, Kunst und Technik*, i: cols. 199–210.

A1907/12   Review of Hébert, *Le divin. Expériences et hypothèses. Études psychologiques* (1907), *DLZ* 28: cols. 1304–6.

A1907/13   [Kant bleibt im Ansatz], *ZThK* 17: 231–3.

A1908/1   'Katholizismus und Reformismus', *Internationale Wochenschrift für Wissenschaft, Kunst und Technik*, 2: cols. 15–26.

A1908/6a   'Glaube, iv. Glaube und Geschichte', *RGG*1, ii: cols. 1447–56. ET, *RH*, 134–45.

A1909/5   Review of Horst Stephan, *Spaldings Bestimmung des Menschen* (1908), *Schleiermachers Sendschreiben* (1908), John Toland, *Christianity not Mysterious* (1908), *TLZ* 34: cols. 245–6.

A1909/7a   'Der Modernismus', *GS* ii: 45–67.

A1909/18a   'Rückblick auf ein halbes Jahrhundert der theologischen Wissenschaft', *GS* ii: 193–226. ET, *MP*, 53–81.

A1909/31a   'Zur Frage des religiösen Apriori', *GS* ii: 754–68. ET, *RH*, 33–45.

A1910/16   'Schleiermacher und die Kirche', in Friedrich Naumann (ed.), *Schleiermacher, der Philosoph des Glaubens* (Berlin: Buchverlag der Hilfe), 9–35.

A1910/20a   'Contingency', *ERE* iv: cols. 87–9.

A1911/1a   'Die Zukunftsmöglichkeiten des Christentums im Verhältnis zur modernen Philosophie', *GS* ii: 837–62.

A1911/8a   'Die Kirche im Leben der Gegenwart', *GS* ii: 91–108.

A1912/2   *Die Soziallehren der christlichen Kirchen und Gruppen. Gesammelte Schriften, i [GS i]* (Tübingen: J. C. B. Mohr (Paul Siebeck)). ET: *The Social Teaching [sic] of the Christian Churches*, tr. Olive Wyon (London: George Allen and Unwin, 1931).

A1912/6   'Empiricism and Platonism in the Philosophy of Religion—to the Memory of William James', *Harvard Theological Review*, 5: 401–22.

A1912/8   Review of Th. Kaftan, *Ernst Tröltsch. Eine kritische Zeitstudie* (1912), *TLZ* 37: cols. 724–8.

A1913/2   'The Dogmatics of the "Religionsgeschichtliche Schule"', *American Journal of Theology*, 17: 1–21.

A1913/2a   'Die Dogmatik der religionsgeschichtlichen Schule', *GS* ii: 500–24.

A1913/8a   'Logos und Mythos in Theologie und Religionsphilosophie', *GS* ii: 805–36. ET, *RH*, 46–72.

A1913/11   Review of Andrew White, *Geschichte der Fehde zwischen Wissenschaft und Theologie* (1911), *TLZ* 38: cols. 271–3.

A1913/12   Review of L. Nelson, *Die Unmöglichkeit der Erkenntnistheorie* (1911), *TLZ* 38: cols. 341–2.

A1913/13   *Zur religiösen Lage, Religionsphilosophie und Ethik [GS ii]* (Tübingen: J. C. B. Mohr (Paul Siebeck)).

A1913/18   'Prinzip, religiöses', *RGG*[1] iv: cols. 1499–1503.

A1913/24   Review of Paul Mezger, *Die Absolutheit des Christentums und die Religionsgeschichte* (1912), *TLZ* 38: col. 502.

A1913/28   Review of Karl Přibram, *Die Entstehung der individualistischen Sozialphilosophie* (1912), *TLZ* 38: cols. 594–6.

A1913/35   'Historiography', *ERE* vi: cols. 716–23.

A1913/36a   'Das neunzehnte Jahrhundert', *GS* iv: 614–49.

A1913/37a   'Die Religion im deutschen Staate', *GS* ii: 68–90.

A1913/38a   'Die Restaurationsepoche am Anfang des 19. Jahrhunderts', *GS* iv: 587–614.

A1914/15   'Kant', *ERE* vii: cols. 653–9.

A1915/6a   *Augustin, die christliche Antike und das Mittelalter. Im Anschluß an die Schrift 'De Civitate Dei'* (Munich and Berlin: Oldenbourg).

A1916/4   Review of H. Cohen, *Über das Eigentümliche des deutschen Geistes* (1914), *TLZ* 41: cols. 89–90.

A1916/22   Review of W. Günther, *Die Grundlagen der Religionsphiloso-*
                phie Ernst Troeltsch' (1914), *TLZ* 41: cols. 448–50.

A1916/13a   'Glaube und Ethos der hebräischen Propheten', *GS* iv: 34–65.

A1917/1   Review of G. Lasson, *Was heißt Hegelianismus?* (1916), *TLZ* 42:
                cols. 16–17.

A1917/4   Review of Aug. Dorner, *Die Metaphysik des Christentums*
                (1913), *TLZ* 42: cols. 84–7.

A1917/12   Review of Johannes Wendland, *Handbuch der Sozialethik*
                (1916), *TLZ* 42: cols. 295–8.

A1917/24   Review of R. Wlassak, *Ernst Mach* (1916), *TLZ* 42: col. 468.

A1918/18   Review of S. Marck, *Kant und Hegel* (1917), *TLZ* 43: cols.
                258–9.

A1918/21   'Zur Religionsphilosophie. Aus Anlaß des Buches von Rudolf
                Otto über "Das Heilige"', *Kant–Studien*, 23: 65–76.

A1919/41   'Religiöser Subjektivismus', *Die Hilfe*, 25: 697–701.

A1920/8   'Die "kleine Göttinger Fakultät" von 1890', *CW* 34: cols. 281–3.

A1920/14   'Kritik am System: Das Parteiwesen, ii', *Der Kunstwart und*
                Kulturwart, 33: 209–15.

A1921/5a   'Ein Apfel vom Baume Kierkegaards', in J. Moltmann (ed.),
                Anfänge der dialektischen Theologie, Theologische Bücherei,
                17 (Munich: Kaiser, 1963), 134–40. ET: 'An Apple from the
                Tree of Kierkegaard', in J. M. Robinson (ed.), *The Beginnings*
                of Dialectical Theology (Richmond, John Knox Press,
                1968).

A1921/11   *Der Berg der Läuterung: Zur Erinnerung an den 600–jährigen*
                Todestag Dantes (Berlin: Mittler).

A1921/28a   'Die Revolution in den Wissenschaften: Eine Besprechung
                von Kahlers *Der Beruf der Wissenschaft* and Salz' *Für die Wis-*
                senschaft gegen die Gebildeten unter ihren Verächten', *GS* iv:
                653–77.

A1921/29b   'Meine Bücher', *GS* iv: 3–18. ET, *RH*, 365–78.

A1922/22   *Der Historismus und seine Probleme* [*GS* iii] (Tübingen: J. C. B.
                Mohr (Paul Siebeck)).

A1922/23b   'Naturrecht und Humanität in der Weltpolitik', *DGW*, 3–27.
                ET: 'The Idea of Natural Law and Humanity in World Pol-
                itics', in Otto Gierke, *Natural Law and the Theory of Society*
                1500–1800, 201–22.

A1922/27   *Die Sozialphilosophie des Christentums* (Zürich: Seldwyla). ET,
                RH, 210–34.

A1923/1   Review of Emanuel Hirsch, *Die Reich-Gottesbegriffe des*
                neueren europäischen Denkens (1921), *TLZ* 48: 23–4.

C1905/1   'Main Problems in the Philosophy of Religion: Psychology
                and Theory of Knowledge in the Science of Religion', tr. J. H.
                Woods, in H. J. Rogers (ed.), *Proceedings of the Congress of Arts*
                and Sciences, Universal Exposition, i: 275–88.

C1911/2b   'Religiöser Individualismus und Kirche', *GS* ii: 109–33.

E1923/7	Christian Thought: Its History and Applications, ed. Friedrich von Hügel (London: University of London Press).
E1923/7a	Der Historismus und seine Überwindung (Berlin: Rolf Heise, 1924).
F1925/2	Glaubenslehre. Nach Heidelberger Vorlesungen aus den Jahren 1911 und 1912 (München and Leipzig: Duncker and Humblot). ET: The Christian Faith, tr. Garrett Paul (Minn.: Fortress, 1991).
G1974/1	Ernst Troeltsch. Briefe an Friedrich von Hügel, 1901–1923, ed. Karl-Ernst Apfelbacher and Peter Neuner (Paderborn: Bonifacius-Druckerei).
G1976/2	'Ernst Troeltsch. Briefe aus der Heidelberger Zeit an Wilhelm Bousset 1894–1914', ed. Erika Dinkler–von Schubert, Heidelberger Jahrbücher, 20: 19–52.
G1978/1	Various letters from Troeltsch cited in Karl-Ernst Apfelbacher, Frömmigkeit und Wissenschaft.
H1924/3	Spektatorbriefe. Aufsätze über die deutsche Revolution und die Weltpolitik 1918/22, ed. Hans Baron (Tübingen: J. C. B. Mohr (Paul Siebeck)).
H1925/1a	Aufsätze zur Geistesgeschichte und Religionssoziologie [GS iv], ed. Hans Baron (Tübingen: J. C. B. Mohr (Paul Siebeck)).
H1925/3a	Deutscher Geist und Westeuropa [DGW], ed. Hans Baron, repr. (Aalen: Scientia, 1966).

SECONDARY WORKS

ADICKES, ERICH, Kant Contra Haeckel; Erkenntnistheorie gegen naturwissenschaftlichen Dogmatismus (Berlin: Reuther and Reichard, 1901).

ALDENHOFF, RITA, 'Max Weber and the Evangelical Social Congress', in Mommsen and Osterhammel (eds.), Max Weber and his Contemporaries, 193–202.

ALMOND, PHILIP C., 'Rudolf Otto and the Kantian Tradition', NZSThRph, 25 (1983), 52–67.

—— 'Rudolf Otto: Life and Work', Journal of Religious History, 12 (1983), 305–21.

—— 'Rudolf Otto: The Context of His Thought', SJT, 36 (1983), 347–62.

ANDERSON, M. L., 'Voter, Junker, Landrat, Priest: The Old Authorities and the New Franchise in Imperial Germany', American Historical Review, 98 (1993), 1448–74.

'An die evangelischen Christen im Auslande' (August, 1914), Die Eiche, 3 (1914), 49–53.

'An die Kulturwelt', Berliner Tageblatt, 4 October 1914.

APFELBACHER, KARL-ERNST, Frömmigkeit und Wissenschaft. Ernst Troeltsch und sein theologisches Programm, Beiträge zur Ökumenischen Theologie, 18 (Munich Paderborn/Vienna: Verlag Ferdinand Schöningh, 1978).

BAILEY, CHARLES, 'Gott mit uns: Germany's Protestant Theologians in the First World War' (Univ. of Virginia Ph.D. thesis 1978).

BAILEY, CHARLES, 'The British Protestant Theologians in the First World War: Germanophobia Unleashed', *Harvard Theological Review*, 77 (1984), 195–221.

BAILLIE, JOHN, *The Interpretation of Religion* (Edinburgh: T. & T. Clark, 1929).

BARMANN, LAWRENCE, F., *Baron Friedrich von Hügel and the Modernist Crisis in England* (Cambridge: Cambridge University Press, 1972).

BARNOUW, D., *Weimar Intellectuals and the Threat of Modernity* (Bloomington and Indianapolis: Indiana University Press, 1988).

BARTH, KARL, 'Evangelical Theology in the Nineteenth Century (1956)', in *The Humanity of God* (London: Collins, 1961), 11–33.

—— *Protestant Theology in the Nineteenth Century* (London: SCM, 1972).

Karl Barth–Rudolf Bultmann Letters, 1922–1966, tr. Geoffrey Bromiley (Grand Rapids, Mich.: Eerdmans, 1981).

BARTH, ULRICH, 'Ethische Aspekte der Kapitalismus-Deutung Max Webers', *Zeitschrift für Evangelische Ethik*, 35 (1991), 187–204.

BAUMGARTEN, E., *Max Weber: Werk und Person* (Tübingen: J. C. B. Mohr (Paul Siebeck), 1964).

BAUR, JÖRG, 'Albrecht Ritschl: Herrschaft und Versöhnung', in Bernd Moeller (ed.), *Theologie in Göttingen*, 256–70.

BECKER, G., *Neuzeitliche Subjektivität und Religiosität. Die religionsphilosophische Bedeutung von Heraufkunft und Wesen der Neuzeit im Denken Ernst Troeltschs* (Regensburg: Pustet, 1982).

BEETHAM, DAVID, *Max Weber and the Meaning of Modern Politics* (London: George Allen and Unwin, 1974).

BEINTKER, MICHAEL, *Die Gottesfrage in der Theologie Wilhelm Herrmanns* (Berlin: Evangelische Verlagsanstalt, 1976).

BENCKERT, H., 'Der Begriff der Entscheidung bei Ernst Troeltsch: Ein Beitrag zum Verständnis seines Denkens', *ZThK*, NF 12 (1931), 422–42.

—— *Ernst Troeltsch und das ethische Problem* (Göttingen: Vandenhoeck and Ruprecht, 1932).

BENSON, CONSTANCE, L., *God and Caesar: Troeltsch's Social Teaching as Legitimation*, with a foreword by Cornel West (New Brunswick and London: Transaction Publishers, 1998).

BENZ, ERNST (ed.), *Rudolf Ottos Bedeutung für die Religionswissenschaft und die Theologie heute* (Leiden: Brill, 1971).

BERGER, KLAUS, 'Nationalsoziale Religionsgeschichte: Wilhelm Bousset', in F. W. Graf (ed.), *Profile des neuzeitlichen Protestantismus*, ii/2: 279–94.

BLACKBOURN, D., and ELEY, S., *The Peculiarities of German History: Bourgeois Society and Politics in Nineteenth-Century Germany* (Oxford: Oxford University Press, 1984).

BODENSTEIN, WALTER, *Neige des Historismus: Ernst Troeltschs Entwicklungsgang* (Gütersloh: Gerd Mohn, 1959).

BOEKE, R., 'Rudolf Otto, Leben und Werk', *Numen*, 14 (1967), 130–43.

BOELSCHE, WILHELM, *Haeckel, His Life and Work: With Introduction and Supplementary Chapter By the Translator*, tr. Joseph McCabe (London: Fisher Unwin, 1906).

BOHATEC, JOSEF, *Die Religionsphilosophie Kants in der 'Religion innerhalb der Grenzen der bloßen Vernunft'. Mit besonderer Berücksichtigung ihrer theologisch-dogmatischen Quellen* (1938), reprint (Hildesheim: Georg Olms, 1966).

BOOZER, JACK, S., 'Rudolf Otto', in I. Schnack (ed.), *Marburger Gelehrte in der ersten Hälfte des 20. Jahrhunderts.*

BORNHAUSEN, KARL, 'Das religiöse Apriori bei Ernst Troeltsch und Rudolf Otto', test lecture in Marburg, 11 Jan. 1910, *Zeitschrift für Philosophie und Philosophische Kritik,* 139 (1910), 193–206.

—— 'Wider den Neofriesianismus in der Theologie', *ZThK* 20 (1910), 341–405.

—— 'In Sachen des Neofriesianismus, ii. Duplik des Kritikers', *ZThK* 21 (1911), 159–65.

BOSSE, HANS, *Marx–Weber–Troeltsch* (Munich: Kaiser, 1970).

BOUQUET, A. C., *Is Christianity the Final Religion?* (London: Macmillan, 1921).

BOUSSET, WILHELM, 'Die Lehre des Apostels Paulus vom Gesetz' (Univ. of Göttingen Habilitationsschrift, 1890), ed. Horst Renz, *MdETG,* iv (1989), 84–139.

—— *Der Antichrist in der Überlieferung des Judentums, des neuen Testaments und der alten Kirche. Ein Beitrag zur Auslegung der Apokalypse* (Göttingen: Vandenhoeck and Ruprecht, 1895). ET: *The Antichrist Legend: A Chapter in Christian and Jewish Folklore,* tr. A. H. Keane, introd. by D. Frankfurter (Atlanta, Ga.: Scholars Press, 1999).

—— 'Die Religionsgeschichte und das neue Testament', *ThR* vii (1904), 265–77, 311–18, 353–65.

—— *Das Wesen der Religion,* 3rd edn. (Halle: Gebauer–Schwetschke, 1906).

—— *Die Mission und die sogenannte religionsgeschichtliche Schule* (Göttingen: Vandenhoeck and Ruprecht, 1907).

—— *What is Religion?,* tr. F. B. Law (London: Unwin, 1907).

—— *Unser Gottesglaube* (Tübingen: J. C. B. Mohr (Paul Siebeck), 1908).

—— 'Kantisch-Fries'sche Religionsphilosophie und ihre Anwendung auf die Theologie', *ThR* 11 (1909), 419–36, 471–88.

—— 'Der religiöse Liberalismus', in L. Nelson (ed.), *Was ist Liberal?* (Munich: Buchhandlung Nationalverein, 1910).

—— *Die Bedeutung der Person Jesu für den Glauben. Historische und rationale Grundlagen des Glaubens* (Berlin/Schöneberg: Protestantischen Schriftenvertrieb, 1910).

—— Foreword to J. F. Fries, *Julius und Evagoras. Neu herausgegeben und mit Einleitung versehen von Wilhelm Bousset* (Göttingen: Vandenhoeck and Ruprecht, 1910).

—— 'In Sachen des Neofriesianismus, i. Wider unsern Kritiker', *ZThK* 21 (1911), 141–59.

—— *Kyrios Christos. Geschichte des Christusglaubens von den Anfängen des Christentums bis Irenaeus,* foreword by Rudolf Bultmann, 5th edn. (Göttingen: Vandenhoeck and Ruprecht, 1965). ET by John E. Steely: *Kyrios Christos: A History of the Belief in Christ from the Beginnings of Christianity to Irenaeus* (Nashville, Tenn.: Abingdon, 1970).

—— 'Religion und Theologie', in Anthonie F. Verheule (ed.), *Religionsgeschichtliche Studien. Aufsätze zur religionsgeschichtlichen Studien des hellenistischen Zeitalters,* Novum Testamentum, supplement 50 (Leiden: Brill, 1979), 29–43.

BRAKELMANN, G., *Protestantische Kriegstheologie im ersten Weltkrieg, Reinhold Seeberg* (Bielefeld: Luther–Verlag, 1974).

BROWN, W. A., *The Essence of Christianity: A Study in the History of Definition* (NY: Scribner, 1902).

BRUCH, RÜDIGER VON, GRAF, F. W., and HÜBINGER, G. (eds.), *Kultur und Kulturwissenschaften um 1900* (Stuttgart: Franz Steiner, 1989).

BUSCH, EBERHARD, *Karl Barth*, tr. John Bowden (London: SCM, 1976).

BUTTERFIELD, HERBERT, *Man on His Past* (Cambridge: Cambridge University Press, 1969).

CASSIRER, ERNST, *The Problem of Knowledge: Philosophy, Science and History Since Hegel* (New Haven, Conn.: Yale University Press, 1950).

CHAMBERLAIN, H. S., *Immanuel Kant*, tr. Lord Redesdale, 2 vols. (London: The Bodley Head, 1904).

CHAPMAN, MARK D., 'Apologetics and the Religious *A Priori*: The Use and Abuse of Kantianism in German Theology, 1900–1920', *Journal of Theological Studies*, 43 (1992), 470–510.

—— 'Theology Within the Walls: Wilhelm Herrmann's Religious Reality', *NZSThRph* 34 (1992), 69–84.

—— 'Polytheism and Personality—Aspects of the Intellectual Relationship between Weber and Troeltsch', *History of the Human Sciences*, 6 (1993), 1–33.

—— 'Religion, Ethics and the History of Religion School', *SJT* 46 (1993), 43–78.

—— Review of Drescher, *Ernst Troeltsch: Leben und Werk* in *Journal of Theological Studies*, 44 (1993): 437–40.

—— 'A Theology for Europe: Universality and Particularity in Christian Theology', *Heythrop Journal*, 25 (1994), 125–39.

—— 'The "Sad Story" of Ernst Troeltsch's Proposed British Lectures of 1923', *Zeitschrift für neuere Theologiegeschichte*, 1 (1994), 96–121.

—— 'Concepts of the Voluntary Church in England and Germany, 1890–1920: A Study of J. N. Figgis and Ernst Troeltsch', *Zeitschrift für neuere Theologiegeschichte*, 2 (1995), 37–59.

—— 'Ideology, Theology and Sociology: From Kautsky to Meeks', in J. W. Rogerson (ed.), *The Use of the Bible in Ethics*, 42–65.

—— 'Theology, Nationalism and the First World War: Christian Ethics and the Constraints of Politics', *Studies in Christian Ethics*, 8 (1995), 13–35.

—— 'Troeltsch, Kant and the Quest for a Critical Public Theology', *Zeitschrift für neuere Theologiegeschichte*, 5 (1998), 29–59.

—— 'Why the Enlightenment Project Doesn't have to Fail', *Heythrop Journal*, 39 (1998), 379–93.

CLAYTON, J. P. (ed.), *Ernst Troeltsch and the Future of Theology* (Cambridge: Cambridge University Press, 1976).

COAKLEY, SARAH, *Christ Without Absolutes* (Oxford: Clarendon Press, 1988).

COLPE, CARSTEN, *Die Religionsgeschichtliche Schule. Darstellung und Kritik ihres Bildes vom gnostischen Erlösermythus*, Forschungen zur Religion und Literatur des Alten und Neuen Testaments, NF, lx (Göttingen: Vandenhoeck and Ruprecht, 1961).

—— (ed.), *Die Diskussion um das 'Heilige'* (Darmstadt: Wissenschaftliche Buchgesellschaft, 1977).

CROCE, B., 'Antihistorismus' (lecture delivered at Oxford in 1931), *Historische Zeitschrift*, 143 (1931), 457–66.

DAHRENDORFF, RALF, *Society and Democracy in Germany* (London: Weidenfeld and Nicholson, 1968).

DAVIDSON, R. F., *Rudolf Otto's Interpretation of Religion* (Princeton, NJ: Princeton University Press, 1947).

DIEHL, H., 'Herrmann und Troeltsch', *ZThK* 18 (1908), 473–8.

DIETRICH, W. S., *Cohen and Troeltsch: Ethical Monotheistic Religion and Theory of Culture* (Atlanta, Ga.: Scholars Press, 1986).

DILTHEY, WILHELM, 'The Interpretation and Analysis of Man in the Fifteenth and Sixteenth Centuries', in L. W. Spitz (ed.), *The Reformation: Material or Spiritual*, 8–16.

DOBSCHÜTZ, ERNST VON, *Probleme des apostolischen Zeitalters* (Leipzig: J. C. Hinrichs, 1904).

DÖRING, A., and GERICKE, C., 'Namenregister zu Troeltschs *Die Soziallehren der christlichen Kirchen und Gruppen*', *MdETG* 4 (1989), 140–68.

DORNER, AUGUST, *Grundriß der Religionsphilosophie* (Leipzig: Dürr, 1903).

DRESCHER, H.-G., 'Glaube und Vernunft bei Ernst Troeltsch. Eine kritische Deutung seiner Religionsphilosophischen Grundlegung' (Univ. of Marburg diss. 1957).

—— 'Ernst Troeltsch's Intellectual Development', in J. P. Clayton (ed.), *Ernst Troeltsch and the Future of Theology*, 3–32.

—— 'Entwicklungsdenken und Glaubensentscheidung', *ZThK* NF 79 (1982), 80 ff.

—— 'Ernst Troeltsch und Paul de Lagarde', *MdETG* 3 (1984), 95–115.

—— *Ernst Troeltsch: Leben und Werk* (Göttingen: Vandenhoeck and Ruprecht, 1991). ET: *Ernst Troeltsch: His Life and Work*, tr. John Bowden (London: SCM, 1992).

—— 'Zur Entstehung von Troeltschs "Sozialiehren" ', *TS* vi: 11–26.

DUHM, BERNHARD, *Die Theologie der Propheten als Grundlage für die innere Entwicklungsgeschichte der Israelitischen Religion* (Bonn: Marcus, 1875).

—— *Über Ziel und Methode der theologischen Wissenschaft. Antrittsvorlesung* (Basel: Schweigerhauser, 1889).

DUNKMANN, K., *Religionsphilosophie. Kritik der religiösen Erfahrung als Grundlegung christlicher Theologie*, Systematische Theologie, i (Gütersloh: Bertelsmann, 1917).

ECKE, GUSTAV, *Die theologische Schule Albrecht Ritschls und die evangelische Kirche der Gegenwart*, 3 vols. (Berlin: Reuther and Reichard, 1897).

EICHHORN, A., *Das Abendmahl im neuen Testament*, supplement to *CW* 36 (Freiburg and Leipzig: J. C. B. Mohr (Paul Siebeck), 1898).

ERDMANN, K., *Die Weimarer Republik*, 5th edn. (Munich: Gebhardt, 1985).

EUCKEN, RUDOLF, *Geistige Strömungen der Gegenwart*, 4th edn. (Leipzig: Veit, 1909).

EVANG, MARTIN, *Rudolf Bultmann in seiner Frühzeit*, Beiträge zur historischen Theologie, 74 (Tübingen: J. C. B. Mohr (Paul Siebeck), 1988).

FISCHER, HERMANN, 'Theologie des positiven und kritischen Paradoxes: Paul Tillich und Karl Barth im Streit um die Wirklichkeit', *NZSThRph* 31 (1989), 195–212.

FISCHER, KUNO, *Kants Leben und die Grundlagen seiner Lehre* (Mannheim: F. Bassermann, 1860–1).

FISHER, SIMON, *Revelatory Positivism? Barth's Earliest Theology and the Marburg School* (Oxford: Clarendon Press, 1988).

FISCHER-APPELT, PETER, *Metaphysik im Horizont der Theologie Wilhelm Herrmanns* (Munich: Kaiser, 1965).

FRANK, F. H. R., *System der christlichen Gewißheit*, 2 vols. (Erlangen: A. Deichert, 1870–3).

FREI, HANS, 'The Relation of Faith and History in the Thought of Ernst Troeltsch', in Paul Ramsey (ed.), *Faith and Ethics*, 53–64.

FRIES, J. F., *Wissen, Glaube und Ahndung*, ed. L. Nelson (Göttingen: Vandenhoeck and Ruprecht, 1905). The original 1805 edn. has been reprinted in J. F. Fries, *Sämtliche Schriften*, 3 (Aalen: Scientia, 1973), 413–755.

—— *Julius und Evagoras. Neu herausgegeben und mit Einleitung versehen von Wilhelm Bousset* (Göttingen: Vandenhoeck and Ruprecht, 1910).

GASMAN, DANIEL, *The Scientific Origins of National Socialism: Social Darwinism in Ernst Haeckel and the German Monist League* (London: MacDonald, 1971).

GIDDENS, A., 'Positivism and its Critics', in *Studies in Social and Political Theory* (London: Hutchinson, 1977), 29–88.

GIERKE, O., *Natural Law and the Theory of Society 1500–1800* (Cambridge: Cambridge University Press, 1950).

GOGARTEN, FRIEDRICH, *Verhängnis und Hoffnung der Neuzeit. Die Säkularisierung als theologisches Problem* (Stuttgart: Friedrich Vorwerk Verlag, 1953).

GÖHRE, P., *Drei Monate Fabrikarbeiter und Handwerksbursche* (Leipzig: Grunow, 1891).

GRAF, F. W., 'Profile: Spuren in Bonn', *TS* i: 103–31.

—— 'Friendship between Experts: Notes on Weber and Troeltsch', in W. Mommsen and J. Osterhammel (eds.), *Max Weber and his Contemporaries*, 215–31.

—— '"Kierkegaards junge Herren". Troeltschs Kritik der "geistigen Revolution" im frühen zwanzigsten Jahrhundert', *TS* iii: 172–92.

—— 'Religion und Individualität', *TS* iii: 207–30.

—— 'Der "Systematiker" der "kleinen Göttinger Fakultät". Ernst Troeltschs Promotionsthesen und ihr Göttinger Kontext', *TS* i: 235–90.

—— 'Kulturprotestantismus. Zur Begriffsgeschichte einer theologischen Chiffre', *Archiv für Begriffsgeschichte*, 28 (1986), 214–68.

—— 'Max Weber und die protestantische Theologie seiner Zeit', *Zeitschrift für Religions- und Geistesgeschichte*, 40 (1987), 122–47.

—— 'Rettung der Persönlichkeit. Protestantische Theologie als Kulturwissenschaft des Christentums', in Rüdiger von Bruch, F. W. Graf, and G. Hübinger (eds.), *Kultur und Kulturwissenschaften um 1900*, 103–31.

—— (ed.), *Profile des neuzeitlichen Protestantismus* (Gütersloh: Gerd Mohn, vol i, 1990, vol ii, pt 1, 1992, vol ii, pt 2, 1993).

—— '"endlich grosse Bücher schreiben". Marginalien zur Werkgeschichte der "Soziallehren"', *TS* vi: 27–50.

—— (ed.), 'Ernst Troeltschs Briefe und Karten an Paul Wernle', *Zeitschrift für neuere Theologiegeschichte*, 2 (1995), 85–147.

—— 'Das Laboratorium der religiösen Moderne. Zur "Verlagsreligion" des Eugen Diederichs Verlags', in Gangolf Hübinger (ed.), *Versammlungsort moderner Geister*, 243–98.

—— and RUDDIES, H., *Ernst Troeltsch Bibliographie* (Tübingen: J. C. B. Mohr (Paul Siebeck), 1982).

—— and RUDDIES, H., 'Religiöser Historismus: Ernst Troeltsch', in F. W. Graf (ed.), *Profile des neuzeitlichen Protestantismus*, ii/2: 295–335.

GRESCHAT, MARTIN (ed.), *Theologen des Protestantismus im 18. und 19. Jahrhundert* (Stuttgart: Kohlhammer, 1978).

GRESSMANN, HUGO, *Eichhorn und die religionsgeschichtliche Schule* (Göttingen: Vandenhoeck and Ruprecht, 1914).

GRIEVE, W., *Der Grund des Glaubens. Die Christologie Wilhelm Herrmanns* (Göttingen: Vandenhoeck and Ruprecht, 1976).

GUNKEL, HERMANN, *Die Wirkungen des heiligen Geistes nach der populären Anschauung der apostolischen Zeit und der Lehre des Apostels Paulus* (Göttingen: Vandenhoeck and Ruprecht, 1888, 2nd edn. 1899).

—— *Schöpfung und Chaos in Urzeit und Endzeit. Eine religionsgeschichtliche Untersuchung über Gen. I und Ap. Joh. XII* (Göttingen: Vandenhoeck and Ruprecht, 1895).

—— *Israel und Babylonien* (Göttingen: Vandenhoeck and Ruprecht, 1903).

—— *Zum religionsgeschichtlichen Verständnis des neuen Testaments* (Göttingen: Vandenhoeck and Ruprecht, 1903).

—— Review of Reischle, *Theologie und Religionsgeschichte*, DLZ 25 (1904), cols. 1100–10.

—— 'Das alte Testament im Lichte der modernen Forschung', in A. Deißmann *et al.* (eds.), *Beiträge zur Weiterentwicklung der christlichen Religion* (Munich: Lehmann, 1905), 40–76.

—— Review of Ernst Sellin, *Die biblische Urgeschichte*, CW 20 (1906), cols. 176–7.

—— *Reden und Aufsätze* (Göttingen: Vandenhoeck and Ruprecht, 1913).

—— 'Was will die "religionsgeschichtliche" Bewegung?', *Deutsch-Evangelisch*, 5 (1914), 385–97.

—— 'Gedächtnisrede an Wilhelm Bousset', *Evangelische Freiheit*, 10 (1920), 141–62. (also published separately: Tübingen: J. C. B. Mohr (Paul Siebeck), 1920).

GUNTON, COLIN, *Enlightenment and Alienation: An Essay Towards a Trinitarian Theology* (London: Marshall, Morgan and Scott, 1985).

—— *The One, The Three and The Many* (Cambridge: Cambridge University Press, 1993).

HABERMAS, J., *Strukturwandel der Öffentlichkeit* (Berlin: Leuchterhand, 1962).

—— *Knowledge and Human Interests* (Boston: Beacon Press, 1971).

HAECKEL, ERNST, *Generelle Morphologie*, 2 vols. (Berlin: Reimer, 1866).

—— *Der Monismus als Band zwischen Religion und Wissenschaft* (Bonn: Emil Strauss, 1892). ET: *Monism as Connecting Religion and Science: The Confession of Faith of a Man of Science* (London: A. & C. Black, 1894).

—— *Die Welträtsel. Gemeinverständliche Studien über monistische Philosophie* (Bonn: Emil Strauss, 1899). ET: *The Riddle of the Universe at the Close of the Nineteenth Century*, tr. John McCabe (NY: Harper, 1900). References are to the Rationalist Press Association trans. of the fifth edn. (London: Watts and Co., 1909).

HÄLFTER, WILLIAM JULIUS, 'The Religious A Priori in the Writings of Professor Ernst Troeltsch and Professor Rudolf Otto' (Univ. of Yale Ph.D. thesis 1941).

HANHART, ROBERT, 'Paul Anton de Lagarde und seine Kritik an der Theologie', in Bernd Moeller (ed.), *Theologie in Göttingen*, 271–305.

HARNACK, A. VON, 'Die Aufgabe der theologischen Fakultäten und die allgemeine Religionsgeschichte', in Harnack, *Reden und Aufsätze*, ii (Gießen: Ricker, 1904), 159–87.

—— 'Ritschl und seine Schule', in Harnack, *Reden und Aufsätze*, ii (Gießen: Ricker, 1904), 345–68.

—— *Wesen des Christentums* (Leipzig: J. C. Hinrichs, 1901). ET: *What is Christianity?*, tr. T. B. Saunders (London: Williams and Norgate, 1904).

HARNACK, A. VON, *Dogmengeschichte*, 4th edn. (Tübingen: J. C. B. Mohr (Paul Siebeck), 1909). ET of 3rd edn.: *History of Dogma* (London: Williams and Norgate, 1897).

—— 'Über die Sicherheit und die Grenzen geschichtlicher Erkenntnis', in Harnack, *Erforschtes und Erlebtes, Reden und Aufsätze*, NF, iv (Gießen: Töpelmann, 1923), 3–23.

HARVEY, VAN, A., *The Historian and the Believer: The Morality of Historical Knowledge and Christian Belief* (NY: Macmillan, 1966).

HASLER, U., *Die beherrschte Natur: Die Anpassung der Theologie an die bürgerliche Naturauffassung im 19. Jahrhundert* (Bern: Peter Lang, 1982).

HASTINGS, JAMES (ed.), *Encyclopaedia of Religion and Ethics*, 13 vols. (Edinburgh: T. & T. Clark, 1914).

HEIDLER, IRMGARD, *Der Verleger Eugen Diederichs und seine Welt (1896–1930)* (Wiesbaden: Harrassowitz, 1998).

HEITMÜLLER, W., *'Im Namen Jesu'. Eine sprach- und religionsgeschichtliche Untersuchung zum neuen Testament, speziell zur altchristlichen Taufe* (Göttingen: Vandenhoeck and Ruprecht, 1903).

—— *Taufe und Abendmahl bei Paulus. Darstellung und religionsgeschichtliche Beleutung* (Göttingen: Vandenhoeck and Ruprecht, 1903).

HENNIS, W., *Max Weber: Essays in Reconstruction*, tr. Keith Tribe (London: Allen and Unwin, 1988).

HERMS, EILERT, and RINGLEBEN, JOACHIM (eds.), *Vergessene Theologen des 20. Jahrhunderts; Studien zur Theologiegeschichte*, Göttinger Theologische Arbeiten, 32 (Göttingen: Vandenhoeck and Ruprecht, 1984).

HERRING, H., 'Max Weber und Ernst Troeltsch als Geschichtsdenker', *Kant-Studien*, 59 (1968), 410–34.

HERRMANN, WILHELM, *Die Metaphysik in der Theologie* (Halle: M. Niemayer, 1876).

—— *Die Religion im Verhältnis zum Welterkennen und zur Sittlichkeit* (Halle: M. Niemeyer, 1879).

—— *Die Gewißheit des Glaubens und die Freiheit der Theologie* (Freiburg im Breisgau: J. C. B. Mohr (Paul Siebeck), 1889).

—— 'Religion und Sozialdemokratie', *ZThK* 1 (1891), 254–86.

—— Review of Otto Pfleiderer, *Die Ritschl'sche Theologie*, and J. Claravallensis, *Die falschmünzerische Theologie Albrecht Ritschl's und die christliche Wahrheit*, *TLZ* 17 (1892), cols. 382–7.

—— Review of Troeltsch, *Die Absolutheit des Christentums*, *TLZ* 27 (1902), cols. 330–4.

—— 'Die Lage und Aufgabe der evangelischen Dogmatik', *ZThK* 17 (1907), 1–33, 172–201.

—— 'Die Religion und das Allgemeingültige. Zur Verständigung mit Sulze', *ZThK* 18 (1908), 228–32.

—— *The Communion of the Christian with God*, reprint of 4th edn. of 1909 (London: SCM, 1971).

—— *Ethik*, 5th edn. (Tübingen: J. C. B. Mohr (Paul Siebeck), 1913).

—— *Gesammelte Aufsätze*, ed. F. W. Schmidt (Tübingen: J. C. B. Mohr (Paul Siebeck), 1923).

—— 'Wilhelm Herrmann über Ernst Troeltsch', *ZThK* NF57 (1960), 232–7.

—— *Schriften zur Grundlegung der Theologie*, ed. Peter Fischer-Appelt, 2 vols. (Munich: Kaiser, 1966–7).

—— and RADE, MARTIN, 'In Sachen des Neofriesianismus, iii. Nachwort der Redaktion', *ZThK* 21 (1911).

HINTZE, OTTO, 'Troeltsch und die Probleme des Historismus', in Gerhard Oestreich (ed.), *Soziologie und Geschichte*, 2nd edn. (Göttingen: Vandenhoeck and Ruprecht, 1964), 323–73. ET: 'Historicism as a Philosophy and a Methodology', in *The Historical Essays of Otto Hintze* (NY, Oxford University Press, 1975), 370–421.

HODGSON, SHADWORTH, H., 'The Centenary of Kant's Death', *Proceedings of the British Academy*, i (1903–4), 169–82.

HOLM, SØREN, 'Apriori und Urphänomen bei Rudolf Otto', in Ernst Benz (ed.), *Rudolf Ottos Bedeutung für die Religionswissenschaft und die Theologie heute*, 70–83.

HONIGSHEIM, P., *On Max Weber*, tr. Joan Rytina (NY: Free Press, 1968).

HÜBINGER, GANGOLF, 'Kulturkritik und Kulturpolitik des Eugen-Diederichs-Verlags im Wilhelminismus. Auswege aus der Krise der Moderne', *TS* iv: 92–114.

—— *Kulturprotestantismus und Politik. Zum Verhältnis von Liberalismus und Protestantismus im wilhelminischen Deutschland* (Tübingen: J. C. B. Mohr (Paul Siebeck), 1994).

—— (ed.), *Versammlungsort moderner Geister. Der Eugen Diederichs Verlag—Aufbruch ins Jahrhundert der Extreme* (Munich: Eugen Diederichs Verlag, 1996).

HUNZINGER, A.W., *Die religionsgeschichtliche Methode* (Lichterfelde/Berlin: Runge, 1908).

IGGERS, GEORG, *The German Conception of History* (Middletown, Conn.: Wesleyan University Press, 1968).

IRLE, GÜNTER, 'Theologie als Wissenschaft bei Georg Wobbermin' (Univ. of Marburg doctoral thesis 1976).

ITTEL, G. W., 'Die Hauptgedanken der "religionsgeschichtlichen Schule"', *Zeitschrift für Religions- und Geistesgeschichte*, 10 (1958), 20–55.

JACKE, J., *Kirche Zwischen Monarchie und Republik. Der Preußische Protestantismus nach dem Zusammenbruch von 1918* (Hamburg: Christians, 1976).

JAMES, WILLIAM, *Varieties of Religious Experience* (London: Longmans, Green and Co., 1904). German trans. Georg Wobbermin, *Die religiöse Erfahrung in ihrer Mannigfaltigkeit* (Leipzig: Hinrichs, 1907, 2nd edn., 1914).

JARAUSCH, KONRAD, H., *Students, Society and Politics in Imperial Germany: The Rise of Academic Illiberalism* (Princeton, NJ: Princeton University Press, 1982).

JELKE, R. J., 'Das religiöse Apriori und die Aufgaben der Religionsphilosophie: Ein Beitrag zur Kritik der religionsphilosophischen Position Ernst Troeltschs' (Univ. of Gütersloh doctoral thesis 1917).

JENKINS, JULIAN, 'War Theology, 1914 and Germany's *Sonderweg*: Luther's Heirs and Patriotism', *Journal of Religious History*, 15 (1989), 292–310.

JENSEN, OLE, *Theologie zwischen Illusion und Restriktion. Analyse und Kritik der existenzkritischen Theologie bei dem jungen Wilhelm Herrmann und bei Rudolf Bultmann*, Beiträge zur evangelischen Theologie, 71 (Munich: Kaiser Verlag, 1975).

JONES, L. J., *German Liberalism and the Dissolution of the Weimar Party System, 1918–1933* (Chapel Hill, NC: University Press of North Carolina, 1988).

KAFTAN, JULIUS, *Die religionsphilosophische Anschauung Kants in ihrer Bedeutung für die Apologetik. Antrittsrede gehalten den 6. Nov. 1873* (Basel: Bahnmaier, 1874).

KAFTAN, JULIUS, *Das Wesen der christlichen Religion* (Basel: Bahnmaier, 1881). ET: *The Truth of the Christian Religion*, tr. G. Ferries (Edinburgh: T. & T. Clark, 1894).

—— Review of Troeltsch, *Vernunft und Offenbarung* (A1891/3), *TLZ* 17 (1892), cols. 208–12.

—— 'Die Selbständigkeit des Christentums', *ZThK* vi (1896), 379–94.

—— *Kant, der Philosoph des Protestantismus* (Berlin: Reuther and Reichard, 1904).

—— *Dogmatik*, 5th edn. (Tübingen: J. C. B. Mohr (Paul Siebeck), 1909).

—— *Philosophie des Protestantismus. Eine Apologetik des evangelischen Glaubens* (Tübingen: J. C. B. Mohr (Paul Siebeck), 1917).

KAFTAN, THEODOR, *Ernst Tröltsch. Eine kritische Zeitstudie* (Schleswig: Julius Bergas, 1912).

KAHLERT, HEINRICH, *Der Held und seine Gemeinde. Untersuchungen zum Verhältnis von Stifterpersönlichkeit und Verehrergemeinschaft in der Theologie des freien Protestantismus* (Frankfurt: Peter Lang, 1984).

KANT, IMMANUEL, 'What is Enlightenment?', in Kant, *On History*.

—— *Critique of Pure Reason*, tr. Norman Kemp Smith (London and Basingstoke: Macmillan, 1929). Page numbers refer to the original first two German editions: A = 1781, B = 1787.

—— *The Critique of Judgement*, tr. James Creed Meredith (Oxford: Clarendon Press, 1952).

—— 'Conjectural Beginning of Human History', in Kant, *On History*.

—— *On History*, ed. Lewis White Beck (Indianapolis and NY: Bobbs–Merrill, 1963).

KANTZENBACH, F. W., *Die Erlanger Theologie* (Munich: Evangelische Presseverband für Bayern, 1960).

KÄSLER, D., *Max Weber*, tr. Philippa Hurd (Cambridge: Polity Press, 1988).

KATTENBUSCH, F., *Die deutsche evangelische Theologie seit Schleiermacher*, 4th edn. (Gießen: Töpelmann, 1924).

KITIGAWA, JOSEPH, M., and STRONG, JOHN, S., 'Friedrich Max Müller and the Comparative Study of Religion', in Ninian Smart et al. (eds.), *Nineteenth-Century Religious Thought in the West*, iii, 179–214.

KLATT, H., *Hermann Gunkel. Zu seiner Theologie der Religionsgeschichte und zur Entstehung der formgeschichtlichen Methode*, Forschungen zur Religion und Literatur des Alten und Neuen Testaments, 100 (Göttingen: Vandenhoeck and Ruprecht, 1969).

KLEMPERER, KLEMENS VON, *Germany's New Conservatism: Its History and Dilemma in the Twentieth Century*, 2nd edn. (Princeton, NJ: Princeton University Press, 1968).

KOCH, DIETRICH, and RUDDIES, HARTMUT (eds.), *Wahrheit und Versöhnung* (Gütersloh: Gerd Mohn, 1989).

KOCH, TRAUGOTT, 'Theologie unter den Bedingungen der Moderne. W. Herrmann, Die "Religionsgeschichtliche Schule" und die Genese der Theologie R. Bultmanns' (Univ. of Munich doctoral thesis 1970).

KÖHLER, RUDOLF, *Der Begriff Apriori in der modernen Religionsphilosophie: Eine Untersuchung zur religionsphilosophischen Methode* (Leipzig: Hinrich, 1920).

KÖHLER, WALTER, *Ernst Troeltsch* (Tübingen: J. C. B. Mohr (Paul Siebeck), 1941).

KÖHNKE, KLAUS CHRISTIAN, *Entstehung und Aufstieg des Neukantianismus: Die deutsche Universitätsphilosophie zwischen Idealismus und Positivismus* (Frankfurt-am-Main: Suhrkamp, 1986).

KOLLMAN, E. C., 'Eine Diagnose der Weimarer Republik', *Historische Zeitschrift*, 182 (1956), 291–318.

KÖPF, ULRICH, 'Die Idee der "Einheitskultur" des Mittelalters', *TS* vi: 103–21.

KRAUS, H. J., *Geschichte der historischen-kritischen Erforschung des alten Testaments von der Reformation bis zur Gegenwart*, 2nd edn. (Neukirchen: Neukirchner Verlag, 1969).

KUHLMANN, HELGA, *Die theologische Ethik Albrecht Ritschls* (Munich: Kaiser, 1992).

KÜLPE, OSWALD, *Die Philosophie der Gegenwart in Deutschland. Eine Charakteristik ihrer Hauptrichtungen nach Vorträgen gehalten im Ferienkurs für Lehrer 1901 zu Würzburg*, 2nd edn. (Leipzig: B. C. Teubner, 1904).

KÜMMEL, W. G., *The New Testament: The History of the Investigation of its Problems* (London: SCM Press, 1972).

LAGARDE, PAUL DE, 'Über das Verhältnis des deutschen Staates zu Theologie, Kirche und Religion. Ein Versuch Nicht-theologen zu orientieren', in *Deutsche-Schriften*.

—— *Deutsche-Schriften*, 5th edn. (Göttingen: Dieterich, 1920).

LANGE, F. A., *Geschichte des Materialismus*, new edn. (Frankfurt: Suhrkamp, 1974).

LANNERT, BERTHOLD, *Die Wiederentdeckung der neutestamentlichen Eschatologie durch Johannes Weiss* (Tübingen: Francke Verlag, 1989).

LASSMAN, P., and VELODY, I. (eds.), *Max Weber's 'Science as a Vocation'* (London: Unwin Hyman, 1989).

LE FORT, GERTRUD VON, *Hälfte des Lebens* (Munich: Ehrenwirth, 1965).

LEHMANN, G., *Die deutsche Philosophie der Gegenwart* (Stuttgart: Kroner, 1943).

LESSING, E., 'Die Bedeutung des religiösen Apriori für wissenschaftstheoretische Überlegungen innerhalb der Theologie', *Evangelische Theologie*, 30 (1970), 355–67.

LEWKOWITZ, A., 'Die Religionsphilosophie des Neukantianismus', *Zeitschrift für Philosophie und philosophische Kritik*, 144 (1911), 10–33.

LEXIS, W., *Das Unterrichtswesen im Deutschen Reich* (Berlin: Ascher, 1904).

LIEBERSOHN, Harry, *Religion and Industrial Society: The Protestant Social Congress in Wilhelmine Germany*, Transactions of the American Philosophical Society, 76 (Phil.: American Philosophical Society, 1986).

—— *Fate and Utopia in German Sociology, 1870–1923* (Cambridge, Mass.: MIT Press, 1988).

LIEBMANN, OTTO, *Kant und die Epigonen* (Stuttgart: C. Schober, 1865).

LITTLE, H. G., 'Ernst Troeltsch and the Scope of Historicism', *Journal of Religion*, 46 (1966), 343–64.

LOISY, A. F., *L'Évangile et l'Église* (Bellevue: Chez L'Auteur, 1902). ET: *The Gospel and the Church* (London: Isbister, 1903).

LOOFS, FRIEDRICH, *Anti-Haeckel: An Exposure of Haeckel's Views of Christianity*, tr. H. R. Mackintosh (Hodder and Stoughton: London, 1903).

LOTZ, DAVID, *Ritschl and Luther* (Nashville, Tenn.: Abingdon, 1974).

LÜDEMANN, GERD, *Die Religionsgeschichtliche Schule in Göttingen. Eine Dokumentation* (Göttingen: Vandenhoeck and Ruprecht, 1987).

—— 'Die Religionsgeschichtliche Schule', in Bernd Moeller (ed.), *Theologie in Göttingen*.

McCORMACK, BRUCE, L., *Karl Barth's Critical Realistic Dialectical Theology: Its Genesis and Development 1909–1936* (Oxford: Clarendon Press, 1995).

McGRATH, A. E., *The Genesis of Doctrine* (Oxford: Blackwell, 1990).

MacINTOSH, D. C., 'Troeltsch's Theory of Religious Knowledge', *American Journal of Theology*, 23 (1919), 274–89.

MACKINTOSH, H. R., 'Does the Historical Study of Religion Yield a Dogmatic Theology?', *American Journal of Theology*, 13 (1909), 505–19.

—— *The Doctrine of the Person of Jesus Christ* (Edinburgh: T. & T. Clark, 1912).

—— 'The Philosophical Presuppositions of Ritschlianism', in *Some Aspects of Christian Belief* (London: Hodder and Stoughton, 1923).

—— *Types of Modern Theology* (London: Nisbet, 1937).

MACKINTOSH, ROBERT, *Albrecht Ritschl and his School* (London: Chapman and Hall, 1915).

MacINTYRE, ALASTAIR, *After Virtue: A Study in Moral Theory* (London: Duckworth, 1981).

MANDELBAUM, MAURICE, *History, Man and Reason: A Study in Nineteenth-Century Thought* (Baltimore, Md. / London: Johns Hopkins Press, 1971).

MARQUARDT, MANFRED, 'Karl Bornhausen', in Eilert Herms and Joachim Ringleben (eds.), *Vergessene Theologen des 20. Jahrhunderts; Studien zur Theologiegeschichte*, 104–28.

MARSH, CLIVE, *Albrecht Ritschl and the Problem of the Historical Jesus* (San Francisco, Calif.: Mellen Research University Press, 1992).

MAYER, E.W., 'Wesen der Religion', *RGG*[1] 5: cols. 1949–67.

—— 'Über den gegenwärtigen Stand der Religionsphilosophie und deren Bedeutung für die Theologie', *ZThK* 22 (1912), 41–71.

MEBUST, JOHN LELAND, 'Wilhelm Dilthey's Philosophy of History and its Influence on Wilhelm Herrmann and Ernst Troeltsch' (Univ. of Princeton Ph.D. thesis 1973).

MEINECKE, FRIEDRICH, *Historism: The Rise of a New Historical Outlook*, tr. J. E. Anderson (London: Routledge and Kegan Paul, 1972).

MERZ, JOHN THEODORE, *A History of European Thought in the Nineteenth Century* (1912), reprint (New York: Dover, 1965).

MOELLER, BERND (ed.), *Theologie in Göttingen: Eine Vorlesungsreihe* (Göttingen: Vandenhoeck and Ruprecht, 1987).

MÖLLER, HORST, *Vernunft und Kritik. Deutsche Aufklärung im 17. und 18. Jahrhundert* (Frankfurt: Suhrkamp, 1986).

MOMMSEN, WOLFGANG, *Max Weber and German Politics, 1890–1920*, tr. Michael S. Steinberg (Chicago, Ill. and London: University of Chicago Press, 1984).

—— *The Political and Social Theory of Max Weber* (Cambridge: Polity Press, 1989).

—— and OSTERHAMMEL, J. (eds.), *Max Weber and his Contemporaries* (London: Allen and Unwin, 1987).

MORGAN, ROBERT, 'Troeltsch and the Dialectical Theology', in J. P. Clayton (ed.), *Ernst Troeltsch and the Future of Theology*, 33–77.

—— and PYE, MICHAEL (eds.), *Ernst Troeltsch: Writings on Theology and Religion* (Atlanta, Ga.: John Knox, 1977).

MOSES, JOHN, A., 'The British and German Churches and the Perception of War', in *War and Society*, 5 (1987), 23–44.

MUELLER, D. L., *An Introduction to the Theology of Albrecht Ritschl* (Phil.: Westminster, 1969).

MUNDLE, WILHELM, 'Das religiöse Apriori in der Religionsphilosophie Tröltschs in seinem Verhältnis zu Kant', *Theologische Studien und Kritiken*, 89 (1916), 427–70.

NATHUSIUS, M. V., *Die Mitarbeit der Kirche an der Lösung der sozialen Frage: Auf Grund einer kurzgefaßten Volkswirtschaftslehre und eines Systems der christlichen Gesellschaftslehre (Sozialethik)* (Leipzig: Hinrichs, 1897).

NEILL, STEPHEN, *The Interpretation of the New Testament, 1861–1961* (Oxford: Oxford University Press, 1964).

NELSON, L., *Über das sogenannten Erkenntnisproblem* (1908), 2nd edn. (Göttingen: Vandenhoeck and Ruprecht, 1930).

NEUMANN, S., *Die Parteien der Weimarer Republik*, 2nd edn. (Stuttgart: Kohlhammer, 1970).

NIEBERGALL, FRIEDRICH, 'Über die Absolutheit des Christentums', *Theologische Arbeiten aus dem rheinischen wissenschaftlichen Predigerverein*, NF, 4 (1900), 46–86.

NIEBUHR, H. RICHARD, 'Ernst Troeltsch's Philosophy of Religion' (Univ. of Yale Ph.D. thesis 1924).

—— *Christ and Culture* (London: Faber and Faber, 1957).

NIPPERDEY, THOMAS, *Deutsche Geschichte 1866–1918* (Munich: C. H. Beck, 1991–2).

NOWAK, KURT, *Evangelische Kirche und Weimarer Republik* (Weimar: Böhlhaus, 1981).

—— 'Die "antihistoristische Revolution". Symptome und Folgen der Krise historischer Weltorientierung nach dem ersten Weltkrieg im Deutschland', *TS* iv: 133–71.

—— 'Bürgerliche Bildungsreligion? Zur Stellung Adolf von Harnacks in der protestantischen Frömmigkeitsgeschichte der Moderne', *Zeitschrift für Kirchengeschichte*, 99 (1988), 326–53.

NYGREN, GOTTHART, 'Die Religionsphilosophie Rudolf Ottos', in Ernst Benz (ed.), *Rudolf Ottos Bedeutung für die Religionswissenschaft und die Theologie heute* (Leiden: Brill, 1971), 84–96.

OGLETREE, THOMAS, *Christian Faith and History* (NY and Nashville, Tenn.: Abingdon, 1965).

OLLIG, HANS-LUDWIG, *Der Neukantianismus* (Stuttgart: Metzler, 1979).

O'NEILL, J. C., *The Bible's Authority: A Portrait Gallery of Thinkers from Lessing to Bultmann* (Edinburgh: T. & T. Clark, 1991).

ORR, JAMES, *The Ritschlian Theology and the Evangelical Faith* (London: Hodder and Stoughton, 1898).

—— *Ritschlianism: Expository and Critical Essays* (London: Hodder and Stoughton, 1903).

OTTO, RUDOLF, 'Geist und Wort nach Luther' (Univ. of Göttingen doctoral thesis 1898).

—— *Leben und Wirken Jesu nach historisch-kritischer Auffasssung* (Göttingen: Vandenhoeck and Ruprecht, 1902). ET: *Life and Ministry of Jesus according to the Historical and Critical Method* (Chicago, Ill.: Open Court, 1908).

—— 'Wie Schleiermacher die Religion wiederentdeckte', *CW* 17 (1903), 506–12. ET: 'How Schleiermacher Rediscovered the Sensus Numinous', in *Religious Essays: A Supplement to 'The Idea of the Holy'*, 68–77.

—— *Naturalistische und religiöse Weltansicht* (Tübingen: J. C. B. Mohr (Paul Siebeck), 1904). ET: *Naturalism and Religion*, tr. J. Arthur Thomson and Margaret R. Thomson (London: Williams and Norgate, 1907).

OTTO, RUDOLF, Review of L. Nelson, *Über das sogenannte Erkenntnis problem* (1908), *CW* 22 (1909), cols. 475–6.

—— 'Jakob Fries' Religionsphilosophie', *ZThK* 19 (1909), 31–56, 108–61, 204–42.

—— *Kantisch-Fries'sche Religionsphilosophie und ihre Anwendung auf die Theologie. Zur Einleitung in die Glaubenslehre für Studenten der Theologie* (Tübingen: J. C. B. Mohr (Paul Siebeck), 1909). ET: *The Philosophy of Religion based on Kant and Fries* (London: Williams and Norgate, 1931).

—— 'Mythus und Religion in Wundt's *Völkerpsychologie*', *ThR* 13 (1910), 251–75, 293–305; published in a revised form in English translation as 'The Sensus Numinis as the Historical Basis of Religion', *Hibbert Journal*, 30 (1931–2), 283–97, 415–30.

—— *Das Heilige* (Breslau: Trewendt and Ganier, 1917). ET: *The Idea of the Holy*, tr. John W. Harvey (London: Oxford University Press, 1923).

—— *Religious Essays: A Supplement to 'The Idea of the Holy'*, tr. Brian Linn (London: Oxford University Press, 1931).

—— *Gottheit und Gottheiten der Arier* (Gießen: Töpelmann, 1932).

—— *Mysticism East and West: A Comparative Analysis of the Nature of Mysticism*, tr. Bertha L. Braces and Richenda C. Payne (London: Macmillan, 1932).

—— *The Kingdom of God and the Son of Man*, tr. Floyd V. Filson and Bertram Lee-Wolf, 2nd edn. (London: Lutterworth, 1943).

—— *Aufsätze zur Ethik*, ed. Jack Stewart Boozer (Munich: Beck, 1981).

OUTKA, GENE, and REEDER, JOHN, P., jun. (eds.), *Religion and Morality: A Collection of Essays* (Garden City, NY: Anchor Press, 1973).

PANNENBERG, WOLFHART, 'Redemptive Event and History', in *Basic Questions in Theology*, i (London: SCM, 1970), 15–80.

—— 'Kontingenz und Naturgesetz', in W. Pannenberg and A. M. Klaus Müller, *Erwägungen zu einer Theologie der Natur* (Gütersloh: Mohn, 1970).

—— 'Toward a Theology of the History of Religions', in *Basic Questions in Theology*, ii (London: SCM, 1971), 65–118.

—— 'Die Begründung der Ethik bei Ernst Troeltsch', in *Ethik and Ekklesiologie* (Göttingen: Vandenhoeck and Ruprecht, 1977), 70–96. ET by Keith Crim in *Ethics* (Phil. and Tunbridge Wells: Westminster, 1981), 87–111.

PAUL, GARRETT, ' "Religionswissenschaft": The Development of Ernst Troeltsch's Philosophy of Religion, 1895–1914' (Univ. of Chicago Ph.D. thesis 1980).

PAULSEN, FRIEDRICH, *Kant, Der Philosoph des Glaubens* (Berlin: Reuther and Reichard, 1899).

—— 'Haeckel als Philosoph', *Preußische Jahrbücher*, 101 (1900), 29–72.

PAUS, ANSGAR, *Religiöser Erkenntnisgrund. Herkunft und Wesen der Aprioritheorie Rudolf Ottos* (Leiden: Brill, 1966).

PERKINS, D. D., jun., 'Explicating Christian Faith in a Historically Conscious Age: The Method of Ernst Troeltsch's Glaubenslehre' (Univ. of Nashville Ph.D. thesis 1981).

PRESSEL, W., *Die Kriegspredigt 1914–1918 in der evangelischen Kirche* (Göttingen: Vandenhoeck and Ruprecht, 1967).

PRETZEL, U., 'Ernst Troeltschs Berufung an die Berliner Universität', in Hans Leussink (ed.), *Studium Berolinense: Aufsätze und Beiträge zu Problemen der*

Wissenschaft und zur Geschichte der Friedrich-Wilhelms-Universität zu Berlin (Berlin: de Gruyter, 1960), 507–14.

RADE, MARTIN, 'Religionsgeschichte', *RGG*[1] iv: cols. 2183 ff.

[Martin Rade], *Vierzig Jahre 'Christliche Welt': Festgabe für Martin Rade* (Gotha: Klotz, 1927).

RAMSEY, PAUL (ed.), *Faith and Ethics: The Theology of H. Richard Niebuhr* (NY: Harper and Row, 1957).

RATHJE, JOHANNES, *Die Welt des freien Protestantismus. Ein Beitrag zur deutsch-evangelischen Geistesgeschichte. Dargestellt an Leben und Werk von Martin Rades* (Stuttgart: E. Klotz, 1952).

REEDER, JOHN, P., jun., 'The Relation of the Moral and the Numinous in Otto's Notion of the Holy', in Gene Outka and John P. Reeder, jun. (eds.), *Religion and Morality: A Collection of Essays*, 255–92.

REISCHLE, MAX, *Die Frage nach dem Wesen der Religion. Grundlegung zu einer Methodologie der Religionsphilosophie* (Freiburg im Breisgau: J. C. B. Mohr (Paul Siebeck), 1889).

—— 'Historische und dogmatische Methode in der Theologie', *ThR* 4 (1901), 261–75, 305–24.

—— 'Kant und die Theologie der Gegenwart', *ZThK* 14 (1904), 357–88.

—— *Theologie und Religionsgeschichte. Fünf Vorlesungen* (Tübingen: J. C. B. Mohr (Paul Siebeck), 1904).

REIST, BENJAMIN, A., *Towards a Theology of Involvement: The Thought of Ernst Troeltsch* (London: SCM, 1966).

RENDTORFF, TRUTZ, 'The Modern Age as a Chapter in the History of Christianity', *Journal of Religion*, 65 (1985), 478–99.

—— 'Theologische Orientierung im Prozeß der Aufklärung. Eine Erinnerung an Ernst Troeltsch', in R. Vierhaus (ed.), *Aufklärung als Prozeß*, 19–33.

—— '"Meine eigene Theologie ist spiritualistisch". Zur Funktion der "Mystik" als Sozialform des modernen Christentums', *TS* vi: 178–92.

RENZ, HORST, 'Albert Eichhorn und die Anfänge der religionsgeschichtlichen Schule' (Univ. of Augsburg doctoral thesis 1985).

—— 'Eine unbekannte Preisarbeit über Lotze', *TS* i: 33–47.

—— 'Troeltschs Theologiestudium', *TS* i: 48–59.

RICHES, JOHN K., *A Century of New Testament Study* (Cambridge: Lutterworth Press, 1993).

RICHMOND, JAMES, *Ritschl: A Reappraisal* (London: Collins, 1978).

RITSCHL, ALBRECHT, *Unterricht in der christlichen Religion*, (Bonn: Marcus, 1875). ET: 'Instruction in the Christian Religion', in Albert Swing, *The Theology of Albrecht Ritschl*, tr. Alice Swing and rev. Philip Hefner, in Albrecht Ritschl, *Three Essays*, 221–91.

—— *Geschichte des Pietismus*, 3 vols. (Bonn: Marcus, 1880–6). ET of the Prolegomena in Ritschl, *Three Essays*.

—— *Theologie und Metaphysik. Zur Verständigung und Abwehr* (Bonn: Marcus, 1881). ET in Albrecht Ritschl, *Three Essays*, 150–217.

—— *Die christliche Lehre von der Rechtfertigung und Versöhnung*, i, 2nd edn. (Bonn: Marcus, 1882). ET: *The Christian Doctrine of Justification and Reconciliation*, i: 'A Critical History of the Christian Doctrine of Justification and Reconciliation', tr. J. S. Black (Edinburgh: Edmondston and Douglas, 1872).

208 *Bibliography*

RITSCHL, ALBRECHT, *Die christliche Lehre von der Rechtfertigung und Versöhnung*, ii, 4th edn. (Bonn: Marcus, 1900).
—— *Die christliche Lehre von der Rechtfertigung und Versöhnung*, iii, 4th edn. (Bonn: Marcus, 1900). ET: The *Christian Doctrine of Justification and Reconciliation: The Positive Development of the Doctrine*, tr. H. R. Mackintosh and A. B. Macaulay (Edinburgh: T. & T. Clark, 1902).
—— 'Festrede for the 400th Birthday of Luther', in Lotz, *Ritschl and Luther*, 187–202.
—— *Three Essays*, ed. Philip Hefner (Phil.: Fortress, 1972).
RITSCHL, OTTO, *Albrecht Ritschls Leben*, 2 vols. (Freiburg im Breisgau and Leipzig: J. C. B. Mohr (Paul Siebeck), 1896).
RITZERT, G., 'Die Religionsphilosophie Ernst Troeltschs', in A. Messer (ed.), *Friedrich Manns Pädagogisches Magazin*, 993: *philosophische und pädagogische Schriften*, 4 (Langensalza: Bayer and Mann, 1924).
ROBERTS, RICHARD, H., 'Ideal and the Real in the Theology of Karl Barth', in Stephen Sykes and Derek Holmes (eds.), *New Studies in Theology*, i (London: Duckworth, 1980), 163–80.
ROBINSON, JAMES, M., 'Das Problem des heiligen Geistes bei Wilhelm Herrmann' (Univ. of Basel doctoral thesis 1952).
—— (ed.), *The Beginnings of Dialectical Theology* (Richmond: John Knox, 1968).
ROGERS, H. J. (ed.), *Congress of Arts and Sciences: Universal Exposition, St. Louis, 1904, Proceedings* (Boston, Mass. and NY: Houghton, Mifflin and Co., 1905).
ROGERSON, JOHN, W., *Old Testament Criticism in the Nineteenth Century* (London: SPCK, 1984).
—— (ed.), *The Use of the Bible in Ethics* (Sheffield: JSOT Press, 1995).
ROLLMANN, HANS, 'Troeltsch, von Hügel and Modernism', *The Downside Review*, 96 (1978), 35–60.
—— 'Theologie und Religionsgeschichte: religionsgechichtliche Methode und die Einführung religionsgeschichtlicher Lehrstühle', *ZThK* NF 80 (1983), 69–84.
—— 'From Baur to Wrede', *Studies in Religion*, 17 (1988) 443–54.
ROTH, G., and SCHUCHTER, W., *Max Weber's Vision of History* (Berkeley, Calif.: University of California Press, 1979).
RUBANOWICE, R., *Crisis in Consciousness* (Tallahassee, Fla.: University of Florida Press, 1982).
RUDDIES, H., 'Mystische Theologie? Bemerkungen zur Interpretation Karl-Ernst Apfelbachers', *MdETG* 2 (1983) 95–108.
—— 'Soziale Demokratie und freier Protestantismus in den Anfängen der Weimarer Republik', *TS* iii: 145–74.
—— 'Karl Barth im Kulturprotestantismus. Eine theologische Problemanzeige', in Dietrich Koch and Hartmut Ruddies (eds.), *Wahrheit und Versöhnung* (Gütersloh: Gerd Mohn, 1989), 193–231.
RÜHLE, OTTO, *Der theologische Verlag J.C.B. Mohr* (Tübingen: J. C. B. Mohr (Paul Siebeck), 1926).
RUNZO, JOSEPH, *Reason, Relativism and God* (London and Basingstoke: Macmillan, 1986).
RUPP, G., *Culture Protestantism: German Liberal Theology at the Turn of the Twentieth Century*, AAR Studies, 15 (Missoula, Mont.: Scholars Press, 1977).

SÄNGER, DIETER, 'Phänomenologie oder Geschichte. Methodische Anmerkungen zur religionsgeschichtlichen Schule', *Zeitschrift für Religions- und Geistesgeschichte*, 32 (1980), 13–27.

SATO, SHINICHI, 'Ernst Troeltsch und die soziale Frage im Wilhelminischen Zeitalter unter besonderer Berücksichtigung des Zusammenhangs zwischen Troeltsch und Gottfried Traub', *MdETG* 4 (1989), 6–21.

—— 'Ernst Troeltsch and Ernst Haeckel', *MdETG* 8 (1994), 53–104.

SCAFF, L., *Fleeing the Iron Cage* (Berkeley, Calif.: University of California Press, 1989).

SCHAAF, J. J., *Geschichte und Begriff: Eine kritische Studie zur Geschichtsphilosophie von Ernst Troeltsch und Max Weber* (Tübingen: J. C. B. Mohr (Paul Siebeck), 1946).

SCHEEL, O., 'Die moderne Religionspsychologie', *ZThK* 18 (1908), 1–38.

SCHELLONG, D., *Bürgertum und christliche Religion. Anpassungsprobleme der Theologie seit Schleiermacher* (Munich: Kaiser, 1975).

SCHENK, WILHELM, 'Ernst Troeltsch's Conception of History', *The Dublin Review*, 108 (1944), 25–34.

SCHINZER, R., 'Rudolf Otto—Entwurf einer Biographie', in Ernst Benz (ed.), *Rudolf Ottos Bedeutung für die Religionswissenschaft und die Theologie heute* (Leiden: Brill, 1971).

SCHLEIERMACHER, F. D. E., *Über die Religion. Reden an die Gebildeten unter ihren Verächtern. Zum hundertjahr-Gedächtnis ihres ersten Erscheinens in ihrer ursprünglichen Gestalt neu herausgegeben mit Übersichten und Vor- und Nachwort versehen von Lic. Rudolf Otto* (Göttingen: Vandenhoeck and Ruprecht, 1899).

—— *Kurze Darstellung des Theologischen Studiums zum Behuf einleitender Vorlesungen*, reprint of third critical edn. by Heinrich Holz of 1910 (Darmstadt: Wissenschaftlice Buchgesellschaft, 1993). ET: *Brief Outline on the Study of Theology*, tr. T. N. Tice (Richmond: John Knox, 1966).

SCHLESINGER, RUTH, 'Probleme eines religiösen Apriori' (Univ. of Berlin doctoral thesis 1959).

SCHLIPPE, G. VON, *Die Absolutheit des Christentums bei Ernst Troeltsch auf dem Hintergrund der Denkfelder des 19. Jahrhunderts* (Neustadt: Degener, 1966).

SCHMIDT, F. W. (ed.), *Luther, Kant, Schleiermacher in ihrer Bedeutung für den Protestantismus*, Festschrift for seventieth birthday of Georg Wobbermin (Berlin: Collignon, 1939).

SCHMIDT, G., *Deutscher Historismus und der Übergang zur parlamentarischen Demokratie*, Historische Studien, 389 (Lübeck and Hamburg: Matthiesen, 1964).

SCHMIDT, HANS (ed.), *ΕΥΧΑΡΙΣΤΗΡΙΟΝ. Studien zur Religion und Literatur des alten Testaments und neuen Testaments* (Göttingen: Vandenhoeck and Ruprecht, 1923).

SCHMIDT, HEINRICH, 'Ernst Haeckel als Theolog', *Der Monismus*, 6 (1911).

SCHNACK, I. (ed.), *Marburger Gelehrte in der ersten Hälfte des 20. Jahrhunderts* (Marburg: Elwert, 1977).

SCHNÄDELBACH, H., *Philosophy in Germany, 1831–1933*, tr. Eric Matthews (Cambridge: Cambridge University Press, 1984).

SCHUCHTER, W., 'Value-Neutrality and the Ethic of Responsibility', in G. Roth and W. Schuchter (eds.), *Max Weber's Vision of History*, 113 ff.

SCHÜTTE, H.-W., *Religion und Christentum in der Theologie Rudolf Ottos* (Berlin: Walter de Gruyter, 1969).

SCHWEITZER, ALBERT, *Die Religionsphilosophie Kant's von der 'Kritik der reinen Vernunft' bis zur 'Religion innerhalb der Grenzen der blossen Vernunft'* (Freiburg im Breisgau/ Leipzig/Tübingen: J. C. B. Mohr (Paul Siebeck), 1899).

SCHWÖBEL, CHRISTOPH (ed.), *An die Freunde. Vertrauliche d.i. nicht für die Öffentlichkeit bestimmte Mitteilungen (1903–1934)* (Berlin: Walter de Gruyter, 1993).

SEEBERG, AMANDA, 'Lebensbild von Reinhold Seeberg', unpublished typescript in the Bundesarchiv, Koblenz.

SHEEHAN, JAMES J., *German History 1770–1866* (Oxford: Clarendon Press, 1989).

SIEGFRIED, THEODOR, 'Theologie als Wissenschaft bei Rudolf Otto', *ZThK* NF 19 (1938), 16–45.

SLEIGH, R. S., *The Sufficiency of Christianity: An Enquiry Concerning the Nature and the Modern Possibilities of the Christian Religion, with Special Reference to the Religious Philosophy of Dr Ernst Troeltsch* (London: James Clarke, 1923).

SMART, NINIAN, *et al.* (eds.), *Nineteenth-Century Religious Thought in the West*, 3 vols. (Cambridge: Cambridge University Press, 1985).

SMEND, F., *Adolf von Harnack. Verzeichnis seiner Schriften bis 1930* (Leipzig: Zentralantiquariat der DDR, 1990).

SOCKNESS, BRENT, *Against False Apologetics: Wilhelm Herrmann and Ernst Troeltsch in Conflict*, Beiträge Zur Historischen Theologie, 105 (Tübingen: J. C. B. Mohr (Paul Siebeck), 1998).

SÖSEMANN, BERND, 'Das "erneute Deutschland". Ernst Troeltschs politische Engagement im ersten Weltkrieg', *TS* iii: 120–44.

SPARN, WALTER, 'Vernünftiges Christentum. Über die geschichtliche Aufgabe der theologischen Aufklärung im 18. Jahrhundert in Deutschland', in R. Vierhaus (ed.), *Wissenschaften im Zeitalter der Aufklärung im 18. Jahrhundert in Deutschland* (Göttingen: Vandenhoeck and Ruprecht, 1985).

SPIEß, PAUL, 'Zur Frage des religiösen Apriori', *Zeitschrift für Religion und Geisteskultur*, 3 (1909), 207–15.

SPITZ, L. W. (ed.), *The Reformation: Material or Spiritual* (Boston, Mass.: Heath, 1962).

STARR, BRADLEY, E., 'Individualism and Reform in Troeltsch's View of the Church', *Modern Theology*, 7 (1991), 447–63.

STECK, K. G., 'Karl Barths Absage an die Neuzeit', in K. G. Steck and Dieter Schellong, *Karl Barth und die Neuzeit*, Theologische Existenz Heute, 173 (Munich: Kaiser, 1973).

STEINER, RUDOLF, *Haeckel, die Welträtsel und die Theosophie* (Dornach, Switzerland: Philosophisch-Anthropologischer Verlag, 1926).

STEPHAN, HORST, 'Albrecht Ritschl und die Gegenwart', *ZThK* NF 15 (1935), 21–43.

STEPHAN, W., *Aufstieg und Verfall der Linksliberalismus, 1918–1933. Geschichte der Deutschen Demokratischen Partei* (Göttingen: Vandenhoeck and Ruprecht, 1973).

STERN, FRITZ, *The Politics of Cultural Despair*, 2nd edn. (Berkeley, Calif.: University of California Press, 1974).

STRECKER, G., 'William Wrede', *ZThK* 57 (1960), 67–91.

SYKES, STEPHEN, 'Ernst Troeltsch and Christianity's Essence', in J. P. Clayton (ed.), *Ernst Troeltsch and the Future of Theology*, 139–70.

TENBRUCK, F., 'The Problem of the Thematic Unity in the Works of Max Weber', *British Journal of Sociology*, 31 (1980), 316–51.

TIMM, H., *Theorie und Praxis in der Theologie Albrecht Ritschls und Wilhelm Herrmanns* (Gütersloh: Mohn, 1967).

TITIUS, ARTHUR, 'Albrecht Ritschl und die Gegenwart', *Theologische Studien und Kritiken*, 86 (1913).

—— 'Julius Kaftan', *ZThK* NF 8 (1927), 1–20.

To the Christian Scholars of Europe and America: A Reply from Oxford to the German Address to Evangelical Christians (London: Oxford University Press, 1914).

TRACY, DAVID, *The Analogical Imagination: Christian Theology and the Culture of Pluralism* (NY: Crossroad, 1981).

TRAUB, FRIEDRICH, 'Die religionsgeschichtliche Methode und die systematische Theologie: Eine Auseinandersetzung mit Tröltschs theologischen Reformprogramm', *ZThK* 11 (1901), 301–40.

—— 'Zur Frage des religiösen Apriori', *ZThK* 24 (1914), 181–99.

TRILLHAAS, WOLFGANG, 'Albrecht Ritschl', in Martin Greschat (ed.), *Theologen des Protestantismus im 18. und 19. Jahrhundert*, i: 113–29.

VAIHINGER, HANS, 'An die Freunde der Kantischen Philosophie: Bericht über die Begründung einer "Kantgesellschaft" und die Errichtung einer "Kantstiftung" zum hundertjährigen Todestag des Philosophen', in Hans Vaihinger and Bruno Bauch (eds.), *Kant-Studien Festheft* (1904), 344–50.

—— 'Das Kantjubiläum im Jahre 1904', *Kant-Studien*, 9 (1904), 105–55.

VERHEULE, A. F. *Wilhelm Bousset. Leben und Werk. Ein Theologiegeschichtlicher Versuch* (Amsterdam: Ton Bolland, 1973).

VIERHAUS, R., (ed.), *Wissenschaften im Zeitalter der Aufklärung im 18. Jahrhundert in Deutschland* (Göttingen: Vandenhoeck and Ruprecht, 1985).

—— (ed.), *Aufklärung als Prozeß* (Hamburg: Meiner, 1988).

—— 'Aufklärung als Emanzipationsprozeß', in R. Vierhaus (ed.), *Aufklärung als Prozeß*, 3–8.

VORBORDT, G., 'Religionspsychologie als Methode und Objekt der Dogmatik', *ZThK* 18 (1908), 60–7.

WAGENHAMMER, HANS, *Das Wesen des Christentums: Eine begriffsgeschichtliche Untersuchung* (Mainz: Matthias Grünewald Verlag, 1973).

WAGNER, FALK, 'Aspekte der Rezeption Kantischer Metaphysik-Kritik in der evangelischen Theologie des 19. und 20. Jahrhunderts', *NZSysThRph* 27 (1985), 25–41.

—— 'Lutherische Erfahrungstheologie. F. H. R. Frank (1827–1894)', in F. W. Graf (ed.), *Profile des neuzeitlichen Protestantismus*, ii/2: 205–30.

—— 'Theologischer Neukantianismus. Wilhelm Herrmann (1846–1922)', in F. W. Graf (ed.), *Profile des neuzeitlichen Protestantismus*, ii/2: 251–78.

WALTHER, CHRISTIAN, *Typen des Reich-Gottes-Verständnis. Studien zur Eschatologie und Ethik im 19. Jahrhundert* (Munich: Kaiser, 1961).

WARD, W. R., *Theology, Sociology and Politics: The German Protestant Social Conscience, 1890–1933* (Berne: University of Durham Publications (Peter Lang), 1979).

WAY, DAVID, *The Lordship of Christ: A Critical Analysis of Ernst Käsemann's Interpretation of Pauline Theology* (Oxford: Clarendon Press, 1987).

WEBER, MARIANNE, *Max Weber: A Biography*, tr. Harry Zohn (NY: Wiley, 1975).

WEBER, MAX, 'Die deutschen Landarbeiter', *Verhandlungen des 5. Evangelischen Sozialen Kongreßes* (1894), 61–82, 92–4.

—— 'Die sozialen Gründe des Untergangs der antiken Kultur', *Die Wahrheit*, 6 (1896), 57–77.

—— 'Agrarverhältnisse im Altertum', *Handwörterbuch der Staatswissenschaften*, ed. J. Conrad (Jena: Fischer, 1897), 1–18.

—— 'Die Protestantische Ethik und der Geist des Kapitalismus', *Archiv für Sozialwissenschaft und Sozialpolitik*, 20 (1905), 1–54; 21 (1905), 1–110. ET: *The Protestant Ethic and the Spirit of Capitalism*, trs. Talcott Parsons (London: George Allen and Unwin, 1976).

—— 'Kirchen und Sekten in Nordamerika', *CW* 20 (1906), 558–62, 577–83.

—— 'R. Stammlers Überwindung der materialistischen Geschichtsauffassung', *Archiv für Sozialwissenschaft und Sozialpolitik*, 24 (1907), 94–151.

—— 'Antikritisches zum Geist des Kapitalismus', *Archiv für Sozialwissenschaft und Sozialpolitik*, 30 (1910), 176–202.

—— 'Antikritisches Schlußwort zum Geist des Kapitalismus', *Archiv für Sozialwissenschaft und Sozialpolitik*, 31 (1910), 554–99.

—— *Gesammelte Aufsätze zur Soziologie und Sozialpolitik*, ed. Marianne Weber (Tübingen: J. C. B. Mohr (Paul Siebeck), 1924).

—— *The Methodology of the Social Sciences* (Glencoe, Ill.: Free Press, 1949).

—— *Die Protestantische Ethik*, ii, ed. J. Winckelmann (Munich and Hamburg: Siebernstern-Taschenbuch, 1968).

—— *Gesammelte Politische Schriften*, ed. J. Winckelmann, 3rd edn. (Tübingen: J. C. B. Mohr (Paul Siebeck), 1971).

—— *Gesammelte Aufsätze zur Religionssoziologie*, 6th edn. (Tübingen: J. C. B. Mohr (Paul Siebeck), 1972).

—— *Gesammelte Aufsätze zur Wissenschaftslehre*, ed. J. Winckelmann, 4th edn. (Tübingen: J. C. B. Mohr (Paul Siebeck), 1973).

—— *Max Weber Gesamtausgabe*, xv/1, ed. W. J. Mommsen (Tübingen: J. C. B. Mohr (Paul Siebeck), 1984).

WEHLER, H.-U., *The German Empire 1871–1918* (Leamington Spa: Berg Publishers, 1985).

—— *Deutsche Sozialgeschichte*, i (Munich: Beck, 1987).

WEINEL, H., *Die Wirkungen des Geistes und der Geister im nachapostolischen Zeitalter bis auf Irenäus* (Freiburg im Breisgau: J. C. B. Mohr (Paul Siebeck), 1899).

WEINHARDT, JOACHIM, *Wilhelm Herrmanns Stellung in der Ritschlschen Schule* (Tübingen: J. C. B. Mohr (Paul Siebeck), 1996).

WEISS, JOHANNES, *Die Predigt Jesu vom Reiche Gottes* (Göttingen: Vandenhoeck and Ruprecht, 1892; 2nd edn. 1900).

—— *Earliest Christianity: A History of the Period AD 30–150* (NY: Harper, 1959; trans. of *Das Urchristentum*, Göttingen: Vandenhoeck and Ruprecht, 1914–17).

WENDLAND, J., *Albrecht Ritschl und seine Schüler im Verhältnis zur Theologie, zur Philosophie und zur Frömmigkeit unserer Zeit* (Berlin: Reimer, 1889).

—— 'Wesen des Christentums', *RGG*[1] v: cols. 1967–73.

WERNLE, PAUL, *Die Anfänge unserer Religion* (Tübingen: J. C. B. Mohr (Paul Siebeck), 1901).

—— 'Paul Wernle', in Martin Dibelius *et al.* (eds.), *Die Religionswissenchaft der Gegenwart in Selbstdarstellungen*, 5 (Leipzig: Meiner, 1929), 207–51.

WIEFEL, W., 'Zur Würdigung William Wredes', *Zeitschrift für Religions- und Geistesgeschichte*, 23 (1971), 60–83.

WIESENBERG, WALTER, 'Das Verhältnis von Formal- und Materialethik erörtert an dem Streit zwischen Wilhelm Herrmann und Ernst Troeltsch' (Univ. of Leipzig doctoral thesis 1934).

WILL, H., 'Ethik als allgemeine Theorie des geistigen Lebens. Troeltsch' Erlanger Lehrer Gustav Claß', *TS* i: 175–202.

WILLEY, THOMAS, E., *Back to Kant: The Revival of Kantianism in German Social and Historical Thought (1860–1914)* (Detroit, Mich.: Wayne State University Press, 1978).

WINDELBAND, WILHELM, *Präludien*, 7th edn., 2 vols. (Tübingen: J. C. B. Mohr (Paul Siebeck), 1921).

—— 'Nach hundert Jahren', *Kant-Studien*, 9 (1904), 5–20.

WOBBERMIN, GEORG, *Zwei akademische Vorlesungen über Grundprobleme der systematischen Theologie: Die Wahrheitsbeweis für die christliche Religion* (Berlin: Theology Faculty, 1899).

—— *Theologie und Metaphysik. Das Verhältnis der Theologie zur modernen Erkenntnistheorie und Psychologie* (Berlin: Alexander Duncker, 1901).

—— *Das Wesen des Christentums* (Munich: Lehmann, 1905).

—— *Aufgabe und Bedeutung der Religionspsychologie*, lecture given at the fifth World Congress for Free Christianity and Religious Progress (Berlin: Protestantische Schriftenvertrieb, 1910).

—— *Monismus und Monotheismus: Vorträge und Abhandlungen zum Kampf an die monistische Weltanschauung* (Tübingen: J. C. B. Mohr (Paul Siebeck), 1911).

—— *Systematische Theologie nach religionspsychologischer Methode* (Tübingen: J. C. B. Mohr (Paul Siebeck), 1913–25).

WOLFES, MATTHIAS, *Protestantische Theologie und Modern Welt. Studien zur Geschichte der liberalen Theologie nach 1918* (Berlin: Walter de Gruyter, 1999).

WREDE, W., *Paulus*, Religionsgeschichtliche Volksbücher, i / 5, 6 (Tübingen: J. C. B. Mohr (Paul Siebeck), 1904). ET: *Paul* (Boston, Mass.: American Unitarian Association, 1908).

—— *Vorträge und Studien* (Tübingen: J. C. B. Mohr (Paul Siebeck), 1907).

WRIGHT, J. R. C., 'Ernst Troeltsch als parlamentarischer Unterstaatssekretär im Preußischen Ministerium für Wissenschaft, Kunst und Volksbildung. Seine kirchenpolitische Auseinandersetzung mit den Beamten', *TS* iii: 175–206.

WRZECIONKO, P., *Die philosophischen Wurzeln der Theologie Albrecht Ritschls. Ein Beitrag zum Problem des Verhältnisses von Theologie und Philosophie im 19. Jahrhundert* (Berlin: Töpelmann, 1964).

WUNDT, W., *Völkerpsychologie. Eine Untersuchung der Entwicklungsgesetze von Sprache, Mythus und Sitte* (Leipzig: Wilhelm Engelmann, 1905–9).

—— 'Die Tabugebote. Das Heilige und das Unreine', in *Völkerpsychologie*, ii: 300–18, repr. in Carsten Colpe (ed.), *Die Diskussion um das 'Heilige'*, 57–75.

WYMAN, WALTER, Review of Apfelbacher, *Frömmigkeit und Wissenschaft*, *Journal of Religion*, 60 (1980), 353–5.

WYMAN, WALTER, *The Concept of Glaubenslehre: Ernst Troeltsch and the Theological Heritage of Schleiermacher*, American Academy of Religion series, 44 (Chico, Calif.: Scholars Press, 1983).

YASUKATA, TOSHIMASA, *Ernst Troeltsch: Systematic Theologian of Radical Historicality*, American Academy of Religion series, 55 (Atlanta, Ga.: Scholars Press, 1986).

ZAHN-HARNACK, AGNES VON, *Adolf von Harnack* (Berlin: Bott, 1936; 2nd edn., Berlin: de Gruyter, 1951).

ZAHRNT, HEINZ, *The Question of God* (London: Collins, 1969).

ZELGER, MANUEL, 'Modernisierte Gemeindetheologie': Albrecht Ritschl, in F. W. Graf (ed.), *Profile des neuzeitlichen Protestantismus*, ii/1: 183–204.

Index

Index

Printed in the United States
106486LV00002B/220/A

9 780199 246823